Renault Fuego Owners Workshop Manual

A K Legg T Eng (CEI), AMIMI

Models covered
Renault Fuego TL, 1397 cc
Renault Fuego Turbo, 1565 cc
Renault Fuego TS and GTS, 1647 cc
Renault Fuego Automatic and GTS Automatic, 1647 cc
Renault Fuego TX and GTX, 1995 cc

Covers automatic and four- & five-speed manual transmissions

ISBN 1 85010 318 6

© Haynes Publishing Group 1984, 1987

Printed in England *(764-11M1)*

ABCDE
FGHIJ
KLMNO
PQ

Haynes Publishing Group
Sparkford Nr Yeovil
Somerset BA22 7JJ England

Haynes Publications, Inc
861 Lawrence Drive
Newbury Park
California 91320 USA

Acknowledgements

Special thanks are due to Régie Renault for the supply of technical information and certain illustrations, to the Champion Sparking Plug Company who supplied the illustrations showing the various spark plug conditions and also to Castrol Limited who supplied lubrication data. Sykes-Pickavant provided some of the workshop tools. Thanks are also due to all those people at Sparkford who helped in the production of this manual.

About this manual

Its aim

The aim of this manual is to help you get the best value from your vehicle. It can do so in several ways. It can help you decide what work must be done (even should you choose to get it done by a garage), provide information on routine maintenance and servicing, and give a logical course of action and diagnosis when random faults occur. However, it is hoped that you will use the manual by tackling the work yourself. On simpler jobs it may even be quicker than booking the car into a garage and going there twice, to leave and collect it. Perhaps most important, a lot of money can be saved by avoiding the costs a garage must charge to cover its labour and overheads.

The manual has drawings and descriptions to show the function of the various components so that their layout can be understood. Then the tasks are described and photographed in a step-by-step sequence so that even a novice can do the work.

Its arrangement

The manual is divided into thirteen Chapters, each covering a logical sub-division of the vehicle. The Chapters are each divided into Sections, numbered with single figures, eg 5; and the Sections into paragraphs (or sub-sections), with decimal numbers following on from the Section they are in, eg 5.1, 5.2, 5.3 etc.

It is freely illustrated, especially in those parts where there is a detailed sequence of operations to be carried out. There are two forms of illustration; figures and photographs. The figures are numbered in sequence with decimal numbers, according to their position in the Chapter — eg Fig. 6.4 is the fourth drawing/illustration in Chapter 6. Photographs carry the same number (either individually or in related groups) as the Section or sub-section to which they relate.

There is an alphabetical index at the back of the manual as well as a contents list at the front. Each Chapter is also preceded by its own individual contents list.

References to the 'left' or 'right' of the vehicle are in the sense of a person in the driver's seat facing forwards.

Unless otherwise stated, nuts and bolts are removed by turning anti-clockwise, and tightened by turning clockwise.

Vehicle manufacturers continually make changes to specifications and recommendations, and these, when notified, are incorporated into our manuals at the earliest opportunity.

Whilst every care is taken to ensure that the information in this manual is correct, no liability can be accepted by the authors or publishers for loss, damage or injury caused by any errors in, or omissions from, the information given.

Introduction to the Renault Fuego

The Renault Fuego was introduced in the UK in 1980 and in North America in 1982. It is the FH Coupé version of the Renault 18 and incorporates many identical mechanical components. UK versions are fitted with carburettor engines and North American versions with fuel injection engines; the 1565 cc engine is a turbocharged unit. The transmission is of either manual or automatic type driving the front wheels. Power steering and electrically-operated windows are fitted to certain models.

Although special tools are required for some work on the Fuego, the DIY home mechanic should find that most work on the car is straightforward. However, there is very little unoccupied space in the engine compartment and this has resulted in rather less working room than is found on many other cars.

Contents

Renault Fuego GTS

Renault Fuego GTX

General dimensions, weights and capacities

Dimensions

	UK	North America
Overall length	4358 mm (171.7 in)	4489 mm (176.9 in)
Overall width	1692 mm (66.7 in)	1692 mm (66.7 in)
Overall height (at kerb weight)	1315 mm (51.8 in)	1333 mm (52.5 in)
Wheelbase	2438 mm (96.1 in)	2442 mm (96.2 in)
Track:		
Front	1426 mm (56.2 in)	1425 mm (56.1 in)
Rear	1344 mm (53.0 in)	1346 mm (53.0 in)
	or 1346 mm (53.0 in)	
Turning circle (between walls):		
Manual gearbox models	11.0 m (36.0 ft)	
Automatic transmission models	11.9 m (39.0 ft)	

Weights

UK models:	
TL and GTL	1010 kg (2227 lb)
TS and GTS	1035 kg (2282 lb)
TX and GTX	1080 kg (2381 lb)
Automatic versions	1055 kg (2326 lb)
North American models:	
1368	
Manual gearbox models	1080 kg (2381 lb)
Automatic transmission models	1090 kg (2403 lb)
136A	1110 kg (2447 lb)
Maximum roof rack load	60 kg (132 lb)

Capacities

Engine oil:	
847	3.25 litre (5.72 Imp pt, 3.44 US qt)
A5L, A7L, A2M, 843, and A6M	4.25 litre (7.48 Imp pt, 4.49 US qt)
829, J6R and 851	5.25 litre (9.24 Imp pt, 5.55 US qt)
Cooling system:	
847	6.0 litre (10.56 Imp pt, 6.34 US qt)
All except 847	7.0 litre (12.32 Imp pt, 7.40 US qt)
Fuel tank	57.0 litre (12.5 Imp gal, 15.0 US gal)
Manual gearbox	2.0 litre (3.5 Imp pt, 2.1 US qt)
Automatic transmission (total)	5.0 litre (8.8 Imp pt, 5.29 US qt)

Use of English

As this book has been written in England, it uses the appropriate English component names, phrases, and spelling. Some of these differ from those used in America. Normally, these cause no difficulty, but to make sure, a glossary is printed below. In ordering spare parts remember the parts list may use some of these words:

English	American	English	American
Accelerator	Gas pedal	Leading shoe (of brake)	Primary shoe
Aerial	Antenna	Locks	Latches
Anti-roll bar	Stabiliser or sway bar	Methylated spirit	Denatured alcohol
Big-end bearing	Rod bearing	Motorway	Freeway, turnpike etc
Bonnet (engine cover)	Hood	Number plate	License plate
Boot (luggage compartment)	Trunk	Paraffin	Kerosene
Bulkhead	Firewall	Petrol	Gasoline (gas)
Bush	Bushing	Petrol tank	Gas tank
Cam follower or tappet	Valve lifter or tappet	'Pinking'	'Pinging'
Carburettor	Carburetor	Prise (force apart)	Pry
Catch	Latch	Propeller shaft	Driveshaft
Choke/venturi	Barrel	Quarterlight	Quarter window
Circlip	Snap-ring	Retread	Recap
Clearance	Lash	Reverse	Back-up
Crownwheel	Ring gear (of differential)	Rocker cover	Valve cover
Damper	Shock absorber, shock	Saloon	Sedan
Disc (brake)	Rotor/disk	Seized	Frozen
Distance piece	Spacer	Sidelight	Parking light
Drop arm	Pitman arm	Silencer	Muffler
Drop head coupe	Convertible	Sill panel (beneath doors)	Rocker panel
Dynamo	Generator (DC)	Small end, little end	Piston pin or wrist pin
Earth (electrical)	Ground	Spanner	Wrench
Engineer's blue	Prussian blue	Split cotter (for valve spring cap)	Lock (for valve spring retainer)
Estate car	Station wagon	Split pin	Cotter pin
Exhaust manifold	Header	Steering arm	Spindle arm
Fault finding/diagnosis	Troubleshooting	Sump	Oil pan
Float chamber	Float bowl	Swarf	Metal chips or debris
Free-play	Lash	Tab washer	Tang or lock
Freewheel	Coast	Tappet	Valve lifter
Gearbox	Transmission	Thrust bearing	Throw-out bearing
Gearchange	Shift	Top gear	High
Grub screw	Setscrew, Allen screw	Trackrod (of steering)	Tie-rod (or connecting rod)
Gudgeon pin	Piston pin or wrist pin	Trailing shoe (of brake)	Secondary shoe
Halfshaft	Axleshaft	Transmission	Whole drive line
Handbrake	Parking brake	Tyre	Tire
Hood	Soft top	Van	Panel wagon/van
Hot spot	Heat riser	Vice	Vise
Indicator	Turn signal	Wheel nut	Lug nut
Interior light	Dome lamp	Windscreen	Windshield
Layshaft (of gearbox)	Countershaft	Wing/mudguard	Fender

Buying spare parts and vehicle identification numbers

Buying spare parts

Spare parts are available from many sources, for example: Renault dealers, other garages and accessory shops, and motor factors. Our advice regarding spare part sources is as follows:

Officially appointed Renault garages – This is the best source of parts which are peculiar to your car and are otherwise not generally available (eg complete cylinder heads, internal gearbox components, badges, interior trim etc). It is also the only place at which you should have repairs carried out if your car is still under warranty – non-Renault components may invalidate the warranty. To be sure of obtaining the correct parts it will always be necessary to give the storeman your car's vehicle identification number, and if possible, to take the old part along for positive identification. It obviously makes good sense to go straight to the specialists on your car for this type of part for they are best equipped to supply you.

Other garages and accessory shops – These are often very good places to buy materials and components needed for the maintenance of your car (eg spark plugs, bulbs, fanbelts, oils and greases, filler paste etc). They also sell general accessories, usually have convenient opening hours, charge reasonable prices and can often be found not far from home.

Motor factors – Good factors will stock all the more important components which wear out relatively quickly (eg clutch components, pistons, valves, exhaust systems, brake cylinders/pipes/hoses/shoes and pads etc). Motor factors will often provide new or reconditioned components on a part exchange basis – this can save a considerable amount of money.

Vehicle identification numbers

Modifications are a continuous and unpublicised process carried out by the vehicle manufacturers, so accept the advice of the parts storeman when purchasing components. Spare parts lists and manuals are compiled upon a numerical basis and individual vehicle numbers are essential to the supply of the correct component.

The *vehicle identification plate* is a rectangular plate secured to the heating/ventilating block on the RH side of the engine compartment on UK models or on the left-hand centre pillar on North American models. An oval plate is also secured to the right-hand inner wing panel.

The *engine identification plate* will be found riveted to the cylinder block, the position depending upon the space available (photo). Two types of plate may be employed.

The *transmission identification plate* will be found on manual gearboxes, under the head of one of the bolts which secure the end cover. Where automatic transmission is concerned, the plate is riveted to the upper face of the converter housing.

Engine identification plate

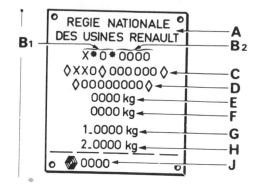

Vehicle identification plate (rectangular) on UK models

A	Maker's name	E	Maximum all-up weight
B1	Country number	F	Maximum gross train weight
B2	Reception number	G	Maximum front axle load
C	French Ministry of Mines number	H	Maximum rear axle load
D	Chassis number	J	Model year

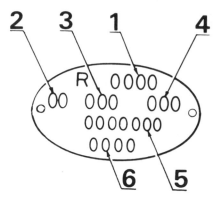

Vehicle identification plate (oval)

1 Vehicle type
2 Transmission and appearance code
3 Basic equipment code
4 Optional equipment code
5 Fabrication number
6 Model year (not always present)

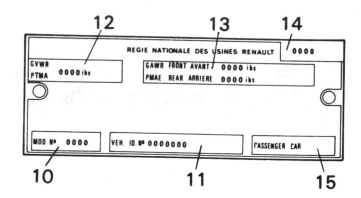

Vehicle identification plate (rectangular) on North American models

10 Model number
11 Serial number
12 Maximum allowable load (total)
13 Maximum allowable load (front and rear axles)
14 Month/year of manufacture
15 Vehicle class

Tools and working facilities

Introduction

A selection of good tools is a fundamental requirement for anyone contemplating the maintenance and repair of a motor vehicle. For the owner who does not possess any, their purchase will prove a considerable expense, offsetting some of the savings made by doing-it-yourself. However, provided that the tools purchased are of good quality, they will last for many years and prove an extremely worthwhile investment.

To help the average owner to decide which tools are needed to carry out the various tasks detailed in this manual, we have compiled three lists of tools under the following headings: *Maintenance and minor repair, Repair and overhaul,* and *Special.* The newcomer to practical mechanics should start off with the *Maintenance and minor repair* tool kit and confine himself to the simpler jobs around the vehicle. Then, as his confidence and experience grow, he can undertake more difficult tasks, buying extra tools as, and when, they are needed. In this way, a *Maintenance and minor repair* tool kit can be built-up into a *Repair and overhaul* tool kit over a considerable period of time without any major cash outlays. The experienced do-it-yourselfer will have a tool kit good enough for most repair and overhaul procedures and will add tools from the *Special* category when he feels the expense is justified by the amount of use to which these tools will be put.

It is obviously not possible to cover the subject of tools fully here. For those who wish to learn more about tools and their use there is a book entitled *How to Choose and Use Car Tools* available from the publishers of this manual.

Maintenance and minor repair tool kit

The tools given in this list should be considered as a minimum requirement if routine maintenance, servicing and minor repair operations are to be undertaken. We recommend the purchase of combination spanners (ring one end, open-ended the other); although more expensive than open-ended ones, they do give the advantages of both types of spanner.

Combination spanners - 10, 11, 12, 13, 14 & 17 mm
Adjustable spanner - 9 inch
Engine sump/gearbox drain plug key
Spark plug spanner (with rubber insert)
Spark plug gap adjustment tool
Set of feeler gauges
Brake adjuster spanner
Brake bleed nipple spanner
Screwdriver - 4 in long x $\frac{1}{4}$ in dia (flat blade)
Screwdriver - 4 in long x $\frac{1}{4}$ in dia (cross blade)
Combination pliers - 6 inch
Hacksaw (junior)
Tyre pump
Tyre pressure gauge
Oil can
Fine emery cloth (1 sheet)
Wire brush (small)
Funnel (medium size)

Repair and overhaul tool kit

These tools are virtually essential for anyone undertaking any major repairs to a motor vehicle, and are additional to those given in the *Maintenance and minor repair* list. Included in this list is a comprehensive set of sockets. Although these are expensive they will be found invaluable as they are so versatile - particularly if various drives are included in the set. We recommend the $\frac{1}{2}$ in square-drive type, as this can be used with most proprietary torque wrenches. If you cannot afford a socket set, even bought piecemeal, then inexpensive tubular box spanners are a useful alternative.

The tools in this list will occasionally need to be supplemented by tools from the *Special* list.

Sockets (or box spanners) to cover range in previous list
Reversible ratchet drive (for use with sockets)
Extension piece, 10 inch (for use with sockets)
Universal joint (for use with sockets)
Torque wrench (for use with sockets)
'Mole' wrench - 8 inch
Ball pein hammer
Soft-faced hammer, plastic or rubber
Screwdriver - 6 in long x $\frac{5}{16}$ in dia (flat blade)
Screwdriver - 2 in long x $\frac{5}{16}$ in square (flat blade)
Screwdriver - 1$\frac{1}{2}$ in long x $\frac{1}{4}$ in dia (cross blade)
Screwdriver - 3 in long x $\frac{1}{8}$ in dia (electricians)
Pliers - electricians side cutters
Pliers - needle nosed
Pliers - circlip (internal and external)
Cold chisel - $\frac{1}{2}$ inch
Scriber
Scraper
Centre punch
Pin punch
Hacksaw
Valve grinding tool
Steel rule/straight-edge
Allen keys
Selection of files
Wire brush (large)
Axle-stands
Jack (strong scissor or hydraulic type)

Special tools

The tools in this list are those which are not used regularly, are expensive to buy, or which need to be used in accordance with their manufacturers' instructions. Unless relatively difficult mechanical jobs are undertaken frequently, it will not be economic to buy many of these tools. Where this is the case, you could consider clubbing together with friends (or joining a motorists' club) to make a joint purchase, or borrowing the tools against a deposit from a local garage or tool hire specialist.

The following list contains only those tools and instruments freely available to the public, and not those special tools produced by the vehicle manufacturer specifically for its dealer network. You will find occasional references to these manufacturers' special tools in the text of this manual. Generally, an alternative method of doing the job without the vehicle manufacturers' special tool is given. However, sometimes, there is no alternative to using them. Where this is the case and the relevant tool cannot be bought or borrowed, you will have to entrust the work to a franchised garage.

Valve spring compressor
Piston ring compressor
Balljoint separator
Universal hub/bearing puller
Impact screwdriver
Micrometer and/or vernier gauge
Dial gauge
Stroboscopic timing light
Dwell angle meter/tachometer
Universal electrical multi-meter
Cylinder compression gauge
Lifting tackle
Trolley jack
Light with extension lead

Buying tools

For practically all tools, a tool factor is the best source since he will have a very comprehensive range compared with the average garage or accessory shop. Having said that, accessory shops often offer excellent quality tools at discount prices, so it pays to shop around.

Remember, you don't have to buy the most expensive items on the shelf, but it is always advisable to steer clear of the very cheap tools. There are plenty of good tools around at reasonable prices, so ask the proprietor or manager of the shop for advice before making a purchase.

Care and maintenance of tools

Having purchased a reasonable tool kit, it is necessary to keep the tools in a clean serviceable condition. After use, always wipe off any dirt, grease and metal particles using a clean, dry cloth, before putting the tools away. Never leave them lying around after they have been used. A simple tool rack on the garage or workshop wall, for items such as screwdrivers and pliers is a good idea. Store all normal wrenches and sockets in a metal box. Any measuring instruments, gauges, meters, etc, must be carefully stored where they cannot be damaged or become rusty.

Take a little care when tools are used. Hammer heads inevitably become marked and screwdrivers lose the keen edge on their blades from time to time. A little timely attention with emery cloth or a file will soon restore items like this to a good serviceable finish.

Working facilities

Not to be forgotten when discussing tools, is the workshop itself. If anything more than routine maintenance is to be carried out, some form of suitable working area becomes essential.

It is appreciated that many an owner mechanic is forced by circumstances to remove an engine or similar item, without the benefit of a garage or workshop. Having done this, any repairs should always be done under the cover of a roof.

Wherever possible, any dismantling should be done on a clean, flat workbench or table at a suitable working height.

Any workbench needs a vice: one with a jaw opening of 4 in (100 mm) is suitable for most jobs. As mentioned previously, some clean dry storage space is also required for tools, as well as for lubricants, cleaning fluids, touch-up paints and so on, which become necessary.

Another item which may be required, and which has a much more general usage, is an electric drill with a chuck capacity of at least $\frac{5}{16}$ in (8 mm). This, together with a good range of twist drills, is virtually essential for fitting accessories such as mirrors and reversing lights.

Last, but not least, always keep a supply of old newspapers and clean, lint-free rags available, and try to keep any working area as clean as possible.

Spanner jaw gap comparison table

Jaw gap (in)	Spanner size
0.250	$\frac{1}{4}$ in AF
0.276	7 mm
0.313	$\frac{5}{16}$ in AF
0.315	8 mm
0.344	$\frac{11}{32}$ in AF; $\frac{1}{8}$ in Whitworth
0.354	9 mm
0.375	$\frac{3}{8}$ in AF
0.394	10 mm
0.433	11 mm
0.438	$\frac{7}{16}$ in AF
0.445	$\frac{3}{16}$ in Whitworth; $\frac{1}{4}$ in BSF
0.472	12 mm
0.500	$\frac{1}{2}$ in AF
0.512	13 mm
0.525	$\frac{1}{4}$ in Whitworth; $\frac{5}{16}$ in BSF
0.551	14 mm
0.563	$\frac{9}{16}$ in AF
0.591	15 mm
0.600	$\frac{5}{16}$ in Whitworth; $\frac{3}{8}$ in BSF
0.625	$\frac{5}{8}$ in AF
0.630	16 mm
0.669	17 mm
0.686	$\frac{11}{16}$ in AF
0.709	18 mm
0.710	$\frac{3}{8}$ in Whitworth; $\frac{7}{16}$ in BSF
0.748	19 mm
0.750	$\frac{3}{4}$ in AF
0.813	$\frac{13}{16}$ in AF
0.820	$\frac{7}{16}$ in Whitworth; $\frac{1}{2}$ in BSF
0.866	22 mm
0.875	$\frac{7}{8}$ in AF
0.920	$\frac{1}{2}$ in Whitworth; $\frac{9}{16}$ in BSF
0.938	$\frac{15}{16}$ in AF
0.945	24 mm
1.000	1 in AF
1.010	$\frac{9}{16}$ in Whitworth; $\frac{5}{8}$ in BSF
1.024	26 mm
1.063	$1\frac{1}{16}$ in AF; 27 mm
1.100	$\frac{5}{8}$ in Whitworth; $\frac{11}{16}$ in BSF
1.125	$1\frac{1}{8}$ in AF
1.181	30 mm
1.200	$\frac{11}{16}$ in Whitworth; $\frac{3}{4}$ in BSF
1.250	$1\frac{1}{4}$ in AF
1.260	32 mm
1.300	$\frac{3}{4}$ in Whitworth; $\frac{7}{8}$ in BSF
1.313	$1\frac{5}{16}$ in AF
1.390	$\frac{13}{16}$ in Whitworth; $\frac{15}{16}$ in BSF
1.417	36 mm
1.438	$1\frac{7}{16}$ in AF
1.480	$\frac{7}{8}$ in Whitworth; 1 in BSF
1.500	$1\frac{1}{2}$ in AF
1.575	40 mm; $\frac{15}{16}$ in Whitworth
1.614	41 mm
1.625	$1\frac{5}{8}$ in AF
1.670	1 in Whitworth; $1\frac{1}{8}$ in BSF
1.688	$1\frac{11}{16}$ in AF
1.811	46 mm
1.813	$1\frac{13}{16}$ in AF
1.860	$1\frac{1}{8}$ in Whitworth; $1\frac{1}{4}$ in BSF
1.875	$1\frac{7}{8}$ in AF
1.969	50 mm
2.000	2 in AF
2.050	$1\frac{1}{4}$ in Whitworth; $1\frac{3}{8}$ in BSF
2.165	55 mm
2.362	60 mm

General repair procedures

Whenever servicing, repair or overhaul work is carried out on the car or its components, it is necessary to observe the following procedures and instructions. This will assist in carrying out the operation efficiently and to a professional standard of workmanship.

Joint mating faces and gaskets

Where a gasket is used between the mating faces of two components, ensure that it is renewed on reassembly, and fit it dry unless otherwise stated in the repair procedure. Make sure that the mating faces are clean and dry with all traces of old gasket removed. When cleaning a joint face, use a tool which is not likely to score or damage the face, and remove any burrs or nicks with an oilstone or fine file.

Make sure that tapped holes are cleaned with a pipe cleaner, and keep them free of jointing compound if this is being used unless specifically instructed otherwise.

Ensure that all orifices, channels or pipes are clear and blow through them, preferably using compressed air.

Oil seals

Whenever an oil seal is removed from its working location, either individually or as part of an assembly, it should be renewed.

The very fine sealing lip of the seal is easily damaged and will not seal if the surface it contacts is not completely clean and free from scratches, nicks or grooves. If the original sealing surface of the component cannot be restored, the component should be renewed.

Protect the lips of the seal from any surface which may damage them in the course of fitting. Use tape or a conical sleeve where possible. Lubricate the seal lips with oil before fitting and, on dual lipped seals, fill the space between the lips with grease.

Unless otherwise stated, oil seals must be fitted with their sealing lips toward the lubricant to be sealed.

Use a tubular drift or block of wood of the appropriate size to install the seal and, if the seal housing is shouldered, drive the seal down to the shoulder. If the seal housing is unshouldered, the seal should be fitted with its face flush with the housing top face.

Screw threads and fastenings

Always ensure that a blind tapped hole is completely free from oil, grease, water or other fluid before installing the bolt or stud. Failure to do this could cause the housing to crack due to the hydraulic action of the bolt or stud as it is screwed in.

When tightening a castellated nut to accept a split pin, tighten the nut to the specified torque, where applicable, and then tighten further to the next split pin hole. Never slacken the nut to align a split pin hole unless stated in the repair procedure.

When checking or retightening a nut or bolt to a specified torque setting, slacken the nut or bolt by a quarter of a turn, and then retighten to the specified setting.

Locknuts, locktabs and washers

Any fastening which will rotate against a component or housing in the course of tightening should always have a washer between it and the relevant component or housing.

Spring or split washers should always be renewed when they are used to lock a critical component such as a big-end bearing retaining nut or bolt.

Locktabs which are folded over to retain a nut or bolt should always be renewed.

Self-locking nuts can be reused in non-critical areas, providing resistance can be felt when the locking portion passes over the bolt or stud thread.

Split pins must always be replaced with new ones of the correct size for the hole.

Special tools

Some repair procedures in this manual entail the use of special tools such as a press, two or three-legged pullers, spring compressors etc. Wherever possible, suitable readily available alternatives to the manufacturer's special tools are described, and are shown in use. In some instances, where no alternative is possible, it has been necessary to resort to the use of a manufacturer's tool and this has been done for reasons of safety as well as the efficient completion of the repair operation. Unless you are highly skilled and have a thorough understanding of the procedure described, never attempt to bypass the use of any special tool when the procedure described specifies its use. Not only is there a very great risk of personal injury, but expensive damage could be caused to the components involved.

Jacking and towing

Jacking

The jack supplied with the vehicle is not designed for service or repair operations, but purely for changing a wheel in the event of a puncture. A strong pillar or trolley jack should be employed for maintenance and repair tasks requiring the vehicle to be raised. The jacking point is of particular importance.

At the front use a block to take the load under the side members behind the undertray. Do not bear on the exhaust pipe, and before lifting ensure that the handbrake is applied and the rear wheels are chocked.

At the side, take the load under the sill in the centre of the front door, using a wooden block to spread the load. Ensure that the wheels are chocked.

At the rear, position the jack head under the centre of the rear axle beams. Ensure that the front wheels are chocked.

When using stands, do not omit to use a reinforcement block between the vehicle and the stand.

Do not lift the vehicle by the towing attachment points.

When jacking the vehicle in an emergency situation, such as changing a wheel at the roadside, remove the jack and brace from the

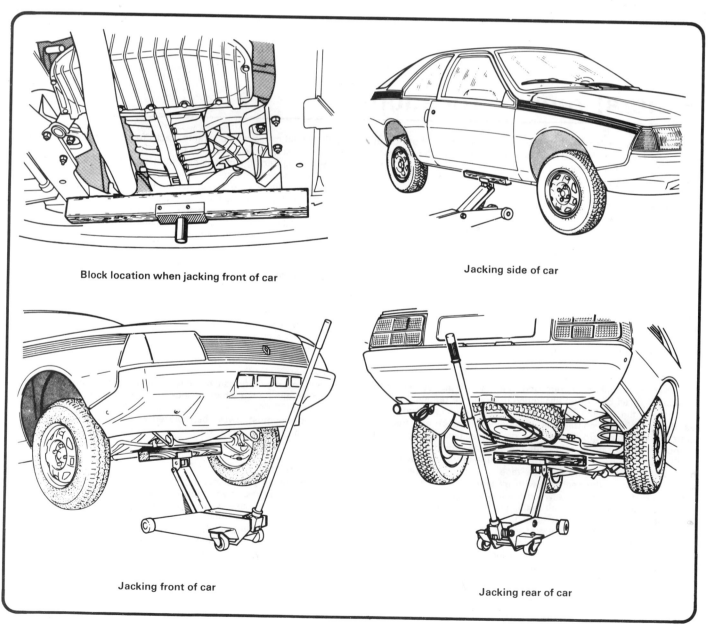

Block location when jacking front of car

Jacking side of car

Jacking front of car

Jacking rear of car

engine compartment (UK models) or luggage compartment (North American models). Remove the spare wheel using the brace to lower it from inside the luggage compartment (photos). Make sure that the tongue on the jack head is located correctly in the slot on the sill. The jacking points are to be found one behind each front wheel, and one in front of each rear wheel.

Towing

Towing eyes are provided at the front and rear of the car (photos). Never attach the tow rope to suspension or body parts. Do not use the towing eyes for operations of a heavy nature, such as pulling other vehicles from ditches. Ensure when being towed that the steering is unlocked, and note that more effort will be required when braking if the engine is off and the servo therefore inoperative.

Towing of automatic transmission models requires special care since, if the engine is stopped, the transmission is not lubricated. For this reason it is preferable to raise the front wheels from the ground when towing; if this is not possible, add an extra 2 litres (3.5 Imp pt/2.1 US qt) of fluid to the transmission and do not tow the car at speeds of more than 20 mph (30 kph) or for a distance of more than 30 miles (50 km). After towing, drain the additional fluid.

Push or tow starting is not possible on cars fitted with automatic transmission.

Lifting jack location (R1363)

Brace – arrowed (R1363)

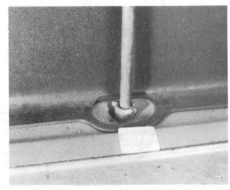
Lowering the spare wheel

Front towing eye

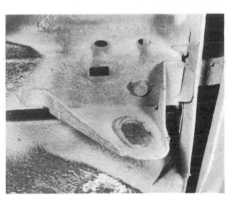
Rear towing eye

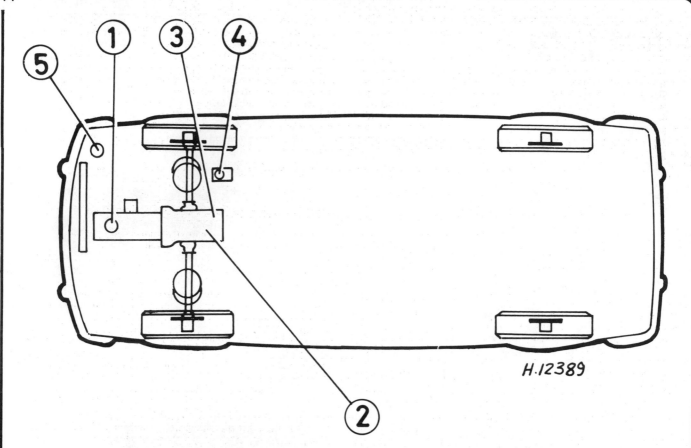

H.12389

Recommended lubricants and fluids

Component or system	Lubricant type or specificaion
Engine (1)	15W/40, 20W/40 or 10W/40 multigrade engine oil
Manual gearbox (2)	SAE 80W gear oil
Automatic transmission (3)	ATF or TQ Dexron II
Brake fluid (4)	SAE J1703 F, DOT3 or DOT4 hydraulic fluid
Power steering (5)	ATF

Safety first!

Professional motor mechanics are trained in safe working procedures. However enthusiastic you may be about getting on with the job in hand, do take the time to ensure that your safety is not put at risk. A moment's lack of attention can result in an accident, as can failure to observe certain elementary precautions.

There will always be new ways of having accidents, and the following points do not pretend to be a comprehensive list of all dangers; they are intended rather to make you aware of the risks and to encourage a safety-conscious approach to all work you carry out on your vehicle.

Essential DOs and DON'Ts

DON'T rely on a single jack when working underneath the vehicle. Always use reliable additional means of support, such as axle stands, securely placed under a part of the vehicle that you know will not give way.

DON'T attempt to loosen or tighten high-torque nuts (e.g. wheel hub nuts) while the vehicle is on a jack; it may be pulled off.

DON'T start the engine without first ascertaining that the transmission is in neutral (or 'Park' where applicable) and the parking brake applied.

DON'T suddenly remove the filler cap from a hot cooling system – cover it with a cloth and release the pressure gradually first, or you may get scalded by escaping coolant.

DON'T attempt to drain oil until you are sure it has cooled sufficiently to avoid scalding you.

DON'T grasp any part of the engine, exhaust or catalytic converter without first ascertaining that it is sufficiently cool to avoid burning you.

DON'T allow brake fluid or antifreeze to contact vehicle paintwork.

DON'T syphon toxic liquids such as fuel, brake fluid or antifreeze by mouth, or allow them to remain on your skin.

DON'T inhale dust – it may be injurious to health (see *Asbestos* below).

DON'T allow any spilt oil or grease to remain on the floor – wipe it up straight away, before someone slips on it.

DON'T use ill-fitting spanners or other tools which may slip and cause injury.

DON'T attempt to lift a heavy component which may be beyond your capability – get assistance.

DON'T rush to finish a job, or take unverified short cuts.

DON'T allow children or animals in or around an unattended vehicle.

DO wear eye protection when using power tools such as drill, sander, bench grinder etc, and when working under the vehicle.

DO use a barrier cream on your hands prior to undertaking dirty jobs – it will protect your skin from infection as well as making the dirt easier to remove afterwards; but make sure your hands aren't left slippery.

DO keep loose clothing (cuffs, tie etc) and long hair well out of the way of moving mechanical parts.

DO remove rings, wristwatch etc, before working on the vehicle – especially the electrical system.

DO ensure that any lifting tackle used has a safe working load rating adequate for the job.

DO keep your work area tidy – it is only too easy to fall over articles left lying around.

DO get someone to check periodically that all is well, when working alone on the vehicle.

DO carry out work in a logical sequence and check that everything is correctly assembled and tightened afterwards.

DO remember that your vehicle's safety affects that of yourself and others. If in doubt on any point, get specialist advice.

IF, in spite of following these precautions, you are unfortunate enough to injure yourself, seek medical attention as soon as possible.

Asbestos

Certain friction, insulating, sealing, and other products – such as brake linings, brake bands, clutch linings, torque converters, gaskets, etc – contain asbestos. *Extreme care must be taken to avoid inhalation of dust from such products since it is hazardous to health.* If in doubt, assume that they *do* contain asbestos.

Fire

Remember at all times that petrol (gasoline) is highly flammable. Never smoke, or have any kind of naked flame around, when working on the vehicle. But the risk does not end there – a spark caused by an electrical short-circuit, by two metal surfaces contacting each other, by careless use of tools, or even by static electricity built up in your body under certain conditions, can ignite petrol vapour, which in a confined space is highly explosive.

Always disconnect the battery earth (ground) terminal before working on any part of the fuel or electrical system, and never risk spilling fuel on to a hot engine or exhaust.

It is recommended that a fire extinguisher of a type suitable for fuel and electrical fires is kept handy in the garage or workplace at all times. Never try to extinguish a fuel or electrical fire with water.

Fumes

Certain fumes are highly toxic and can quickly cause unconsciousness and even death if inhaled to any extent. Petrol (gasoline) vapour comes into this category, as do the vapours from certain solvents such as trichloroethylene. Any draining or pouring of such volatile fluids should be done in a well ventilated area.

When using cleaning fluids and solvents, read the instructions carefully. Never use materials from unmarked containers – they may give off poisonous vapours.

Never run the engine of a motor vehicle in an enclosed space such as a garage. Exhaust fumes contain carbon monoxide which is extremely poisonous; if you need to run the engine, always do so in the open air or at least have the rear of the vehicle outside the workplace.

If you are fortunate enough to have the use of an inspection pit, never drain or pour petrol, and never run the engine, while the vehicle is standing over it; the fumes, being heavier than air, will concentrate in the pit with possibly lethal results.

The battery

Never cause a spark, or allow a naked light, near the vehicle's battery. It will normally be giving off a certain amount of hydrogen gas, which is highly explosive.

Always disconnect the battery earth (ground) terminal before working on the fuel or electrical systems.

If possible, loosen the filler plugs or cover when charging the battery from an external source. Do not charge at an excessive rate or the battery may burst.

Take care when topping up and when carrying the battery. The acid electrolyte, even when diluted, is very corrosive and should not be allowed to contact the eyes or skin.

If you ever need to prepare electrolyte yourself, always add the acid slowly to the water, and never the other way round. Protect against splashes by wearing rubber gloves and goggles.

When jump starting a car using a booster battery, for negative earth (ground) vehicles, connect the jump leads in the following sequence: First connect one jump lead between the positive (+) terminals of the two batteries. Then connect the other jump lead first to the negative (–) terminal of the booster battery, and then to a good earthing (ground) point on the vehicle to be started, at least 18 in (45 cm) from the battery if possible. Ensure that hands and jump leads are clear of any moving parts, and that the two vehicles do not touch. Disconnect the leads in the reverse order.

Mains electricity

When using an electric power tool, inspection light etc, which works from the mains, always ensure that the appliance is correctly connected to its plug and that, where necessary, it is properly earthed (grounded). Do not use such appliances in damp conditions and, again, beware of creating a spark or applying excessive heat in the vicinity of fuel or fuel vapour.

Ignition HT voltage

A severe electric shock can result from touching certain parts of the ignition system, such as the HT leads, when the engine is running or being cranked, particularly if components are damp or the insulation is defective. Where an electronic ignition system is fitted, the HT voltage is much higher and could prove fatal.

Routine maintenance

Maintenance is essential for ensuring safety and desirable for the purpose of getting the best in terms of performance and economy from your car. Over the years the need for periodic lubrication – oiling, greasing and so on – has been drastically reduced if not totally eliminated. This has unfortunately tended to lead some owners to think that because no such action is required, components either no longer exist, or will last forever. This is a serious delusion. It follows therefore that the largest initial element of maintenance is visual examination. This may lead to repairs or renewal.

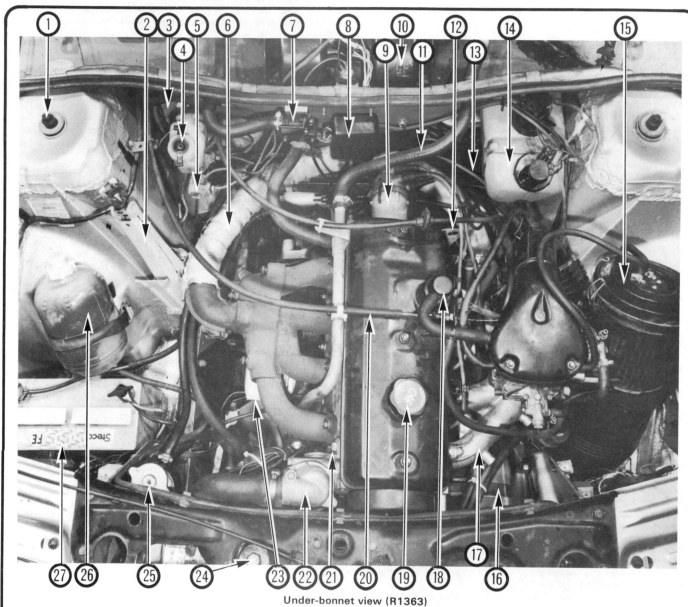

Under-bonnet view (R1363)

1	Front shock absorber upper mounting	7	Heater valve	14	Washer fluid reservoir
2	Lifting jack	8	Engine wiring harness connector cover	15	Air cleaner unit
3	Servo unit	9	Distributor	16	Alternator
4	Brake fluid reservoir filler cap	10	Heater motor	17	Inlet manifold
5	Brake master cylinder	11	Heater return hose	18	Crankcase ventilation outlet
6	Warm air hose for air inlet temperature control	12	Rear engine hanger	19	Oil filler cap
		13	Steering gear	20	Accelerator cable
				21	Front engine hanger

22 Thermostat cover
23 Oil filter
24 Radiator cap
25 Power steering fluid reservoir filler cap
26 Coolant expansion bottle
27 Battery

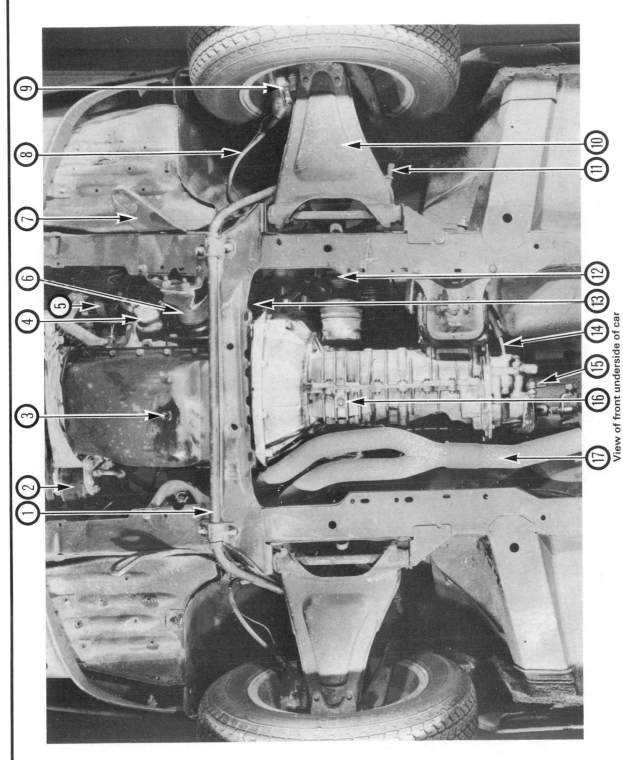

View of front underside of car

1 Front anti-roll bar
2 Power steering pump
3 Engine oil drain plug
4 Fuel pump

5 Alternator
6 Engine mounting
7 Front towing eye
8 Brake hydraulic hose

9 Front brake caliper
10 Front suspension lower arm
11 Track rod end

12 Driveshaft
13 Starter motor
14 Speedometer cable

15 Gearchange linkage
16 Manual gearbox oil drain plug
17 Exhaust front downpipe

View of rear underside of car

1 Rear suspension side arm
2 Handbrake cable (RH section)
3 Brake pressure limiter
4 Rear suspension centre arm
5 Exhaust intermediate silencer
6 Exhaust mounting
7 Handbrake cable (LH section)
8 Rear anti-roll bar
9 Exhaust rear silencer
10 Coil spring
11 Spare wheel
12 Rear axle beam
13 Rear shock absorber lower mounting

The summary below gives a schedule of routine maintenance operations. More detailed information on the respective items is given in the Chapter concerned. Before starting on any maintenance procedures, make a list and obtain any items or parts that may be required. Make sure you have the necessary tools to complete the servicing requirements. Where the vehicle has to be raised clear of the ground pay particular attention to safety and ensure that chassis stands and/or blocks supplement the jack. Do not rely on the jack supplied with the car — it was designed purely to raise the car for changing a wheel in the event of a puncture.

Every 250 miles (400 km) or weekly – whichever occurs first

Engine
    Check the oil level and top up if necessary (photos)
    Check the coolant level and top up if necessary (photo)

Tyres
    Check and adjust the tyre pressures (photo)

Every 5000 miles (8000 km) or six monthly

Engine
    Change the oil
    Check for oil, fuel and water leaks

Brakes
    Check hydraulic fluid level and top up if necessary (Chapter 9)

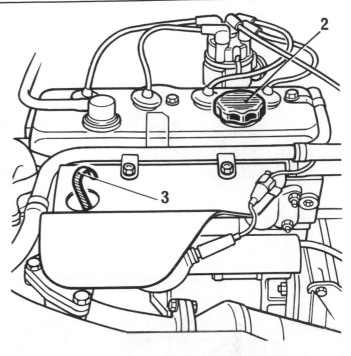

Checking oil level on type 843 engine

    2   *Filler cap*   3   *Dipstick*

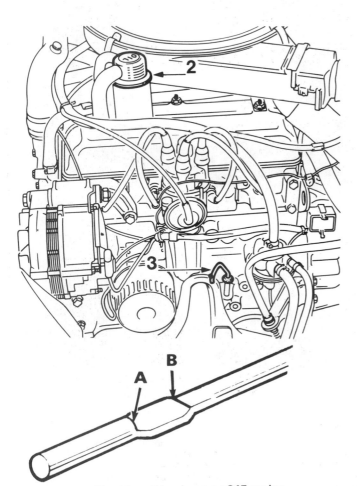

Checking oil level on type 847 engine

    A   *Minimum*   2   *Filler cap*
    B   *Maximum*   3   *Dipstick*

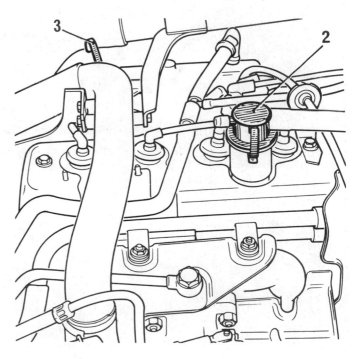

Checking oil level on type A7L engine

    2   *Filler cap*   3   *Dipstick*

Electrical
    Check battery electrolyte level and top up if necessary
    Check washer fluid levels and top up if necessary (photo)
    Check operation of all lights

Tyres
    Check the tyres for wear and damage

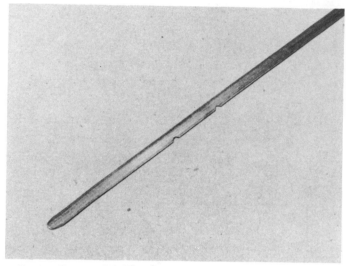

Engine oil level dipstick markings (approx 1 litre min to max)

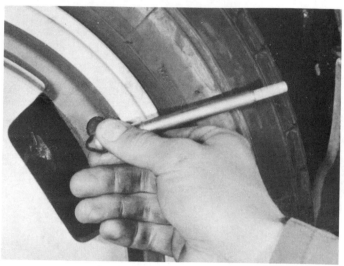

Checking the tyre pressures

Topping-up the engine oil level

Washer fluid reservoir (R1363)

Topping-up the coolant level

Every 10 000 miles (16 000 km) or once a year

Engine

Change the oil and filter
Check and adjust the dwell angle (conventional ignition) (Chapter 4)
Adjust the ignition timing (Chapter 4)
Check and adjust or renew the spark plugs (conventional ignition) (Chapter 4)
Adjust the idling speed and mixture (Chapter 3)
Adjust all drivebelt tensions

Automatic transmission

Check the fluid level and top up if necessary (Chapter 7)

Brakes

Check the disc pads for wear (Chapter 9)

Electrical

Check and adjust main beam alignment (Chapter 10)

Suspension and steering

Check the power steering fluid level and top up if necessary (Chapter 11)

Bodywork
 Check the underbody and wheel arches for damage and repair as necessary
 Lubricate sparingly door and bonnet hinges and catches

Every 20 000 miles (32 000 km) or every 2 years

Engine
 Visually check all components for condition
 Check and adjust or renew the contact breaker points (conventional ignition) (Chapter 4)
 Check and adjust or renew the spark plugs (electronic ignition) (Chapter 4)
 Renew the fuel filter (Chapter 3)
 Renew the air cleaner element (Chapter 3)

Every 30 000 miles (50 000 km) or every 3 years

Automatic transmission
 Renew the fluid and the filter

Every 40 000 miles (65 000 km) or every 4 years

Engine
 Drain, flush and refill the cooling system (Chapter 2)

Clutch
 Check and adjust the clutch cable (Chapter 5)

Manual gearbox
 Change the oil

Brakes
 Check the rear brake shoe linings for wear and renew if necessary (Chapter 9)
 Adjust the handbrake cable (Chapter 9)

Suspension and steering
 Check all joints and linkages for wear

Every 80 000 miles (130 000 km) or every 8 years

Engine (ohc type)
 Renew the timing belt (Chapter 1)

Fault diagnosis

Introduction

The vehicle owner who does his or her own maintenance according to the recommended schedules should not have to use this section of the manual very often. Modern component reliability is such that, provided those items subject to wear or deterioration are inspected or renewed at the specified intervals, sudden failure is comparatively rare. Faults do not usually just happen as a result of sudden failure, but develop over a period of time. Major mechanical failures in particular are usually preceded by characteristic symptoms over hundreds or even thousands of miles. Those components which do occasionally fail without warning are often small and easily carried in the vehicle.

With any fault finding, the first step is to decide where to begin investigations. Sometimes this is obvious, but on other occasions a little detective work will be necessary. The owner who makes half a dozen haphazard adjustments or replacements may be successful in curing a fault (or its symptoms), but he will be none the wiser if the fault recurs and he may well have spent more time and money than was necessary. A calm and logical approach will be found to be more satisfactory in the long run. Always take into account any warning signs or abnormalities that may have been noticed in the period preceding the fault — power loss, high or low gauge readings, unusual noises or smells, etc — and remember that failure of components such as fuses or spark plugs may only be pointers to some underlying fault.

The pages which follow here are intended to help in cases of failure to start or breakdown on the road. There is also a Fault Diagnosis Section at the end of each Chapter which should be consulted if the preliminary checks prove unfruitful. Whatever the fault, certain basic principles apply. These are as follows:

Verify the fault. This is simply a matter of being sure that you know what the symptoms are before starting work. This is particularly important if you are investigating a fault for someone else who may not have described it very accurately.

Don't overlook the obvious. For example, if the vehicle won't start, is there petrol in the tank? (Don't take anyone else's word on this particular point, and don't trust the fuel gauge either!) If an electrical fault is indicated, look for loose or broken wires before digging out the test gear.

Cure the disease, not the symptom. Substituting a flat battery with a fully charged one will get you off the hard shoulder, but if the underlying cause is not attended to, the new battery will go the same way. Similarly, changing oil-fouled spark plugs for a new set will get you moving again, but remember that the reason for the fouling (if it wasn't simply an incorrect grade of plug) will have to be established and corrected.

Don't take anything for granted. Particularly, don't forget that a 'new' component may itself be defective (especially if it's been rattling round in the boot for months), and don't leave components out of a fault diagnosis sequence just because they are new or recently fitted. When you do finally diagnose a difficult fault, you'll probably realise that all the evidence was there from the start.

Electrical faults

Electrical faults can be more puzzling than straightforward mechanical failures, but they are no less susceptible to logical analysis if the basic principles of operation are understood. Vehicle electrical wiring exists in extremely unfavourable conditions — heat, vibration and chemical attack — and the first things to look for are loose or corroded connections and broken or chafed wires, especially where the wires pass through holes in the bodywork or are subject to vibration.

All metal-bodied vehicles in current production have one pole of the battery 'earthed', ie connected to the vehicle bodywork, and in nearly all modern vehicles it is the negative (−) terminal. The various electrical components — motors, bulb holders etc — are also connected to earth, either by means of a lead or directly by their mountings. Electric current flows through the component and then back to the battery via the bodywork. If the component mounting is loose or corroded, or if a good path back to the battery is not available, the circuit will be incomplete and malfunction will result. The engine and/or gearbox are also earthed by means of flexible metal straps to the body or subframe; if these straps are loose or missing, starter motor, generator and ignition trouble may result.

Assuming the earth return to be satisfactory, electrical faults will be due either to component malfunction or to defects in the current supply. Individual components are dealt with in Chapter 10. If supply wires are broken or cracked internally this results in an open-circuit, and the easiest way to check for this is to bypass the suspect wire temporarily with a length of wire having a crocodile clip or suitable connector at each end. Alternatively, a 12V test lamp can be used to verify the presence of supply voltage at various points along the wire and the break can be thus isolated.

If a bare portion of a live wire touches the bodywork or other earthed metal part, the electricity will take the low-resistance path thus formed back to the battery: this is known as a short-circuit. Hopefully a short-circuit will blow a fuse, but otherwise it may cause burning of the insulation (and possibly further short-circuits) or even a fire. This is why it is inadvisable to bypass persistently blowing fuses with silver foil or wire.

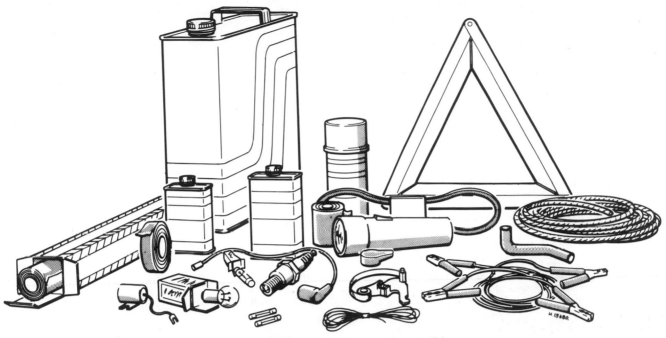

Carrying a few spares can save you a long walk!

Spares and tool kit

Most vehicles are supplied only with sufficient tools for wheel changing; the *Maintenance and minor repair* tool kit detailed in *Tools and working facilities,* with the addition of a hammer, is probably sufficient for those repairs that most motorists would consider attempting at the roadside. In addition a few items which can be fitted without too much trouble in the event of a breakdown should be carried. Experience and available space will modify the list below, but the following may save having to call on professional assistance:

Spark plugs, clean and correctly gapped
HT lead and plug cap — long enough to reach the plug furthest from the distributor
Distributor rotor, condenser and contact breaker points
Drivebelt(s) — emergency type may suffice
Spare fuses
Set of principal light bulbs
Tin of radiator sealer and hose bandage
Exhaust bandage
Roll of insulating tape
Length of soft iron wire
Length of electrical flex
Torch or inspection lamp (can double as test lamp)
Battery jump leads
Tow-rope
Ignition waterproofing aerosol
Litre of engine oil
Sealed can of hydraulic fluid
Emergency windscreen
Worm drive clips
Tube of filler paste

If spare fuel is carried, a can designed for the purpose should be used to minimise risks of leakage and collision damage. A first aid kit and a warning triangle, whilst not at present compulsory in the UK, are obviously sensible items to carry in addition to the above.

When touring abroad it may be advisable to carry additional spares which, even if you cannot fit them yourself, could save having to wait while parts are obtained. The items below may be worth considering:

Clutch and throttle cables
Cylinder head gasket
Alternator brushes
Fuel pump repair kit
Tyre valve core

One of the motoring organisations will be able to advise on availability of fuel etc in foreign countries.

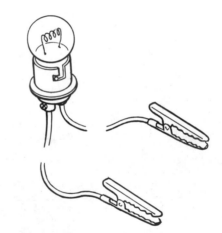

A simple test lamp is useful for tracing electrical faults

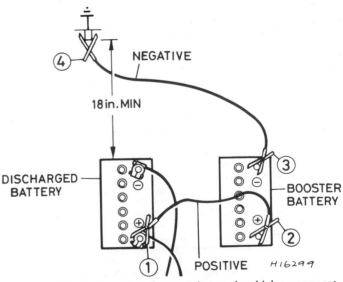

Jump start lead connections for negative earth vehicles – connect leads in order shown

Engine will not start

Engine fails to turn when starter operated

Flat battery (recharge, use jump leads, or push start where possible)
Battery terminals loose or corroded
Battery earth to body defective
Engine earth strap loose or broken
Starter motor (or solenoid) wiring loose or broken
Automatic transmission selector in wrong position, or inhibitor switch faulty
Ignition/starter switch faulty
Major mechanical failure (seizure)
Starter or solenoid internal fault (see Chapter 10)

Starter motor turns engine slowly

Partially discharged battery (recharge, use jump leads, or push start where possible)
Battery terminals loose or corroded
Battery earth to body defective
Engine earth strap loose
Starter motor (or solenoid) wiring loose
Starter motor internal fault (see Chapter 10)

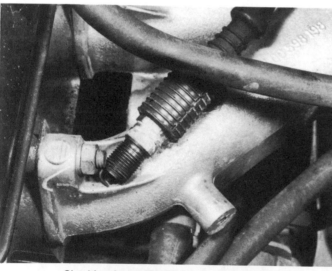

Checking for an HT spark (see Chapter 4)

Engine turns normally but fails to start

Damp or dirty HT leads and distributor cap (crank engine and check for spark) (photo)
Dirty or incorrectly gapped distributor points (if applicable)
No fuel in tank (check for delivery)
Excessive choke (hot engine) or insufficient choke (cold engine)
Fouled or incorrectly gapped spark plugs (remove, clean and regap)
Other ignition system fault (see Chapter 4)
Other fuel system fault (see Chapter 3)
Poor compression (see Chapter 1)
Major mechanical failure (eg camshaft drive)

Engine fires but will not run

Insufficient choke (cold engine)
Air leaks at carburettor or inlet manifold

Fuel starvation (see Chapter 3)
Ballast resistor defective, or other ignition fault (see Chapter 4)

Engine cuts out and will not restart

Engine cuts out suddenly — ignition fault

Loose or disconnected LT wires
Wet HT leads or distributor cap (after traversing water splash)
Coil or condenser failure (check for spark)
Other ignition fault (see Chapter 4)

Engine misfires before cutting out — fuel fault

Fuel tank empty
Fuel pump defective or filter blocked (check for delivery)
Fuel tank filler vent blocked on UK models (suction will be evident on releasing cap)
Carburettor needle valve sticking where applicable
Carburettor jets blocked (fuel contaminated)
Other fuel system fault (see Chapter 3)

Engine cuts out — other causes

Serious overheating
Major mechanical failure (eg camshaft drive)

Engine overheats

Ignition (no-charge) warning light illuminated

Slack or broken drivebelt — retension or renew (Chapter 2)

Ignition warning light not illuminated

Coolant loss due to internal or external leakage (see Chapter 2)
Thermostat defective
Low oil level
Brakes binding
Radiator clogged externally or internally
Electric cooling fan not operating correctly
Engine waterways clogged
Ignition timing incorrect or automatic advance malfunctioning
Mixture too weak

Note: *Do not add cold water to an overheated engine or damage may result*

Low engine oil pressure

Gauge reads low or warning light illuminated with engine running

Oil level low or incorrect grade
Defective gauge or sender unit
Wire to sender unit earthed
Engine overheating
Oil filter clogged or bypass valve defective
Oil pressure relief valve defective
Oil pick-up strainer clogged
Oil pump worn or mountings loose
Worn main or big-end bearings

Note: *Low oil pressure in a high-mileage engine at tickover is not necessarily a cause for concern. Sudden pressure loss at speed is far more significant. In any event, check the gauge or warning light sender before condemning the engine.*

Engine noises

Pre-ignition (pinking) on acceleration

Incorrect grade of fuel
Ignition timing incorrect
Distributor faulty or worn (where applicable)

Incorrect mixture adjustment
Excessive carbon build-up in engine

Whistling or wheezing noises
  Leaking vacuum hose
  Leaking manifold gasket
  Blowing head gasket

Tapping or rattling
  Incorrect valve clearances
  Worn valve gear

Worn timing chain or belt
Broken piston ring (ticking noise)

Knocking or thumping
  Unintentional mechanical contact (eg fan blades)
  Worn fanbelt
  Peripheral component fault (generator, water pump etc)
  Worn big-end bearings (regular heavy knocking, perhaps less under load)
  Worn main bearings (rumbling and knocking, perhaps worsening under load)
  Piston slap (most noticeable when cold)

Chapter 1 Engine

For modifications, and information applicable to later models, see Supplement at end of manual

Contents

Specifications

Type .... Four-cylinder in-line, overhead valve or overhead camshaft

Application
Model:

	Capacity	Engine code
R1360	1397 cc	847
R1365	1565 cc	A5L
R136A	1565 cc	A7L
R1361	1647 cc	A2M
R1362 and B1368	1647 cc	843 or A6M
R1363	1995 cc	829 or J6R
*R1279	2165 cc	851

These engines are fitted to vehicles marketed in N. America

Overhead valve engines (ohv)
Bore
1397 cc .... 76.0 mm (2.994 in)
1565 cc .... 77.0 mm (3.034 in)
1647 cc .... 79.0 mm (3.113 in)

Stroke
1397 cc .... 77.0 mm (2.034 in)
1565 cc .... 84.0 mm (3.310 in)
1647 cc .... 84.0 mm (3.310 in)

Compression ratio
847 .... 9.25 to 1
A5L .... 8.1 to 1
A7L .... 8.0 to 1
A2M .... 9.3 to 1
843 (UK) .... 9.25 to 1
843 (North America) .... 8.6 to 1
A6M .... 9.3 to 1

Firing order .... 1-3-4-2 (No 1 at flywheel end)

Cylinder head
Valve clearances:
  847 hot:
    Inlet .... 0.18 mm (0.007 in)
    Exhaust .... 0.25 mm (0.010 in)
  847 cold:
    Inlet .... 0.15 mm (0.006 in)
    Exhaust .... 0.20 mm (0.008 in)
  All except 847 (hot or cold):
    Inlet .... 0.20 mm (0.008 in)
    Exhaust .... 0.25 mm (0.010 in)
Maximum face distortion .... 0.05 mm (0.002 in)
Maximum resurfacing depth .... 0.50 mm (0.020 in)
Minimum height:
  847:
    Early models .... 71.3 mm (2.809 ln)
    Late models .... 71.7 mm (2.825 in)
  A5L, A7L, 843 and J6R .... 93.0 mm (3.664 in)
  A2M .... 80.5 mm (3.172 in)
Head and seat valve angles (included):
  847 inlet .... 120°
  All except 847 inlet (including exhaust) .... 90°
Valve guides:
  Bore:
    847 .... 7.0 mm (0.276 in)
    All except 847 .... 8.0 mm (0.315 in)
  External diameter:
    847 .... 11.0 mm (0.433 in)
    All except 847 .... 13.0 mm (0.512 in)
  Oversizes:
    1 groove .... + 0.10 mm (0.004 in)
    2 grooves .... + 0.25 mm (0.010 in)
Valve spring free length:
  847 .... 42.0 mm (1.655 in)
  A5L and A6M .... 42.2 mm (1.663 in)
  A7L .... 54.3 mm (2.139 in)
  A2M .... 48.4 mm (1.907 in)
  843:
    Outer .... 54.3 mm (2.139 in)
    Inner .... 46.8 mm (1.844 in)

Cylinder liners
Protrusion (without O-rings):
  847 .... 0.02 to 0.09 mm (0.0008 to 0.0035 in)
  All except 847 .... 0.10 to 0.17 mm (0.0039 to 0.0067 in)

Crankshaft
Endfloat .... 0.05 to 0.23 mm (0.002 to 0.009 in)
Thrust washer thicknesses .... 2.80, 2.85, 2.90 and 2.95 mm (0.1103, 0.1123, 0.1143 and 0.1162 in)

	Standard	Regrind
Crankpin diameter:		
847	43.98 mm (1.7328 in)	43.73 mm (1.7230 in)
All except 847	48.00 mm (1.8812 in)	47.75 mm (1.8814 in)
Main bearing journal diameter	54.80 mm (2.1591 in)	54.55 mm (2.1493 in)

Camshaft
Endfloat:
  847 .... 0.06 to 0.11 mm (0.0024 to 0.0043 in)
  All except 847 .... 0.05 to 0.12 mm (0.0020 to 0.0047 in)

Valve timing

	Inlet opens	Inlet closes	Exhaust opens	Exhaust closes
847	22° BTDC	62° ABDC	65° BBDC	25° ATDC
A5L and A7L	10° BTDC	50° ABDC	50° BBDC	10° ATDC
A2M	10° BTDC	54° ABDC	54° BBDC	10° ATDC
843	21° BTDC	59° ABDC	59° BBDC	21° ATDC
A6M	30° BTDC	72° ABDC	72° BBDC	30° ATDC

Tappets

External diameter:
- 847 .... 19.0 mm (0.7486 in)
- A51, A2M and A6M .... 12.0 mm (0.4728 in)
- A7L and 843 .... 19.0 mm (0.7486 in)

Oversize .... + 0.20 mm (0.0079 in)

Pistons

Type .... Alloy with 3 rings

Connecting rods:
- Small-end play .... 0.31 to 0.57 mm (0.0122 to 0.0225 in)

Lubrication system

Oil capacity:
- Total:
  - 847 .... 3.25 litre (5.72 Imp pt; 3.44 US qt)
  - All except 847 .... 4.25 litre (7.48 Imp pt; 4.49 US qt)
- Filter .... 0.25 litre (0.44 Imp pt; 0.26 US qt)

Oil pressure (hot):

	Idling	4000 rpm
847	0.7 bar (10 lbf/in^2)	3.5 bar (50.75 lbf/in^2)
All except 847	2.0 bar (29 lbf/in^2)	4.0 bar (58 lbf/in^2)

Torque wrench settings

	lbf ft	Nm
Cylinder head bolts:		
Pre-tightening value (all models)	28	38
847	40 to 47	54 to 64
All except 847:		
Hot	61 to 65	83 to 88
Cold	56 to 59	76 to 80
Flywheel bolts	37	50
Driveplate bolts	48 to 52	65 to 71
Main bearing cap bolts:		
847	41 to 48	56 to 65
All except 847	48	65
Crankshaft pulley bolt:		
847	Not specified	Not specified
All except 847:		
40 mm (1.6 in) bolt	44 to 59	60 to 80
45 mm (1.8 in) bolt	66	89
Big-end bearing cap nuts/bolts:		
847	30 to 33	41 to 45
All except 847	33	45
Camshaft bolt (847)	22	30
Rocker assembly bolts (847)	11 to 15	15 to 20
Valve cover bolts (all except 847)	6	8

Overhead camshaft engines (ohc)

Bore
- 1995 cc .... 88.0 mm (3.467 in)
- 2165 cc .... 88.0 mm (3.467 in)

Stroke
- 1995 cc .... 82.0 mm (3.231 in)
- 2165 cc .... 89.0 mm (3.507 in)

Compression ratio .... 9.2 to 1

Firing order .... 1-3-4-2 (No 1 at flywheel end)

Cylinder head

Valve clearances (cold – stopped for at least 2.5 hours):
- Inlet .... 0.10 mm (0.004 in)
- Exhaust .... 0.25 mm (0.010 in)

Maximum face distortion .... 0.05 mm (0.002 in)

*(Note: Resurfacing **not** permitted.*

Head and seat valve angles (included):
    Inlet .... 120°
    Exhaust .... 90°
Valve guides:
    Bore .... 8.0 mm (0.3152 in)
    External diameter .... 13.0 mm (0.5122 in)
    Oversizes:
        1 groove .... + 0.10 mm (0.004 in)
        2 grooves .... + 0.25 mm (0.010 in)
    Interference fit .... 0.10 mm (0.004 in)
Valve spring free length:
    829 and J6R
        Early .... 47.2 mm (1.860 in)
        Late .... 46.0 mm (1.812 in)
    851 .... Not specified

Camshaft
Endfloat:
    829 and J6R .... 0.07 to 0.13 mm (0.003 to 0.005 in)
    851 .... 0.07 to 0.15 mm (0.003 to 0.006 in)

Valve timing

	Inlet opens	Inlet closes	Exhaust opens	Exhaust closes
829 and J6R	17° BTDC	63° ABDC	63° BBDC	17° ATDC
851	17° BTDC	63° ABDC	63° BBDC	17° ATDC

Note: Valve timing with valve clearance of 0.35 mm (0.014 in)

Pistons
Type .... Alloy with 3 rings
Connecting rods:
    Small-end play .... 0.31 to 0.57 mm (0.012 to 0.022 in)

Cylinder liners
Protrusion (without O-rings) .... 0.08 to 0.15 mm (0.0032 to 0.0059 in)

Crankshaft
Endfloat:
    829 and J6R .... 0.07 to 0.25 mm (0.003 to 0.010 in)
    851 .... 0.13 to 0.30 mm (0.005 to 0.012 in)
Main bearing journal diameter:
    Standard .... 62.892 mm (2.4779 in)
    Regrind .... 62.642 mm (2.4681 in)

Crankpin diameter:	Standard	Regrind
829 and J6R	52.296 mm (2.0605 in)	52.046 mm (2.0506 in)
851	56.296 mm (2.2181 in)	56.046 mm (2.2082 in)

Lubrication system
Oil capacity:
    Total .... 5.5 litre (9.7 Imp pt; 5.8 US qt)
    Filter .... 0.5 litre (0.9 Imp pt; 0.53 US qt)
Oil pressure (hot):
    Idling .... 0.8 bar (11.6 lbf/in^2)
    At 3000 rpm .... 3.0 bar (43.5 lbf/in^2)
Oil pump clearances:
    Rotor-to-inner housing .... 0.05 to 0.10 mm (0.002 to 0.004 in)
    Gear endfloat .... 0.02 to 0.10 mm (0.001 to 0.004 in)

Torque wrench settings

	lbf ft	Nm
Cylinder head bolts (cold)	65 to 72	88 to 98
Big-end bearing cap nuts/bolts:		
829 and J6R	33 to 37	45 to 50
851	44 to 48	60 to 65
Oil pump	30 to 33	41 to 45
Oil pump cover	10	14
Sump	6 to 7	8 to 9
Camshaft sprocket	37	50
Rocker filter	15	20
Flywheel bolts	44	60
Driveplate bolts	48 to 52	65 to 71
Main bearing cap bolts	65 to 72	88 to 98
Crankshaft pulley bolt:		
829 and J6R	55 to 63	75 to 85
851	89 to 100	121 to 136
Valve cover nuts	3 to 4	4 to 5
Intermediate shaft sprocket nut	37	50

PART A – ALL ENGINES

1   General description

The engine is of four-cylinder in-line type mounted at the front of the car. Drive to the front wheels is through a manual gearbox or automatic transmission attached to the rear of the engine. Both overhead valve and overhead camshaft engines are fitted.

The crankshaft incorporates five main bearings with thrust washers located on the centre bearing on overhead valve engines or on the second main bearing from the flywheel/driveplate on overhead camshaft engines.

The crankshaft is driven by a chain on overhead valve engines and by a rubber drivebelt on overhead camshaft engines. The cylinder head may be of crossflow or sideflow design, according to model.

Lubrication is by means of a gear or rotor oil pump located in the crankcase.

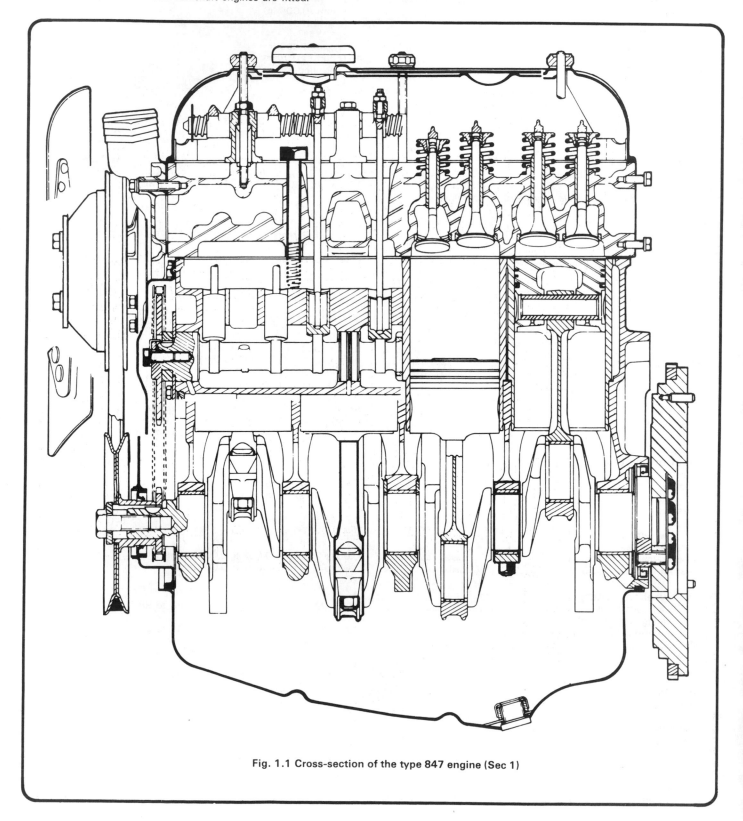

Fig. 1.1 Cross-section of the type 847 engine (Sec 1)

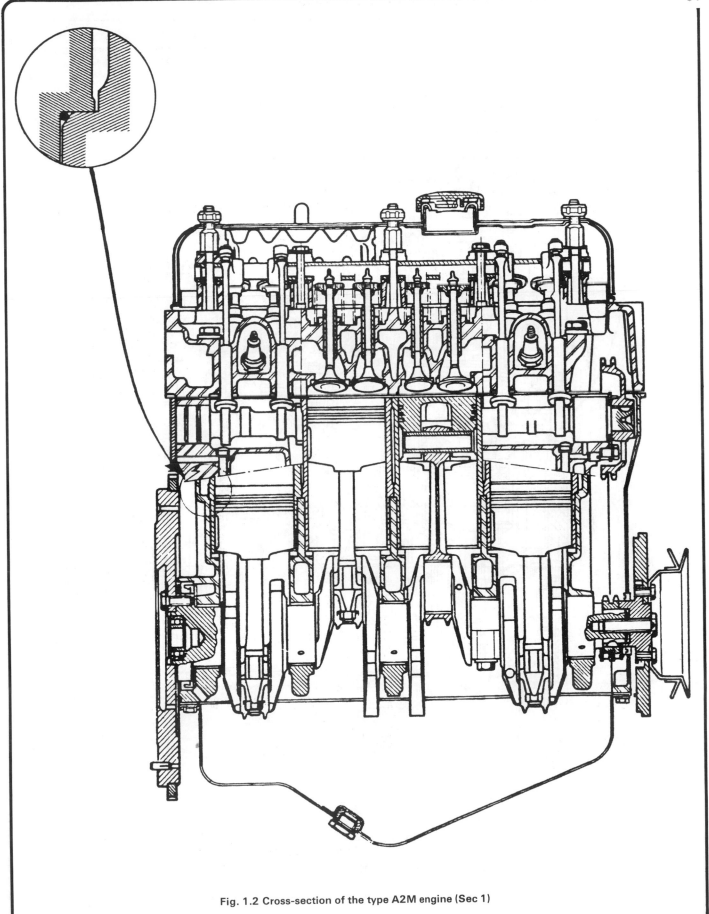

Fig. 1.2 Cross-section of the type A2M engine (Sec 1)

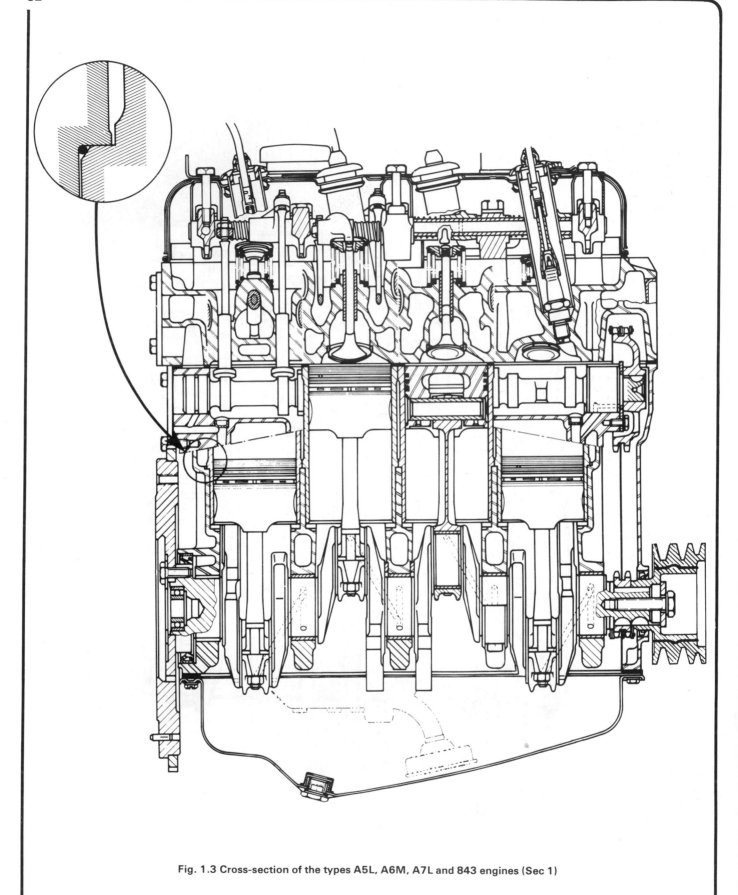

Fig. 1.3 Cross-section of the types A5L, A6M, A7L and 843 engines (Sec 1)

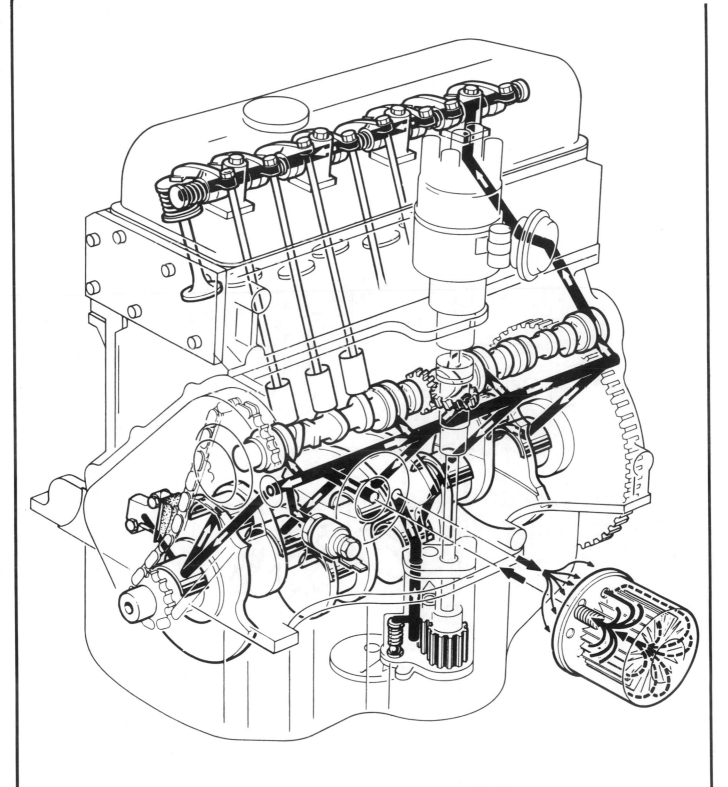

Fig. 1.4 Lubrication circuit for the type 847 engine (Sec 1)

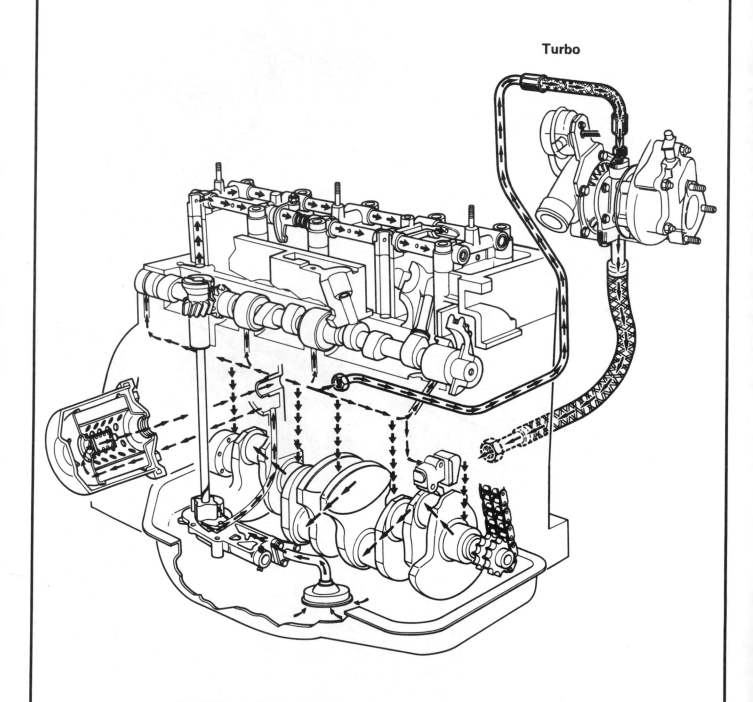

Turbo

Fig. 1.5 Lubrication circuit for the types A5L, A6M, A7L and 843 engines (Sec 1)

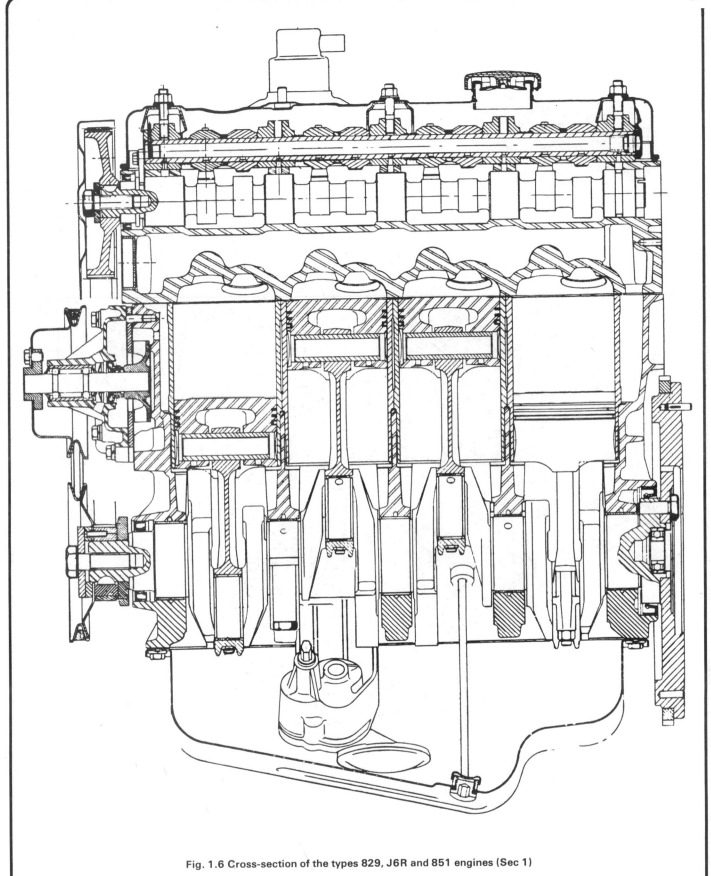

Fig. 1.6 Cross-section of the types 829, J6R and 851 engines (Sec 1)

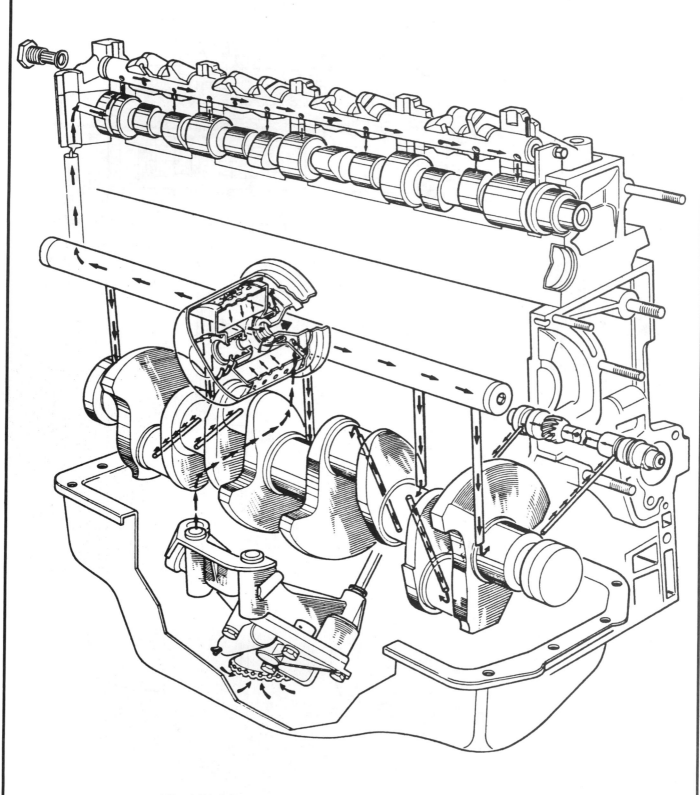

Fig. 1.7 Lubrication circuit for the types 829, J6R and 851 engines (Sec 1)

2 Routine maintenance

1 Every 5000 miles (8000 km) change the engine oil. Renew the oil filter every 10 000 miles (16 000 km).
2 Check and adjust all ancillary drivebelts every 10 000 miles (16 000 km).
3 Renew the timing belt on the overhead camshaft engines every 80 000 miles (130 000 km).
4 Adjust the valve clearances every 20 000 miles (32 000 km) and, where applicable, renew the rocker assembly filter at the same time.

PART B – OHV ENGINE

3 Major operations possible with the engine in the car

The following operations can be carried out without having to remove the engine from the car:

(a) *Removal of the cylinder head*
(b) *Removal of the sump and oil pump*
(c) *Removal of the pistons and liners*
(d) *Removal of the timing cover, timing chain and sprockets, tensioner and camshaft*
(e) *Removal of the flywheel*
(f) *Renewal of the crankshaft oil seals*
(g) *Removal of the engine mountings*

4 Major operations only possible after removal of the engine from the car

The following operations can only be carried out after removal of the engine from the car:

(a) *Removal of the crankshaft*
(b) *Renewal of the main bearings*

5 Engine – removal

Note: *The engine may be removed either separately or together with the transmission. The following paragraphs describe both methods*

Method 1 (engine unit only)
1 Disconnect the battery.
2 Protect the wings with a suitable non-abrasive material, to prevent accidental scratching.
3 Remove the engine undertray, by taking out the three securing bolts.
4 Remove the sump plug using the correct sized square key, and allow the oil to drain.
5 Drain the cooling system (see Chapter 2).
6 Remove the air cleaner assembly (see Chapter 3).
7 Where applicable, remove the air conditioning components with reference to Chapter 12.
8 Disconnect the accelerator cable at the engine end (see Chapter 3). We discovered that the tongues on the compensator could be closed by pressing a 12 mm socket over them. The compensator can then be pulled out.
9 Disconnect the choke cable at the carburettor, where applicable.
10 Disconnect the bonnet release cable.
11 Remove the bonnet release platform, by taking out the 6 bolts, two at each end and two in the front centre. Take away the two top radiator mountings thereby released.
12 Remove the front grille, by taking out the screws in the top corners.
13 Remove the radiator (see Chapter 2).
14 Remove the top and bottom radiator hoses.
15 Pull the fuel pipes off the pump, and plug or clamp them to prevent fuel loss.
16 On North American models remove the exhaust heat shields, EGR hose and catalytic converter, as applicable.
17 Remove the distributor vacuum pipe.

18 Disconnect the clutch cable at the bellhousing lever on manual gearbox models.
19 Remove the distributor cap and leads.
20 Disconnect the two wiring sockets at the bulkhead.
21 Disconnect the wiring at the reversing light switch, at the coil, and at the white connector.
22 Disconnect the wiring to the distributor.
23 Where applicable, remove the power steering pump with reference to Chapter 11, and the turbo hose and oil line.
24 Remove the heater hoses and all the hoses at the water pump.
25 Disconnect the vacuum hoses, including the brake servo hose.
26 On North American models disconnect the emission control hoses (Chapter 3).
27 Disconnect the automatic transmission leads and cables, as applicable and, where fitted, disconnect the cruise control cable.
28 Remove the electronic ignition module, where applicable.
29 Disconnect the engine earthing strap.
30 Disconnect all wiring to the starter motor solenoid, noting the colour coding.
31 Disconnect the battery (not strictly necessary, but recommended). Put it on charge if necessary.
32 Disconnect the exhaust pipe from the inlet manifold, by removing the clamp (photo).
33 Remove the starter motor (see Chapter 10).
34 Raise the front of the car and support on axle stands, then unbolt and remove the transmission front cover (photo).

5.32 Disconnecting the exhaust downpipe

5.34 Transmission front cover

35 On automatic transmission models remove the torque converter bolts with refererence to Chapter 7.

36 Connect suitable lifting tackle to the engine lifting eyes.

37 Remove the transmission bellhousing-to-engine bolts.

38 Remove the nuts under the engine mountings, one on each side, complete with the cup washers (photo).

39 Lift the engine until the transmission touches the steering crossmember then support the transmission in this position with a trolley jack.

40 Ease the engine forward until it is disconnected from the clutch shaft or torque converter. Where applicable, disconnect the TDC sensor.

41 Lift the engine from the car (photo).

42 On automatic transmission models retain the torque converter, as described in Chapter 7.

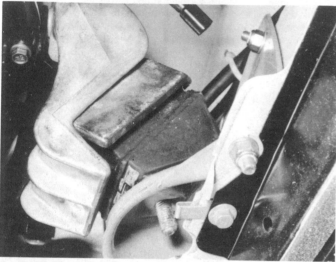

5.38 An engine mounting

5.41 Lifting out the engine

Method 2 (engine and transmission)

43 Follow the procedure given in paragraphs 1 to 32.

44 Where necessary remove the distributor, as described in Chapter 4.

45 Disconnect the driveshafts from the transmission, as described in Chapter 8.

46 Disconnect the speedometer cable from the transmission.

47 Disconnect the gear selector mechanism (see Chapters 6 and 7).

48 Disconnect the wiring from the reversing light switch and auto-

matic transmission, as applicable.

49 Support the rear of the transmission on a jack, and remove the rubber mountings.

50 Connect suitable lifting tackle to the engine lifting eyes, and take the weight.

51 Remove the nuts and cup washers under the engine mountings, one on each side.

52 Raise the engine, lower the transmission as required, and lift out the combined unit.

6   Engine dismantling – general

1   It is best to mount the engine on a dismantling stand, but if one is not available, stand the engine on a strong bench at a comfortable working height. Failing this, the engine can be stripped down on the floor.

2   During dismantling, the greatest care should be taken to keep the exposed parts free from dirt. As an aid to achieving this, it is a sound scheme to first clean down the outside of the engine, removing all traces of oil and congealed dirt.

3   Use paraffin or a good grease solvent. The latter will make the job much easier, as, after the solvent has been applied and allowed to stand for a time, a vigorous jet of water will wash off the solvent and all the grease and filth. If the dirt is thick and deeply embedded, work the solvent into it with a brush.

4   Finally wipe down the exterior of the engine with a rag and only then, when it is quite clean, should dismantling begin. As the engine is stripped, clean each part in a bath of paraffin.

5   Never immerse parts with oilways in paraffin, eg the crankcase, but to clean, wipe down carefully with a solvent dampened rag. Oilways can be cleaned out with wire. If an air line is present all parts can be blown dry and the oilways blown through as an added precaution.

6   Re-use of old engine gaskets is false economy and can give rise to oil and water leaks. To avoid the possibility of trouble after the engine has been reassembled *always* use new gaskets throughout.

7   Do not throw the old gasket away as it sometimes happens that an immediate replacement cannot be found and the old gasket is useful as a template. Hang up the old gaskets as they are removed on a suitable hook or nail.

8   To strip the engine it is best to work from the top down. The sump provides a firm base on which the engine can be supported in an upright position. When this stage where the sump must be removed is reached, the engine can be turned on its side and all other work carried out with it in this position.

9   Whenever possible, refit nuts, bolts and washers fingertight from wherever they were removed. This helps to avoid later loss and muddle. If they cannot be refitted, lay them out so that it is clear where they came from.

7   Ancillary components – removal

Before dismantling the main engine components, the following externally mounted ancillary components can be removed. The removal sequence need not necessarily follow the order given:

Alternator (Chapter 10)
Inlet and exhaust manifolds (Chapter 3 and Sections 18 and 19)
Distributor (Chapter 4)
Emission control components (Chapter 3)
Fuel injection components, if applicable (Chapter 3)
Turbocharger, disconnect if applicable (Chapter 3)
Oil filter (Section 38)
Water pump (Chapter 2)
Thermostat (Chapter 2)
Engine mountings and brackets

8   Cylinder head – removal

If the engine is still in the car disconnect the various components with reference to Sections 5 and 7.

1   Remove the water pump/alternator drivebelt, as described in Chapter 2.

2   Remove the distributor, as described in Chapter 4.

3   Drain the engine oil.

4   Unscrew the nuts and withdraw the valve cover (photos). Remove the diagnostic socket.

5   Free the valve clearance adjusting screws by loosening the locknuts, remove the screws and then the pushrods. Ensure that the components are identified so that they may be refitted in the same positions (photos).

6   Loosen all the cylinder head bolts a little at a time in the order shown in Fig. 1.24. Remove all bolts except that which passes through the locating dowel near the distributor (Fig. 1.8). Leave this one remaining bolt slackened but in contact with the cylinder head. **Do not** lift the cylinder head at this point unless complete dismantling of the engine block and cylinder liners is envisaged, or the watertight seal at the bottom of the liners will be broken, thereby permitting coolant to enter the sump. Instead, tap the head with a suitable soft hammer on each side to unstick it, and pivot it on the locating dowel with the bolt still in place to free the cylinder head surface.

8.4B ... and withdraw the valve cover

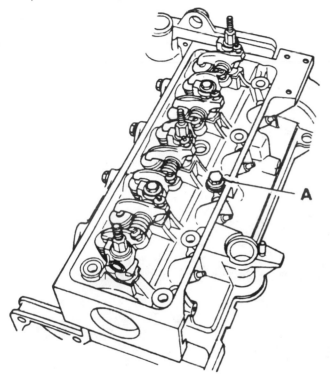
Fig. 1.8 Locating dowel cylinder head bolt (A) (Sec 8)

8.5A The pushrod locations

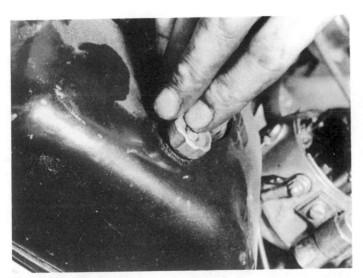
8.4A Unscrew the nuts ...

8.5B Removing a pushrod

8.7A Remove the spark plug tube washers ...

8.7B ... and cups

8.10 Clamping the cylinder liners

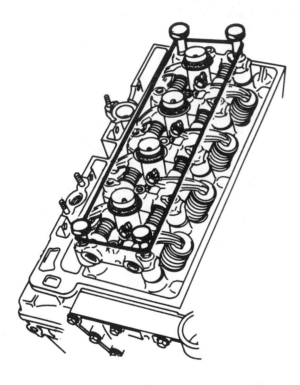

Fig. 1.9 Retaining the rocker assembly using an elastic band – types A5L, A7L, 843 and A6M engines (Sec 8)

7   On engines A5L, A7L, 843 and A6M remove the spark plug tube rubber washers and cups, then fit an elastic band, as shown in Fig. 1.9, and remove the rocker assembly (photos).

8   Remove the remaining bolt and lift the head off; however, on A5L, A7L, 843 and A6M engines after raising the head slightly either push the tappets back into the cylinder head or withdraw them and note their positions.

9   Remove the cylinder head gasket.

10 Clamp the liners down to the cylinder head surface unless they are to be removed. We employed suitable bolts, nuts and plain washers (photo).

11 On the type A6M engine remove the fuel pump plunger.

9   Sump and oil pump – removal

1   Disconnect the battery and drain the engine oil.

2   Remove the engine undertray, and withdraw all the sump bolts. On some models it may be necessary to unbolt the transmission front cover.

3   Partially lower the sump, and turn the engine to place Nos 1 and 4 pistons at BDC.

4   Tilt the front of the sump to the left, and lower it.

5   Remove the bolts securing the oil pump, and withdraw it. On 1565 and 1647 cc engines remove the rotors from the cylinder block (photos).

9.5A Unbolt the oil pump body ...

9.5B ... and remove the rotors from the cylinder block

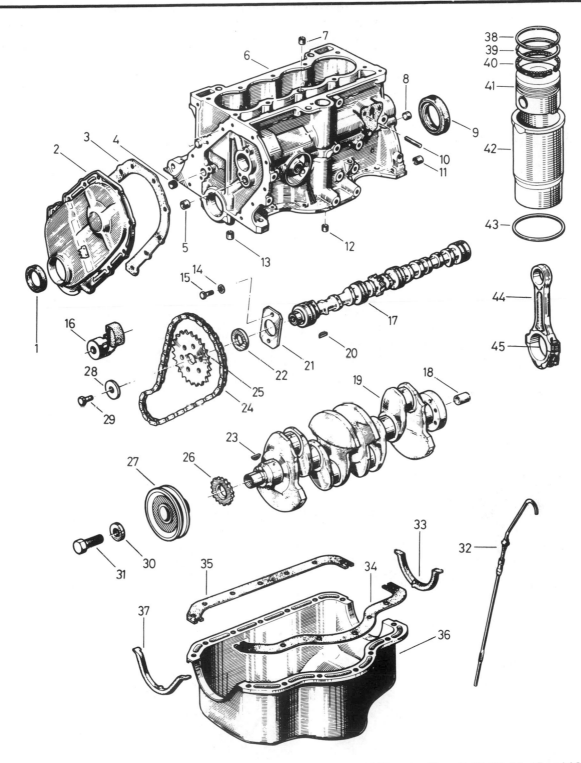

Fig. 1.10 Exploded view of the cylinder block components on the type 847 engine (Secs 9, 10, 12, 14, 15 and 16)

1	Timing cover oil seal	12	Dowel	24	Timing chain
2	Timing cover	13	Dowel	25	Camshaft sprocket
3	Timing cover gasket	14	Spring washer	26	Crankshaft sprocket
4	Oilway plug	15	Bolt	27	Crankshaft pulley
5	Aluminium plug	16	Timing chain tensioner	28	Camshaft washer
6	Cylinder block	17	Camshaft	29	Camshaft bolt
7	Cylinder head locating	18	Crankshaft spigot bearing	30	Pulley washer
	dowel	19	Crankshaft	31	Pulley bolt
8	Aluminium plug	20	Camshaft key	32	Dipstick
9	Crankshaft oil seal	21	Camshaft flange	33	Rubber seal
10	Fuel pump studs	22	Distance piece	34	Sump gasket (half)
11	Dowel	23	Crankshaft key		

35	Sump gasket (half)
36	Sump
37	Rubber seal
38	Top compression ring
39	Taper compression ring
40	Oil control ring
41	Piston
42	Liner
43	Liner seal
44	Connecting rod
45	Connecting rod cap

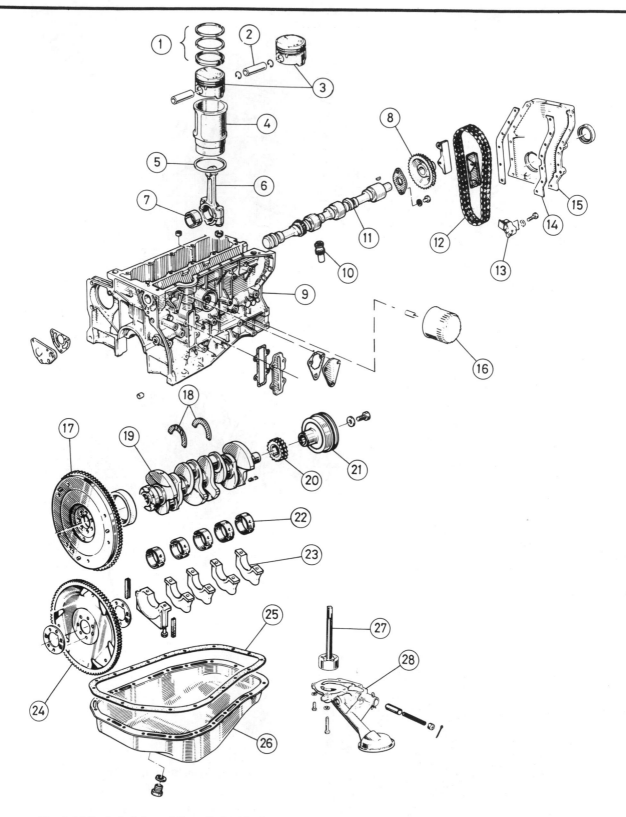

Fig. 1.11 Exploded view of the cylinder block components on the types A2M, A5L, A6M and 843 engines (Secs 9, 11, 13, 14, 15 and 17)

1	Piston rings	8	Sprocket	15	Timing cover	22	Main bearing shells
2	Gudgeon pin	9	Cylinder block	16	Oil filter	23	Main bearing cap
3	Piston	10	Distributor pinion	17	Flywheel	24	Driveplate (Automatic)
4	Liner	11	Camshaft	18	Thrust washers	25	Gasket
5	Seal	12	Timing chain	19	Crankshaft	26	Sump
6	Connecting rod	13	Chain tensioner	20	Sprocket	27	Rotors
7	Big-end bearing shells	14	Gasket	21	Pulley	28	Oil pump

10 Timing chain and sprockets (1397 cc engine) – removal

1   Remove the bonnet release platform, by disconnecting the cable and taking out the bolts, two at each end of the platform and two in the centre.
2   Disconnect the battery.
3   Remove the drivebelt (see Chapter 2).
4   Remove the alternator (see Chapter 10).
5   Take out the retaining bolts, and remove the fan and pulley.
6   Remove the sump, as described in Section 9.
7   Remove the crankshaft pulley bolt. If the flywheel is still fitted, jam it to prevent crankshaft rotation, but if not, screw two of the flywheel retaining bolts into the crankshaft, and jam the shaft by placing a suitable lever between them. Remove the crankshaft pulley (photo).
8   Remove the bolts, and withdraw the timing cover (photo).
9   Carefully prise or tap out the oil seal from the cover.
10 Take the bolt from the centre of the timing chain tensioner, and lift the tensioner off.
11 Remove the camshaft sprocket bolt, and lift the sprocket and chain off (photo).
12 If necessary, draw off the crankshaft sprocket, using either a suitable puller, or a pair of levers carefully applied behind the sprocket (photo).

10.11 Removing the camshaft sprocket bolt

10.7 Crankshaft pulley

10.12 Crankshaft sprocket

10.8 Removing the timing cover

11 Timing chain and sprockets (1565 and 1647 cc engines) – removal

1   Remove the cylinder head (Section 8) and sump (Section 9).
2   Remove the radiator, as described in Chapter 2. If necessary remove the front grille and crossmember.
3   Remove the distributor drive pinion.
4   Remove the bolts securing the crankshaft pulley and damper to the pulley boss, and withdraw the pulley and damper.
5   Lock the flywheel, and remove the pulley hub bolt, followed by the hub.
6   Remove the bolts and withdraw the timing cover.
7   Carefully tap out the oil seal in the cover.
8   Secure the tensioner shoe with a length of soft wire, take out the bolts, and remove the tensioner and plate.
9   Remove the nuts, and take off the chain guides.
10 Set the camshaft sprocket to give the necessary access, and take out the camshaft flange fixing bolts.
11 On the A2M engine, remove the fuel pump (Chapter 3).
12 On models with a power steering pulley on the rear of the camshaft unbolt and pull off the pulley.
13 Using the crankshaft pulley bolt screwed into the crankshaft and a suitable puller, draw off the crankshaft sprocket, camshaft sprocket complete with the camshaft, and chain.

12 Camshaft (1397 cc engine) – removal

1   Drain the sump.
2   Remove the front grille.
3   Remove the radiator (see Chapter 2).
4   Remove the cylinder head and clamp the liners (see Section 8).
5   Lift out the tappets, and ensure that they are identified correctly for refitting purposes (photo).

12.5 Lifting out a tappet

6   Remove the fuel pump (see Section 3). The pipes may be left connected.
7   Lift out the distributor drive pinion, using a bolt 12 mm dia x 1.75 mm pitch (photo).
8   Remove the sump (see Section 9).
9   Remove the camshaft sprocket (see Section 10).
10 Remove the bolts securing the camshaft flange, and draw out the shaft carefully (photos).
11 If necessary, carefully support the camshaft flange and tap the shaft through, thus releasing the collar and flange.

12.7 Distributor drive pinion location

12.10A Camshaft flange and bolts

12.10B Removing the camshaft

13 Camshaft (1565 and 1647 cc engines) – removal and refitting

1   Remove the timing chain and sprockets, as described in Section 11.
2   If the camshaft sprocket has to be removed from the shaft, it must not be re-used. A new sprocket must always be fitted, together with a new flange and key. When pressing on the sprocket, take the load by supporting the camshaft behind the first bearing. Press the sprocket fully home. Always use a new collar and key.
3   Check the clearance at the flange (see Fig. 1.12) and check against the camshaft endfloat as given in the Specifications.
4   Refit the timing chain and sprockets, as described in Section 34.

14 Pistons and cylinder liners – removal

1   The removal of these items is possible, if necessary, with the engine still in the vehicle.
3   Remove the cylinder head (see Section 8).
3   Remove the sump and oil pump (see Section 9).
4   Mark the connecting rods to ensure correct refitting, starting with No 1 at the clutch end, and away from the camshaft side on 1397 cc engines; the same side as the camshaft on 1565 and 1647 cc engines.

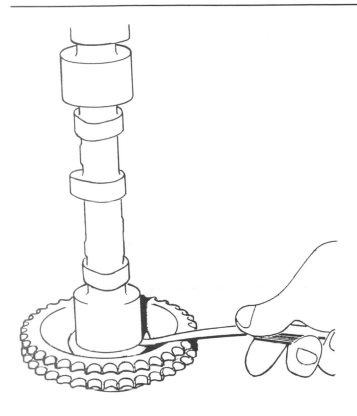

Fig. 1.12 Checking the camshaft flange clearance (Sec 13)

Mark the bearing caps also, so that they are fitted both to the correct rod and the right way round.

5   Remove the big-end nuts/bolts, followed by the caps and bearing shells (photo).

6   Identify the cylinder liners, using a quick drying paint, so that each can be refitted in the same position and the right way round.

7   Withdraw each piston and liner assembly, and temporarily refit the connecting rod caps to the correct rods (photo). Keep the shells with their correct rods and caps if they are to be re-used.

8   Withdraw each piston/connecting rod assembly from the liner. Do not allow the piston rings to jump out sharply or they may break. Instead restrain them with the fingers.

9   Remove the top piston ring by gently springing the ring open far enough to insert a couple of old feeler blades or similar beneath it, then

14.7 Withdrawing a piston and liner assembly from the block

'walking' the ring off the top of the piston. Take care not to scratch the piston – it is made of softer metal than the ring – or to break the ring, which is brittle. Also mind your fingers – piston rings are sharp!

10   Repeat the process with the second and third piston rings, using the feeler blades to stop the rings falling into the grooves above. Keep the rings with the appropriate piston if they are to be re-used.

15 Flywheel/driveplate oil seal and spigot bearing – removal and refitting

1   The flywheel/driveplate may be removed after removing either the engine or transmission.

2   On manual gearbox models remove the clutch (Chapter 5).

3   Lock the starter ring gear by making up a suitable bracket bolted to the cylinder block.

4   Unscrew the bolts and withdraw the flywheel or driveplate, as applicable (photo).

5   Prise out the crankshaft oil seal, taking care not to damage the sealing surface on the shaft.

6   Offer up the oil seal after applying lubricant both to the lip and to the outside diameter. Tap it very gently into place using either the old seal or a suitable piece of tubing. Ensure that all items are thoroughly

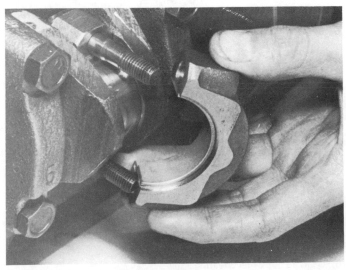

14.5 Removing a big-end bearing cap

15.4 Removing the flywheel

clean, that the seal is tapped in square, and that it is flush with the rear face of the crankshaft block (photo).

7   To renew the spigot bearing on the 1397 cc engine, screw a tap, M14 x 2 mm pitch, into the spigot bush. Grip the tap and pull it out squarely, bringing the bush with it. Use mandrel Emb 319, or a close-fitting home manufactured substitute with a shoulder of suitable size, and gently tap the new bush (coated with locking fluid) into position until it reaches the edge of the chamfer (photo). On 1565 and 1647 cc engines with a long clutch shaft gearbox (see Chapter 5), a suitable tool will be necessary to extract the spigot bearing, which is in fact a ball-race. Tap the new race into position using a suitable diameter piece of tube, bearing only upon the outer bearing track. Do not clean the bearing before fitting, as it is grease-packed ready for use. Note that the spigot bearing can in fact be removed with the flywheel fitted to the crankshaft.

8   Refit all parts in reverse order. Use thread locking fluid on the

threads of the flywheel/driveplate bolts, before tightening them to the specified torque figure (photos).

16 Crankshaft and main bearings (1397 cc engine) – removal

1   The engine must be out of the vehicle to permit this work to be carried out.

2   Remove the clutch and flywheel (see Section 15).

3   Remove the sump and oil pump (see Section 9).

4   Remove the timing chain and sprockets (see Section 10).

5   Mark the connecting rods and big-end caps, number one at the clutch end on the side away from the camshaft, if this has not already been done. Remove the nuts, followed by the big-end caps.

6   Mark the main bearing caps in relation to the cylinder block, remove the nuts, and take off the caps (photo).

15.6 Fitting the rear seal (shown with sump removed)

15.7 Spigot bearing location

15.8A Apply locking fluid to the flywheel bolts

15.8B Tightening the flywheel bolts

16.6 Removing a main bearing cap

16.7A Lifting out the crankshaft

16.7B Removing a thrust washer

16.7C Lifting out a main bearing shell

7 Lift the crankshaft out. Recover all main and big-end bearing shells. Note the thrust washers on either side of the centre (No 3) main bearing (photos). Recover the oil seal.

17 Crankshaft and main bearings (1565 and 1647 cc engines) — removal

1 The engine must be out of the vehicle to permit this work to be carried out.
2 Remove the cylinder head (see Section 8), and take out the distributor drive pinion.
3 Remove the clutch assembly (see Chapter 5).
4 Remove the timing cover, timing chain and sprockets (see Section 11).
5 Mark the connecting rods and big-end caps, number one at the flywheel/driveplate end, on the same side as the camshaft. Remove the bolts, and take off the big-end caps and bearings.
6 Remove the flywheel/driveplate (see Section 15).
7 Mark the main bearing caps relative to the cylinder block (No 1 at the flywheel end), take out the bolts, and remove the bearing caps and bearings, tapping bearing cap number one lightly underneath to remove it if necessary (photo).
8 Remove the oil seal and side seals, and lift out the crankshaft, bearings and thrust washers.

17.7 Identifying a main bearing cap

18 Inlet and exhaust manifold (1397 cc engine) — removal and refitting

1 Disconnect the battery.
2 Remove the air filter assembly, see Chapter 3.
3 Remove the warm air pipe.
4 Remove the carburettor with its heating hoses (as applicable).
5 Remove the accelerator cable swivel.
6 Disconnect the exhaust pipe clamp.
7 Remove the warm air shroud.
8 Disconnect the oil fume hoses.
9 Disconnect the servo vacuum pipe.
10 Remove the fixings and take off the manifold.
11 If a new manifold is to be fitted, remove the vacuum union, and fit to the new part.
12 Clean the manifold mating surfaces, and refit using a new gasket.
13 Refit all parts in reverse order.

19 Inlet and exhaust manifold (1565 and 1647 cc engines) — removal and refitting

1 Disconnect the battery.
2 Remove the air filter elbow and the warm air intake pipe.

3 Disconnect the fuel pipes.
4 Disconnect the oil fume hose.
5 Disconnect all vacuum hoses.
6 Remove the accelerator cable swivel.
7 Clamp the coolant hoses to the carburettor (where fitted), and disconnect them.
8 Remove the exhaust pipe clamp.
9 Remove the warm air pipe and hose clip.
10 If the manifold is being renewed, remove the vacuum unions and the carburettor inlet.
11 Unbolt and remove the manifold.
12 To refit, reverse the removal procedure. Ensure that the manifold mating surfaces are clean, and that a new gasket is used.

20 Oil pump (1397 cc engine) — dismantling and reassembly

1 Holding the cover in position, take out the retaining bolts.
2 Carefully release the cover, and remove the ball seat, ball and pressure spring (photos).
3 Take out the idler gear, driving gear and shaft (photos).
4 Clean all the parts and examine them for visually evident defects.
5 Check the clearance between the gears and the pump body. If this exceeds 0.2 mm (0.008 in), preferably renew the pump, but at least renew the gears (photo).

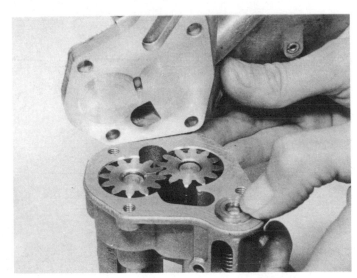

20.2A Removing the oil pump cover ...

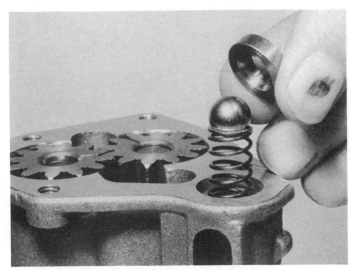

20.2B ... followed by the seat, ball and spring

20.3A Removing the oil pump idler gear ...

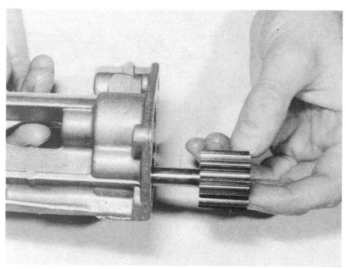

20.3B ... driving gear, and shaft

20.5 Checking the oil pump gear-to-body clearance

6   To reassemble, fit the idler gear, followed by the driving gear. Lubricate all parts before fitting.
7   Fit the spring guide, the spring, ball and seat, and position the cover to retain the parts.
8   Refit the cover bolts, and tighten.

21 Oil pump (1565 and 1647 cc engines) – dismantling and reassembly

1   Remove the bolts, followed by the suction pipe.
2   Take out the split pin from the pressure relief valve, and then the cup, spring and piston (photo).
3   Clean and check all parts.
4   Place the rotors in the cylinder block and check the clearances shown in Figs. 1.13 and 1.14. If either clearance is excessive, discard both rotors complete with the driving spindle (photo).
5   Refit all parts in reverse order, tighten the suction pipe bolts and bend over the locking tabs.
6   Insert the rotors in the block, and refit the pump.
7   Note that on turbo models it is important to fill the turbo oil system before starting the engine. Refer to Chapter 3.

21.2 Oil pump and pressure relief components

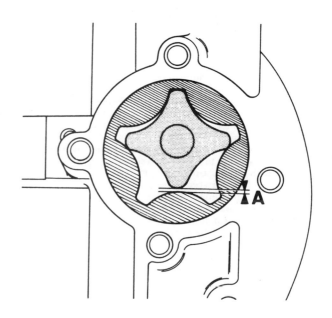

Fig. 1.13 Oil pump rotor clearance (Sec 21)

A = 0.04 to 0.29 mm (0.002 to 0.0011 in)

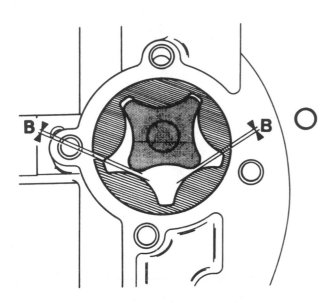

Fig. 1.14 Oil pump rotor clearance (Sec 21)

B = 0.02 to 0.14 mm (0.001 to 0.006 in)

21.4 Checking the oil pump rotor tip clearance

22.7 Removing the valve collets

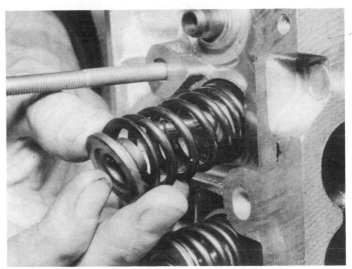

22.8A Removing the top cup and valve spring

22.8B Lifting out a valve

22 Cylinder head (1397 cc engine) – dismantling

1   Remove the fan by removing the fixing screws.
2   If care is exercised, the water pump, temperature transmitter and alternator bracket may be left in place if no work is required upon them.
3   Remove the warm air channel, rear lifting hook, and diagnostic socket bracket.
4   Remove the inlet and exhaust manifold assembly (see Section 18).
5   Remove the core plate and air filter bracket.
6   Remove the bolts and nuts securing the rocker shaft assembly, a little at a time, to avoid distortion of the shaft. Remove the shaft assembly.
7   Compress the valve springs, using a suitable compressor, and extract the collets (2 per valve) (photo).
8   Release and remove the spring compressor, and take out the top cups, springs, base washers and valves. Keep them identified for refitting purposes. Remove each valve similarly (photos).
9   To dismantle the rocker shaft, pull off the circlips at each end and slip off the component parts, noting their positions for refitting.
10   Note that the plugs in the ends of the shaft must not be removed.

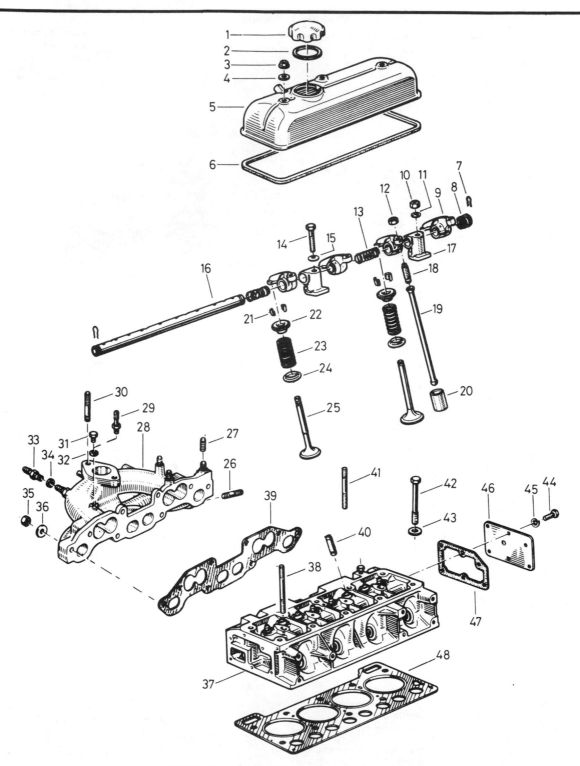

Fig. 1.15 Cylinder head components on the type 847 engine (Sec 22)

1	Oil filler cap	13	Spring	25	Valve
2	Sealing washer	14	Bolt	26	Stud
3	Nut	15	Washer	27	Stud
4	Washer	16	Rocker shaft	28	Manifold, inlet/exhaust
5	Rocker cover	17	Rocker bracket	29	Adaptor
6	Rocker cover gasket	18	Adjustment screw	30	Stud
7	Spring clip	19	Pushrod	31	Plug
8	End spring	20	Tappet	32	Washer
9	Rocker arm	21	Valve collets	33	Adaptor
10	Nut	22	Top cup	34	Washer
11	Washer	23	Valve spring	35	Nut
12	Adjuster locknut	24	Base washer	36	Washer

37	Cylinder head
38	Stud
39	Manifold gasket
40	Valve guide
41	Stud
42	Bolt
43	Washer
44	Bolt
45	Washer
46	Plate
47	Gasket
48	Cylinder head gasket

23 Cylinder head (1565 and 1647 cc engines) – dismantling

1 Refer to Section 22, paragraphs 7 to 10, but note that there are no circlips on the rocker shafts.
2 Remove the inlet and exhaust manifold assembly, as described in Section 19.
3 On models with a rear-mounted power steering pump, unbolt the camshaft rear bearing housing and remove the gasket and small O-ring.
4 Prise off the valve stem seals, where applicable.

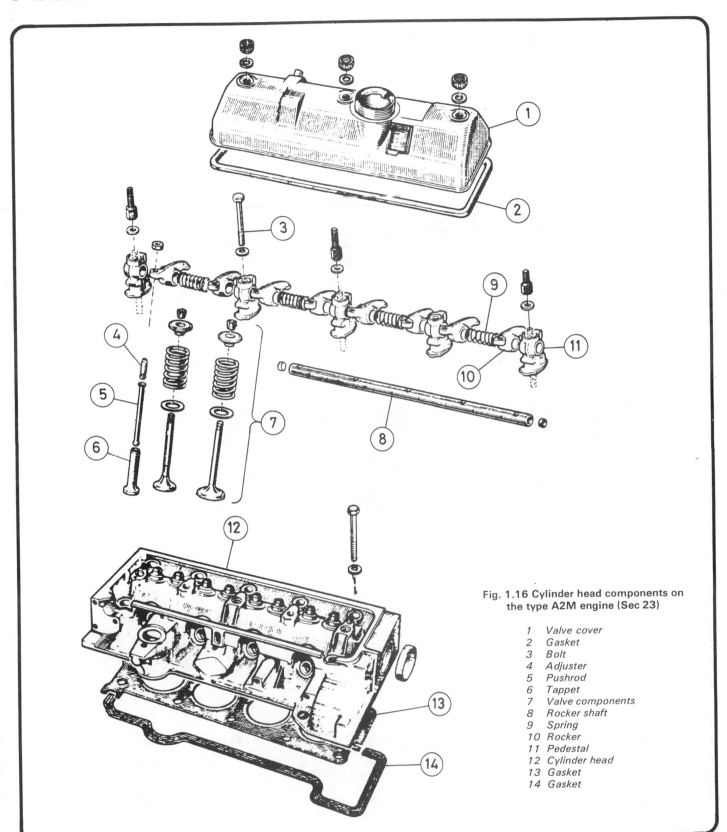

Fig. 1.16 Cylinder head components on the type A2M engine (Sec 23)

1 Valve cover
2 Gasket
3 Bolt
4 Adjuster
5 Pushrod
6 Tappet
7 Valve components
8 Rocker shaft
9 Spring
10 Rocker
11 Pedestal
12 Cylinder head
13 Gasket
14 Gasket

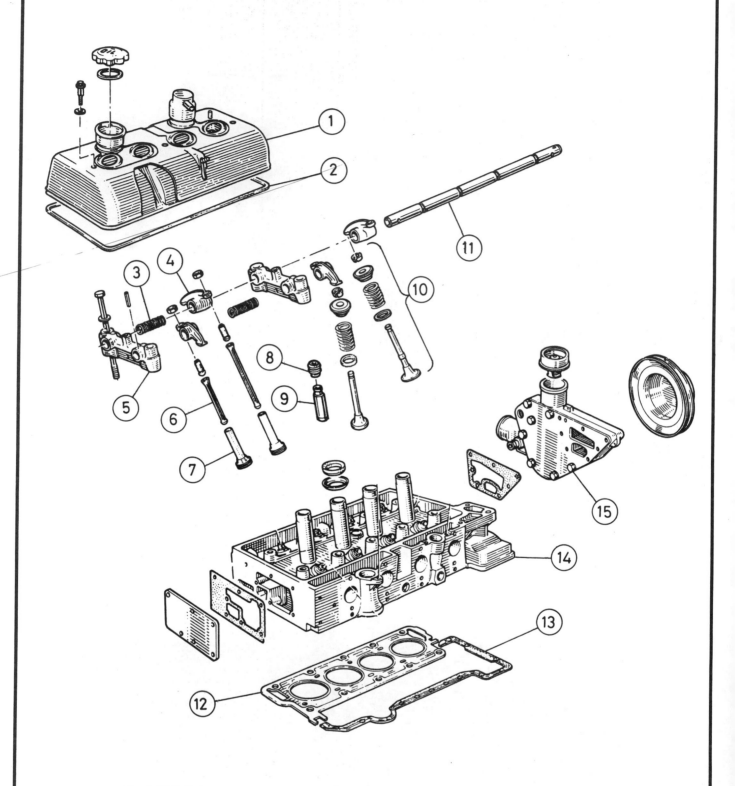

Fig. 1.17 Cylinder head components on the types A5L, A6M, A7L and 843 engines (Sec 23)

1	Valve cover	6	Pushrod	11	Rocker shaft
2	Gasket	7	Tappet	12	Gasket
3	Spring	8	Seal	13	Gasket
4	Rocker	9	Valve guide	14	Cylinder head
5	Pedestal	10	Valve components	15	Water pump

24 Examination and renovation – general

The engine has presumably been dismantled to remedy some specific defect. Before committing yourself to extensive overhauling and the purchase of new parts, compare the cost of overhauling with the cost of an exchange Renault engine.

Truth of cylinder head gasket face

1   Check the gasket mating surface for flatness, by first ensuring that it is completely clean. Either place it face down on a true surface, or invert it and place a known straight-edge such as a good quality steel rule across the gasket mating surface, from end to end.

2   Using a feeler gauge, check for distortion of the face. If the maximum bow exceeds 0.05 mm (0.002 in) have the head face resurfaced (photo).

3   The cylinder head height must not, after resurfacing, be less than a specified minimum dimension. See the Specifications for details.

24.6 Grinding a valve

24.2 Checking for distortion of the cylinder head surface

Cylinder head – general

4   Examine the cylinder heads carefully for any obvious defects such as cracks or defective threads. Any such defects will mean that a specialist engineer or Renault agent should be consulted.

5   It is strongly advised that no scraping of any kind should be carried out on aluminium parts, and instead a cleaning solution (available from Renault dealers) should be employed to clean the cylinder head and other mating surfaces. This liquid should be used according to the instructions supplied, and must not be permitted to contact bare skin or any paintwork.

Valves and valve seats

6   Examine the heads of the valves for pitting and burning, especially the exhaust valves. The valve seatings should be examined at the same time. If pitting is slight, the marks can be removed by grinding the seats and valves together with coarse, and then fine, valve grinding paste (photo). Where bad pitting has occurred to the seats, recut them and fit new valves. If the valve seats are so worn that they cannot be recut, then it will be necessary to fit new valve seat inserts. These latter two jobs should be entrusted to the local Renault agent or engineering works. In practice it is seldom that the seats are so worn that they require renewal. Normally, it is the exhaust valve that is too badly worn for refitting, and the owner can easily purchase a new set of valves and match them to the seats by valve grinding.

7   To grind a valve, smear a trace of coarse carborundum paste on the seat face and apply a suction grinder tool to the valve head. With a semi-rotary motion, grind the head to its seat, lifting the valve occasionally to redistribute the paste. When a dull matt even surface finish is produced on both the valve seat and valve, wipe off the paste and repeat the process with fine carborundum paste, lifting and turning the valve to redistribute the paste as before. A light spring placed under the valve head will greatly ease this operation. When a smooth unbroken ring of light grey matt finish is produced on both valve and valve seats faces, the grinding operation is completed.

8   Scrape all carbon from the valve head and stem. Carefully clean away every trace of grinding compound, taking care to leave none in the ports or valve guides. Clean the valves and seats with a paraffin-soaked rag, then with a clean rag, and finally, if an air line is available, blow the valves, valve guides and valve ports clean.

Valve guides

9   Examine the valve guides internally for wear. If the valves are a very loose fit in the guides and there is the slightest suspicion of lateral rocking using a new valve, then new guides will have to be fitted. Valve guide renewal should be left to a Renault agent who will have the required press and mandrel. Work of this kind in a light alloy head without the correct tools can be disastrous.

Valve springs

10   Compare the old valve springs with new ones. Renew the springs if there is any significant difference in length, or if distortion is evident.

Crankshaft and bearings

11   Wear in the main or big-end bearings will have been noticed before dismantling, evidence being a fall in oil pressure and a rumbling (main bearings) or knocking (big-end bearings) from the engine. If wear is known to exist, take the crankshaft to a motor factor or Renault agent, who will measure the journals and decide whether regrinding is necessary. Serious wear will be evident to the naked eye.

12   The main and big-end bearing shells should be renewed as a matter of course unless they are known to have covered only a nominal mileage. Take the old shells with you when buying new ones and check that you get the same size. Oversize shells (fitted after regrinding) should have the oversize dimension marked on the back.

13   The thrust washers on either side of the centre main bearing are also subject to wear and may need renewal. It may be best to delay purchase until the crankshaft can be temporarily refitted, since several thicknesses are available to give the required endfloat – see Specifications.

Camshaft, timing gears and chain

14   Inspect the camshaft lobes for wear and the bearing surfaces for tracks or other signs of wear. A new camshaft is probably the only answer if much wear has taken place. If there is suspicion that the camshaft bearings in the block are badly worn, consult your Renault dealer. A new block will probably be required.

15   Examine the timing chain and sprockets. Wear in the sprocket teeth will show as hook-shaped teeth, possible bright and sharp on

one side. Renew the sprockets as a pair if necessary. Wear in the chain will show up as side slackness; on a badly worn chain the actual rollers may be grooved or broken. It is sensible to renew the chain anyway if it has covered a high mileage.

16 Do not overlook the timing chain tensioner. This should be renewed if it is badly grooved or seems to have lost its tensioning ability.

Pistons and liners

17 The cylinder bores must be examined for taper, ovality, scoring and scratches. Start by carefully examining the top of the cylinder bores. If they are at all worn a very slight ridge will be found on the thrust side. This marks the top of the piston ring travel. The owner will have a good indication of the bore wear prior to dismantling the engine, or removing the cylinder head. Excessive oil consumption accompanied by blue smoke from the exhaust is a sure sign of worn cylinder bores and piston rings.

18 Measure the bore diameter just under the ridge with an internal micrometer and compare it with the diameter at the bottom of the bore, which is not subject to wear. If the difference between the two measurements is more than 0.1524 mm (0.006 in) then it will be necessary to fit new pistons and liner assemblies. If no micrometer is available remove the rings from a piston and place the piston in each bore in turn about 19 mm (0.75 in) below the top of the bore. If a 0.254 mm (0.010 in) feeler gauge can be slid between the piston and the cylinder wall on the thrust side of the bore then remedial action must be taken.

19 Should the liners have been disturbed they **must** be completely removed from the cylinder block and new seals fitted, otherwise once the seals have been disturbed the chances are that water will leak into the sump.

20 If the old pistons are to be refitted, carefully remove the piston rings and then thoroughly clean them. Take particular care to clean out the piston ring grooves. At the same time do not scratch the aluminium in any way. If new rings are to be fitted to the old pistons then the top ring should be stepped so as to clear the ridge left above the previous top ring. If a normal but oversize new ring is fitted it will hit the ridge and break because the new ring will not have worn in the same way as the old, which will have worn in union with the ridge.

Tappets

21 Check the tappets for scoring and wear and renew them as necessary. Note on 1565 and 1647 cc engines the bores in the cylinder head can be reamed and oversize tappets fitted. This work should be carried out by a Renault dealer or suitably equipped engineering workshop.

General

22 If in doubt as to whether a particular component is serviceable, consider the time and effort which will be required to renew it if it fails prematurely. In a borderline case it is probably best to decide in favour of renewal, but it must be admitted that some degree of compromise is usually inevitable unless funds are unlimited. Obviously, the owner doing a quick 'shell and ring' job will have different standards from the person undertaking a thorough overhaul.

25 Cylinder block (1397 cc engine) – preparation

1   If a new cylinder block is being used, the points mentioned in this Section should be noted and carried out, as applicable.
2   Ensure that the aluminium plugs at the ends of the main oil gallery are in place.
3   Screw the camshaft bearing plugs into place, if necessary, and peen over.
4   Check that the oilway plug behind the timing chain tensioner is in place.
5   Ensure that the following are in place:

(a)   Two timing cover studs
(b)   The engine/gearbox studs and dowels
(c)   Distributor stud
(d)   Fuel pump studs (smear threads with jointing compound before fitting)
(e)   Oil filter threaded mounting
(f)   Coolant drain plug

(g)   Dipstick tube (smear thread locking compound on it before fitting)
(h)   Insert the plug in the camshaft locating bore (hammer the centre to spread it)
(j)   The oil recovery pipe (opposite the dipstick)
(k)   The oil pump locating dowel
(m)   The timing chain tensioner locating peg

26 Cylinder block (1565 and 1647 cc engines) – preparation

1   No scraping of aluminium parts is permissible, and a cleaner as available from Renault agents should be employed, used as directed on the container.
2   Take great care that foreign matter does not cause blockage of any oilways.
3   To ensure that proper tightening of bolts is achieved, suck or blow all remaining oil from the bolt holes and oil feed holes.
4   Do not interfere with the core plugs.
5   Check for freedom of the cylinder head bolts in their threads by screwing them in and out.
6   If necessary, tighten the main oilway screwed plugs.
7   Use a suitable sealant on the fuel pump studs, before fitting.
8   Fit the dipstick tube and oil recovery pipe. Use thread locking compound on them before fitting.
9   Using a new gasket, refit the oil pump driveshaft blanking plate.
10   Clean (but do not scrape) the surfaces for the cylinder liner seals.

27 Cylinder head (1397 cc engine) – reassembly

1   Ensure that all parts are completely clean.
2   Refit each valve in turn into the correct guide, and place over it the base washer, spring (ensuring that the close coils are downwards towards the base washer) and the top cup.
3   Fit the spring compressor and compress the spring, fit the collets around the collet grooves, and gradually release the compressor, ensuring that the collets remain in their groove as the springs are decompressed. Remove the compressor.
4   Note that, if new pillars are required for the rocker assembly, a modified type of pillar will be supplied by the parts department of Renault agents. This pillar, possessing an extra oil hole and possibly a modified drilling for the main clamping bolt also, may be fitted in any position.
5   Refit the component parts of the rocker assembly on the shaft in the proper order, ensuring that the oilways in the rocker shaft face the pushrods, and that those in the rocker shaft pillars are in line with those in the shaft.
6   Refit the circlips to the end of the shaft.
7   Refit the rocker shaft assembly by tightening the holding-down bolts and nuts progressively, a little at a time to avoid distortion, to the correct torque figure (photo).
8   If removed, refit parts in reverse of the order described in Section 22, paragraphs 1 to 5.

28 Cylinder head (1565 and 1647 cc engines) – reassembly

1   Refer to Section 27, paragraphs 1 to 3 and 5 to 7 noting that there are no rocker shaft circlips (photos). Make sure that the end pillars are located on the dowels, where applicable.
2   Refit the inlet and exhaust manifold assembly, as described in Section 19.
3   Where applicable, refit the camshaft rear bearing housing together with a new gasket and O-ring, and tighten the bolts.
4   Fit new valve stem seals, where applicable.

29 Piston and cylinder liners – refitting

1   Thoroughly clean the inside of the cylinder block, particularly the seal locations for the liners. Ensure that the oilways are completely clear in the crankshaft, cylinder block and cylinder head.
2   Dissolve the anti-rust film which will be found on the piston/liner

27.7 The rocker shaft assembly in position

28.1A Inserting a valve

28.1B Fit the seat followed by ...

28.1C ... the valve spring ...

28.1D ... and cup

new parts. Do not scrape them. Use methylated spirit or cellulose thinners as a solvent.

3   Check the oil pump condition, and the cylinder head gasket surface for truth.

4   Mark up the parts in the piston/liner kit, so that they can be kept in four separate sets from this stage onwards.

5   If old pistons and liners are being re-used, ensure that each item is refitted to its former position, that the piston rings are the right way up, and that they do not seize in the grooves when compressed. If they do, it is likely that some carbon still remains in the ring land, and that further cleaning is required.

Cylinder liner protrusion

6   The liners have a designed amount of protrusion above the cylinder block, and this should be checked by fitting the liner into the block without the O-ring seal, placing a straight-edge across the liner top, and checking the gap with a feeler gauge. The protrusion should be within the specified limits (photo).

7   Note that the difference in protrusion between any two adjacent liners must not exceed 0.04 mm (0.0016 in).

8   Note that with a new set of liners, the protrusions should be stepped down from one end or the other. Number the liners from one to four to confirm their positions. If incorrect protrusion is found with a new liner set, the block is probably at fault.

9   With an old block, incorrect protrusion means that either may be faulty. Eliminate one possible fault by retesting using a new liner set.

Gudgeon pin fitting

10 On 1397 cc (Type 847) engines, the removal and refitting of gudgeon pins should be left to your Renault dealer as the pin is an interference fit in the connecting rod small end. The operations require the application of controlled heat and special guides. On other ohv engines, the gudgeon pins are a push fit and retained by circlips, located in grooves in the piston pin bore. If the pin will not push out or in with finger pressure, immerse the piston in hot water. The arrow on the piston crown should point towards the flywheel when the piston/rod is installed with the connecting rod marks (see Sec 14) correctly aligned (photo).

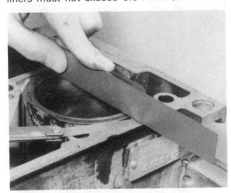

29.6 Checking cylinder liner protrusion

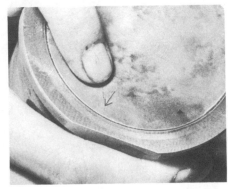

29.10 Arrow location on the piston crown

29.11 Rings fitted to the piston

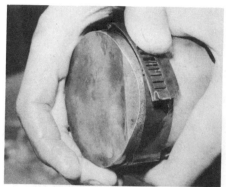
29.14A Fit the ring clamp ...

29.14B ... then push the piston into the liner

29.15 Fitting the liner O-ring

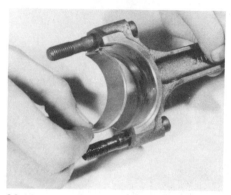
29.16 Fitting the big-end bearing shell to the connecting rod

29.17A Oil the crankpin ...

29.17B ... and fit the big-end cap

Piston rings

11 Fit the oil scraper ring, followed by the tapered compression ring (with the mark upwards), and lastly the top compression ring. Use the method described in Section 14 to assist ring fitting (photo).
12 Do not attempt to adjust the piston ring gaps, which are preset.

Piston fitting to liner

13 Space the rings round the piston so that the gaps are at 120° to one another.
14 Oil the pistons thoroughly and, with the aid of a suitable piston ring clamp, fit each piston to its respective liner, ensuring that the machined sides of the big-end are parallel with the flat on top of the liner (photos).

Fitting the liner and piston assembly to the cylinder block

15 Fit an O-ring to each liner, ensuring that it is not twisted (photo).
16 Fit a half shell bearing to the connecting rod (photo). Insert the piston and liner assembly into its correct bore, and the right way round, ie:

(a) No 1 liner assembly at the flywheel end
(b) The numbers on the big-ends are as indicated in Section 14
(c) The arrows on the pistons are facing the flywheel

17 Fit the liner clamping arrangement (see Section 8, paragraph 10). If the crankshaft is fitted, reassemble the big-end bearings as described in Sections 30 or 31 (photos).

30 Crankshaft and main bearings (1397 cc engine) – refitting

1 Clean all the gasket surfaces on the cylinder block and associated components. Ensure that all parts are clean and all oilways clear.
2 Fit the bearing half shells to the connecting rods, and the main bearing half shells to their recesses in the crankcase. Note the oil hole positions.
3 Lubricate the shells, and lower the crankshaft into place.

4 Slip the thrust washers into place, with the white-metalled sides towards the crankshaft. Squirt oil onto them.
5 Place the main bearing shells in the caps (note that these have no oil feed holes), lubricate the shells, and fit the caps into their proper places. Tighten the bolts to the specified torque. Check for freedom of crankshaft rotation. Some stiffness is to be expected with new components.
6 Measure the endfloat of the crankshaft, using either a dial gauge operating on the flywheel flange, or by testing with feeler gauges between a thrust washer and the adjacent crankshaft abutment (photo). If the endfloat is outside the specified limits, change the thrust washers as necessary for a pair of suitable thickness.
7 Fit the rear oil seal as instructed in Section 15.

30.6 Checking the crankshaft endfloat

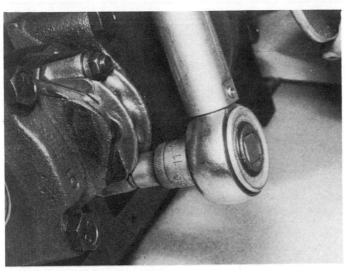

30.8 Tightening the big-end bearing cap nuts

31.1B Lowering the crankshaft into position

8   Lubricate the crankpins, pull the connecting rod big-ends on to them, and fit the big-end caps. Ensure that the caps are fitted to the correct rods, and refit and tighten the nuts to the specified torque (photo). Check again for freedom of crankshaft rotation.
9   Proceed in reverse of the dismantling procedure (Section 16, paragraphs 1 to 4).

31 Crankshaft and main bearings (1565 and 1647 cc engines) — refitting

1   Fit the main bearing shells in the cylinder block, with the oil holes aligned, lubricate the shells and crankshaft journals, and lower the shaft into the block (photos).
2   Slip the thrust washers into place with the white-metalled sides to the crankshaft. Lubricate them.
3   Fit the main bearing shells to bearing caps numbers 2, 3, 4 and 5, lubricate the shells, fit the caps and fit the bolts loosely (photos).
4   Select suitable number one bearing cap side seals, by fitting the bearing to the cap, fitting the cap, and nipping up the cap bolts.

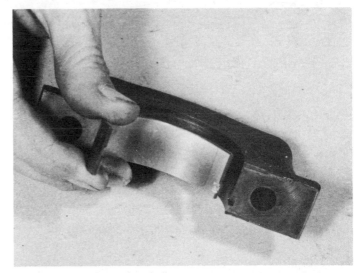

31.3A Fit the main bearing shell ...

31.1A Fitting a main bearing shell in the block

31.3B ... and locate the cap over the crankshaft

31.7A Locate the foil strip ...

31.7B ... fit the No 1 main bearing cap ...

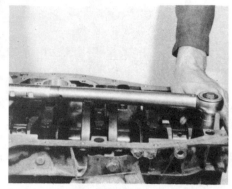

31.7C ... and tighten the bolts

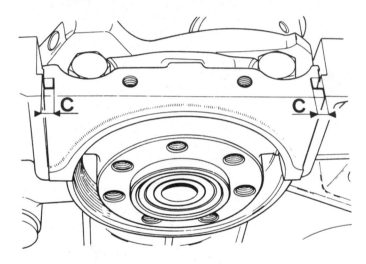

Fig. 1.18 Main bearing side seal checking dimension (C) (Sec 31)

Measure the dimension C (Fig. 1.18), and select suitable seals as follows:

    (a) *Dimension C = 5 mm or less, use 5.10 mm thick seals*
    (b) *Dimension C = more than 5 mm, use 5.4 mm thick seals*
        (coded white)

Remove the bearing cap.
5   Fit both seals to the bearing cap with the seal groove facing outwards. The seal should be approximately 0.2 mm (0.008 in) proud of the joint cap surface.
6   Fit the bearing shell, and lubricate the shell and side seals.
7   Obtain two studs of suitable length, 10 mm diameter by 1.5 mm pitch, screw them into the bearing bolt holes, offer up the bearing cap to the studs, and with two foil strips between the block and seals to prevent damage to the seals, persuade the cap down (photos). As the cap is nearly home, check that the side seals are still projecting by checking with a rule. Take out the foil strips and the studs, fit the cap bolts, and tighten all bolts to the specified torque. Cut off the protruding tips of the seal at the cap and sump surface.
8   Proceed as described in Section 30, paragraphs 6 to 8.
9   Fit the remaining items in reverse of the removal procedure (Section 17).

32 Camshaft (1397 cc engine) – refitting

1   If necessary, fit a new key, a new flange and tap a new distance piece on, using a piece of tube, until the distance piece touches the shoulder.

2   Fit the camshaft sprocket and tighten the bolt to the specified torque. Check dimension (J), see Fig. 1.19.
3   Remove the sprocket. Lubricate the shaft, and refit it. Fit and tighten the camshaft flange bolts.
4   Refit the tensioner, timing chain and sprockets, and the timing cover (see Section 33).
5   Refit the remaining items in reverse of the removal procedure (see Section 12), noting the following paragraphs.
6   Lubricate the tappets before refitting.
7   To refit the distributor driving pinion, first turn the crankshaft to place No 1 piston at TDC on the compression stroke. (Note that the valves on No 4 cylinder will both be open at this point).
8   With a 12 mm dia x 1.75 mm pitch bolt inserted in the distributor drive pinion, insert the pinion so that the slot is at right-angles to the centre-line of the engine, and with the large offset facing the clutch (see Fig. 1.20).

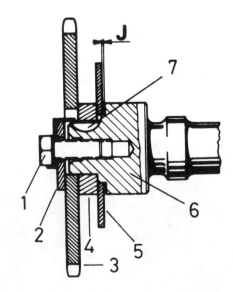

Fig. 1.19 Camshaft flange clearance on the type 847 engine (Sec 32)

1	*Bolt*	*5*	*Flange*
2	*Washer*	*6*	*Camshaft*
3	*Sprocket*	*7*	*Key*
4	*Distance piece*		

J = 0.06 to 0.11 mm (0.002 to 0.004 in)

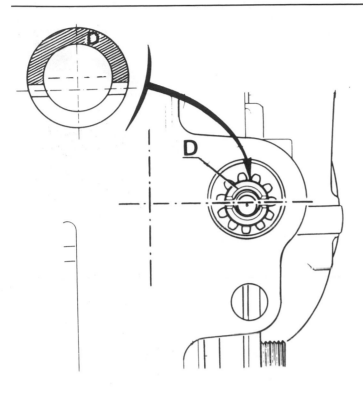

Fig. 1.20 Distributor drive pinion TDC position on the type 847 engine (Sec 32)

D = Large offset

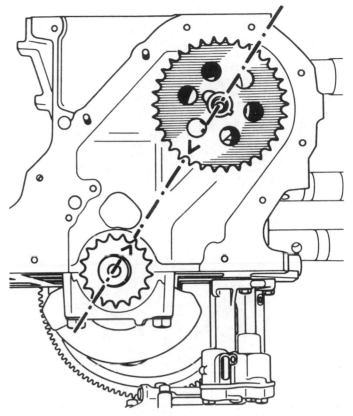

Fig. 1.21 Timing sprocket TDC alignment on the type 847 engine (Sec 33)

33 Timing chain and sprockets (1397 cc engine) – refitting

1   Ensure that all gasket faces on the sump, cylinder block, and timing cover are completely clean.
2   Temporarily fit the camshaft sprocket, refit the crankshaft sprocket, and align the marks as indicated in Fig. 1.21. Remove the camshaft sprocket without disturbing the setting.
3   Fit the timing chain over the crankshaft sprocket, and slip the camshaft sprocket into mesh with the chain. Refit the sprocket to the camshaft, ensuring that the marks remain in line.
4   Refit the timing chain tensioner assembly, with the spindle slot over the pin and the spring tag hooked into the hole in the cylinder block (photo).
5   Support the timing cover adequately and place a little gasket cement around the periphery of the oil seal. Tap the seal carefully into place using a block of wood or other suitable item until the inner edge

of the seal is flush with the inner edge of the cover (photo).
6   Use a new gasket and loosely fit the timing cover, leaving the bolts finger tight.
7   Lubricate the oil seal lips and refit the crankshaft pulley, or the pulley sleeve if fitted, to permit the timing cover to centralise itself about the pulley. Nip up two or three of the cover bolts, and remove the pulley or sleeve (photo).
8   Tighten down all the cover bolts, working progressively and evenly.
9   Refit the crankshaft pulley, jamming the flywheel if necessary to allow the bolt to be tightened.
10 Refit the remaining items in reverse of the removal procedures (see Section 10).

33.4 Fitted timing chain and tensioner

33.5 Timing cover oil seal

33.7 Pulley sleeve located in the timing cover

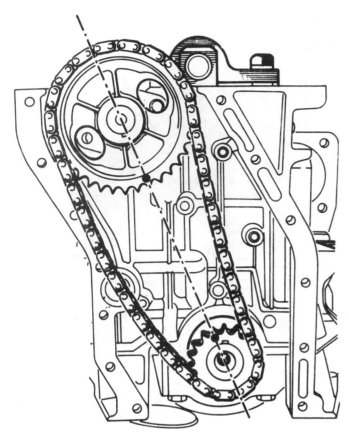

Fig. 1.22 Timing sprocket TDC alignment on the types A2M, A5L, A6M, A7L and 843 engines (Sec 34)

34.3 Inserting the camshaft

34 Timing chain and sprockets (1565 and 1647 cc engines) – refitting

1   Turn the crankshaft to place the key at the top.
2   Fit the chain to the sprockets, with the timing marks and keyway aligned as in Fig. 1.22.
3   Start entering the camshaft, register the crankshaft sprocket with the crankshaft and key at the appropriate point and tap the crankshaft sprocket on gently (photo).
4   Fit and lock the camshaft flange retaining bolts (photo).
5   If re-using the old chain tensioner, take the shoe from the tensioner body and lock the piston in the shoe using a 3 mm Allen key.

Refit the shoe in the body with a shim about 2 mm (0.08 in) thick between body and shoe to prevent premature setting.
6   If using a new chain tensioner, leave the plastic keep plate in position.
7   Fit the tensioner and tighten the securing bolts. Set the tensioner by removing the plastic keep or shim, pressing the shoe to the bottom, and releasing it.
8   Fit the chain guides with the bolts left loose. Place a 0.3 to 0.5 mm (0.012 to 0.020 in) spacer strip between the chain and each guide, tighten the guide bolts and remove the spacer strips.
9   Carefully fit a new oil seal to the crankshaft aperture by supporting the cover at the rear and tapping the seal in from the front, using a piece of tube of suitable diameter. The seal should be flush at the rear of the aperture.
10   Stick the timing cover gaskets to the cylinder block face, using grease or a little jointing compound. Fit the cover, leaving the bolts finger tight (photo).
11   Lubricate the timing cover seal lip, and fit the crankshaft pulley boss, allowing it to centralise the cover (and thus the oil seal) around the boss. Check that the timing cover top face is flush with the cylinder block, and tighten the cover bolts. Trim the edges of the gasket flush at the surface of the timing cover and sump (photo).
12   Refit the remaining items in reverse of the procedure given in Section 11.
13   Refit the power steering pulley to the rear of the camshaft, where applicable. The location roll pin slits should face the direction of rotation.

34.4 Tightening the camshaft flange bolts

34.10 Fitting the timing cover

34.11 Trimming the timing cover gasket

35.2 Refitting the oil pump

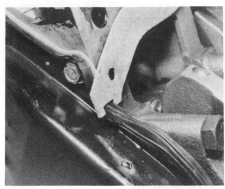

35.4A Sump side gasket and front rubber seal

35.4B Sump side gasket located over the seal

35.4C Applying jointing compound at the gasket ends

35.5 Fitting the sump

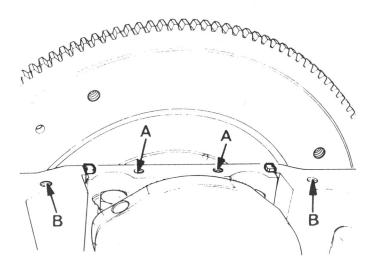

Fig. 1.23 Sump bolt locations on 1565 and 1647 cc engines (Sec 35)

A   Use bolts with deep slotted heads
B   Use bolts with normal slotted heads

35 Sump and oil pump – refitting

1   Ensure that the faces of the cylinder block and sump are thoroughly clean.
2   Refit the oil pump and rotors, as applicable, and tighten the securing bolts (photo).

3   Place the front and rear main bearing rubber seals in position on the 1397cc engine.
4   Smear a suitable jointing compound on the sump side gaskets or single gasket and stick them in place on the sump. Ensure that there is adequate jointing compound at the ends (photos) where applicable.
5   With the pistons of Nos 1 and 4 cylinders at BDC, offer up the sump carefully and fit the bolts (photo). Tighten progressively and evenly (see Fig. 1.23).
6   Refit the undertray and, where necessary, the transmission front cover.
7   Refill the sump with oil.

36 Cylinder head – refitting

1   Do not allow foreign matter to enter the oilways upon the cylinder block and head surfaces, or serious damage due to oil shortage may result.
2   Ensure, before refitting the cylinder head, that all oil in the cylinder head bolt holes on the block surface is removed, thus ensuring that the precise head tightening torques necessary are obtainable.
3   Remove the cylinder liner clamping arrangement, and check that the cylinder liner protrusion is satisfactory (see Section 29).

1397 cc engine

4   Place the new cylinder head gasket in position with the marking 'HAUT-TOP' uppermost. Ensure that the correct gasket has been supplied (photo).
5   Carefully position the cylinder head on the gasket, screw the head bolts in by hand, and tighten them in stages to the specified torque in the order shown in Fig. 1.24.
6   Fit the pushrods, and check the valve clearances (see Section 39).

36.4 1397 cc head gasket in position

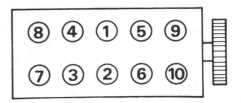

Fig. 1.24 Tightening and loosening sequence for cylinder head bolts on all engines (Sec 36)

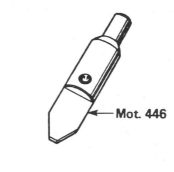

36.5A Fitting the 1397 cc cylinder head

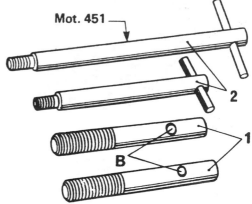

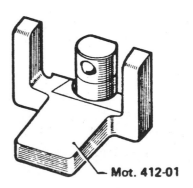

Fig. 1.25 Cylinder head alignment tools for 1565 and 1647 cc engines (Sec 36)

36.5B Tightening the 1397 cc cylinder head bolts

1565 and 1647 cc engines

7   The positioning of the cylinder head is very important, determining as it does the alignment of the distributor drive spindle and pinion. This in itself would present no problem, but Renault say that the head gasket must not be moved once fitted, nor may the head be moved to align it once it has contacted the gasket. To achieve the above conditions, Renault special tools Mot 451, Mot 446 and Mot 402-01 are required (Fig. 1.25). If these tools cannot be hired or borrowed locally – it is unlikely to be economic to buy them – it might be

possible to improvise the locating studs at least, using two long bolts of the same diameter and pitch as the cylinder head bolts.

8 Check that the distributor drive pinion and cylinder head locating dowel are in place in the block. With the No. 1 cylinder at TDC on the firing stroke (ie with the cams for No 4 cylinder both in operation) the slot in the drive pinion should be as in Figs. 1.26, 1.27 or 1.28. Place the cylinder head gasket into position on the block surface, and *do not allow it to move again*. If this should occur, the gasket must be scrapped (photos).

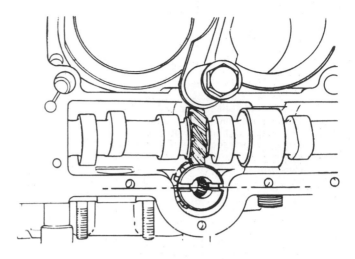

Fig. 1.28 Distributor drive pinion TDC alignment on the UK A2M engine (Sec 36)

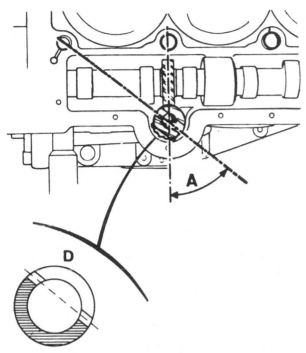

Fig. 1.26 Distributor drive pinion TDC alignment on UK 1565 and 1647 cc engines except A2M (Sec 36)

D   Indicates segment positions

36.8A Distributor drive pinion location

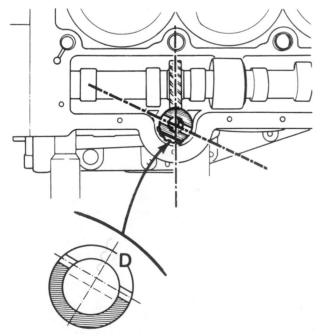

Fig. 1.27 Distributor drive pinion TDC alignment on North American 1565 and 1647 cc engines (Sec 36)

D indicates segment positions

36.8B Fitting the 1565 and 1647 cc cylinder head gasket

9   Screw the studs from tool Mot 451 into the holes (see Figs. 1.29 and 1.30) until the balls just hold the gasket down to the block.

10   On A5L, A7L, 843 and A6M engines locate the Mot 446 gauge in the hole shown in Fig. 1.29.

11   On A2M engines, locate the Mot 412-01 gauge in the hole shown in Fig. 1.30 with the arms (T) parallel to the engine centre-line.

12   Fit the tappet chamber rubber seal, with the ends properly linked into the cylinder head gasket.

13   Clean the cylinder head bolts, and put a little engine oil on the threads. Refit the fuel pump plunger on the A2M engine.

14   Tap each tappet into place in the cylinder head to keep them in position (photos). Smear them with a little grease if necessary. Fit the head, ensuring that the manifold mounting face registers with the arms on gauge Mot 412-01 before the head is permitted to touch the gasket, where applicable. Ensure that the tappet chamber seal does not come out of position.

15   On A5L, A7L, 843 and A6M engines, refit the rocker assembly, making sure that the two bearings with oil holes are located on the dowels (photo).

16   Fit six bolts in the vacant holes, noting the position of the four longest bolts. Remove the two locating studs using the unscrewing tool, and fit the remaining two bolts. Tighten in the proper sequence (Fig. 1.24) to the specified torque figure (photo).

17   Remove the alignment tool.

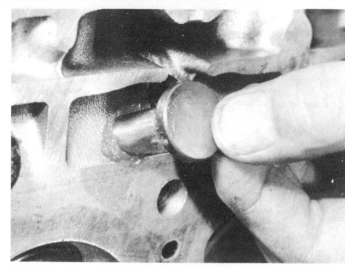

36.14A Inserting the tappets in the cylinder head

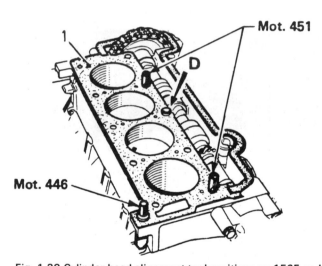

Fig. 1.29 Cylinder head alignment tool positions on 1565 and 1647 cc engines except A2M (Sec 36)

1   Gasket   D   Dowel

36.14B Lightly tap the tappets to retain them in the cylinder head

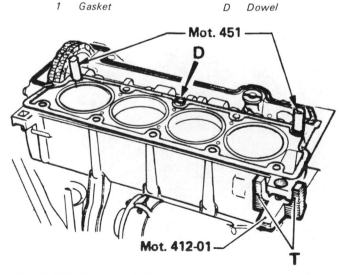

Fig. 1.30 Cylinder head alignment tool positions on the A2M engine (Sec 36)

D   Dowel   T   Alignment arms

36.15 Fit the rocker assembly ...

36.16 ... and tighten the cylinder head bolts

All engines

18 Reverse the procedure given in Section 8, paragraphs 1 to 5, and adjust the valve clearances, as described in Section 39.

37 Ancilliary components – refitting

Refer to Section 7 and refit the listed components with reference to the Chapters indicated, where applicable.

38 Oil filter – removal and refitting

1 It may be possible to unscrew the oil filter by hand, but, if not, a strap wrench of suitable design will be necessary. Be prepared for some spillage as the filter is removed.
2 Clean the seal face on the cylinder block.
3 Smear a little engine oil on the new filter seal then screw on the filter until it just touches the block.
4 Using the hands only tighten the filter a quarter turn, then unscrew it and tighten it a half to three quarters of a turn from the point of contact (photo).

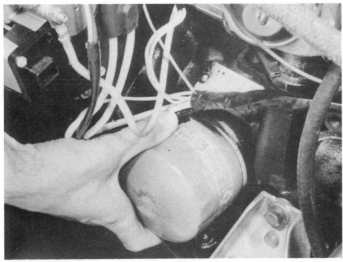

38.4 Tightening the oil filter

39 Valve clearances – adjustment

Correct valve clearances are vital for the correct functioning of the engine. If the clearances are too big, noisy operation and reduced efficiency will result. If the clearances are set too small, the valve may not seat properly when hot, and poor compression and burning of the valve and seat may result. Refer to the Specifications for the clearances.

1 Final adjustment of the valve clearances should be carried out once the engine has run (ie hot). When the engine is in the vehicle and a manual gearbox is fitted, the engine may be rotated by engaging top gear and either pushing the vehicle to and fro or jacking up one front wheel and turning it by hand. If automatic transmission is fitted, the engine will have to be turned a little at a time, using the starter motor, or with a spanner on the crankshaft pulley.
2 Commence by removing the rocker cover. Turn the engine until the exhaust valve on No 1 cylinder is fully open, when the inlet valve on No 3 cylinder and exhaust valve on No 4 cylinder may be adjusted to the appropriate clearance. (Numbering from the flywheel end, exhaust valves are 1-4-5-8, inlet valves are 2-3-6-7) (photo).

39.2 Checking the valve clearances

3 To adjust, loosen the locknut on the rocker arm adjusting screw, place a feeler gauge of the specified thickness between the valve and rocker arm, and turn the adjusting screw until a close sliding fit is obtained on the feeler. Hold the adjusting screw still and tighten the locknut, then recheck the clearance (photos).

39.3A Adjusting the valve clearances (1397 cc engine)

39.3B Adjusting the valve clearances (1565 and 1647 cc engines)

4   Proceed with the remaining valves, so that all of them are adjusted in accordance with the table which follows:

Valve fully open	Check and adjust
1 (EX)	6 (IN), 8 (EX)
5 (EX)	4 (EX), 7 (IN)
8 (EX)	1 (EX), 3 (IN)
4 (EX)	2 (IN), 5 (EX)

5   Refit the rocker cover, using a new gasket if necessary.

40 Engine – refitting

Reverse the procedure given in Section 5, but note the following additional points:

(a) Lightly lubricate the clutch shaft splines (manual gearboxes) or torque converter centre boss (automatic gearboxes) using a suitable grease
(b) On automatic transmission vehicles, the driveplate blade with sharp corners must be lined up with the hole in the converter marked with a paint spot (see Chapter 7). Remove the converter retaining plate fitted during removal of the unit, at the appropriate point
(c) On 1397 cc engines, to ease fitting the clutch shield, use two studs threaded 8 mm dia x 1.25 pitch x 20 mm long inserted in the holes through which the clutch shield bolts pass, thus providing a means of temporarily locating the shield
(d) Adjust the accelerator cable (Chapter 3)
(e) Adjust the clutch cable (Chapter 5) or governor and selector lever (Chapter 7), as applicable
(f) On turbo and North American A7L models, tighten the exhaust or catalytic converter flange bolts then back off one and a half turns
(g) Refill the cooling system (Chapter 2) and fill the engine with oil

41 Engine – adjustment after major overhaul

1   Check that any loose rags or tools are removed from the engine compartment.
2   Start the engine and check that the oil pressure warning light goes out. Check for water and oil leaks.
3   Check and adjust the ignition timing and idle speed.
4   Run the engine for twenty minutes, switch it off, and leave it for two and a half hours before retightening the cylinder head. First loosen

bolt No 1 by half a turn and tighten again to the specified torque figure. Repeat this procedure for all the other bolts in the specified sequence. No further retightening is necessary.
5   Finally check and adjust the valve clearances.

PART C – OHC ENGINES

42 Major operations possible with the engine in the car

The following operations can be carried out without having to remove the engine from the car:

(a) Cylinder head removal
(b) Camshaft removal
(c) Timing sprockets and belt removal
(d) Timing belt tensioner removal
(e) Intermediate shaft removal
(f) Inlet and exhaust manifolds removal
(g) Sump removal
(h) Big end bearings removal
(j) Oil pump removal
(k) Pistons and connecting rod assemblies, and cylinder liners removal

43 Major operations only possible after removal of the engine from the car

The following operations can only be carried out after removal of the engine from the car:

(a) Removal of the crankshaft
(b) Renewal of the main bearings

44 Engine – removal

Note: The engine may be removed either separately, or together with the transmission. The following paragraphs describe both methods.

Method 1 (engine unit only)
1   Disconnect the battery.
2   Drain the engine oil.
3   For better access remove the bonnet (Chapter 12).
4   Remove the front crossmember (Chapter 12), the radiator (Chapter 2) and front grille (Chapter 12).
5   Remove the air cleaner and exhaust warm air duct.
6   Remove the starter motor (Chapter 10).
7   Remove the top and bottom hoses, and disconnect the heater hoses (photos).
8   Loosen the clip and remove the heater intermediate pipe.
9   Remove the exhaust manifold (Chapter 3).
10 Disconnect the earth strap(s) and the wiring connectors on the bulkhead (photos).
11 Disconnect the accelerator cable (Chapter 3).
12 Disconnect all wiring from the engine, identifying each wire for location. These include the wiring to the electronic module, alternator, distributor, temperature sender, reversing light switch and oil pressure switch.
13 Disconnect the vacuum hoses from the electronic module and inlet manifold.
14 Disconnect the fuel pipes from the fuel pump and carburettor, as applicable, plug them and remove the in-line filter.
15 Where applicable, move the air conditioning components with reference to Chapter 12.
16 On North American models, remove the emission control components and catalytic converter, as applicable, with reference to Chapter 3.
17 Disconnect the automatic transmission leads and cables, as applicable (Chapter 7).
18 Remove the distributor cap and rotor arm.
19 Disconnect the clutch cable from the valve cover.

44.7A Heater hose connection to the cylinder head

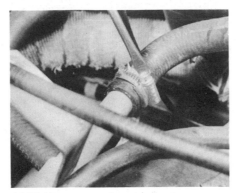

44.7B Heater return hose connection

44.7C Heater hose bracket on front of engine

44.10A Earth straps on the cylinder block

44.10B Remove the cover ...

44.10C ... and disconnect the bulkhead connectors

20 Jack up the front of the car and support on axle stands. Apply the handbrake.

21 Unbolt and remove the transmission front cover.

22 On automatic transmission models remove the torque converter bolts, with reference to Chapter 7.

23 Unscrew the front mounting upper nut and remove the through-bolt (photos).

24 Unscrew the engine side mounting nuts and the left-hand bolts (photos).

25 Connect suitable lifting tackle to the engine lifting eyes (photos).

26 Lift the engine until the transmission touches the steering crossmember, then support the transmission in this position with a trolley jack (photo).

27 Remove the power steering pump (Chapter 11), leaving the hoses connected, and place it on one side.

28 Remove the transmission bellhousing-to-engine bolts, noting the location of the brackets. Note that the top left-hand bolt cannot be removed completely as the steering gear crossmember is in the way. Remember to fit the bolt loosely before refitting the engine.

29 Ease the engine forwards until it is disconnected from the clutch shaft or torque converter. If necessary unbolt one of the engine mountings from the cylinder block.

30 Lift the engine from the car.

31 On automatic transmission models retain the torque converter, as described in Chapter 7.

44.23A Front view of the front engine mounting

44.23B Rear view of the front engine mounting

44.24A Left-hand engine mounting bolts

44.24B Bottom view of the right-hand engine mounting

44.24C Top view of the right-hand engine mounting with the engine installed ...

44.24D ... and with the engine removed

44.25A Front engine lifting eye location

44.25B Rear engine lifting eye location (arrowed)

44.26 Lifting the engine and transmission

Method 2 (engine and transmission)

32 Follow the procedure given in paragraphs 1 to 20, but do not remove the starter motor.

33 Disconnect the clutch cable, where applicable.

34 Disconnect the driveshafts from the transmission, as described in Chapter 8.

35 Disconnect the speedometer cable from the transmission.

36 Disconnect the gear selector mechanism (Chapters 6 or 7).

37 Disconnect the wiring from the reversing light switch and automatic transmission, as applicable.

38 Support the rear of the transmission on a trolley jack and unbolt the rear mounting.

39 Connect suitable lifting tackle to the engine lifting eyes and take the weight.

40 Unscrew the engine side mounting nuts.

41 Raise the engine, lower the transmission and lift out the combined assembly.

42 Separate the transmission from the engine with reference to paragraph 28 (photo).

45 Engine dismantling – general

Refer to Section 6.

46 Ancillary components – removal

Before dismantling the main engine components, the following externally-mounted ancillary components can be removed. The removal sequence need not necessarily follow the order given:

Inlet and exhaust manifolds (Chapter 3)
Oil pressure switch (photo)
Distributor (Chapter 4) (photo)
Engine mountings and brackets (photo)
Alternator (Chapter 10)
Emission control components (Chapter 3)
Fuel injection components, if applicable (Chapter 3)
Oil filter (Section 73)
Water pump (Chapter 2)
Thermostat (Chapter 2)

44.42 Separating the engine and gearbox

46.1A Oil pressure switch location (arrowed)

46.1B Removing the distributor

46.1C Engine mounting bracket

47 Cylinder head – removal

1   If the engine is still in the vehicle, drain, disconnect or remove (as applicable) the following items:

   (a) Disconnect the battery earth lead
   (b) Drain the cooling system (see Chapter 2)
   (c) Disconnect the wires, pipes and leads to the cylinder head, noting the respective connections
   (d) Remove the air filter, carburettor and inlet manifold (see Chapter 3)
   (e) Remove the exhaust manifold, disconnecting it from the cylinder head and exhaust downpipe flange
   (f) Remove the undertray beneath the engine
   (g) Where fitted, detach the power steering pump drivebelt (see Chapter 11)
   (h) Detach the alternator drivebelt
   (i) Remove the diagnostic socket
   (j) If the cylinder head is to be dismantled and the distributor removed, refer to Chapter 4 and check TDC before unbolting the distributor

2   The procedure for cylinder head removal with engine fitted or removed is now the same.
3   Unbolt and remove the timing cover.
4   Remove the rocker cover.
5   With the engine set at TDC, the timing belt tensioner bolts can be loosened and the tensioner pivoted to slacken the belt tension. Remove the timing belt.
6   The cylinder head retaining bolts can now be progressively loosened and, with the exception of the front right-hand bolt, removed. Loosen off the bolts in the sequence shown in Fig. 1.24.
7   The cylinder head is now ready for removal from the block, and it is essential that it is detached in the correct manner. Do not lift the head directly upwards from the block. The head must be swivelled from the rear in a horizontal manner, pivoting on the remaining head bolt at the front. You will probably have to tap the head round on its rear corner, using a soft-headed mallet or wood block to break the seal between the head, gasket and block. Once the head is pivoted round and the seal broken, it can be lifted clear. This action is necessary because if the head were to be lifted directly from the block, the seals at the base of the liners would be disturbed – where the liners are not being removed, it is essential that this seal is not broken or disturbed. If the liners are accidentally disturbed they must be removed and new lower seals fitted.
8   The rocker shaft assembly and final bolt can be removed from the cylinder head once it is withdrawn from the engine.
9   To prevent the possibility of movement by the respective cylinder liners whilst the head is removed, it is advisable to place a clamp plate over the top edges of the liners. A suitable plate (or bar) can be fastened temporarily in position using the existing head bolt holes, using shorter bolts of the desired thread and diameter with large, flat washers under the heads. Alternatively, use a block of wood with two bolts and spacers, clamping it in position in diagonal fashion as shown (photo).

48 Rocker assembly – dismantling

1   Unscrew the end plug from the shaft and extract the plug and filter. This filter must be renewed at 20 000 miles (32 000 km) intervals.
2   Number the rocker arms and pedestals/bearings. Note that

47.9 Clamp the cylinder liners in position

48.2 No 5 rocker bearing pedestal showing rollpin hole

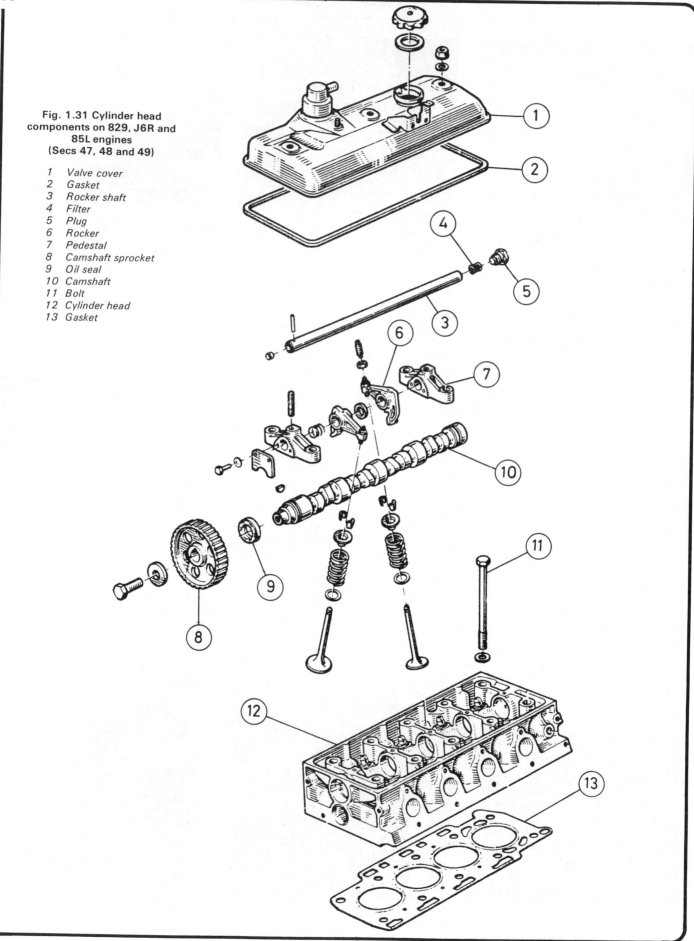

Fig. 1.31 Cylinder head components on 829, J6R and 85L engines (Secs 47, 48 and 49)

1 Valve cover
2 Gasket
3 Rocker shaft
4 Filter
5 Plug
6 Rocker
7 Pedestal
8 Camshaft sprocket
9 Oil seal
10 Camshaft
11 Bolt
12 Cylinder head
13 Gasket

bearing No 5 has two threaded holes to retain the shim which adjusts the rocker shaft endfloat, and a hole for the rollpin which locates the shaft and pedestal (photo).

3   If a rollpin is fitted to No 5 bearing, extract it and obtain a solid type pin before dismantling the assembly. The rollpin can shear when renewing the end filter.

4   Keep the parts in order as they are removed from the shaft and note their respective locations. Note also that the machined flat section on top of pedestals 1 to 4 all face towards the camshaft sprocket.

49 Camshaft – removal

1   The camshaft can be removed with the engine fitted in the car. Where this is the case, proceed as follows in paragraphs 2 to 8. Where the engine/cylinder head are removed, proceed from paragraph 9.

2   Disconnect the battery earth lead.

3   Drain the engine coolant (Chapter 2).

4   Detach the throttle cable from the carburettor and bracket on the rocker cover.

5   Remove the radiator (Chapter 2).

6   Remove the front grille and crossmember (Chapter 12).

7   Remove the engine undertray.

8   Detach the warm air trunking.

9   Remove the drivebelts to the alternator and, where fitted, the power steering pump and air conditioning pump.

10   Unbolt and remove the timing cover.

11   Disconnect the respective HT leads and remove the spark plugs. Next, rotate the crankshaft to locate the No 1 piston (flywheel end) at TDC on firing stroke. This can be checked by ensuring the timing mark on the flywheel is in line with the 'O' graduation marked on the aperture in the clutch housing. Rotate the crankshaft by means of a spanner applied to the crankshaft pulley retaining bolt.

12   Next, turn the crankshaft from the TDC a further quarter of a turn clockwise (viewed from the front).

13   Loosen the timing belt tensioner, release the tension and withdraw the belt.

14   To remove the camshaft sprocket, pass a suitable hardwood dowel rod or screwdriver through a hole in the sprocket and jam against the top surface of the cylinder head to prevent the camshaft from turning. Unscrew the retaining bolt and remove the sprocket. Take great care, as the sprocket is manufactured in sintered metal and is therefore relatively fragile (photo). Also, take care not to damage or distort the cylinder head. Remove the Woodruff key.

15   Remove the rocker cover and unscrew the cylinder head retaining bolts in a progressive manner in the sequence shown in Fig. 1.24. With the bolts extracted, remove the rocker assembly and relocate some of the bolts with spacers to the same depth as the rocker pedestals fitted under the bolt heads, to ensure that the cylinder head is not disturbed during subsequent operations. If for any reason the head is disturbed, then the head gasket and respective liner seals will have to be renewed. Remove the distributor (see Chapter 4).

16   Unscrew and remove the two bolts retaining the camshaft location fork plate. Remove the plate from the groove in the camshaft.

17   The camshaft front oil seal can now be extracted from its housing. Carefully prise out from the front or preferably drift out from the rear. Take great care not to damage the seal location bore in the head.

18   The camshaft can now be withdrawn carefully through the seal aperture in the front of the cylinder head. Take care during its removal not to snag any of the lobe corners on the bearings as they are passed through the cylinder head. On models with a power steering pulley on the rear of the camshaft, remove the pulley first by unscrewing the bolt and pulling the pulley from the location roll pins.

50 Crankshaft pulley, sprocket and front seal – removal and refitting

1   The crankshaft pulley and front oil seal can be removed with the engine fitted as given below. When removing these items with the engine removed, proceed from paragraph 5.

2   Remove the engine undertray panel.

3   Remove the power steering pump driveshaft (where fitted) and the alternator drivebelt.

4   Remove the transmission front cover.

5   Turn the engine over to the TDC position (see Chapter 4), with the mark on the flywheel and 'O' mark on the clutch housing in alignment.

6   Remove the timing cover.

7   Loosen the timing belt tensioner and remove the belt.

8   Now remove the crankshaft pulley which is secured by a large bolt and washer (photo). To prevent the shaft turning when unscrewing the bolt, jam the flywheel starter ring teeth with a large screwdriver blade jammed against a convenient spot on the cylinder block or clutch housing (engine in position).

9   With the pulley bolt removed, the pulley can be withdrawn from the shaft using a puller, or levering free, but take special care (photo). The timing sprocket is located directly onto the pulley rear face and this sprocket, like its counterparts, is relatively fragile, being manufactured of sintered metal. Remove the sprocket from the crankshaft.

10   Prise the key from the keyway in the shaft. Remove the spacer or air conditioning pulley wheel if fitted.

11   Carefully prise out the old seal using a screwdriver blade but do not damage the seal housing or shaft in the process.

12   The timing sprocket is located onto the rear of the pulley by a couple of roll pins, and the two components can be prised apart with care if desired.

13   Seal refitting (engine fitted) is a reversal of the removal process. Lubricate the new seal before fitting with clean engine oil and drive it into position using a suitable pipe drift. The seal must be fitted 'squarely' and accurately or it will leak. If distorted in any way during fitting, renew it.

14   When refitting the pulley retaining bolt, smear the threads with a thread locking compound. Readjust the tension of the timing belt and the respective drivebelts, as applicable. **Note:** *Do not get any oil onto the timing belt during the above operations. If it is oil impregnated it must be renewed before refitting.*

49.14 Removing the camshaft sprocket

50.8 Crankshaft pulley and bolt

50.9 Removing the crankshaft pulley

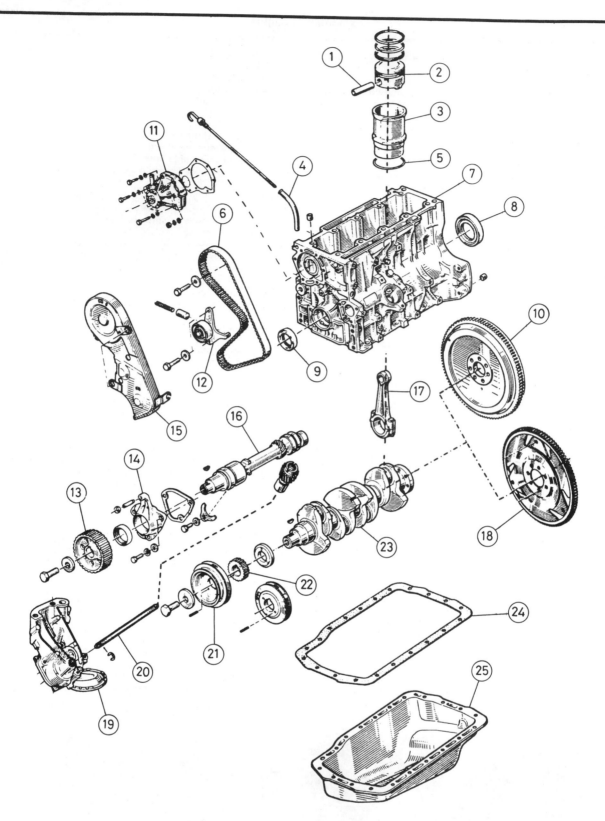

Fig. 1.32 Cylinder block components on 829, J6R and 851 engines (Sec 50)

1	Gudgeon pin	8	Seal	15	Timing cover	22 Sprocket
2	Piston	9	Seal	16	Intermediate shaft	23 Crankshaft
3	Liner	10	Flywheel	17	Connecting rod	24 Gasket
4	Dipstick tube	11	Water pump	18	Driveplate	25 Sump
5	Seal	12	Tensioner	19	Oil pump	26 Distributor pinion
6	Timing belt	13	Sprocket	20	Driveshaft	27 Seal
7	Cylinder block	14	Housing	21	Pulley	

51 Timing belt and tensioner – removal

1   If the engine is fitted and only the timing belt and tensioner are to be removed, proceed as given in paragraphs 2 to 13. Where the engine is being dismantled, as given previously, proceed from paragraph 11.
2   Raise the front of the car so that the wheels clear the ground and support it with suitable stands. Apply the handbrake.
3   Unbolt and remove the engine undertray.
4   Remove the power steering pump drivebelt, loosening the pump retaining/adjuster bolts to loosen the tension.
5   Loosen the alternator retaining bolts and remove its drivebelt.
6   Remove the timing cover.
7   Detach the battery earth terminal.
8   Remove the spark plugs.
9   Turn the engine over to the TDC position.
10 Drain the cooling system or clamp the inlet manifold heater hose close to the manifold and detach the outlet hose from the manifold at the timing case end. Remove the timing cover.
11 Loosen the tensioner retaining bolts and remove the belt.
12 Take care when removing the tensioner as it is operated by a spring and piston in the crankcase side and the tensioner is under considerable pressure. As the tensioner is unbolted, take care that the spring and piston (photo) don't fly out of their aperture at high speed!
13 If the engine is installed, ensure that the timing is not disturbed whilst the belt and tensioner are removed.

51.12 Timing belt tensioner spring and piston

52 Intermediate shaft and oil seal – removal

1   Where the engine is fitted, refer to the previous Section and follow paragraphs 2 to 6, then continue as follows in paragraphs 2 and 3. Where the engine is removed, continue from paragraph 4.
2   Clamp the inlet manifold hose to prevent circulation. Clamp it as close as possible to the inlet manifold and then detach the outlet hose on the manifold.
3   Loosen the timing belt tensioner and remove the timing belt, taking care not to get oil or grease on it.
4   Unscrew the intermediate shaft sprocket bolt, passing a screwdriver shaft or rod through one of the holes in the sprocket to lock against the front of the block and retain the sprocket in position whilst it is being unscrewed.
5   Withdraw the sprocket and remove the Woodruff key from the shaft.
6   Unbolt and remove the intermediate shaft housing.
7   The oil seal can now be extracted. Prise it free with a screwdriver, but take care not to damage the housing.
8   Before the intermediate shaft can be withdrawn remove the fuel pump (Chapter 3) then the oil pump drive pinion must be extracted. To

do this, unscrew the two side cover retaining bolts and remove the cover. The oil pump drive pinion is now accessible and can be extracted (photos).
9   The intermediate shaft can now be removed from the front of the block.

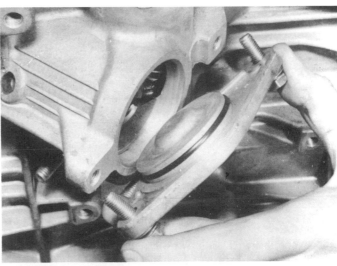

52.8A Remove the side cover ...

52.8B ... and extract the oil pump drive pinion

53 Flywheel/driveplate – removal

1   The flywheel/driveplate is retained in position by seven bolts on the end of the crankshaft.
2   To loosen these bolts, lock the starter ring with a screwdriver blade or similar implement inserted between the teeth of the starter ring against a portion of the block.
3   With the flywheel 'jammed' to prevent it turning, unscrew the retaining bolts. A thread locking compound has been applied during assembly and they will therefore be tight to unscrew.
4   The bolt holes are not equidistant and so there is no need to mark the flywheel and crankshaft flange alignment positions prior to removal.
5   If the flywheel/driveplate is to be removed or inspected and the engine is in the car, the transmission must first be removed (Chapters 6 or 7) and the clutch removed, where applicable.

54 Sump and oil pump – removal

1   If the engine is still fitted, drain the engine oil, remove the engine undertray and the transmission coverplate with TDC pick-up unit.
2   Unscrew the sump bolts and prise the sump free.
3   The oil pump is now accessible for removal. First lift the driveshaft upwards and remove it.
4   Unscrew the two pump unit retaining bolts and withdraw the pump. Note that the pump is also located by dowels.
5   Unscrew the four pump cover bolts to inspect the rotors.
6   Extract the relief valve split pin and withdraw the cup, spring, guide and piston.

55 Pistons and cylinder liners – removal

Refer to Section 14; however, mark the connecting rods on the intermediate shaft side. Remove the cylinder head (Section 47) and the sump and oil pump (Section 54).

56 Crankshaft and main bearings – removal

1   The engine must be removed from the car in order to remove the crankshaft.
2   Remove the flywheel/driveplate (Section 53), sump and oil pump (Section 54) and the crankshaft pulley and sprocket (Section 50.)
3   Remove the crankshaft oil seal and, if necessary, the spigot bearing with reference to Section 15.
4   Disconnect the connecting rods with reference to Sections 55 and 14.
5   Mark the main bearing caps relative to the cylinder block (No 1 at the flywheel end), take out the bolts and remove the bearing caps and bearings, tapping the end caps if necessary to remove them.
6   Remove the side seals and lift out the crankshaft, bearings and thrust washers.

57 Lubrication system – general

1   The engine lubrication system and circuit is shown in Fig. 1.7.
2   Oil from the sump is sucked into the circuit via the pump to the oil filter. From there the oil is passed into the main gallery, where it is distributed under pressure to the crankshaft main bearings, big-end bearings and at the front end is circulated via the intermediate shaft. Oil to the camshaft and rocker shaft assemblies is fed up from the rear end of the main gallery. The rocker shaft has a small gauze filter at its oilway entrance. The oil passes along the oilway in the rocker shaft and is dispersed from various interspaced holes to the lobes and bearings of the camshaft.
3   The oil pressure is regulated by a valve unit within the oil pump unit. The main oil filter is of the disposable cartridge type and is easily accessible for renewal at the specified intervals.

4   The oil pump can be removed with the engine fitted, but due to its location in the underside of the crankcase, the sump must first be removed for access. Once removed, overhaul the sump as described in Section 58, renewing any defective components.

58 Oil pump – dismantling and reassembly

1   It is essential that all parts of the pump are in good condition for the pump to work effectively.
2   To dismantle the pump, remove the cover retaining bolts and detach the cover (photo).

58.2 Removing the oil pump cover

3   Extract the gears and clean the respective components.
4   Inspect for any signs of damage or excessive wear. Use a feeler gauge and check the clearance between the rotor (gear) tips and the inner housing as shown (photo).
5   Also, check the gear endfloat using a straight-edged rule laid across the body of the pump and feeler gauge inserted between the rule and gears.
6   Compare the clearances with the allowable tolerances given in the Specifications at the start of this Chapter and, if necessary, renew any defective parts, or possibly the pump unit.
7   Do not overlook the relief valve assembly. To extract it, remove the split pin and withdraw the cup, spring, guide and piston. Again, look for signs of excessive wear or damage and renew as applicable (photo).
8   Check the pump driveshaft for signs of wear or distortion and renew if necessary (photo).

58.4 Checking the rotor clearance

58.7 Oil pump and relief valve components

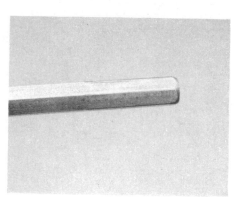

58.8 Check the oil pump driveshaft for wear

59 Cylinder head – dismantling

1 Remove the inlet and exhaust manifolds, as described in Chapter 3.
2 Remove the camshaft with reference to Section 49.
3 Compress the valve springs in turn using a suitable compressor and extract the collets.
4 Release and remove the spring compressor, and take out the cups, spring, seat and valve. Keep them identified for location.
5 Prise the oil seals from the valve guides.
6 On models with a rear-mounted power steering pump remove the rear oil seal.

60 Examination and renovation – general

1 Refer to Section 24, but where reference is made to the timing chain and gears, check the timing belt and sprockets. Ignore the references to the tappets.
2 Check the intermediate shaft components for wear and damage and renew them as necessary.
3 Clean the cylinder block thoroughly and check it for damage.

61 Crankshaft and main bearings – refitting

1 Invert the block and locate the main bearing upper shells into position, engaging the locktabs into the cut-outs in the bearing recesses (photo).
2 Lubricate the shells with clean engine oil and carefully lower the crankshaft into position (photos).
3 Locate the shells to the main bearing caps in a similar manner to that of the block and lubricate (photo). Fit the thrust washers to No 2 main bearing with the dots facing the crankshaft.

4 Fit the respective bearing caps into position (without the side seals at this stage) and torque tighten the retaining bolts.
5 Now check the crankshaft endfloat using a dial gauge or feeler gauges. Note the total endfloat, and then, referring to the Specifications subtract the specified endfloat. Select a thrust washer of suitable thickness to provide the correct endfloat.
6 Before removing the crankshaft bearing caps to insert the selected thrust washers check the clearance between the block and the bottom of the seal groove on the No 1 and No 5 bearing caps. This clearance can be checked using twist drills to gauge the clearance (photo). Where the clearance (C) is 5 mm (0.197 in) or less use a seal of 5.10 mm (0.200 in) thickness. Where the clearance (C) is in excess of 5 mm (0.197 in) select a white code seal of 5.40 mm (0.212 in) thickness.
7 Remove the main bearing caps and insert the selected thrust washers, with their slotted faces towards the crankshaft. When relocating the bearing caps, fit the side seals to the grooves of the Nos 1 and 5 main bearings. The grooved seal must face out and protrude from the joint face of the cap by approximately 0.20 mm (0.008 in).
8 When fitting the No 1 and No 5 main bearing caps, locate a feeler gauge blade or shim between the crankcase and the seal on each side to ensure that the cap and seals are fitted and do not become dislodged (photo). Take due care when tackling this awkward operation. When fitting the seal into the groove each side, leave a small amount of seal protruding at the bottom so that it does not slide up the groove as the bearing cap is being fitted.
9 When the end caps are fitted, insert the retaining bolts and check that the crankshaft rotates freely. Tap the bearing housings with a mallet should the shaft bind. If it continues to bind, a further inspection must be made. Also check that, once in position, there are no gaps between the seals and the crankcase when the shim is removed.
10 Tighten the retaining bolts down to the specified pressure, and recheck the endfloat (photos).
11 Once the shim is removed, the side seals can be trimmed to within 0.5 to 0.7 mm (0.020 to 0.028 in) of the sump joint face. Use a feeler gauge blade of the required thickness to act as a guide when trimming off the seal (photo).

61.1 Locate the main bearing shells in the crankcase ...

61.2A ... and lubricate them

61.2B Lowering the crankshaft into position

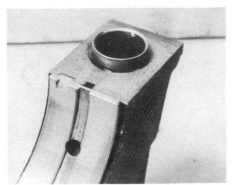

61.3 Main bearing cap and shell showing location tab

61.6 Using a drill to check the main bearing cap seal groove dimension

61.8 Fitting the rear main bearing cap – note the fitting shims (arrowed)

61.10A Tighten the main bearings and ...

61.10B ... recheck the endfloat

61.11 Trimming the main bearing seals

12 Lubricate the new front and rear main bearing oil seals and carefully locate them into their apertures, tapping them fully into position using a tube drift of a suitable diameter (photo). Ensure that the seals face the correct way round, with the cavity/spring side towards the engine. Should the seal lip accidentally become damaged during fitting, remove and discard it and fit another new seal.

13 If a new clutch spigot bearing is being fitted now is the time to do it. Refer to Section 15.

62 Flywheel/driveplate – refitting

1 Locate the flywheel or converter driveplate (as applicable) onto the crankshaft and align the bolt holes (which are not equidistant). Locking fluid should be applied to the mounting face before fitting the flywheel/driveplate.

2 If the retaining bolts are fitted with a lockplate, use a new plate, and when the bolts have been tightened to the specified torque, bend over the tabs to lock each bolt in position.

3 Where no lockplate is fitted, smear the bolt threads with a thread locking compound and tighten to the specified torque (photo).

4 On manual transmission models, refit the clutch unit, as described in Chapter 5.

63 Pistons and cylinder liners – refitting

Refer to Section 29 (photos). The gudgeon pins are an interference fit in the connecting rods on Type 829, J6R and 851 engines. The markings on the connecting rods must be on the intermediate shaft side. Fit the connecting rods to the crankshaft with reference to Section 30, paragraph 8, then refit the cylinder head (Section 70) and the sump and oil pump (Sections 64 and 66).

61.12 Fitting the rear main bearing/crankshaft seal

62.3 Tightening the flywheel bolts

63.1A Checking the liner protrusion

63.1B Piston crown arrows must point to flywheel end

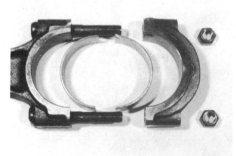

63.1C Big-end bearing components

63.1D Fit the big-end caps and bearings and ...

63.1E ... tighten the nuts

64.2 Inserting the oil pump rotors

64.5 Fitting the oil pump – note the driveshaft and clip (arrowed)

64 Oil pump – refitting

1   Lubricate the component parts of the oil pump and reassemble.
2   Insert the rotors (photo) and refit the cover. No gasket is fitted on this face.
3   Tighten the retaining bolts to secure the cover.
4   Insert the oil pressure relief valve assembly, fitting the piston into the spring and the cup over the spring at the opposing end. Compress into the cylinder and insert a new split pin to retain the valve assembly in place.
5   Fit the assembled pump unit into position, together with the driveshaft. Ensure the driveshaft has the C-clip fitted into its groove, and that this is fitted at the pump end of the shaft (photo). Tighten the retaining bolts.

65 Intermediate shaft and oil seal – refitting

1   Lubricate the shaft and insert it through the front of the crankcase (photo).
2   Slide the lockplate fork into the protruding shaft location groove and secure the plate with bolt and washer (photo). Check that the shaft is free to rotate on completion.
3   Fit the new oil seal into the intermediate shaft front cover and lubricate its lips (photo).
4   The timing belt tensioner can also be fitted at this stage (photo). Insert the spring into its housing in the side of the crankcase and locate the plunger over it. Compress the spring and locate the tensioner jockey wheel arm, retaining it with bolts. The spring tension is quite strong and an assistant will probably be required here.

65.1 Fitting the intermediate shaft

65.2 Fitting the lockplate

65.3 Fitting a new oil seal to the intermediate shaft cover

65.4 Fit the timing belt tensioner ...

65.5 ... the intermediate shaft cover and gasket

65.6 Intermediate shaft sprocket and bolt

5   Fit the front cover carefully into position with a new gasket, and retain it with the bolts (photo).
6   Fit the Woodruff key into its groove in the shaft and carefully locate the intermediate shaft drive sprocket into position with its large offset inner face towards the crankcase (photo). Use a suitable diameter drift to tap the sprocket into position over the key.
7   Prevent the sprocket from rotating by inserting a screwdriver blade or similar through a sprocket hole, and tighten the retaining nut (complete with flat washer) to the specified torque.
8   If not already located, the oil pump drive pinion and shaft can now be inserted through the side cover hole in the crankcase. Make sure

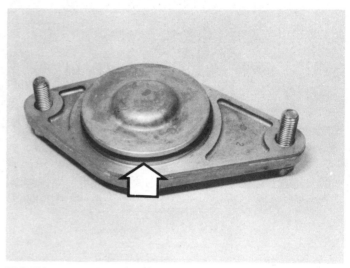

65.9 Side cover and seal (arrowed)

65.8 The oil pump driveshaft circlip location

that the limiting circlip is in position on the oil pump end of the shaft (photo). Once in position, lubricate with engine oil to prevent pinion 'pick-up' on restarting the engine. On models with power steering and air conditioning make sure that the distributor drive slots are as shown in Fig. 1.33 with the intermediate shaft sprocket at TDC (in Section 71).
9   Ensure that the intermediate shaft and oil pump drive rotate freely, then refit the side cover with seal and secure with bolts (photo).
10 Refit the fuel pump.

66 Sump – refitting

1   Check that the mating surfaces of the sump and crankcase are perfectly clean, with no sections of old gasket remaining.
2   Smear an even layer of sealant round the two mating flange surfaces and locate the gasket.
3   Fit the sump carefully into position and locate the retaining bolts (photo). Tighten the bolts progressively by hand in a diagonally opposed sequence, and finally, tighten to the recommended torque setting.
4   Fit and tighten the sump drain plug.

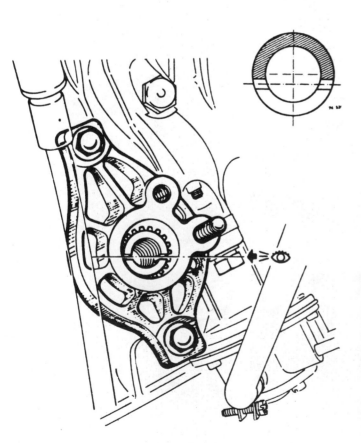

Fig. 1.33 Distributor drive slot position with intermediate shaft sprocket at TDC (Sec 65)

66.3 Refitting the sump

67.1 Inserting the valves

67.3 Fitting the valve springs

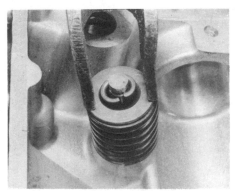
67.4 Compressing the valve springs

67 Valves – refitting

1   Fit the valve stem seals to the guides then lubricate the valve stems and guide bores with clean engine oil prior to inserting the valves into their respective positions. All traces of grinding paste around the valve seat and cylinder head seating faces must be removed – check this before each valve is fitted (photo).
2   As each inlet valve is relocated into its guide, fit a new O-ring seal over the stem. These O-rings are not fitted to the exhaust valves.
3   Fit the base washers, springs and spring cap (photo). The springs must be located with the close coil gaps downwards (to the head).
4   Using a valve spring compressor, compress the valve springs sufficiently to allow the split collets to be located in the groove of the valve stem, then release the compressor (photo). The use of a little grease will retain the collets in position as the compressor is removed.
5   When all the valves are reassembled, tap the end of each stem in turn with a soft-faced hammer to ensure that the collets are correctly seated.

68 Rocker assembly – reassembly

1   Lubricate each component as it is assembled with engine oil. Lay the pedestals, spacers, springs and rockers out in order of appearance.
2   Support the rocker shafts in a soft-jawed vice and insert the new filter into the end of it (photo), fit the retaining bolt and tighten it to the specified torque.
3   Assemble the respective pedestals, rocker arms, springs and spacers onto the shaft. When the shaft assembly is complete, compress the last pedestal to align the retaining pin hole in the shaft and pedestal. Drive a new pin into position to secure (photo). Early models fitted with a hollow type roll-pin should have the later solid type pin fitted on reassembly.

69 Camshaft – refitting

1   Check that the camshaft location bearings in the cylinder head are perfectly clean and lubricate with some engine oil. Similarly lubricate the camshaft journals and lobes.
2   Insert the camshaft carefully into the cylinder head, guiding the cam sections through the bearing apertures so as not to score the bearing surfaces (photo).
3   With the camshaft in position, the front oil seal can be carefully drifted into position. Lubricate the seal lips with oil and drive into its location using a suitable tube drift.
4   Where applicable, refit the power steering pulley to the rear of the camshaft after renewing the oil seal. Note that the location roll pin openings should face the direction of rotation.

70 Cylinder head – refitting

1   Before refitting the cylinder head, check that all the mating surfaces are perfectly clean. Loosen the rocker arm adjuster screws fully. Also ensure that the cylinder head bolt holes in the crankcase are clean and free of oil. Syringe or soak up any oil left in the bolt holes, and in the oil feed hole on the rear left-hand corner of the block. This is most important in order that the correct bolt tightening torque can be applied.
2   Prior to removing the liner clamps, rotate the crankshaft to locate the pistons halfway down the bores. Check that the location dowel is in position at the front right-hand corner.
3   Remove the liner clamps.
4   Fit the cylinder head gasket onto the cylinder block (photo) upper face and ensure that it is exactly located. If possible, screw a couple of guide studs into position. They must be long enough to pass through the cylinder head so that they can be removed when it is in position.

68.2 Rocker assembly and filter

68.3 Rocker pedestal retaining pin

69.2 Inserting the camshaft

70.4 Cylinder head gasket on the block

70.5A Lower the cylinder head into position and ...

70.5B ... fit the rocker assembly

70.7A Fit the camshaft retaining plate ...

70.7B ... and check the camshaft endfloat

70.8 Tightening the camshaft sprocket bolt

5   Lower the cylinder head into position, engaging with the dowel, and then locate the rocker assembly (photos). Remove the guide studs if they were used.

6   Lubricate the cylinder head bolt threads and washers with engine oil, then screw them into position. Tighten them progressively in the sequence given in Fig. 1.24. Tighten all the bolts to the torque specified.

7   Locate the camshaft retaining plate in the groove of the camshaft and retain it with bolts and washers. Check the camshaft endfloat and, if necessary, adjust by fitting a retainer plate of an alternative thickness (photos).

8   Refit the camshaft sprocket and tighten the retaining bolt and flat washer to the specified torque (photo). When fitting the sprocket, ensure that the keyway is in exact alignment with the key. The sprocket inner hub is offset to the camshaft.

9   The valve rocker clearance adjustment can now be made (see Section 74).

71 Timing sprockets and belt – refitting

1   Referring to Chapter 2, refit the water pump with its pulley and outlet pipe.

2   Refit the thermostat (see Chapter 2), and relocate the hose between the water pump housing and the thermostat housing, securing with clips.

3   Refit the timing belt tensioner unit (if not already assembled). Insert the spring and piston into the crankcase aperture. Locate the jockey wheel. Fitting the top bolt first and pushing it inwards, compress the piston and spring, then screw in the lower adjustment bolt. Do not tighten it at this stage.

4   Before fitting the timing belt the clearance between the intermediate shaft housing and the tensioner plate must be set to 0.1 mm (0.004 in). This is to prevent the tensioner tilting when the timing belt is tensioned. Use a feeler blade to check the clearance. On early

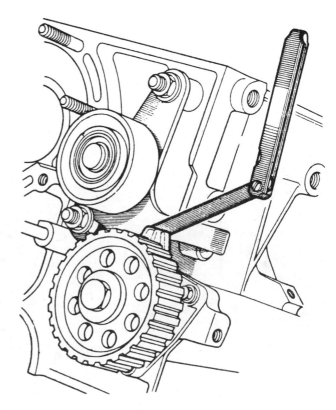
Fig. 1.34 Checking the timing belt tensioner clearance on early models (Sec 71)

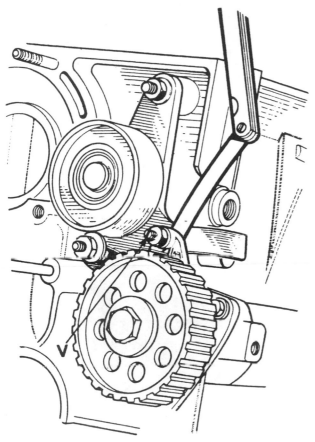

Fig. 1.35 Checking the timing belt tensioner clearance on later models (Sec 71)

V   Adjustment screw

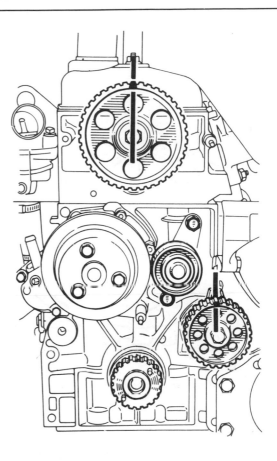

Fig. 1.36 Timing belt sprocket TDC positions (Sec 71)

71.5 Crankshaft pulley spacer washer and key

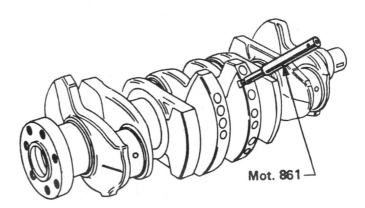

Fig. 1.37 Using a TDC rod inserted through the crankcase (Sec 71)

the timing case retaining stud, as shown in Fig. 1.36. A TDC rod (Fig. 1.37) can be used on some models.

7   Set the camshaft sprocket with its timing mark aligned with the rocker cover stud. Note the two different types of sprocket in use (see Figs. 1.38 and 1.39).

8   Align the intermediate shaft sprocket vertically in line with the crankcase web.

9   The timing belt can now be relocated over the sprockets and with its outer face bearing on the adjuster jockey wheel. If using the old belt (which is *not* recommended), it should be fitted facing the same way as when removed.

10 To adjust the tensioner, loosen the tensioner bolts about a quarter of a turn to allow the tensioner to automatically take up any belt slack under the spring tension. Tighten the tensioner retaining bolts.

models shims are required, but on later models an adjustment screw and locknut are provided.

5   Refit the crankshaft pulley unit comprising a spacer washer, the Woodruff key and the timing sprocket and pulley (photo).

6   Rotate the crankshaft to the TDC piston with No 1 piston on firing stroke. The bottom sprocket timing mark should be in alignment with

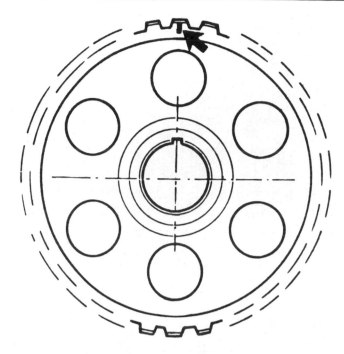

Fig. 1.38 Camshaft sprocket for early types 829 and J6R engines
(Sec 71)

Arrow indicates TDC mark

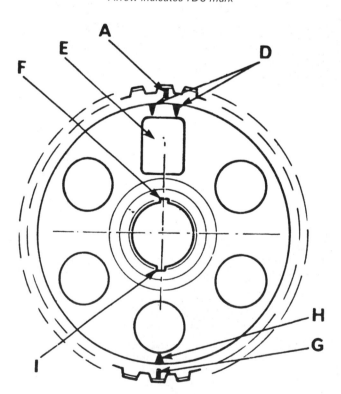

Fig. 1.39 Camshaft sprocket for later types 829, J6R and 851
engines (Sec 71)

A	TDC mark	G	J6R engine valve timing
D	Bosses	H	J6R engine valve timing
E	851 engine valve timing	I	J6R engine valve timing
F	851 engine valve timing		

Note: F or I to be at the top, according to engine type

11 Next check the timing belt tension at the mid-point of its longest run (between the camshaft and intermediate shaft pulleys). The correct amount of deflection is about 6 mm (0.25 in) (photo).

12 As a double check on the tension, turn the engine through two complete revolutions in a clockwise direction (when facing the sprockets), loosen the tensioner bolts and allow the tensioner to readjust itself, if at all. Then recheck the belt tension after retightening the bolts. **Note:** *Do not turn the engine in an anti-clockwise direction.*

13 Refit the timing cover to complete. Do not forget the spacer tube, which fits onto the stud immediately above the crankshaft pulley and the hose clips on the upper left-hand bolt (photo).

71.11 Check the timing belt tension at the point arrowed

71.13 Timing cover location stud

72 Ancillary components – refitting

Refer to Section 46 and refit the listed components with reference to the Chapters indicated, where applicable.

73 Oil filter – removal and refitting

1 The oil filter is a disposable canister type, horizontally located on the cylinder block on the right-hand side (photo).

2   If the old filter proves too tight to be removed by hand pressure, use a strap wrench to unscrew it. Alternatively, a worn drive clip (or two joined together to make up the required diameter) strapped around the canister will provide a better grip point. If necessary, the canister can be tapped round using a small hammer.

3   Once the old filter is removed, wipe clean the joint area in the cylinder block and lubricate the new seal ring.

4   Screw the filter carefully into position by hand, ensuring that the seal does not twist or distort as it is tightened (photo).

5   Do not overtighten the filter; it need only be tightened by firm hand pressure.

6   Check and top up the engine oil as required, then run the engine to check for any signs of leakage around the filter seal.

74 Valve clearances – adjustment

1   The procedure is as given in Section 39.

2   If the clearance requires adjustment; loosen the locknut and, with the feeler in position, turn the adjuster screw until the feeler blade is nipped and will not move. Now unscrew the adjuster until the feeler blade is a stiff sliding fit. Tighten the locknut and recheck the clearance (photo).

75 Engine – refitting

Reverse the procedure given in Section 44, but note the following additional points:

(a)   *Lightly lubricate the clutch shaft splines (manual gearbox models) or converter centre boss (automatic transmission models) with a suitable grease*

(b)   *On automatic transmission models align the torque converter and driveplate, as described in Chapter 7*

(c)   *Adjust the accelerator cable (Chapter 3), clutch cable (Chapter 5) or governor and selector lever (Chapter 7), as applicable*

(d)   *On turbo and North American models tighten the exhaust downpipe/catalytic converter flange bolts then back off one and a half turns*

(e)   *Refill the cooling system (Chapter 2) and fill the engine with oil*

76 Engine – adjustment after major overhaul

Refer to Section 41.

73.1 Oil filter location

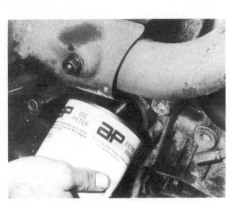

73.4 Fitting the oil filter

74.2 Adjusting the valve clearances

'Fault diagnosis overleaf'

Part D – All engines

77 Fault diagnosis – engine

Symptom	Reason(s)
Engine fails to start	Discharged battery
	Loose battery connection
	Loose or broken ignition leads
	Moisture on spark plugs, distributor cap or HT leads
	Incorrect spark plug gap
	Cracked distributor cap or rotor
	Dirt or water in fuel
	Empty fuel tank
	Faulty fuel pump
	Faulty starter motor
	Low cylinder compression
	Faulty ignition system
Engine idles erratically	Inlet manifold air leak
	Leaking cylinder head gasket
	Incorrect valve clearances
	Loose crankcase ventilation hoses
	Incorrect slow running adjustment
	Uneven cylinder compressions
	Incorrect ignition timing
Engine misfires	Incorrect spark plug gap
	Faulty ignition system
	Distributor cap cracked
	Uneven cylinder compressions
	Moisture on spark plugs, distributor cap or HT leads
Engine stalls	Incorrect slow running adjustment
	Inlet manifold air leak
	Incorrect ignition timing
Excessive oil consumption	Worn pistons and cylinder liners
	Valve guides worn
	Oil leaking from gasket or oil seal

Chapter 2 Cooling system

Contents

Specifications

System type	Pressurised with belt-driven pump; crossflow radiator and expansion tank; pump driven or electric cooling fan; thermostat
Expansion tank cap pressure (stamped on cap)	0.8 or 1.2 bar (12 or 17 lbf/in²)

Thermostat opening temperature
Type 847 engine	75°, 86° or 89°C (167, 187 or 192°F)
Type A5L, A7L, A2M, 843 and A6M engines	75° or 86°C (167 or 187°F)
Type 829 and J6R engines	88°C (190°F)

Water pump/alternator drivebelt tension
Type 847 engine	7 to 8 mm (0.28 to 0.32 in)
Type A5L, A7L, A2M, 843 and A6M engines	3.5 to 4.5 mm (0.14 to 0.18 in)
Type 829 and J6R engines	5.5 to 6.5 mm (0.22 to 0.26 in)

Power steering pump drivebelt tension
Type 829 and J6R engines:	
Models with air conditioning	2.5 to 3.0 mm (0.10 to 0.12 in)
Models without air conditioning	3.0 to 3.7 mm (0.12 to 0.15 in)
Except type 829 and J6R engines	5.5 to 6.5 mm (0.22 to 0.26 in)

Air conditioning compressor drivebelt tension
Type 829 and J6R engines	3.5 to 4.0 mm (0.14 to 0.16 in)
Except type 829 and J6R engines	5.5 to 6.5 mm (0.22 to 0.26 in)

System capacity (including heater)
R1360	6.0 litre (10.6 Imp pt, 6.3 US qt)
All other models	7.0 litre (12.3 Imp pt, 7.4 US qt)

1 General description

The system is of pressurised type and sealed, but with inclusion of an expansion bottle to accept coolant displaced from the system when hot and to return it when the system cools.

Coolant is circulated by thermosyphon action and is assisted by means of the impeller in the belt-driven water pump.

A thermostat is fitted in the outlet from the cylinder head. When the engine is cold, the thermostat valve remains closed so that the coolant flow which occurs at normal operating temperatures through the radiator matrix is interrupted.

As the coolant warms up, the thermostat valve starts to open and allows the coolant flow through the radiator to resume.

The engine temperature will always be maintained at a constant level (according to the thermostat rating) whatever the ambient air temperature.

The coolant circulates around the engine block and cylinder head and absorbs heat as it flows, then travels in an upward direction and out into the radiator to pass across the matrix. As the coolant flows across the radiator matrix, airflow created by the forward motion of the car cools it and it returns via the bottom of the radiator to the water pump. This is a continuous process, assisted by the water pump impeller.

Some models are fitted with an electric cooling fan which is actuated by the thermostat switch according to coolant temperature.

2 Routine maintenance

Apart from renewing the coolant at the prescribed intervals, maintenance is confined to checking the coolant level in the expansion bottle. The level should be between the MIN and MAX lines. The need for persistent topping-up should be investigated.

The hoses and their clamps should also be inspected regularly for security and good condition, and the drivebelt checked and adjusted or renewed as necessary.

3 Cooling system – draining

1 If the coolant is known to be in acceptable condition for further use, have suitable containers available in which to catch it.
2 Set the heater facia controls to 'Hot'.
3 Remove the expansion bottle cap (photo). Take care to avoid scalding if the system is hot.
4 Remove the drain plugs from the cylinder block (photos).
5 Open the drain tap at the base of the radiator, where one is fitted. Alternatively, remove the bottom hose at the radiator stub. When the expansion bottle is empty, remove the filler plug from the radiator (photo). Open all bleed screws.

3.4A Drain plug hole on the right-hand rear of the cylinder block

3.4B Drain plug location on the right-hand front of the cylinder block (arrowed)

3.3 Expansion bottle location

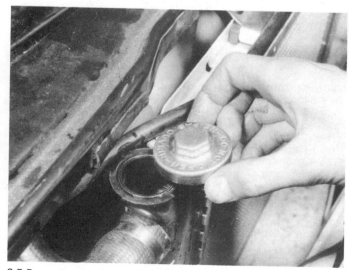

3.5 Removing the radiator filler plug

4 Cooling system – flushing

1 This system will only require flushing if renewal of the antifreeze or corrosion inhibitor has been neglected. In this event, flush the system through with a cold water hose until the water runs clear from the cylinder block and radiator.

2 If the radiator is badly blocked, remove it from the vehicle, and place a hose in the bottom stub, so that the water flows through it in the reverse direction to the normal cooling system flow.

3 The use of chemical descaler should only be used in a cooling system if scale and sludge formation is severe. Adhere strictly to the manufacturer's instructions.

4 Leakage of the radiator or cooling system may be temporarily stopped by the use of a proprietary sealant, but in the long term a new cylinder head or other gasket, water pump, hoses or radiator matrix must be installed. Do not attempt to solder a radiator. The amount of local heat required will almost certainly melt adjacent joints. Take it to a specialist or exchange it for a reconditioned unit.

5 Cooling system – filling

1 Reconnect the hoses and tighten the clips.

2 Refit and tighten the drain plugs.

3 Set the heater facia control to 'Hot'.

4 Prepare a sufficient quantity of coolant.

5 Open the bleed screws located on the top hose, heater return hose, carburettor automatic choke and thermostat housing, as applicable (photos).

6 Temporarily raise the expansion tank as high as possible leaving the tube attached.

7 Fill the radiator with coolant then fit the filler plug (photo).

8 Pour coolant into the expansion tank then tighten each bleed screw when the coolant flows out free of air bubbles.

9 Fit the expansion tank in its correct position and top it up with coolant to the maximum level mark (about 35.0 mm/1.5 in from the bottom). Refit the cap.

10 Run the engine at a fast idling speed until the thermostat opens and the top hose feels warm, then open each bleed screw in turn and check that the coolant flows out free of air bubbles. Tighten the screws fully.

11 Stop the engine and allow it to completely cool down. Top up the coolant in the expansion tank to the maximum mark, if necessary.

6 Coolant mixture – general

1 It is essential that an approved type of antifreeze is employed, in order that the necessary antifreeze and anticorrosion proportions are maintained.

2 Whilst the life of the coolant originally used in the vehicle is stated to be 3 years or 30 000 miles (48 000 km), owners are recommended to consider removing the coolant yearly to ensure that all the essential properties of the solution are fully maintained.

3 Make up the solution, ideally using distilled water or rain water, in the proportions necessary to give protection in the prevailing climate. Percentages of antifreeze necessary are usually found on the container. Do not use too low a percentage of antifreeze, or the anticorrosion properties will not be sufficiently effective. 30% antifreeze should be a minimum.

4 If it is suspected that the coolant strength is unsatisfactory, a check may be made using a hydrometer. Employ the instrument as instructed by the manufacturer, and using the correction tables normally supplied. If the protection is found to be insufficient, drain off some of the coolant and replace it with pure antifreeze. Recheck the coolant with the hydrometer.

5 Even in climates where antifreeze is not required, never use plain water in the system, but mix in a good quality corrosion inhibitor. This is particularly important where the light alloy content of an engine is high.

5.5A Top hose bleed screw (847 engine)

5.5B Heater return hose bleed screw

5.5C Bleed screw located on the carburettor automatic choke

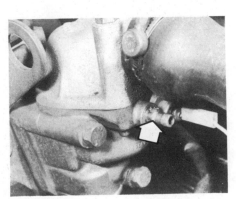
5.5D Thermostat housing bleed screw (arrowed)

5.7 Filling the radiator

7 Radiator – removal, inspection, cleaning and refitting

1   Drain the cooling system, as described in Section 3.
2   Disconnect the battery negative lead.
3   Remove the upper grille crossmember by releasing the expansion bottle supply hose then unscrewing the end bolts, grille and centre stay bolts. If necessary disconnect the bonnet lock cable. Note that the crossmember incorporates the radiator top mounting (photos).
4   Remove the front grille and the screw from the radiator, if applicable (photo).
5   Disconnect the wiring from the electric cooling fan motor and the thermo-switch on the radiator, where applicable (photo).
6   Loosen the clips and disconnect the expansion bottle hose and the top and bottom hoses from the radiator (photos).
7   On models fitted with air conditioning, remove the cooling fans

and disconnect the condenser, placing it to one side on the bumper. Do not attempt to disconnect the refrigerant pipes.
8   Lift the radiator (and cooling fan, where applicable) from the bottom mountings and remove it from the car (photos).
9   Radiator repair is best left to a specialist, however, minor repairs may be made using a proprietary repair kit, soldering or using a coolant additive.
10 Clear the matrix of flies and small leaves with a soft brush or by hosing. Reverse flush the radiator, as described in Section 4. Examine the hoses and clips and renew them if they are damaged or deteriorated. Also check the mounting rubbers and renew them if necessary. If necessary remove the electric cooling fan and the thermo-switch.
11 Refitting is a reversal of removal, but fill the cooling system, as described in Section 5.

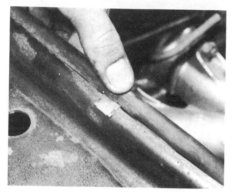
7.3A Releasing the expansion bottle supply hose

7.3B Removing the upper grille crossmember end bolts

7.3C Removing the centre stay bolt

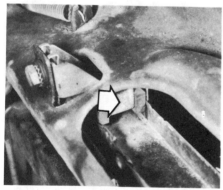
7.3D The radiator upper mounting (arrowed)

7.4 Radiator side screen

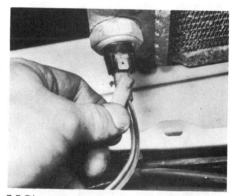
7.5 Disconnecting the wiring from the thermo-switch

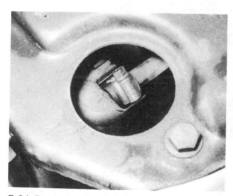
7.6A Expansion bottle hose connection to the radiator

7.6B Disconnecting the top hose

7.8A Radiator bottom mounting

7.8B Removing the radiator and cooling fan assembly

7.8C Radiator and cooling fan removed from the car

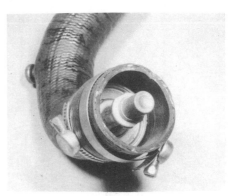

8.1 Thermostat location in the top hose

8.4A Thermostat housing on 829 and J6R engines

8.4B Removing the thermostat on 829 and J6R engines

8 Thermostat – removal, testing and refitting

Type 847, A5L, A7L, A2M, 843 and A6M engines

1 The thermostat is located in the hose attached to the water pump outlet pipe (photo).
2 To remove the thermostat, drain sufficient coolant to allow the level to fall below the pump outlet. Remove the hose, and extract the thermostat.

Type 829 and J6R engines

3 The thermostat is located in a housing on top of the water pump.
4 Before removing the thermostat, drain sufficient coolant to enable the coolant level to fall below the top radiator hose, then unscrew the thermostat housing cover retaining screws and lift the cover clear (whilst still attached to the hose). Extract the thermostat (photos).
5 Test the thermostat by suspending it in a pan of water, together with a thermometer. Commence warming the water, watch when the thermostat begins to open, and check the temperature. Compare the opening temperature with the temperature stamped on the thermostat.
6 Transfer the thermostat to cold water, and check that it closes promptly.
7 If the thermostat does not operate as outlined, it should be renewed.
8 Refit in the reverse order to dismantling, top up the coolant, and bleed the system.
9 In an emergency it is permissible to run the car without a thermostat fitted, but this will lead to prolonged warm-up time, poor heater output and (possibly) poor fuel economy. All these drawbacks are to be preferred to overheating, however!

9 Water pump – removal and refitting

1 Remove the radiator, as described in Section 7.

2 Loosen the alternator pivot and adjustment bolts, swivel the alternator towards the engine, and remove the drivebelt from the water pump pulley.
3 Loosen the clips and disconnect all the hoses from the water

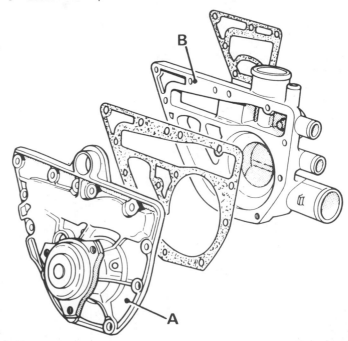

Fig. 2.1 Early water pump fitted to type A5L, A7L, A2M, 843 and A6M engines (Sec 9)

A Cover   B Body

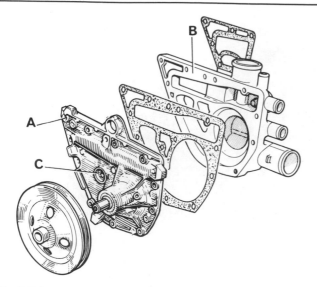

Fig. 2.2 Late water pump fitted to type A5L, A7L, A2M, 843 and A6M engines (Sec 9)

A Cover   C 'Trapped' bolt location
B Body

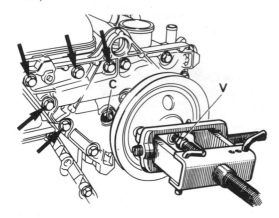

Fig. 2.3 Using a puller to remove the water pump pulley on type A5L, A7L, A2M, 843 and A6M engines (Sec 9)

C 'Trapped' bolt   V Loosely inserted bolt for puller reaction

Arrows indicate retaining bolts

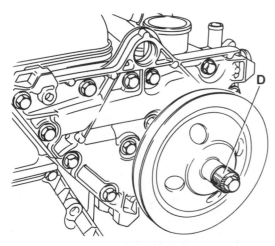

Fig. 2.4 Using a bolt and spacer (D) to press the pulley on the water pump shaft on type A5L, A7L, A2M, 843 and A6M engines (Sec 9)

pump. Also, where applicable, disconnect the temperature sender wire (photos).

4   Where fitted, unbolt the fan blades from the water pump flange and remove the pulley.

5   Unscrew all the pump retaining bolts/nuts (photos). On models with a central pulley bolt the bolt behind the pulley cannot be removed since it is trapped by the pulley itself.

6   On 829 and J6R engines detach the coolant return housing from the rear of the water pump, if necessary (photo).

7   Using a soft-faced mallet, tap the water pump from the front of the cylinder head/block and remove the gasket (photos).

8   Where applicable, unscrew the centre bolt and use a two-legged puller to draw the pulley from the pump shaft. Remove the trapped bolt. Note that some models do not have a centre bolt.

9   No repairs are possible on the water pump except to renew the intermediate gasket in the event of leakage. Obtain a new unit if the pump is faulty.

10 Refitting is a reversal of removal, but always fit a new gasket and tighten the retaining bolts evenly. Tension the drivebelt, as described in Section 10, and fill the cooling system, as described in Section 5. Where the pulley is a press fit on the shaft use a bolt and spacer to press on the pulley until flush with the end of the shaft.

9.3A Hoses connected to the water pump on 829 and J6R engines

9.3B Temperature sender location on the water pump on an 847 engine

9.5A Removing the water pump bolts on an 847 engine

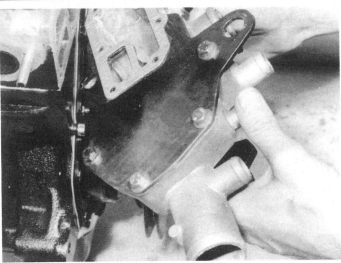
9.7A Removing the water pump on an 847 engine

9.5B Water pump on 829 and J6R engines

9.7B Removing the water pump on 829 and J6R engines

9.6 Coolant return housing on 829 and J6R engines

10 Drivebelts – adjustment and renewal

1 The drivebelts are driven from the engine crankshaft pulley, which is of a single, double or treble track type, depending on the number of belts fitted. The ancillaries depending on the drivebelt(s) are:

(a) Cooling system water pump
(b) Alternator
(c) Air conditioning pump
(d) Power-assisted steering pump

The last two items are not fitted to all models.

2 It is most important that the drivebelt tension be correctly adjusted. A tight fitting will reduce the belt life and also that of the drive bearings of the component concerned. A loose fitting will also reduce the belt life, will slip and consequently also reduce the efficiency of the unit it drives.

3 The belts can be adjusted independently, but the rear one can only be removed after withdrawal of the front belt.

4 Inspect the condition of the belts occasionally and renew them if they show any signs of fraying, or have stretched so that available adjustment has been fully used.

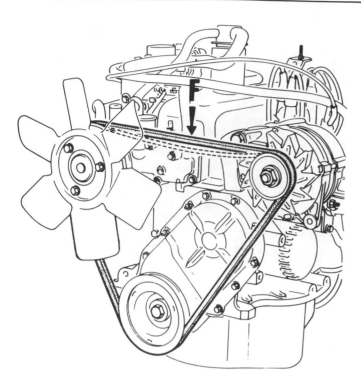

Fig. 2.5 Drivebelt adjustment on the type 847 engine (Sec 10)

F = 7 to 8 mm (0.28 to 0.32 in)

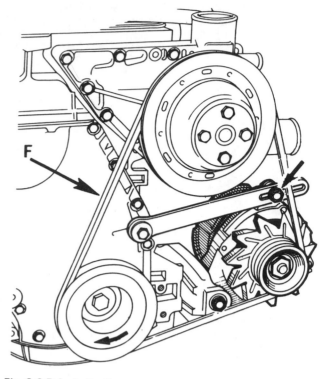

Fig. 2.6 Drivebelt adjustment on type A5L, A7L, A2M, 843 and A6M engines (Sec 10)

F = 3.5 to 4.5 mm (0.14 to 0.18 in)
Arrow indicates adjustment bolt

5   Belts are correctly adjusted when there is a total deflection of the specified amount (see Specifications), under a moderate pressure at the centre of the longest run of the belt concerned (photo).

6   To make adjustment to the drivebelt or a particular system, loosen the alternator/pump/compressor (if applicable) and pivot the unit inwards or outwards to slacken or tighten the tension respectively. Retighten the mounting bolts of the unit concerned and recheck the tension of the belt.

7   Whenever a new belt has been fitted, its tension should be rechecked after the engine has been run for a short initial period. New belts normally stretch a fraction during the early stage of usage and will probably be in need of further adjustment after a short time.

8   To remove and refit a belt, loosen the mounting bolts of the alternator/power-assisted steering pump/compressor, as applicable, and slacken off the adjustment of the belt for removal. Refitting of the belt is a reversal of the above procedure and it must, of course, be adjusted for tension.

11 Coolant temperature and electric cooling fan switches – testing and renewal

1   In the event of a fault occurring in either one of these switches, first check the wiring and connections.

2   A switch can be unscrewed after first having drained the cooling system (photos).

3   The operation of the fan switch can be checked by connecting it to a battery with a test lamp in the circuit and then heating the temperature sensitive end in some water.

4   If the test lamp fails to come on by the time that the water is boiling then the switch should be renewed.

5   Testing of the coolant temperature switch cannot be done without special test instruments and the simplest way to test is by substitution of a new unit.

6   A fault in the coolant temperature gauge must be suspected if the switch is proved functional (refer to Chapter 10 for instrument removal).

10.6 Checking the drivebelt tension

11.2A Temperature sender location on 829 and J6R engines (arrowed)

11.2B Cooling fan thermo-switch location on the radiator

12 Fault diagnosis – cooling system

Symptom	Reason(s)
Overheating	Coolant loss due to leakage Electric cooling fan malfunction (if applicable) Drivebelt slack or broken · Thermostat jammed shut Radiator matrix clogged internally or externally New engine not yet run-in
Overcooling	Thermostat missing or jammed open
Coolant loss	External leakage (hose joints etc) Overheating (see above) Internal leakage (head gasket or cylinder liner) – look for water in oil and/or oil in coolant

Chapter 3
Fuel, exhaust and emission control systems
For modifications, and information applicable to later models, see Supplement at end of manual

Contents

Specifications

General
Fuel system type:
    UK models .... Downdraught carburettor, normally aspirated or turbocharged
    North American models .... Fuel injection, normally aspirated or turbocharged
Fuel tank capacity .... 57.0 litre (12.5 Imp gal, 15.0 US gal)

Carburettor systems
Fuel pump
Static pressure:
    Minimum .... 0.17 bar (2.47 lbf/in^2)
    Maximum .... 0.28 bar (4.06 lbf/in^2)

Carburettors

Solex 32 SEIA-775

Choke tube	24
Main jet	127.5
Idling jet	45
Air compensating jet	160
Needle valve	1.5
Enrichment device – Econostat	70 (pre-1982) or 80 (1982 on)
Initial throttle opening	0.8 mm (0.032 in)
Choke flap part opening	4.2 mm (0.165 in)
Throttle butterfly angle:	
With Mot 522	3.91 mm (0.154 in)
With Solex instrument	9° 15'
Float level	11.7 mm (0.46 in)
Defuming valve gap	3.0 to 4.0 mm (0.118 to 0.158 in)
Idling speed	750 to 800 rpm
CO%	1.5 to 2.5

Solex 32 DIS-805

Choke tube	24
Main jet	110
Air correction jet	135
Idling jet	41
Enricher	65
Boost enrichener open	Over 320 mbar
Needle valve	1.7
Accelerator pump injector	50
Accelerator pump travel gauge	7.0 mm (0.276 in)
Initial throttle opening	0.8 mm (0.032 in)
Pneumatic initial opening	5.5 mm (0.217 in)
Needle valve seal thickness	1.0 mm (0.039 in)
Idling speed	600 to 700 rpm
CO%	1.0 to 2.0

Weber 32 DARA 38:

	Stage 1	Stage 2
Choke tube	24	26
Main jet	132	150
Air compensating jet	180	145
Idling jet	47	45
Mixture centralizer	3.5	4.5
Emulsifier	F53	F6
Initial throttle opening	1.35 mm (0.053 in)	
Throttle butterfly angle:		
With Mot 522	7.37 mm (0.290 in)	
With Solex instrument	17° 30'	
Needle valve	2.00	
Float level	7.0 mm (0.276 in)	
Float travel	8.0 mm (0.315 in)	
Accelerator pump jet	60	
Pneumatic part opening:		
Compensator depressed	5.0 mm (0.197 in) 1980 or 4.5 mm (0.177 in) 1981	
Compensator released	8.0 mm (0.315 in) 1980 or 7.5 mm (0.296 in) 1981	
Deflooding device gap	10.0 mm (0.394 in)	
Idling speed:		
Manual gearbox	775 to 825 rpm	
Automatic transmission	625 to 675 rpm (D selected)	
CO%	1.0 to 2.0	

Weber 32 DARA 39:

	Stage 1	Stage 2
Choke tube	24	26
Main jet	132	150
Air compensating jet	180	145
Idling jet	47	45
Mixture centralizer	3.5	4.5
Emulsifier	F53	F6
Initial throttle opening	1.40 mm (0.055 in)	
Needle valve	2.00	
Float level	7.0 mm (0.276 in)	
Float travel	8.0 mm (0.315 in)	
Accelerator pump jet	60	
Pneumatic part opening:		
Compensator depressed	5.0 mm (0.197 in) 1980 or 4.5 mm (0.177 in) 1981	
Compensator released	8.0 mm (0.315 in) 1980 or 7.5 mm (0.296 in) 1981	
Deflooding device gap	10.0 mm (0.394 in)	
Idling speed:		
Manual gearbox	775 to 825 rpm	
Automatic transmission	625 to 675 rpm (D selected)	
CO%	1.0 to 2.0	

Weber 32 DARA 40:	Stage 1	Stage 2
Choke tube	26	26
Main jet	130 or 132	140
Air compensating jet	155	140
Idling jet	50 or 55	45
Mixture centralizer	3.5	4
Emulsifier	F58	F6
Initial throttle opening	1.3 mm (0.051 in)	
Throttle butterfly angle:		
With Mot 522	5.39 mm (0.212 in)	
With Solex instrument	12° 40'	
Needle valve	2.25	
Float level	7.0 mm (0.276 in)	
Float travel	8.0 mm (0.315 in)	
Accelerator pump jet	60	
Pneumatic part opening:		
Compensator depressed	5.5 mm (0.217 in)	
Compensator released	10.0 mm (0.394 in)	
Deflooding device gap	9.0 mm (0.355 in)	
Idling speed	750 to 850 rpm	
CO%	1.0 to 2.0	

Weber 32 DARA 41:	Stage 1	Stage 2
Choke tube	26	26
Main jet	135	140
Air compensating jet	155	140
Idling jet	57	42/105
Enrichment device	60	110
Mixture centralizer	3.5	4
Emulsifier	F58	F6
Initial throttle opening (medium cold)	1.05 mm (0.041 in)	
Throttle butterfly angle:		
With Mot 522	5.39 mm (0.212 in)	
With Solex instrument	12° 40'	
Needle valve	2.25	
Float level	7.0 mm (0.276 in)	
Float travel	8.0 mm (0.315 in)	
Accelerator pump jet	60	
Pneumatic part opening:		
Compensator depressed	5.5 mm (0.217 in)	
Compensator released	10.0 mm (0.394 in)	
Deflooding device gap	9.0 mm (0.355 in)	
Idling speed:		
Manual gearbox	775 to 825 rpm	
Automatic transmission	875 to 925 rpm (N selected)	
CO%:		
Manual gearbox	1.0 to 2.0	
Automatic transmission	0.5 to 1.5	

Weber 32 DIR 98/98C:	Stage 1	Stage 2
Choke tube	23	24
Main jet	115	125
Air compensating jet	185	145
Idling jet	47	40
Mixture centralizer	3.5	4.5
Initial butterfly opening	0.90 mm (0.035 in)	
Enrichment device	50	90
Emulsifier	F20	F6
Accelerator pump jet	50	
Needle valve	1.75	
Float level	7.0 mm (0.276 in)	
Float travel	8.0 mm (0.315 in)	
Pneumatic part opening	4.0 mm (0.158 in)	
Mechanical part opening	4.5 to 5.5 mm (0.177 to 0.217 in)	
Idling speed	600 to 700 rpm	
CO%	1.0 to 2.0	

Zenith 32 IF 7		
Choke tube	24	
Main jet	121	
Idling jet	70	
Needle valve	1.25	
Initial throttle opening	0.95 mm (0.037 in)	
Auxiliary jet	0.7	
Accelerator pump stroke	22.8 mm (0.90 in)	
Accelerator pump jet	0.50	
Accelerator pump tube height	64.0 mm (2.522 in)	
Fuel level	11.85 to 12.05 mm (0.467 to 0.475 in)	
Econostat	0.60	

Defuming valve gap	0.4 to 0.8 mm (0.016 to 0.032 in)
Auxiliary jet tube height	0.75 to 1.25 mm (0.030 to 0.050 in)
Idling speed	750 to 800 rpm
CO%	2.0 to 3.0

Fuel injection systems
Type .... Bosch L-Jetronic with Lamda oxygen sensor

Idling speed
843 engine:
Manual gearbox .... 750 to 850 rpm
Automatic transmission .... 600 to 700 rpm (D selected)
A7L engine .... 700 to 800 rpm

CO settings
843 engine:
Manual gearbox .... 0.4 to 1.0%
Automatic transmission .... Integrator voltage 5.0 to 6.0 volt
A7L engine .... Integrator voltage 6.5 to 7.5 volt

Fuel pump
Pressure .... 2.3 to 2.7 bar (33.4 to 39.2 lbf/in^2)
Delivery .... 1 litre (1.8 Imp pt, 1.06 US qt) per minute

Turbo system
Type .... Garrett T3 with pressure check valve

Torque wrench settings

	lbf ft	Nm
Turbocharger to catalytic converter	22	30
Turbocharger to exhaust manifold	33	45

PART A – ALL SYSTEMS

1 General description

The fuel system consists of a rear-mounted fuel tank, fuel pump and a downdraught carburettor on UK models or fuel injection system on North American models.

The air cleaner is of automatic temperature control type with a renewable element.

Turbocharged models incorporate an exhaust driven compressor to charge the induction air/fuel mixture.

Before working on the fuel system read the precautions given in Safety first! at the front of this manual.

2 Routine maintenance

1 Every 10 000 miles (16 000 km) adjust the idle speed and mixture setting.

2 Every 20 000 miles (32 000 km) renew the fuel filter and air filter elements.

PART B – CARBURETTOR SYSTEMS

3 Air cleaner element – renewal

1 Unscrew the wing nut(s)/bolts or prise back the spring clips (as applicable) retaining the cover on the air cleaner.
2 Remove the cover and, where applicable, the seal (photo).
3 Withdraw the element from the air cleaner body (photo).
4 Clean the inside surfaces of the body and cover.
5 Fit the new element using a reversal of the removal procedure.

4 Air cleaner – removal and refitting

1 Remove the element, as described in Section 3.
2 Disconnect the inlet and warm air hoses (photo).

3.2 Removing the air cleaner cover (top-mounted)

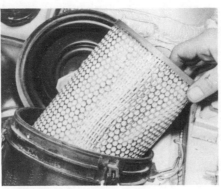

3.3 Removing the air cleaner element (side-mounted)

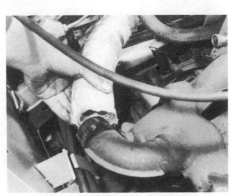

4.2 Disconnecting the warm air hose at the exhaust manifold end

4.4 Releasing the air cleaner strap (side-mounted)

4.6C ... then disconnect the hoses

4.6A Unscrew the nuts ...

3   Disconnect the crankcase ventilation hoses, where applicable, noting their locations.
4   Release the strap on side-mounted air cleaners (photo).
5   Withdraw the air cleaner.
6   Where applicable remove the remaining inlet hoses and ducts (photos).
7   Refitting is a reversal of removal.

5   Air inlet temperature control – testing

All except A5L engines
1   Remove the air cleaner (Section 4) and element (Section 3).
2   To test the control unit immerse it in a container of water at the following temperatures:
3   With a water temperature of 17.5°C (63.5°F), the flap should close the cold air intake after 5 minutes.
4   With a water temperature of 26°C (79°F), the flap should close the warm air intake after 5 minutes.

4.6B ... and remove the inlet elbow ...

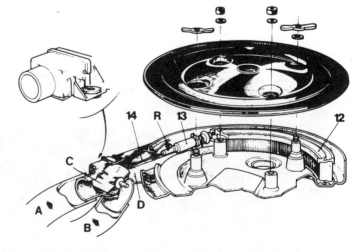

Fig. 3.1 Air inlet temperature control components on a type 847 engine (Sec 5)

A   Cold air intake   R   Spindle adjustment screw
B   Warm air intake   12 Filter
C   Flap   13 Thermostat
D   Mixed air stream   14 Spindle

5   If adjustment is necessary alter the length of the spindle as required.

A5L engines

6   The control is located in the top of the intercooler. Test the control by immersion in water at the following temperatures:
7   With a water temperature of 43°C (109°F), the flap should bypass the intercooler after 5 minutes.
8   With a water temperature of 47°C (117°F), the flap should direct all the air through the intercooler after 5 minutes.

---

6   Fuel pump – testing, servicing, removal and refitting

A5L engines

1   Refer to Section 21 as the fuel pump is identical to the one fitted to the A7L engine.

All except A5L engines

2   The fuel pump is located on either the right- or left-hand side of the cylinder block, according to the engine type (photo).
3   To test its operation, disconnect the outlet hose and hold a wad of rag by the outlet. Disconnect the coil HT lead at the distributor and connect it to earth, then have an assistant spin the engine on the starter. Check that well defined spurts of fuel are ejected.
4   If a pressure gauge is available, check that the output pressure is as given in the Specifications.
5   To clean the gauze filter, remove the screw(s) and withdraw the cover (photos). Clean the filter and seal, and the interior surfaces of the pump and cover. Check the seal for condition then refit the components in reverse order, taking care not to over-tighten the screw(s).
6   To remove the fuel pump, first remove the air cleaner and engine splash panels, as required.
7   Identify the supply and return hoses for location then disconnect them. Plug or clamp the supply hose.

6.2 Fuel pump on a type 829 engine

8   Unscrew the nuts/bolts and withdraw the fuel pump from the cylinder block (photos).
9   Remove the gaskets and insulating washer. Clean the mating faces of the pump and block.
10 Refitting is a reversal of removal, but fit new gaskets.

---

7   Fuel in-line filter – removal and refitting

---

1   Clamp the fuel lines on either side of the filter.
2   Loosen the filter clips, and remove the filter (photo).

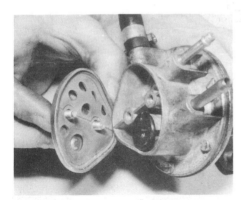

6.5A Remove the fuel pump cover (829 engine) ...

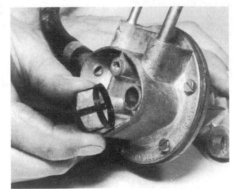

6.5B ... and take out the gauze filter

6.5C Removing the fuel pump cover on a type 847 engine

6.8A Removing the fuel pump on a type 847 engine

6.8B Removing the fuel pump on a type 829 engine

7.2 In-line fuel filter

3 To fit a new filter, connect it to the fuel pipes with the arrow on the body pointing in the direction of the carburettor (ie in the direction of flow).

4 Tighten the clips, and remove the clamps.

8 Fuel tank (except A5L) – removal, servicing and refitting

Note: *For safety always remove the fuel tank in a well ventilated area, never over a pit. For type A5L engines refer to Section 30.*

1 Disconnect the battery.

2 Preferably choose a time when the fuel level in the tank is low, and syphon off the remaining contents of the tank via the filler cap.

3 Jack up the rear of the car and support on axle stands. Chock the front wheels.

4 Remove the spare tyre.

5 Remove the rear luggage compartment mat, prise up the cover, and disconnect the wiring to the fuel gauge sender unit.

6 Identify the fuel supply and return hoses for location then disconnect them from the sender unit.

7 Remove the filler neck from the fuel tank by removing the screws (cap removed).

8 Where applicable, unclip the hoses from the tank.

8.9 Fuel tank mounting bolt location

9 Support the fuel tank with a trolley jack and block of wood then unscrew the mounting bolts/nuts (photo).

10 Push the filler side out in order to release the opposite side, then withdraw the fuel tank at an angle. Where applicable, disconnect the vent hoses.

11 If the tank is contaminated with sediment or water, swill it out with clean fuel after removing the fuel gauge sender unit. Never attempt to solder or weld a leaking fuel tank unless it has been thoroughly steamed or boiled first. Fuel tank repair is a specialist field. Temporary repairs with the tank *in situ* can sometimes be made using proprietary plugging compounds, but these are unlikely to prove satisfactory in the long run.

12 Refitting is a reversal of removal, but make sure that all the hoses are securely fitted.

9 Fuel gauge sender unit – removal and refitting

1 Open the tailgate and remove the luggage compartment mat.

2 Disconnect the battery negative lead.

3 Prise up the cover and disconnect the wiring plug (photos).

4 Using a screwdriver, turn the retaining ring anti-clockwise then withdraw the sender unit.

5 Refitting is a reversal of removal, but clean the retaining ring and tank mating surfaces, and apply a little sealing compound to them.

10 Accelerator cable – removal, refitting and adjustment

1 Disconnect the battery.

2 At the carburettor end, free the locknut and the cable clamping screw (photo).

3 At the pedal end, remove the split pin, extract the clevis, and take the scuttle fitting from its location.

4 Pass the clevis through into the engine compartment, and withdraw the cable.

5 To refit, reverse the removal procedure. Check that the scuttle fitting is properly in place, and ensure that no sharp bends are present in the cable run, then adjust as follows:

6 Have an assistant hold the throttle pedal down to the floor, whilst you hold the throttle butterfly on the carburettor wide open.

7 Tension the cable against the compensator spring, so that the spring is compressed about 2.0 mm (0.08 in). Tighten the cable securing screw at the carburettor trunnion, and lock with the nut.

8 Where automatic transmission is fitted, check for correct operation of the kickdown switch (see Chapter 7).

9 Ensure that where the cable leaves the sleeve, at the stop adjacent to the carburettor, it makes good alignment with the carburettor lever. The stop may be bent if necessary to this end. Poor alignment causes excessive friction, producing heavy operation and wear. Make sure also that, when the throttle pedal is released, the cable has enough tension to prevent the sleeve from jumping out of the stop.

11 Choke cable – removal, refitting and adjustment

1 Disconnect the battery earth lead.

2 Slacken the bolt at the carburettor which retains the outer cable. Withdraw the cable from the carburettor.

3 The choke cable and control can be withdrawn from the steering column lower surround after releasing the surround. Note the wire connector for the choke warning light.

4 Refitting is the reverse of the removal procedure. Adjust the cable

9.3A Lift the cover ...

9.3B ... and disconnect the wiring from the fuel gauge sender

10.2 Accelerator cable end and adjuster (type 829 engine)

so that with the choke control fully home, there is a small amount of slack in the inner cable. Check for correct operation on completion.

12 Idling speed and mixture – adjustment

1   Accurate adjustment is only possible using an exhaust gas analyser. Connect the analyser, together with a tachometer, to the engine.
2   Run the engine at approximately 2000 rpm until it reaches the normal operating temperature with the thermostat open.
3   Where applicable, remove the tamperproof cap from the mixture adjustment screw, but check first that local legislation permits this.
4   Allow the engine to idle, then adjust the idling/volume screw to achieve the specified idling speed (photo).
5   Turn the mixture screw to achieve the specified CO percentage.
6   Repeat the procedure in paragraph 5 as required.
7   Fit a new tamperproof cap, where applicable.

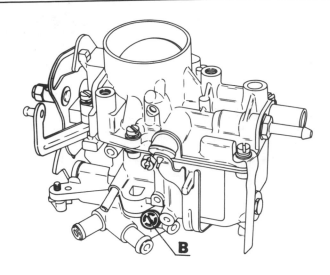

Fig. 3.3 Mixture screw (B) on the Solex carburettor (Sec 12)

12.4 Adjusting the idling/volume screw on the Weber 32 DARA

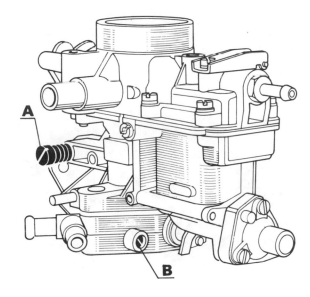

Fig. 3.4 Idling/volume screw (A) and mixture screw (B) on the Zenith carburettor (Sec 12)

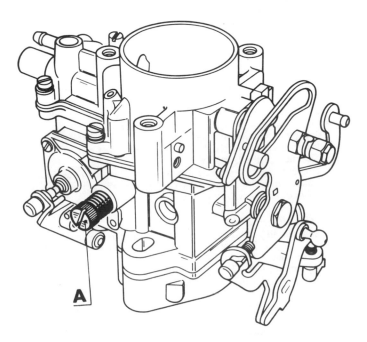

Fig. 3.2 Idling/volume screw (A) on the Solex carburettor (Sec 12)

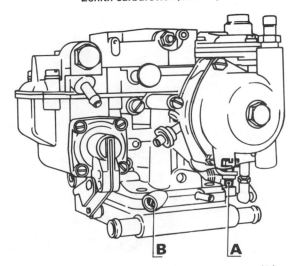

Fig. 3.5 Idling/volume screw (A) and mixture screw (B) on the Weber carburettor (Sec 12)

13.3A Coolant hoses on the automatic choke ...

13.5 Location of mounting nuts on the Weber 32 DARA (arrowed)

13.3B ... and carburettor base – arrowed (Weber 32 DARA)

13 Carburettor – removal and refitting

1   Remove the air cleaner (Section 4).
2   Disconnect the accelerator linkage and choke cable (Section 11), as applicable.
3   Clamp the coolant hoses to the carburettor base and automatic choke, as applicable, then disconnect them (photos).
4   Disconnect the fuel supply and crankcase ventilation hoses (photo). Also disconnect the vacuum hose.
5   Unscrew the mounting nuts, remove the washers, and withdraw the carburettor from the inlet manifold studs (photo).
6   Remove the gaskets and insulating washer.
7   Clean the carburettor and inlet manifold mating faces.
8   Refitting is a reversal of removal, but use new gaskets, and tighten the nuts evenly.

14 Carburettor (Solex 32 SEIA) – adjustment

Throttle butterfly angle
1   Either Renault tool Mot 522 or the special Solex tool is required to make this adjustment, the former measuring movement in mm and the latter measuring degrees.
2   Using tool Mot 522, invert the carburettor and fit the tool. Zero the clock gauge in the position shown in Fig. 3.7, then turn the gauge through 180° and read off the difference in height of each side of the butterfly.
3   Using the Solex gauge, first zero it on a flat surface plate then, with the carburettor inverted, fit the gauge with the fixed probe on the highest section of the butterfly. Read off the angle.
4   If the reading obtained in paragraph 2 or 3 is not as given in the Specifications turn the screw shown in Fig. 3.8 as required. Note that a tamperproof cap may be fitted.

Initial throttle opening
5   Fully close the choke flap by turning the flap lever clockwise.
6   Using a twist drill of the specified diameter, check the gap between the butterfly and the bore (Fig. 3.9).
7   If adjustment is necessary, turn the screw shown in Fig. 3.9. Note that a tamperproof cap may be fitted.

Accelerator pump stroke
8   With the throttle butterfly shut, move the pump lever roller into contact with the operating cam.
9   Turn the adjusting screw (Fig. 3.10) so that it just touches the plunger, then turn it an additional half turn.

13.4 Disconnecting the fuel supply hose

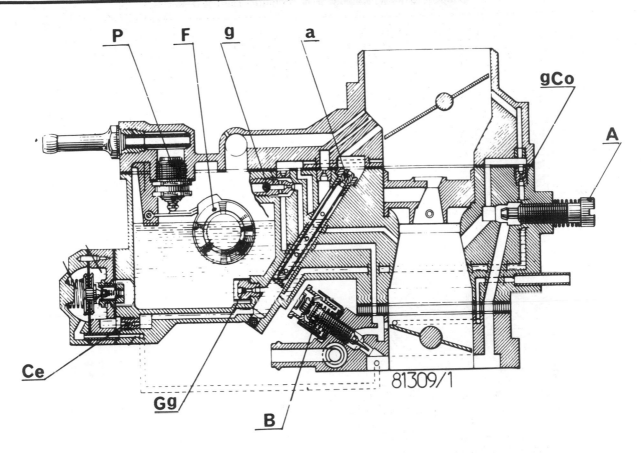

Fig. 3.6 Cross-section of the Solex 32 SEIA carburettor (Sec 14)

A	Idling/volume screw	*Ce*	Econostat	*g*	Idling jet	*Gg*	Main jet
a	Air compensating jet	*F*	Float	*gCo*	Air bleed jet	*P*	Needle valve
B	Mixture screw						

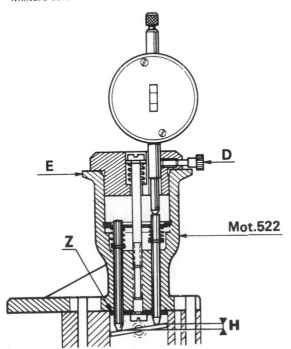

Fig. 3.7 Adjusting the throttle butterfly angle (Sec 14)

D	Screw	*H*	Dimension
E	Lug	*Z*	Locating washer

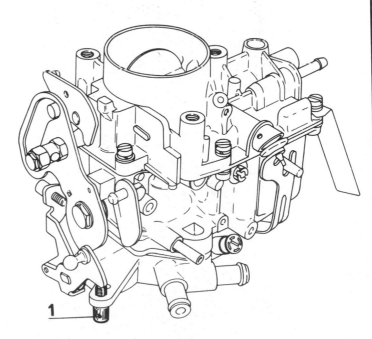

Fig. 3.8 Throttle butterfly angle adjustment screw (1) on the Solex 32 SEIA carburettor (Sec 14)

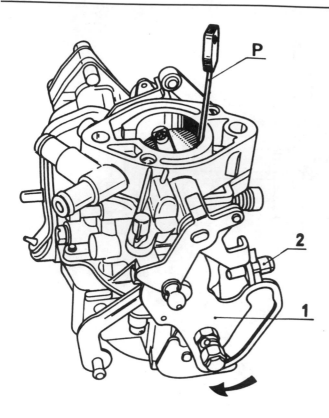

Fig. 3.9 Checking initial throttle opening on the Solex 32 SEIA carburettor (Sec 14)

P Gauge
1 Lever

2 Adjustment screw

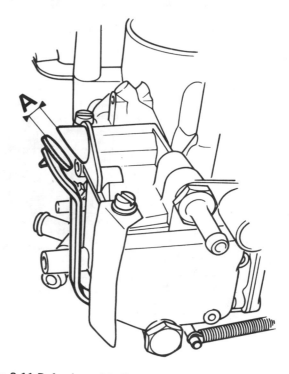

Fig. 3.11 Defuming valve dimension (A) on the Solex 32 SEIA carburettor (Sec 14)

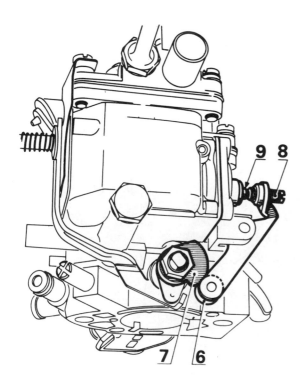

Fig. 3.10 Accelerator pump stroke adjustment on the Solex 32 SEIA carburettor (Sec 14)

6 Roller
7 Cam

8 Adjustment screw
9 Plunger

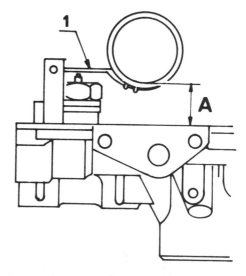

Fig. 3.12 Float level dimension (A) on the Solex 32 SEIA carburettor (Sec 14)

1   Float arm

Defuming valve position
10 With the throttle butterfly shut, check the gap shown in Fig. 3.11.
11 To adjust the gap, bend the valve stem as required.

Float level (ball type needle valve only)
12 Remove the carburettor cover and hold it inverted without the gasket.
13 Check that the dimension shown in Fig. 3.12 is as given in the Specifications. If not, bend the float arm as required.
14 Before refitting the cover and gasket check that the float pivots freely.

15 Carburettor (Zenith 32 IF) – adjustment

Initial throttle opening

1 Fully close the choke flap by turning the flap lever anti-clockwise.
2 Using a twist drill of the specified diameter, check the gap between the butterfly and the bore (Fig. 3.14).
3 If adjustment is necessary turn the screw shown in Fig. 3.14.

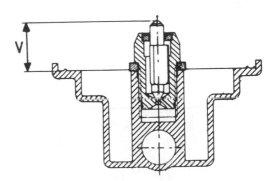

Fig. 3.13 Zenith 32 IF carburettor components (Sec 15)

g	Idling jet	I	Accelerator pump jet
Ga	Auxiliary jet	K	Choke tube
Gg	Main jet		

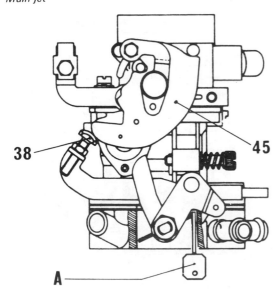

Fig. 3.14 Checking initial throttle opening on the Zenith 32 IF carburettor (Sec 15)

A	Gauge	45	Lever
38	Adjustment screw		

Fuel level

4 Remove the float chamber cover and gasket.
5 With the cover inverted, and without depressing the ball, check the dimension shown in Fig. 3.15. If excessive, screw in the needle valve, as required, compressing the seal. However, if the dimension is

too small it is not acceptable to simply unscrew the valve – instead a new seal must be fitted.

Auxiliary jet tube height

6 Check the dimension from the top of the tube to the top of the carburettor (Fig. 3.16).
7 If necessary bend the tube slightly to obtain the correct dimension.

Accelerator pump delivery tube height

8 Check the dimension from the tip of the tube to the carburettor flange (Fig. 3.17).
9 Bend the tube slightly if necessary and make sure that the jet of fuel strikes the diffuser, as indicated in Fig. 3.17.

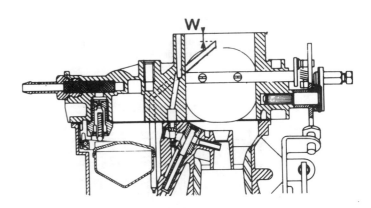

Fig. 3.15 Fuel level dimension (V) on the Zenith 32 IF carburettor (Sec 15)

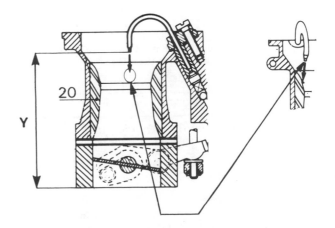

Fig. 3.16 Auxiliary jet tube dimension (W) on the Zenith 32 IF carburettor (Sec 15)

Fig. 3.17 Accelerator pump delivery tube position dimension (Y) on the Zenith 32 IF carburettor (Sec 15)

20 Diffuser

Accelerator pump stroke
10 Remove the check valve body.
11 With the choke flap fully open and the throttle butterfly closed, use vernier calipers to measure the dimension shown in Fig. 3.18.
12 If necessary, turn the adjusting nut as required.

Defuming valve position
13 Fully close the choke flap by turning the lever anti-clockwise.
14 Check the dimension between the spindle and valve arm (Fig. 3.19), and bend the arm as required.

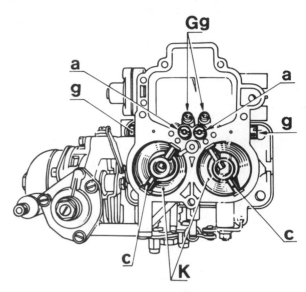

Fig. 3.20 Weber 32 DARA carburettor components (Sec 16)

a	Air compensating jet	*Gg*	Main jet
C	Mixture centralizer	*K*	Choke tube
g	Idling jet		

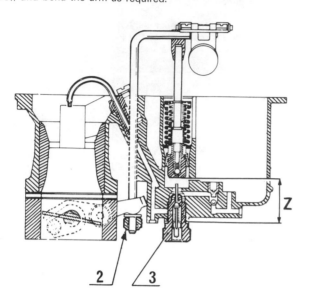

Fig. 3.18 Accelerator pump stroke dimension (Z) on the Zenith 32 IF carburettor (Sec 15)

2   Adjustment nut   *3   Check valve body*

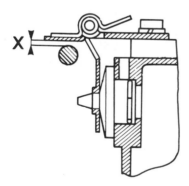

Fig. 3.19 Defuming valve gap dimension (X) on the Zenith 32 IF carburettor (Sec 15)

---

16 Carburettor (Weber 32 DARA) – adjustment

Throttle butterfly angle (829 engine only)
1   Remove the carburettor heating flange and disconnect the fast idle link.
2   Follow the procedure given in Section 14, paragraphs 1 to 3.
3   If adjustment is necessary turn the screw shown in Fig. 3.21.

Initial throttle opening
4   Fully close the choke flaps by hand, and position the adjustment screw (Fig. 3.22) on the highest part of the fast idle cam on pre-1982 models or on the second highest part on 1982-on models.
5   Using a twist drill, check that the gap between the throttle butterfly (1st stage) and bore is as given in the Specifications. If not, turn the adjustment screw as required.

Fig. 3.21 Throttle butterfly angle adjustment on the Weber 32 DARA carburettor fitted to the 829 engine (Sec 16)

L   Fast idle link   *1   Adjustment screw*

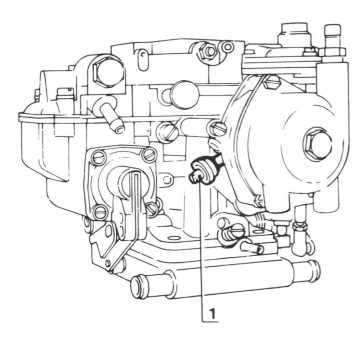

Fig. 3.22 Initial throttle opening adjustment screw (1) on the Weber 32 DARA carburettor (Sec 16)

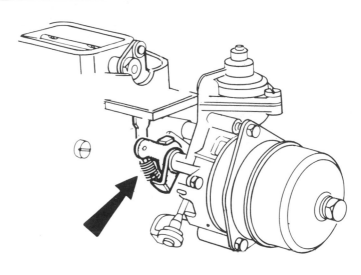

Fig. 3.24 Intermediate spring location on the Weber 32 DARA carburettor (Sec 16)

Automatic choke

6   Fully close the choke flaps by hand.

7   With the automatic choke cover and spring removed, lift the vacuum pull-off spindle until it touches the stopscrew, at the same time keeping the choke lever in contact with the spindle.

8   Using a twist drill, check the gap between the large section side of the choke flaps and the body.

9   If adjustment is necessary, turn the adjustment screw in the top of the vacuum capsule.

10 Check that the intermediate spring (Fig. 3.24) is correctly fitted.

11 When refitting the automatic choke cover make sure that the bi-metallic spring is correctly attached and position the cover so that the assembly marks are aligned.

Deflooding device setting

12 Fully close the choke flaps by hand, then fully open the throttles and release the flaps.

13 Using a twist drill, check that the gap between the large section side of the choke flaps and the body is as given in the Specifications. If not, turn the adjustment screw (Fig. 3.25) as required.

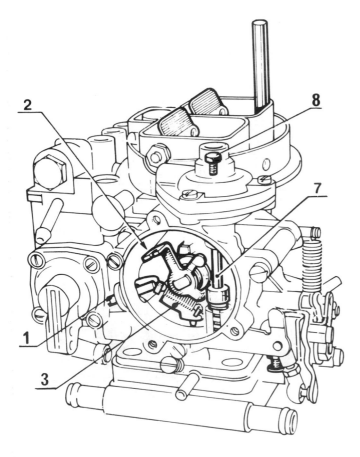

Fig. 3.23 Automatic choke adjustment on the Weber 32 DARA carburettor (Sec 16)

1	Screw	7	Spindle
2	Lever	8	Adjustment/stop screw
3	Cam		

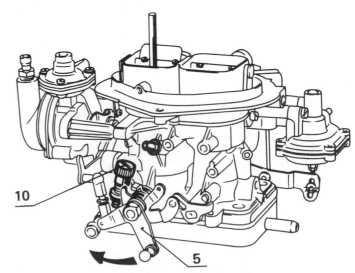

Fig. 3.25 Deflooding device adjustment on the Weber 32 DARA carburettor (Sec 16)

5	Throttle lever	10	Adjustment screw

Float level

14   Remove the carburettor top cover and hold it vertically so that the needle valve is closed by the float, but the spring-tensioned ball is not depressed.

15   With the gasket in place, measure the distance between the float and the gasket. If it is not as given in the Specifications bend the float arm, making sure that the tongue remains at right-angles to the needle valve.

16   Check that the float travel is as given in the Specifications, and if necessary bend the tab on the end of the float arm.

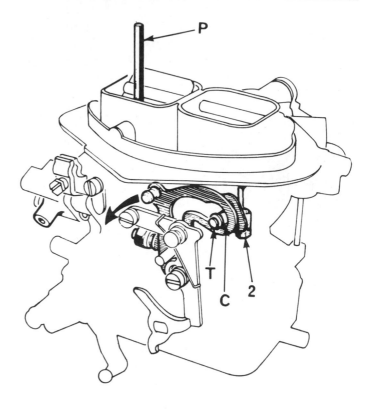

Fig. 3.27 Choke flap part opening adjustment on the Weber 32 DIR carburettor (Sec 17)

C	Camplate	T	Spindle
P	Gauge	2	Adjustment screw

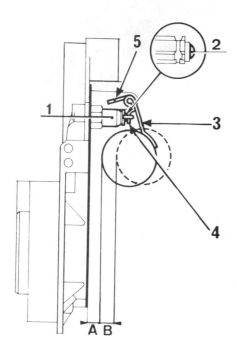

Fig. 3.26 Float level adjustment on the Weber 32 DARA carburettor (Sec 16)

A	Float level	3	Float arm
B	Float travel	4	Tongue
1	Needle valve	5	Tab
2	Spring-tensioned ball		

17 Carburettor (Weber 32 DIR) – adjustment

Float level

1   Refer to Section 16, paragraphs 14 to 16.

Choke flap part open setting (mechanical)

2   Move the control lever to the cold start position (Fig. 3.27), making sure that the operating spindle is touching the end of the opening in the camplate.

3   Using a twist drill, check that the gap between the choke flap and the body is as given in the Specifications. If not, turn the adjustment screw as required.

18 Carburettor (Solex 32 DIS) – adjustment

Initial throttle opening

1   Fully close the choke flap by turning the lever clockwise.

2   Using a twist drill, check the gap between the throttle and the bore on the side opposite the progression slot (Fig. 3.30).

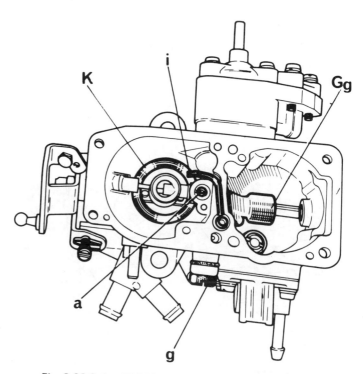

Fig. 3.28 Solex 32 DIS carburettor components (Sec 18)

a	Air correction jet	i	Accelerator pump injector
g	Idling jet	K	Choke tube
Gg	Main jet		

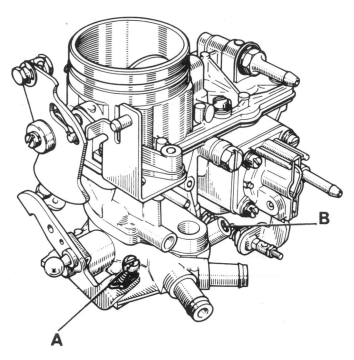

Fig. 3.29 Idling/volume adjustment screw (A) and mixture screw (B) on the Solex 32 DIS carburettor (Sec 18)

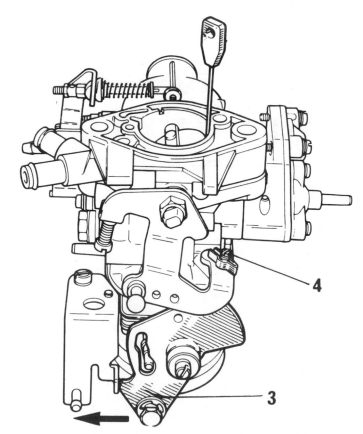

Fig. 3.30 Initial throttle opening adjustment on the Solex 32 DIS carburettor (Sec 18)

3   Lever   4   Adjustment screw

3   If the gap is not as given in the Specifications turn the adjustment screw as required.

Accelerator pump stroke

4   Locate a twist drill of the specified diameter as shown in Fig. 3.31, then check that the accelerator pump is just at the end of its stroke. If not, turn the adjustment nut as required.

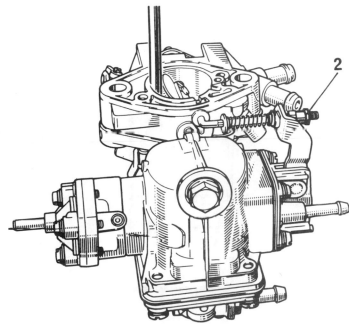

Fig. 3.31 Accelerator pump stroke adjustment on the Solex 32 DIS carburettor (Sec 18)

2   Adjustment nut

PART C – FUEL INJECTION SYSTEMS

19 Fuel injection system – description and precautions

1   The fuel injection system fitted to North American R1368 and R136A models is shown in Figs. 3.32, 3.33 and 3.34.
2   Fuel from the pump passes through the filter to the injector ramp assembly, the pressure being controlled by a pressure regulator.
3   The injectors inject fuel twice for each camshaft revolution, the injection period being determined by the electronic control unit.
4   The control unit is fed information in the form of electronic signals from the airflow meter, ignition circuit, coolant temperature, throttle position switch, oxygen sensor and air temperature sensor.
5   The cold start injector provides extra fuel for starting the engine from cold.
6   The auxiliary air regulator increases the engine speed during the warm-up period.
7   On models with air conditioning a fast idle valve compensates for the additional load on the engine at idling when the air conditioning compressor operates.
8   As the system incorporates sensitive electronic components the following precautions should be heeded:

   (a) *Switch off the igniton before disconnecting any wiring*
   (b) *Disconnect the battery leads before charging it*
   (c) *Remove the electronic control unit if the ambient temperature is likely to exceed 80°C (176°F).*

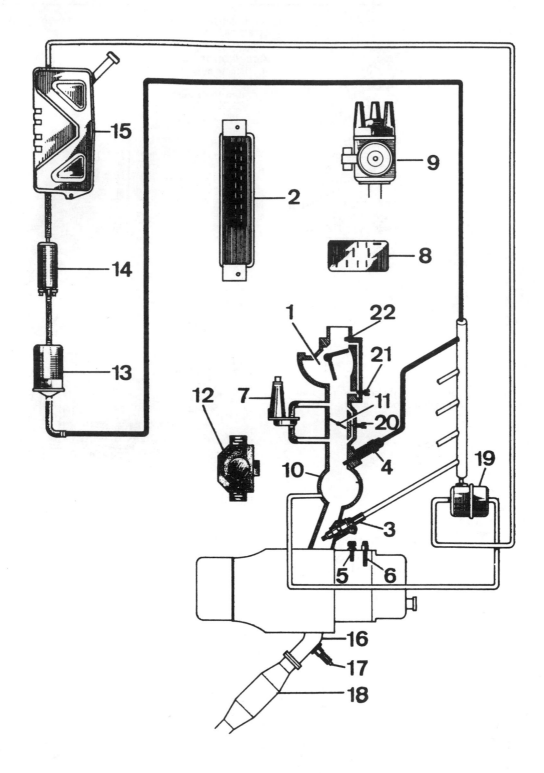

Fig. 3.32 Diagram of the Bosch L-Jetronic fuel injection system (Sec 19)

1 Airflow meter	9 Ignition distributor or integral	16 Exhaust manifold
2 Electronic control unit	electronic ignition (AEI)	17 Oxygen sensor
3 Injector	10 Intake manifold chamber	18 3-way catalytic converter
4 Cold start injector	11 Throttle plate assembly	19 Fuel pressure regulator
5 Coolant temperature sensor	12 Throttle position switch	20 Throttle plate bypass screw
6 Coolant thermotime switch	13 Fuel filter	21 Airflow meter bypass screw
7 Auxiliary air regulator	14 Fuel pump	22 Air temperature sensor
8 Relay	15 Fuel tank	

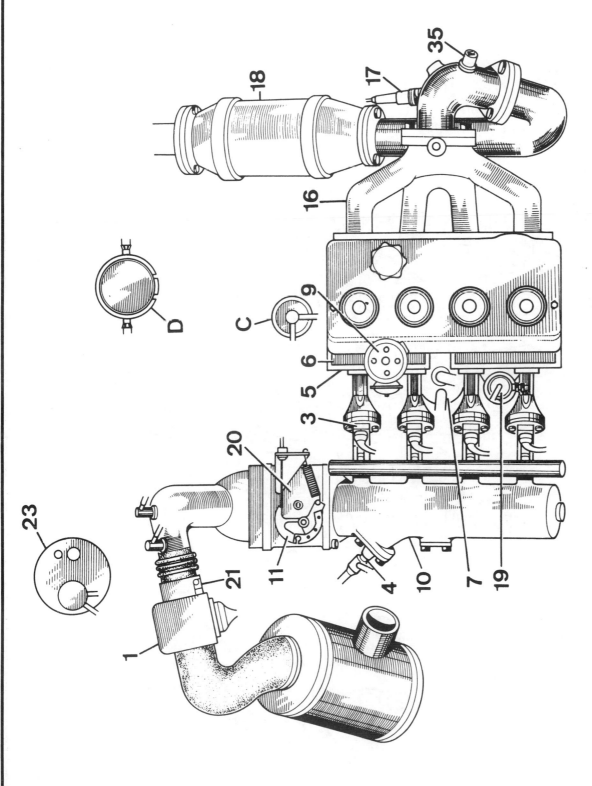

Fig. 3.33 Fuel injection component location diagram for the type 843 engine (Sec 19)

C   Oil condenser
D   Oxygen sensor maintenance
    indicator
1   Airflow meter
3   Injector

4   Cold start injector
5   Coolant temperature sensor
6   Coolant thermotime switch
7   Auxiliary air regulator

9   Ignition distributor
10 Intake manifold chamber
11 Throttle plate assembly
16 Exhaust manifold

17 Oxygen sensor
18 3-way catalytic converter
19 Fuel pressure regulator
20 Throttle valve bypass
    screw

21 Airflow sensor bypass
    screw
23 Charcoal canister
35 Carbon monoxide socket
    plug

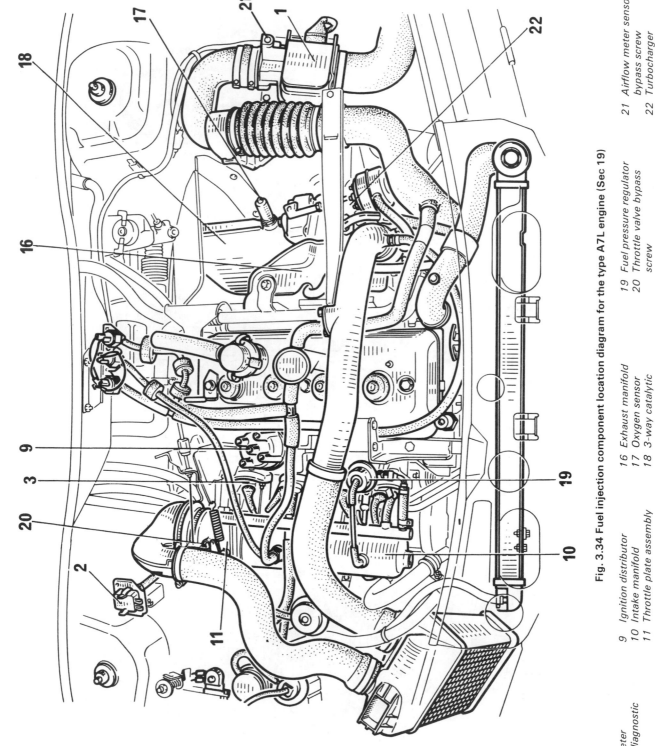

Fig. 3.34 Fuel injection component location diagram for the type A7L engine (Sec 19)

1 Airflow meter
2 Injection diagnostic
   connector
3 Injector

9 Ignition distributor
10 Intake manifold
11 Throttle plate assembly

16 Exhaust manifold
17 Oxygen sensor
18 3-way catalytic
   converter

19 Fuel pressure regulator
20 Throttle valve bypass
   screw

21 Airflow meter sensor
   bypass screw
22 Turbocharger

20 Fuel filter – removal and refitting

1   Jack up the rear of the car and support on axle stands. Chock the front wheels.
2   Clamp the hoses connected to the filter, then disconnect them.
3   Unbolt the mounting clamp and withdraw the filter.
4   Refitting is a reversal of removal, but make sure that the fuel flow arrow is pointing in the right direction.

21 Fuel pump – removal and refitting

1   Jack up the rear of the car and support on axle stands. Chock the front wheels.
2   Clamp the input and output hoses.
3   Disconnect the battery negative lead.
4   Disconnect the wiring from the pump, noting its location.
5   Unbolt the mounting clamp and withdraw the fuel pump.
6   Refitting is a reversal of removal.

22 Auxiliary air regulator – removal and refitting

1   Disconnect the wiring.
2   Disconnect the input and output hoses.
3   Unbolt and remove the regulator, but plug the bolt holes in the cylinder head to prevent the loss of coolant.
4   Refitting is a reversal of removal, but apply a little sealing compound to the threads of the bolts.

23 Injector ramp assembly – removal and refitting

1   On the A7L engine disconnect the air-to-air chamber hoses.
2   Unbolt the injector ramp then disconnect the fuel lines and wiring and withdraw the assembly.
3   Refitting is a reversal of removal.

24 Temperature sensor and thermotime switch – removal and refitting

1   Disconnect the wiring.
2   Obtain a suitable rubber or cork plug, then unscrew the sensor and quickly plug the cylinder head.
3   Refitting is a reversal of removal.

25 Airflow meter – removal and refitting

1   Unplug the wiring connector.
2   Disconnect the intake and output hoses.
3   Release the clip and withdraw the airflow meter.
4   Refitting is a reversal of removal.

26 Oxygen sensor – removal and refitting

Type 843 engine

1   The sensor must be renewed between 29 686 and 30 106 miles (47 774 and 48 450 km). A maintenance indicator warning lamp on the instrument panel is operated by a mechanism connected to the speedometer cable.
2   To remove the sensor, disconnect the wiring and unscrew the unit from the exhaust.
3   Insert and tighten the new sensor and reconnect the wiring.
4   If local legislation permits, break the seals on the cable mechanism, remove the cover and turn the button a quarter turn toward the reset 'O' mark. Refit and seal the cover.

Type A7L engine

5   Unlike the 843 engine the sensor does not require renewing at periodic intervals. However, the removal and refitting procedure is as given in paragraphs 2 and 3 except that a heat resistant lubricant (MIL specification A-907B) must be applied to the sensor threads.

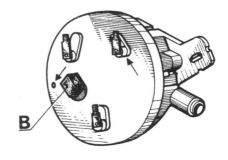

Fig. 3.35 Oxygen sensor maintenance indicator reset button (B) on type 843 engine models (Sec 26)

27 Idle speed and mixture – adjustment

Note: *Before carrying out the following work, check that local legislation permits it.*
1   On the 843 engine fit an exhaust gas analyser probe in the exhaust manifold elbow.
2   On all engines, connect a 20 000 ohm per volt voltmeter between terminals 2 and 8 of the diagnostic socket (Fig. 3.36). Also connect a tachometer.
3   Run the engine to normal operating temperature (but after the cooling fan has stopped).

Front view

Fig. 3.36 Diagnostic socket terminals (Sec 27)

Type 843 engine	Type A7L engine
1 Not used	1 Not used
2 Ground	2 Ground
3 Locator	3 Locator
4 and 5 Altitude compensator	4 and 5 Not used
6 Positive (+) to electronic control unit	6 Positive (+) to electronic control unit
7, 9 and 10 Throttle position switch	7, 9 and 10 Throttle position switch
8 Integrator voltage	8 Integrator voltage
11 and 12 Coolant thermotime switch	11 and 12 Coolant thermotime switch

843 engine

4   Check that the idling speed is as given in the Specifications. Note that on automatic transmission models this check must be with the selector lever in D. If adjustment is required, turn the throttle valve bypass screw.

5   With the oxygen sensor disconnected (but **not** earthed) check that the integrator voltage on the meter is 6.5 volt.

6   Reconnect the oxygen sensor, then adjust the airflow meter bypass screw until the integrator voltage returns as near as possible to the 6.5 volt with the CO percentage as specified.

A7L engine

7   With the oxygen sensor energised, check that the integrator voltage fluctuates $\pm$ 0.5 volt. If the meter reads a stable 6.4 volt the engine is not at normal operating temperature.

8   Adjust the throttle valve bypass screw to achieve the specified idle speed.

9   Adjust the airflow meter sensor bypass screw until the integrator voltage is 6.5 to 7.5 volt. If more than one complete turn of the screw is necessary check for air leaks between the airflow meter and manifold, vacuum circuit leaks or grounding of the oxygen sensor wire.

28 Fuel injection system – checking

Note: *A full check of the system should be made by a fuel injection specialist – the following paragraphs describes procedures which are considered within the scope of the home mechanic.*

1   Disconnect the pressure regulator-to-injector ramp assembly hose or the cold start injector input hose and connect a pressure gauge.

2   Turn on the ignition.

3   On the 843 engine open the airflow meter sensor flap through the intake opening to start the fuel pump. If the pump does not start, bridge terminals 36 and 39 in the airflow meter connector.

4   On the A7L engine bridge terminals 2 and 8 on the tachometer relay connector.

5   Check that the fuel pump pressure is as given in the Specifications.

6   Apply a vacuum of 0.53 bar (7.7 lbf/in^2) to the pressure regulator vacuum hose. The fuel pressure should now drop by 0.5 bar (7.3 lbf/in^2).

7   Disconnect the injector connectors, then remove the injector ramp assembly complete with injectors and cold start injector.

8   Start the fuel pump and make sure that the injectors do not leak.

9   Position the injectors over a container then momentarily apply a 12 volt supply to each injector in turn and check that the fuel sprays out.

10 Disconnect the fuel tank return hose at the pressure regulator and direct it into a calibrated beaker.

11 Run the fuel pump for 1 minute and check that 1 litre (1.8 Imp pt/1.06 US qt) is delivered. If the quantity is less, check the filter, pressure regulator and fuel pump.

29 Throttle positon switch – adjustment

1   Loosen the two fixing screws.

2   With the throttle closed in the idle position, turn the switch in the direction of throttle opening until the inner stop can be felt. The switch contacts can be heard slightly before the inner stop is reached.

3   Tighten the fixing screws.

30 Fuel tank – removal, servicing and refitting

Follow the procedure given in Section 8, but since the fuel pump and filter are located beneath the floor, clamp and disconnect the hoses as required. Also disconnect the exhaust silencer mounting.

31 Air cleaner element – renewal

The procedure is basically the same as that described in Section 3.

PART D – TURBOCHARGER, INLET AND EXHAUST SYSTEMS

32 Turbocharger – description and precautions

1   The turbocharger utilizes the flow of exhaust gases in the exhaust manifold to rotate a turbine and pressurize the intake air to a nominal 0.88 bar (13 lbf/in^2). The pressure is registered by a pressure gauge on the instrument panel.

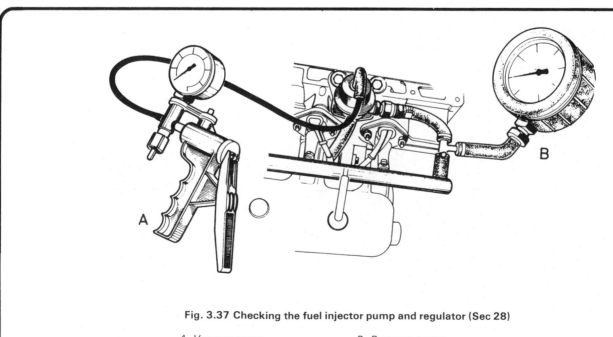

Fig. 3.37 Checking the fuel injector pump and regulator (Sec 28)

A *Vacuum pump*   B *Pressure gauge*

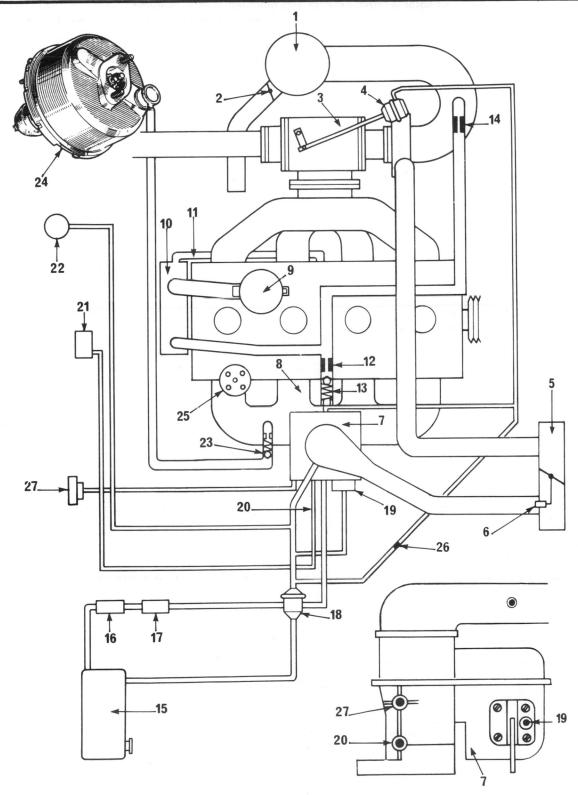

Fig. 3.38 Diagram of the turbocharger circuit on the type A5L engine (Sec 32)

1 Air filter	8 Inlet manifold	16 Pump	22 Instrument panel boost pressure gauge
2 Air temperature control flap	9 Oil filler cap	17 Fuel filter	23 Valve
3 Turbocharger	10 Oil separator	18 Intake pressure regulator	24 Brake servo
4 Wastegate (boost pressure regulator)	11 Oil return pipe	19 Accelerator pump	25 Distributor
5 Intercooler	12 Jet	20 Jet	26 Jet
6 Thermostatic capsule	13 Valve	21 Ignition cut-off pressure switch	27 Integral electronic ignition unit
7 Carburettor	14 Jet		
	15 Fuel tank		

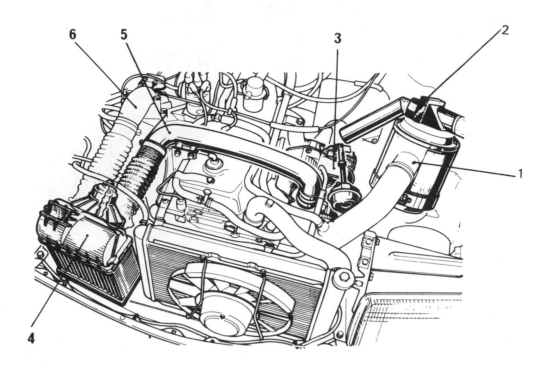

Fig. 3.39 Turbocharger component location diagram on the type A5L engine (Sec 32)

1	Air temperature control flap	3	Turbocharger	5	Air duct
2	Air filter	4	Intercooler	6	Air duct

2   The intake air is cooled by an intercooler incorporating an electric fan.

3   The turbocharger **must not** be operated with any of the hoses and ducts disconnected.

4   The oil circuit must be primed after disconnecting the oil pipes **before** starting the engine.

5   When stopping the engine allow it to idle for approximately 30 seconds before switching off the ignition.

33 Turbocharger – removal and refitting

UK models

1   Remove the air cleaner assembly (Section 4).

2   Disconnect the air cleaner hose and remove the exhaust pipe support bolts.

3   Remove the intake duct.

4   Disconnect the oil input and return pipes.

5   Loosen the mounting bracket lower bolt and remove the upper bolts.

6   Using a spanner, as shown in Fig. 3.40 unscrew the mounting nuts and withdraw the turbocharger from the exhaust manifold. **Do not** lift it by the wastegate control rod.

7   Clean the mating faces then refit the unit in reverse order, but renew the self-locking nuts, the gasket and the input and return pipe seals. Prime the lubrication circuit by injecting oil in the input aperture. Disconnect the ignition module three terminal plug and operate the starter until oil runs from the input pipe, then reconnect the pipe and plug. Allow the engine to run at idling speed for several minutes. Note that the downpipe flange bolts should first be fully tightened then backed off one and a half turns.

North American models

8   Disconnect the hoses and ducts from the turbocharger.

9   Unbolt and remove the heat shields.

10 Disconnect the heating ducts and vacuum hose.

Fig. 3.40 Special spanner for unscrewing the turbocharger mounting nuts (Sec 33)

11 Remove the oxygen snsor then unbolt the catalytic converter from the unit.

12 Disconnect the oil input and return pipes.

13 Disconnect the EGR hose and loosen the front retainers.

14 Unbolt the lower support bracket clamp.

15 Unbolt the exhaust manifold and withdraw it, together with the turbocharger.

16 Unbolt the exhaust manifold from the turbocharger. **Do not** lift the unit by the wastegate control rod.

17 Clean the mating faces and refit the unit in reverse order with reference also to paragraph 7. Apply a heat resistant lubricant (Specification MIL-A-907B) to the EGR line coupling nut. Tighten the catalytic converter lower flange bolts until the spring is coil bound, then back off one and a half turns.

34 Intercooler – removal and refitting

1   Unscrew the upper mounting bolt.

2   Disconnect the air hoses and the fan wiring.

3   Lift the intercooler from the engine compartment.

4   Refitting is a reversal of removal.

35 Manifolds and exhaust system – general

1   The inlet and exhaust manifolds are shown in Figs. 3.41 to 3.46.

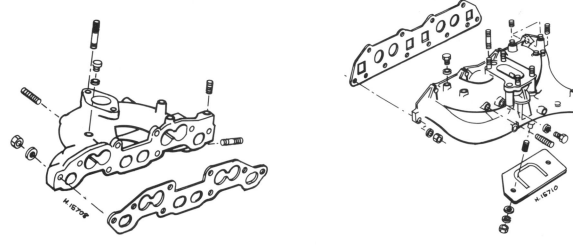

Fig. 3.41 Inlet and exhaust manifolds on the type 847 engine (Sec 35)

Fig. 3.42 Inlet and exhaust manifolds on the type A2M engine (Sec 35)

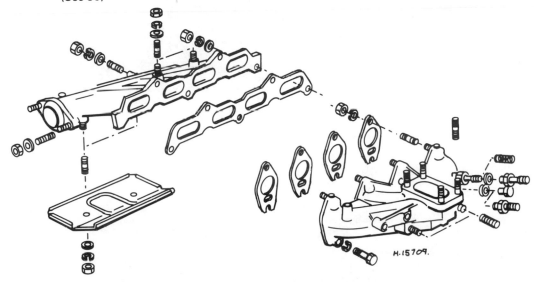

Fig. 3.43 Inlet and exhaust manifolds on the types A6M and 843 engines (Sec 35)

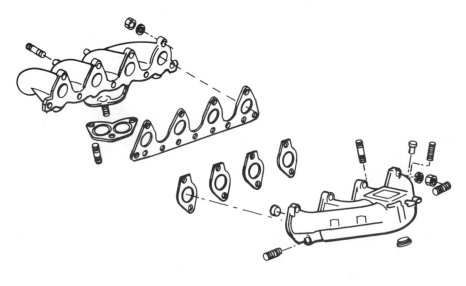

Fig. 3.44 Inlet and exhaust manifolds on the types 829 and J6R engines (Sec 35)

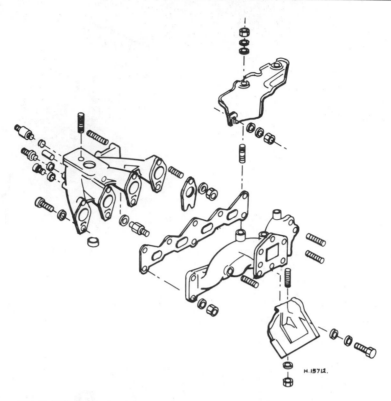

Fig. 3.45 Inlet and exhaust manifolds on the type A5L engine (Sec 35)

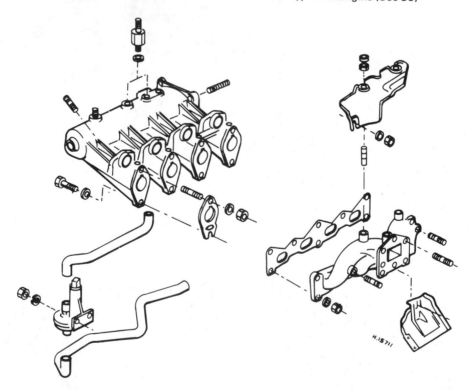

Fig. 3.46 Inlet and exhaust manifolds on the type A7L engine (Sec 35)

2   Removal and refitting is straightforward, but always use new gaskets and tighten the nuts/bolts evenly (photos).

3   The exhaust systems are shown in Figs. 3.47 and 3.48.

4   Each section can be removed, thus providing for renewal of individual sections as these become worn out. Corrosion at the joints can sometimes make separation of the sections difficult, and this problem can sometimes be eased by using a wire brush and penetrating oil. Corroded bolts are probably best cut off with a hacksaw, and replaced with new parts (photo).

5   Check the condition of the rubber mountings and rings, and renew them if necessary (photos).

6   The downpipe rear joint bolts should be fully tightened until the springs are coil bound, then backed off one and a half turns (photo).

35.2A Coolant hose connection to the inlet manifold

35.2B Removing the inlet manifold gasket (type 829 engine)

35.2C Exhaust manifold (type 829 engine)

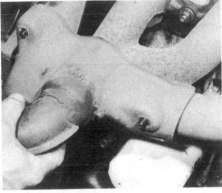

35.2D Removing the exhaust manifold hot air shroud (type 829 engine)

35.2E Unscrew the nuts ...

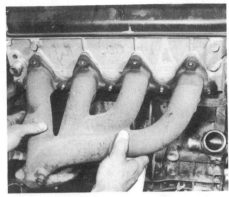

35.2F ... and remove the exhaust manifold (type 829 engine)

35.4 Fitting the exhaust manifold-to-downpipe gasket (type 829 engine)

35.5A Exhaust intermediate section mounting (type 829 engine)

35.5B Exhaust front silencer mounting (type 829 engine)

35.5C Exhaust tailpipe mounting (type 829 engine)

35.6 Exhaust downpipe rear joint (type 829 engine)

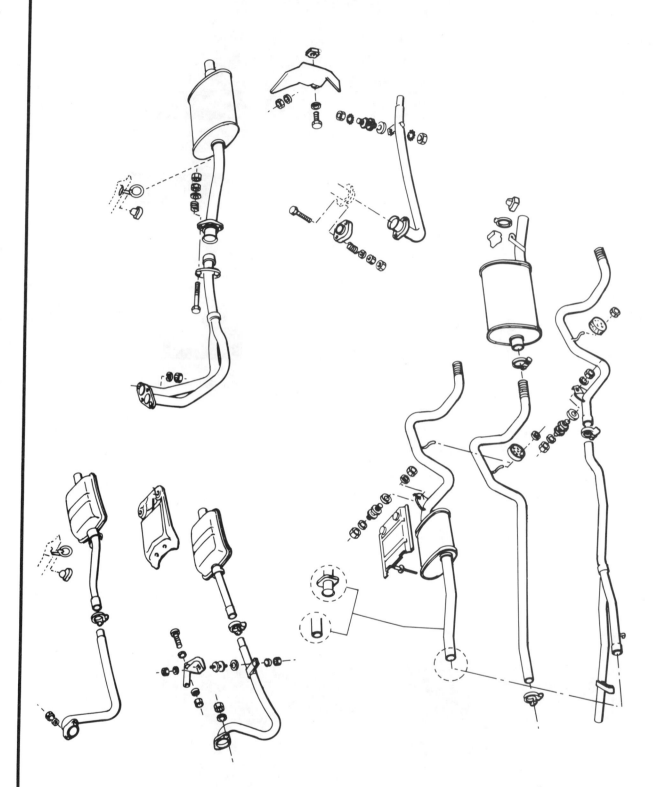

Fig. 3.47 Exhaust system components on UK models (Sec 35)

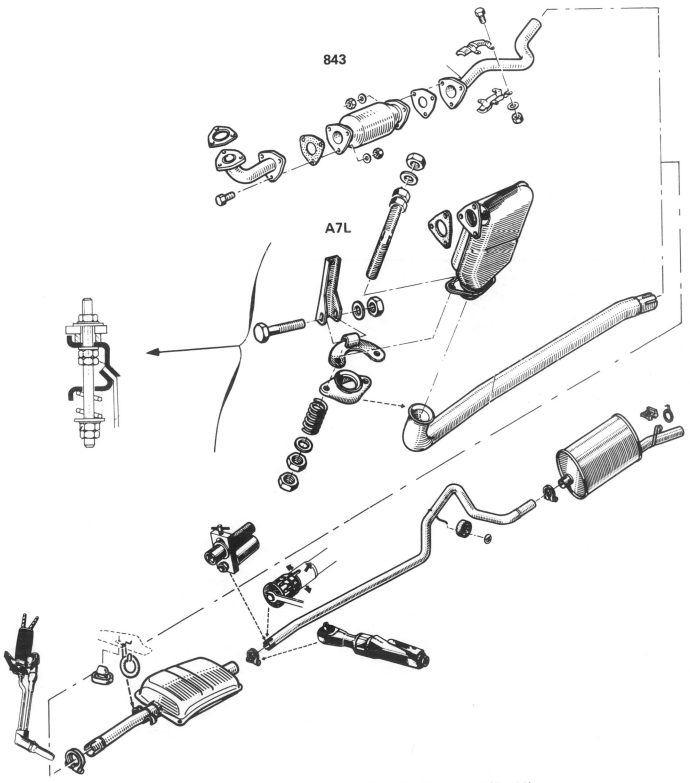

843

A7L

Fig. 3.48 Exhaust system components on North American models (Sec 35)

PART E – EMISSION CONTROL SYSTEMS

36 Crankcase ventilation system (PCV)

General description

1   Crankcase blow-by gases are drawn into the engine again for burning in the combustion chambers. The positive ventilation system is fully enclosed and the hose arrangements are shown in Figs. 3.49 to 3.52 (photo).

Checking

2   Periodically check the condition of the hoses and their security and renew them as required. Also check the calibrated jets for blockage.

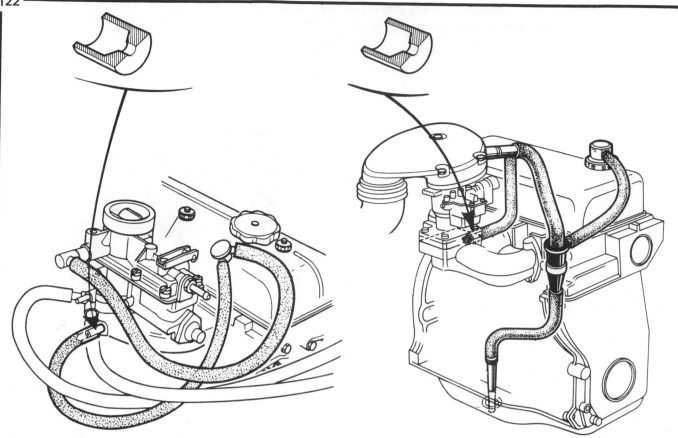

Fig. 3.49 Crankcase ventilation system on the type 847 engine (Sec 36)

Fig. 3.50 Crankcase ventilation system on the types 843 (UK) and A6M engines (Sec 36)

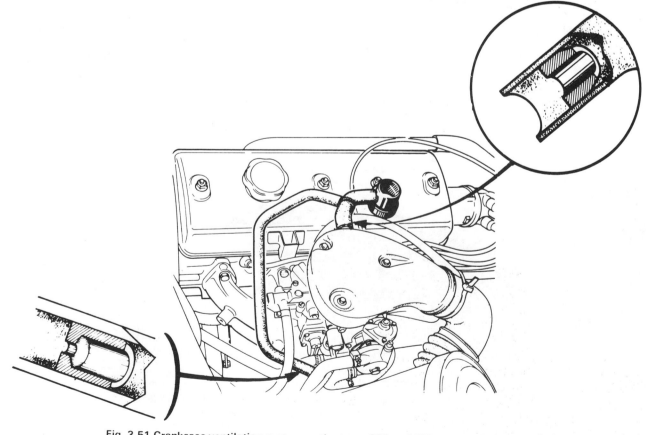

Fig. 3.51 Crankcase ventilation system on the types 829 and J6R engines (Sec 36)

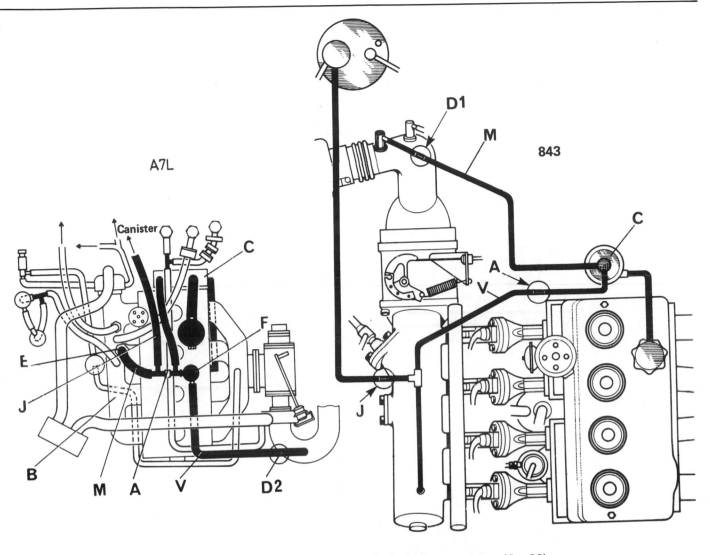

Fig. 3.52 Crankcase ventilation system on North American engines (Sec 36)

A	Calibrated jet 1.7 mm (0.066 in)	D1	Calibrated jet 5.0 mm (0.19 in)	E	One-way check valve	J	Calibrated jet 2.0 mm (0.08 in)
B	Air intake manifold	D2	Calibrated jet 7.0 mm (0.27 in)	F	Vacuum regulator check valve	M	Upstream circuit
C	Receptacle					V	Downstream circuit

36.1 Crankcase ventilation outlet on the valve cover (type 829 engine)

37 Fuel evaporative control system

General description

1   The system prevents evaporation of fuel into the atmosphere. It comprises an airtight fuel tank filler cap, charcoal canister and valves.

2   Vapours collecting in the fuel tank are channelled to the canister where the charcoal retains them while the engine is stopped. When the engine is started the intake vacuum draws the vapours into the engine.

3   If the car overturns, a one-way valve prevents fuel leaking into the canister and engine.

Checking

4   Periodically check the condition of the hoses and their security, and renew them as required.

5   With the engine at normal operating temperature and idling, disconnect the canister hose at the throttle and check that the idle speed increases by approximately 100 rpm. If not, check for leaks.

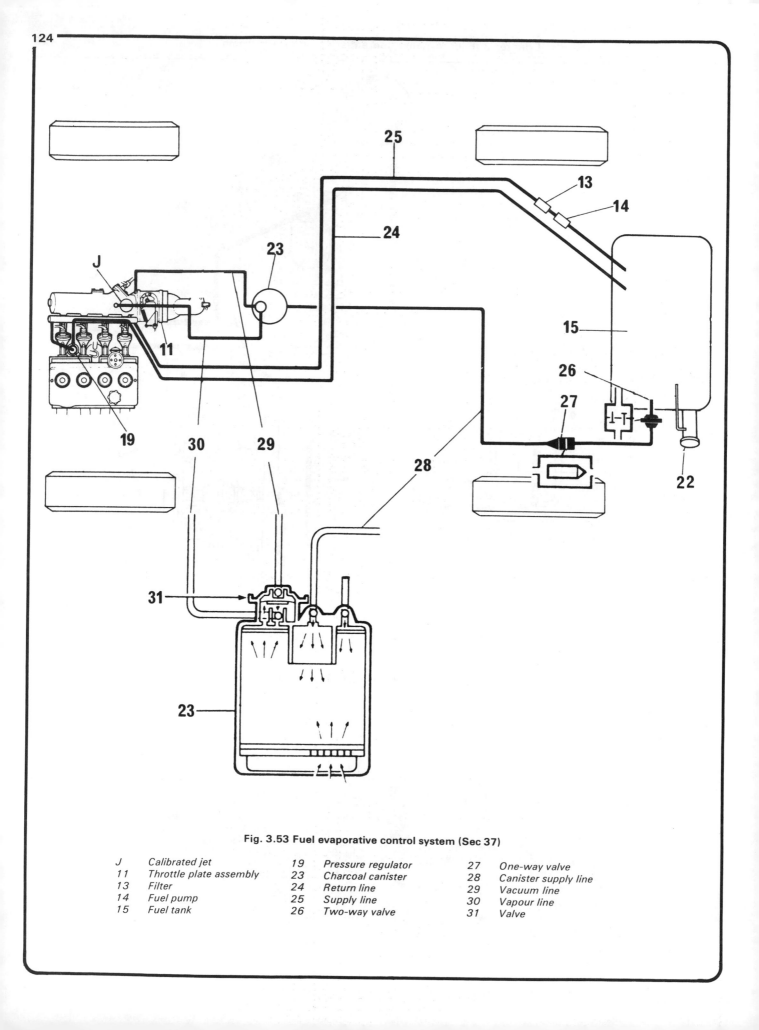

Fig. 3.53 Fuel evaporative control system (Sec 37)

J	Calibrated jet	19	Pressure regulator	27	One-way valve
11	Throttle plate assembly	23	Charcoal canister	28	Canister supply line
13	Filter	24	Return line	29	Vacuum line
14	Fuel pump	25	Supply line	30	Vapour line
15	Fuel tank	26	Two-way valve	31	Valve

38 Exhaust gas recirculation system (EGR)

General description

1 A proportion of exhaust gas is diverted into the inlet manifold under certain engine operating conditions. This inert gas prevents local hot spots in the combustion chambers and reduces nitrous oxide emissions. The system is only fitted to the A7L engine.

2 A solenoid controls the system only under the following conditions.

(a) 5th gear is not engaged
(b) The coolant temperature exceeds 45°C (113°F)
(c) The pressure differential switch contacts are closed, ie during acceleration

Checking

3 The EGR valve can be checked visually or with a vacuum gauge.

4 With the engine cold (ie below 45°C/113°F) accelerate the

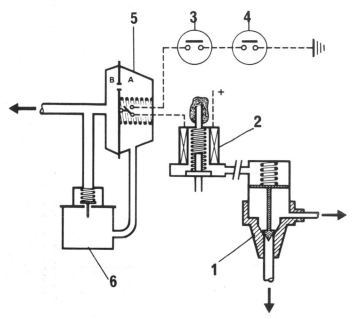

Fig. 3.55 Exhaust gas recirculation system solenoid operating circuit (Sec 38)

1 EGR valve
2 Solenoid
3 5th gear switch
4 Coolant temperature switch
5 Pressure differential switch (A and B vacuum chambers)
6 Vacuum reservoir

engine. The EGR valve should remain closed (no vacuum). If not renew the coolant temperature switch.

5 With the engine hot (ie above 45°C/113°F) accelerate the engine. The EGR valve should open for 5 to 6 seconds (vacuum reading).

6 If the check in paragraph 5 results in a different time value, renew the pressure differential switch.

7 Repeat the check in paragraph 5, this time with 5th gear engaged. The EGR valve should remain closed.

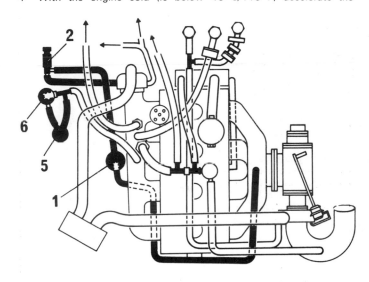

Fig. 3.54 Exhaust gas recirculation system circuit (Sec 38)

1 EGR valve
2 Solenoid
5 Pressure differential switch
6 Vaccum reservoir

PART F – ALL SYSTEMS

39 Fault diagnosis – fuel, exhaust and emission control systems

Symptom	Reason(s)
Carburettor systems	
Fuel consumption excessive	Air cleaner element dirty
	Fuel leak
	Incorrect float level
	Worn carburettor
	Idling adjustment incorrect
Insufficient fuel delivery or weak mixture	Fuel filter dirty
	Fuel pump faulty
	Manifold air leak
Fuel injection system	
Engine fails to start	Fuse blown
	Pump relay faulty
	Cold start injector faulty
	Auxiliary air regulator not opening
	Intake leaks
	Faulty control unit
Engine starts and stalls	Airflow meter sensor faulty
Poor acceleration	Faulty throttle position switch
Excessive fuel consumption	Leaking injectors
	Airflow meter sensor faulty
	Fuel pressure regulator faulty
	Faulty control unit
Turbocharger	
Noisy operation	Worn bearings
	Intake or exhaust leaks
	Poor lubrication
Poor acceleration	Air filter clogged
	Pressure regulator faulty
	Leaks in manifold or ducts
Blue smoke in exhaust	Internal oil seals leaking
EGR system	
Poor idling	EGR valve stuck open
	Faulty solenoid circuit

Chapter 4 Ignition system

For modifications, and information applicable to later models, see Supplement at end of manual

Contents

Specifications

System type	Conventional with coil and contact breaker points, transistorized with distributor pulse generator and electronic module or fully electronic with computerised module; fllywheel magnetic sensor and spark knock detector

Distributor

Firing order	1-3-4-2 (No 1 at flywheel end)
Rotation:	
ohv engine	Clockwise
ohc engine	Anti-clockwise (from cap end)
Contact breaker points gap on conventional system (initial setting only)	0.4 mm (0.016 in)
Dwell angle on conventional system	57° ± 3° (equal to dwell percentage of 63 ± 3%)
Rotor air gap on transistorized system	0.3 to 0.6 mm (0.012 to 0.024 in)

Diagnostic system

Sensor-to-flywheel gap	0.5 to 1.0 mm (0.020 to 0.039 in)
Ignition timing (with vacuum pipe disconnected from capsule):	
A5L engine	12° BTDC
All engines except A5L	10° BTDC
Spark knock detector retard (full electronic system)	6°

Spark plugs

Engine code:	Type
847	AC 43XLS, Champion N12Y, Eyquem 600 LS or Marchal GT35H
843 and A6M	AC 42XLS, Champion N7Y, Eyquem 755 LS, Marchal GT342H or Bosch WR7DS
829 and J6R	Champion S279YC or Marchal SCGT 345H
A5L	Champion N3G or Eyquem 805LP
A2M	AC 43XLS or Champion N9Y
A7L	Champion RN3G
Gap:	
All engines except USA/Canadian 1647 cc	0.55 to 0.65 mm (0.022 to 0.026 in)
USA/Canadian 1647 cc engine	0.6 to 0.7 mm (0.024 to 0.028 in)

Torque wrench settings

Spark plugs:	lbf ft	Nm
829, J6R and A2M engines	11 to 15	15 to 20
All except 829, J6R and A2M engines	23	31

1 General description

The ignition system may be one of three different types depending on the engine type and operating territory. The conventional system incorporates contact breaker points to switch the coil primary circuit on and off, but on the transistorized system the circuit is switched by a pulse generator and electronic module. On the fully electronic system a computerised module incorporating a vacuum capsule performs the complete function of the primary circuit independently (photo).

1.1 Computerised module on the fully electronic ignition system

In order that the engine may run correctly it is necessary for an electrical spark to ignite the fuel/air mixture in the combustion chambers at exactly the right moment in relation to engine speed and loading. The ignition system is based on feeding low tension voltage from the battery to the coil where it is converted to high tension voltage. The high tension voltage is powerful enough to jump the gap between the electrodes of the spark plugs in the cylinders many times a second under high compression, providing that the system is in good condition and all the adjustments are correct.

The system is divided into two circuits; the low tension and high tension. Low tension voltage is changed in the coil to high tension voltage by the alternate switching on and off of the primary circuit. The high tension voltage is fed to the relevant spark plug via the distributor cap and rotor arm. The ignition is advanced and retarded automatically to ensure that the spark occurs at the correct instant in relation to the engine speed and load. On the fully electronic system this is accomplished within the electronic module by using sensors to monitor the engine speed and vacuum. This system also incorporates a spark knock detector which retards the ignition timing by 6° under certain engine operating conditions. On the conventional and transistorized systems centrifugal weights in the distributor advance the ignition timing in relation to engine speed, and a vacuum unit on the side of the distributor controls the timing in relation to engine load.

When working on electronic ignition systems remember that the high tension voltage can be considerably higher than on a conventional system and in certain circumstances could prove fatal.

2 Routine maintenance

Conventional ignition system
1   Every 20 000 miles (32 000 km) *starting at 10 000 miles (16 000 km)* check and adjust the contact points dwell angle.
2   Every 10 000 miles (16 000 km) check and adjust the ignition timing. At the same interval check and adjust or renew the spark plugs.
3   Every 20 000 miles (32 000 km) check and adjust or renew the contact points.

Transistorized or fully electronic ignition system
4   Every 20 000 miles (32 000 km) check and adjust or renew the spark plugs.

3 Contact breaker points (conventional system) – adjustment

ohv engines (conventional contacts)
1   Prise back the retaining clips or unscrew the two screws, and lift the cap from the distributor.
2   Withdraw the rotor arm from the cam spindle and remove the dust shield.
3   The contact points are now accessible for inspection and if necessary adjustment (photo). Prise the points apart by levering the moving contact away from the fixed contact, using a small screwdriver. If the contact faces are pitted or badly worn they cannot be accurately adjusted and must therefore be removed for cleaning or renewal, as applicable.

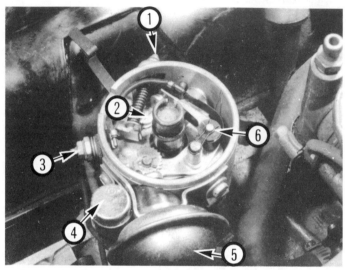

3.3 Distributor components on the conventional ignition ohv engine
1   Adjuster nut   4   Condenser
2   Retaining screw   5   Vacuum unit
3   LT terminal   6   Moving contact pivot

4   Assuming the contact faces to be in order, turn the engine to position the moving contact arm cam lug against the peak of one of the four cam spindle lobes. The engine can be turned by engaging a gear and moving the car, or by turning the crankshaft pulley bolt.
5   Select a feeler gauge blade of the specified clearance, and insert it between the contact faces. The selected blade should be a firm sliding fit (photo). If the gap is correct, rotate the adjuster nut on the outside of the distributor, shown in Fig. 4.1, in the desired direction to open or close the points as required.
6   Check the inside of the distributor cap before replacing it, and verify that the four contact segments are clean, and also that the central spring-loaded carbon brush is clean and moves freely in its housing.
7   Refit the dust shield and rotor arm followed by the cap.
8   To adjust the dwell angle, connect a dwell meter to the engine as recommended by the instrument manufacturer.
9   Start the engine, and run it at idling speed, or crank it on the starter motor (according to the type of instrument used).
10 Adjust as necessary using the adjuster nut until the correct dwell angle is achieved. Stop the engine, and disconnect the test instrument.

ohv engines (cassette contacts)
11 Remove the contact cassette, as described in Section 4.
12 Insert a length of ground bar 16.95 mm (0.6677 in) diameter through the cassette, to take the place of the drive spindle. (This diameter corresponds to the maximum diameter across the cams).
13 Using a 3 mm Allen key in the adjusting screw, adjust the points to give the specified clearance (photo).

3.5 Checking the points gap on an ohv engine

3.13 Using an Allen key to adjust the cassette contacts

3.17 Checking the points gap on an ohc engine

14 Refit the contact cassette with reference to Section 4 and check the distributor cap with reference to paragraph 6.
15 Adjust the dwell angle with reference to paragraphs 8 to 10, but use the 3 mm Allen key to make any adjustment.

ohc engines

16 Where the distributor is mounted on the left-hand side of the engine (ie models with power steering and air conditioning), proceed as in paragraphs 1 to 15.
17 Where the distributor is mounted on the rear of the camshaft, access to the contact points is limited and it is therefore suggested that if the points are to be inspected and adjusted using feeler gauges, the distributor be removed. Otherwise proceed as in paragraphs 1 to 10 (photo).

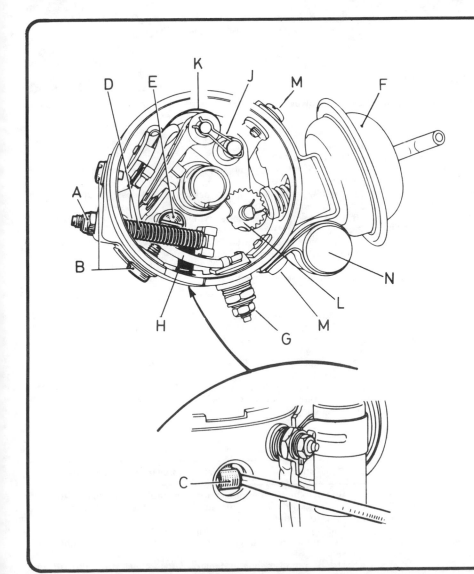

Fig. 4.1 Distributor with conventional contacts (Secs 3 and 4)

A   Adjuster nut
B   Adjuster bracket screws
C   Retaining lug
D   Adjuster spring and rod
E   Fixed contact screw
F   Vacuum capsule
G   LT terminal
H   LT lead
J   Clip
K   Spring blade
L   Serrated cam
M   Vacuum capsule retaining screws
N   Condenser

4.3A Removing the upper bearing plate screws on ohc engines

4.3B Distributor components on an ohc engine

1	Moving contact	3	Retaining screw
	pivot	4	Adjuster nut
2	Contact points		

4.15 Removing the condenser support assembly and cassette

4.16A Disconnecting the wiring connector

4.16B Disconnecting the cassette (lower view)

4.16C Distributor with condenser and cassette assembly removed

4 Contact breaker points (conventional system) – removal and refitting

1 On ohc engines with the distributor mounted on the rear of the camshaft remove the distributor, as described in Section 7.
2 Prise back the retaining clips or unscrew the two screws, and lift the cap from the distributor. Remove the rotor arm and dust shield (where fitted).

Conventional contacts

3 On ohc engines, where applicable, remove the screws and lift off the upper bearing plate (photos). Also pull the low tension lead grommet from the distributor body.
4 Remove the adjuster nut (A), see Fig. 4.1.
5 Unscrew screws (2) each side of the adjuster nut , where applicable.
6 Take out the small plug covering retaining lug (C), using a suitable small tool to prise out the lug.
7 Remove adjustment rod and spring (D).
8 Take out screw (E) and remove the fixed contact.
9 Loosen the LT terminal (G), and detach the LT lead (H), where applicable.
10 Free clip (J) from the pivot post and take off the insulating washer. Remove the moving contact whilst keeping the spring blade (K) pressed inwards, thereby releasing it from its mounting.
11 Examine the point faces for a pip on one, for a corresponding pit on the other and for generally poor condition. Where necessary, contacts may be resurfaced using an oil stone, with care being taken to maintain the original contours. However, where the overall condition is poor, or where considerable burning has occurred, they should be renewed.
12 Clean the contact surfaces, whether old or new, with methylated spirit, to ensure complete freedom from greasy deposits.
13 Refit in the reverse order to removal.

Cassette contacts

14 Pull off the electrical connections to the condenser support assembly.
15 Lift the condenser support assembly and cassette upwards and out of the body (photo).
16 Disconnect the cassette wiring connector, and remove the cassette (photos).
17 Fit a new cassette in the reverse order to the removal procedure, ensuring when placing the cassette over the cam that the contact point heel is not in line with the high point of a cam, as this might cause damage to the heel.

Conventional and cassette contacts

18 Adjust the contact breaker gap, as described in Section 3; however, where a new cassette has been fitted the gap is set at manufacture.
19 Refit the dust shield (where applicable), the rotor arm, and the cap. If removed, refit the distributor.
20 Adjust the dwell angle (Section 3) then check and adjust the ignition timing (Section 8). Always adjust the dwell angle *before* the ignition timing.

5 Pulse rotor air gap (transistorized system) – adjustment

1 Remove the distributor cap and dust cap and dust cover. **Note:** on ohc engines with a rear-mounted distributor, the distributor should be removed for better access.
2 Loosen the screws indicated in Fig. 4.3.
3 Rotate the engine until one of the pulse rotor arms is aligned with the sensor.
4 Using a non-magnetic feeler gauge, check that the air gap

Measuring plug gap. A feeler gauge of the correct size (see ignition system specifications) should have a slight 'drag' when slid between the electrodes. Adjust gap if necessary

Adjusting plug gap. The plug gap is adjusted by bending the earth electrode inwards, or outwards, as necessary until the correct clearance is obtained. Note the use of the correct tool

Normal. Grey-brown deposits, lightly coated core nose. Gap increasing by around 0.001 in (0.025 mm) per 1000 miles (1600 km). Plugs ideally suited to engine, and engine in good condition

Carbon fouling. Dry, black, sooty deposits. Will cause weak spark and eventually misfire. Fault: over-rich fuel mixture. Check: carburettor mixture settings, float level and jet sizes; choke operation and cleanliness of air filter. Plugs can be re-used after cleaning

Oil fouling. Wet, oily deposits. Will cause weak spark and eventually misfire. Fault: worn bores/piston rings or valve guides; sometimes occurs (temporarily) during running-in period. Plugs can be re-used after thorough cleaning

Overheating. Electrodes have glazed appearance, core nose very white – few deposits. Fault: plug overheating. Check: plug value, ignition timing, fuel octane rating (too low) and fuel mixture (too weak). Discard plugs and cure fault immediately

Electrode damage. Electrodes burned away; core nose has burned, glazed appearance. Fault: pre-ignition. Check: as for 'Overheating' but may be more severe. Discard plugs and remedy fault before piston or valve damage occurs

Split core nose (may appear initially as a crack). Damage is self-evident, but cracks will only show after cleaning. Fault: pre-ignition or wrong gap-setting technique. Check: ignition timing, cooling system, fuel octane rating (too low) and fuel mixture (too weak). Discard plugs, rectify fault immediately

between the pulse rotor arm and sensor is as given in the Specifications.
5   Adjust the base until the gap is correct, then tighten the screws.
6   Rotate the engine and check the gap is correct for the remaining pulse rotor arms.
7   Refit the distributor cap and, where applicable, the distributor.

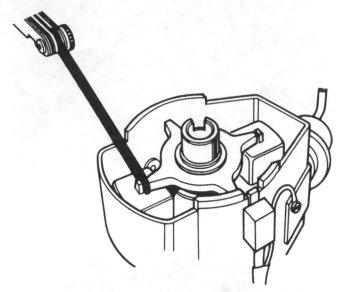

Fig. 4.4 Checking the pulse rotor air gap (Sec 5)

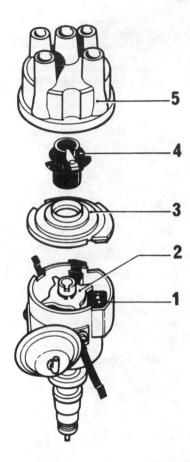

Fig. 4.2 Transistorized ignition distributor components (Sec 5)

1	Sensor coil (two on some models)	3	Dust cover
2	Pulse rotor	4	Rotor arm
		5	Cap

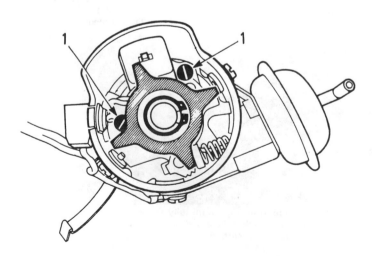

Fig. 4.3 Sensor coil base screws (1) (Sec 5)

6   Condenser (conventional system) – removal and refitting

1   Failure to start, misfiring, or excessive burning or pitting of the contact breaker point faces, can be caused by a failed condenser.

Conventional contacts
2   To remove the condenser, disconnect the wire at the terminal post, and remove the condenser mounting screw.
3   Remove the condenser, and fit a new part.

Cassette contacts
4   Remove the condenser support/cassette assembly (see Section 4), and disconnect the cassette.
5   Push out the condenser form the support (photo).
6   Fit a new condenser, and reassemble in the reverse order to the dismantling procedure.

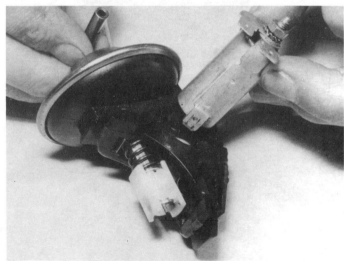

6.5 Removing the condenser from the support

7   Distributor – removal and refitting

1   Turn the engine to bring No 1 piston (nearest flywheel/driveplate) to TDC on the firing stroke.
2   Remove the distributor cap. Make a mark on the rim of the

7.2A Remove the distributor cap

7.2B Rotor arm alignment marks – arrowed (ohc engine)

7.2C Distributor body alignment marks – arrowed (ohv engine)

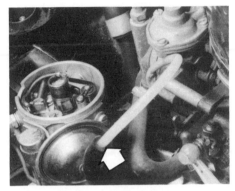

7.4 Disconnect the vacuum hose – arrowed (ohv engine)

7.6A Removing the distributor (ohv engine)

7.6B The distributor (ohc engine) showing offset driving dog

distributor body to show the position of the tip of the rotor arm. Make further alignment marks on the distributor body and on the engine so that the distributor can be refitted in the same position (photos).

3 Disconnect the wiring from the distributor.

4 Disconnect the vacuum hose where fitted (photo).

5 Unscrew the retaining nut or bolt(s), as applicable, and, where fitted, remove the clamp.

6 Remove the distributor from the block or head as applicable (photos).

7 Renew the seal, if necessary.

8 If the crankshaft has been turned since the distributor was removed, turn it to bring No 1 piston to TDC on the firing stroke.

9 To refit the distributor, insert it so that the marks made in paragraph 2 are aligned, then lightly tighten the nut or bolt(s).

10 Reconnect the vacuum hose and wiring, then refit the distributor cap.

11 Check and adjust the ignition timing, as described in Section 8, then tighten the nut or bolt(s).

8 Ignition timing – adjustment

1 In the following paragraphs the initial setting method should be used to start the engine or for emergency roadside repairs; however, the final setting must always be made using a stroboscopic timing light. A diagnostic socket is fitted on the engine on some models for connecting a special Renault instrument in order to check the ignition timing and engine speed, but the instrument will not normally be available to the home mechanic.

Initial setting

2 Remove the No 1 spark plug (flywheel/driveplate end).

3 Turn the engine in the normal running direction (clockwise from front) until pressure is felt in No 1 cylinder, indicating that the piston

is commencing its compression stroke. Use a spanner on the crankshaft pulley bolt.

4 Continue turning the engine until the correct ignition timing marks are aligned in the aperture on the top of the transmission bellhousing. The ignition timing for the engine is on a clip attached to one of the spark plug HT leads but details are also given in the Specifications (photo). On automatic transmission models a hole is provided in the driveplate, and on manual transmission models a slot is provided in the flywheel.

8.4 Ignition timing clip location (ohc engine)

5   Remove the distributor cap and check that the rotor arm is pointing in the direction of the No 1 terminal of the cap. If not, loosen the distributor retaining nut or bolt(s) and turn the distributor as required, then retighten.

6   On conventional ignition models the instant when the contact points open can be checked by connecting a 12 volt test lamp across the points. Turn the distributor body slightly in the direction of the rotor arm rotation so that the points are closed, then, with the ignition on, slowly return the body. The test lamp will light when the points open and, at this instant, the retaining nut or bolt(s) should be tightened.

7   On transistorized ignition models the distributor body must be positioned so that the pulse rotor arm is aligned with the sensor.

8   On the full electronic system models no further check is possible other than that described in paragraph 5.

9   Refit the distributor cap and No 1 spark plug.

Final setting

10 Connect a timing light and tachometer to the engine in accordance with the manufacturer's instructions.

11 Disconnect and plug the vacuum hose at the distributor or electronic module, as applicable.

12 Start the engine and run it at the idle speed given in Chapter 3.

13 Point the timing light at the aperture on the top of the transmission bellhousing and check that the timing marks are correctly aligned (refer to paragraph 4). If adjustment is necessary (not possible on full eelctronic system) loosen the nut or bolt(s) and turn the distributor as necessary. Tighten the nut or bolt(s) when the setting is correct.

14 If the timing marks appear unsteady and will not stay in alignment, this may be due to wear in the distributor, or to wear in the timing gear generally (except on full electronic system).

15 Increasing the engine speed above idle should make the timing marks appear to drift apart as the centrifugal or electronic advance mechanisms come into operation.

16 Applying suction to the vacuum unit should similarly cause the timing marks to move in the direction showing advance.

17 Switch off the engine, reconnect the vacuum hose and remove the tachometer and timing light.

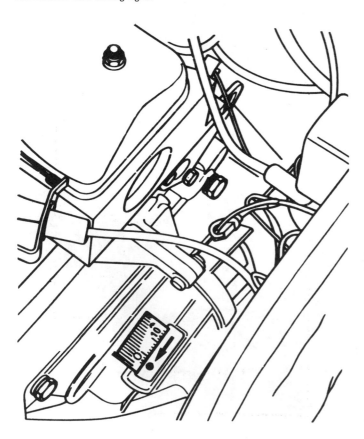

Fig. 4.5 Automatic transmission timing marks (Sec 8)

Fig. 4.6 Manual transmission timing marks (Sec 8)

9   Diagnostic socket – removal and refitting

1   Disconnect the battery earth lead.

2   Remove the diagnostic socket, leaving the supporting plate in place (photo).

9.2 Diagnostic socket location (ohv engine)

3   Remove the socket cover, and disconnect the earth wire, contact breaker wire, and ignition coil wire.

4   Working under the vehicle, remove the sensor retaining screw and withdraw the sensor.

5   If required, the sensor can be disconnected from the socket by removing the wire clamp then using a suitable tube to release the terminals (Fig. 4.7). Note the location of the terminals.

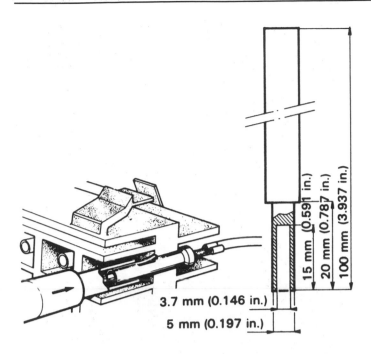

Fig. 4.7 Tube dimensions for releasing the TDC sensor terminals (Sec 9)

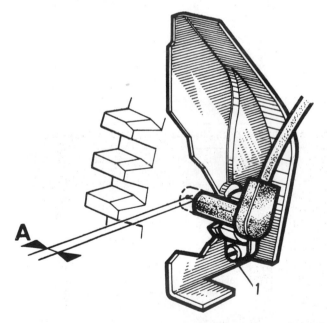

Fig. 4.8 TDC sensor-to-flywheel/driveplate clearance A (Sec 9)

1 Clamp

6 Refitting is a reversal of removal, but adjust the sensor so that the clearance from the flywheel/driveplate is as given in the Specifications. New sensors are provided with three pegs to give the required clearance, but if the old sensor is being refitted, mark the sensor in the fully inserted position then back off by the required amount.

10 Spark plugs, HT leads and distributor cap – general

1 The correct functioning of the spark plugs is vital for the correct running and efficiency of the engine. At the interval given in Section 2 the spark plugs must be cleaned and re-gapped.

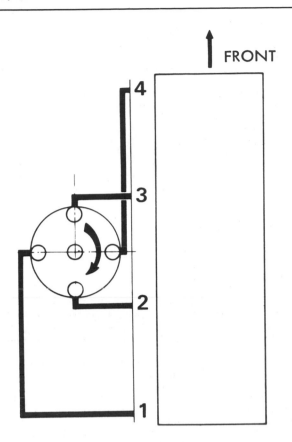

Fig. 4.9 Spark plug HT lead positions on the 847 engine (Sec 10)

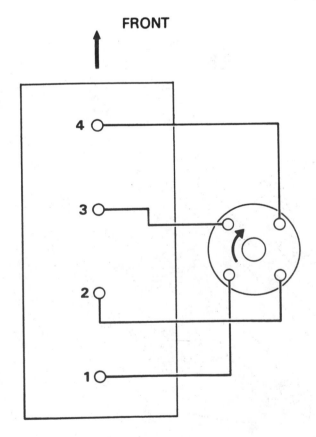

Fig. 4.10 Spark plug HT lead positions on ohv engines except the 847 (Sec 10)

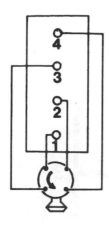

Fig. 4.11 Spark plug HT lead positions on ohc engines (Sec 10)

2   To remove the spark plugs, disconnect the HT leads and identify them for position. Clean any debris from around the spark plugs then unscrew and remove them using a plug spanner, preferably fitted with a rubber insert.

3   The removed spark plug is a good indication of engine condition, particularly as regards the fuel mixture being used and the state of the pistons and cylinder bores. Check each plug as it is possible that one cylinder condition is different from the rest. Plugs come in different types to suit the particular type of engine. A 'hot' plug is for engines which run at lower temperatures than normal and a 'cold' plug is for the hotter running engines. If plugs of the wrong rating are fitted they can either damage the engine or fail to operate properly. Under normal running conditions a correctly rated plug in a properly tuned engine will have a light deposit of brownish colour on the electrodes. A dry black, sooty deposit indicates an over-rich fuel mixture. An oily, blackish deposit indicates worn bores or valve guides. A dry, hard, whitish deposit indicates too weak a fuel mixture. If plugs of the wrong heat ranges are fitted they will have similar symptoms to a weak mixture together with burnt electrodes (plug too hot) or to an over-rich mixture caked somewhat thicker (plug too cold).

4   Clean the plugs, preferably with a sand blasting machine, then set the gaps to the amount given in the Specifications using a feeler gauge (photo). Bend the outer electrodes to make the adjustment.

5   Before fitting the spark plugs, check that the threaded connector sleeves are tight and that the plug exterior surfaces and threads are clean.

6   Screw in the spark plugs, by hand where possible, then tighten

10.4 Adjusting a spark plug gap

them to the specified torque. Take extra care to enter the plugs in the threads correctly as the cylinder head is of aluminium.

7   The HT leads and their connections at both ends should always be clean and dry and, as far as possible, neatly arranged away from each other and nearby metallic parts which could cause shorting. The end connectors should be a firm fit and free from deposits. If any lead shows signs of cracking or chafing of the insulation it should be renewed.

8   Check the distributor cap whenever it is removed. If there are any very thin black lines running between the electrodes this indicates tracking and in this case a new cap should be fitted. Check the rotor arm in a similar way (photo).

10.8 Removing the rotor arm (ohc engine)

11 Fault diagnosis – ignition system

1   If the engine fails to start and the car was running normally when it was last used, first check that there is fuel in the fuel tank. If the engine turns over normally on the starter motor and the battery is evidently well charged first check the HT circuit.

2   One of the commonest reasons for bad starting is wet or damp spark plug leads and distributor cap. Check both items and wipe dry, if necessary.

3   If the engine still fails to start, disconnect an HT lead from any spark plug and hold the end of the cable approximately 5.0mm (0.2 in) away from the cylinder head using well insulated pliers. While an assistant spins the engine on the starter motor check that a regular blue spark occurs. If so the spark plugs are probably the cause of the engine not starting and they should be closed and re-gapped or renewed.

4   If no spark occurs, disconnect the main feed HT lead from the distributor cap and check for a spark as in paragraph 3. If sparks now occur, check the distributor cap, rotor arm, and HT leads, as described in Section 10, and renew them as necessary.

Conventional ignition system

5   Using a 12 volt voltmeter or 12 volt test lamp, test between the low tension wire to the coil (it is marked 15 or +) and earth with the ignition switched on and the points open. No reading indicates a break in the supply from the ignition switch.

6   Test between the low tension coil terminal marked 1 or − and earth. If there is no reading suspect the condenser or coil.

Transistorized ignition system

7   Remove the distributor cap and also hold the coil output HT lead as described in paragraph 3.

8   With the ignition switched on, quickly move a magnet down and

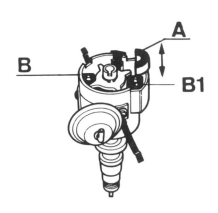

Fig. 4.12 Initial test for transistorized ignition system (Sec 11)

A Magnet   *B and B1 Sensors*

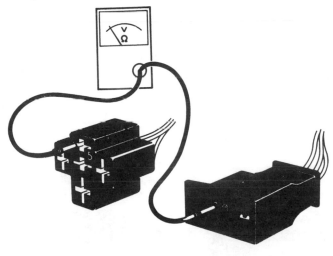

Fig. 4.13 Checking the sensor coil for continuity (Sec 11)

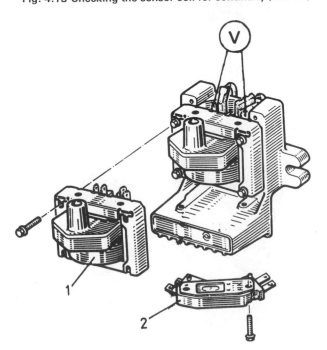

Fig. 4.14 Checking the coil (Sec 11)

1 Coil   *2 Electronic module*

back from the sensor (Fig. 4.12) and check that an HT spark occurs. If not, check the individual components as follows:

9   Connect an ohmmeter across the sensor coil (Fig. 4.13) and check for continuity.

10 Connect the ohmmeter between one of the sensor coil terminals and the distributor body. If the needle moves, the coil is short circuited to earth and should be renewed.

11 Connect a voltmeter as shown in Fig. 4.14 then, with the ignition on, use a magnet as described in paragraph 8. If the voltmeter needle moves, renew the coil, if it remains still renew the electronic module.

12 Disconnect the distributor wiring and connect a TDC sensor to the electronic module (Fig. 4.15). Move a magnet as shown in Fig. 4.15. If a spark occurs, renew the distributor.

13 Note that the spark plug leads should not be disconnected with the engine running, otherwise the rotor arm may be damaged.

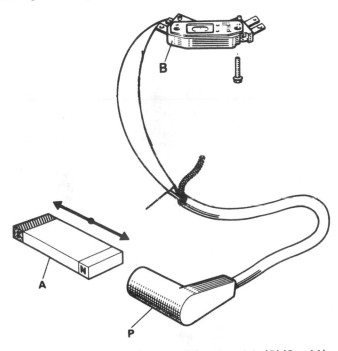

Fig. 4.15 Checking TDC sensor (P) and module (B) (Sec 11)

A Magnet

Fully electronic ignition system

14 First check that all the wiring and connectors are intact and correctly fitted.

15 Refer to Fig. 4.16. With the ignition on, check that there is 9.5 volts at terminal 7.

16 Disconnect A, switch on the ignition and spin the engine on the starter. There should be 9.5 volts at terminal 1. If not, check the battery.

17 With the ignition off, connect an ohmmeter between terminal 2 and earth. If the needle moves, check the module earth.

18 Connect the ohmmeter between terminals 9 and 11. If the needle moves renew the module.

19 Reconnect A and switch on the ignition. Connect a voltmeter between terminal 9 and earth. If 9.5 volts is not recorded move the connector to check for bad contacts.

20 Disconnect B and switch off the ignition. Connect the ohmmeter between terminals 4 and 5. If 100 to 200 ohms is not recorded renew the sensor.

21 Connect the ohmmeter between terminals 5 and 6. If infinity is not recorded, renew the sensor.

22 Connect the ohmmeter between terminals 4 and 6. If infinity is not recorded, renew the sensor.

23 Check that the sensor-to-flywheel/driveplate clearance is 1.0 mm (0.04 in).

24 Connect A and B and connect a test lamp between wires 9 and 10 (disconnected). If the test lamp does not flicker when spinning the engine on the starter, renew the module.

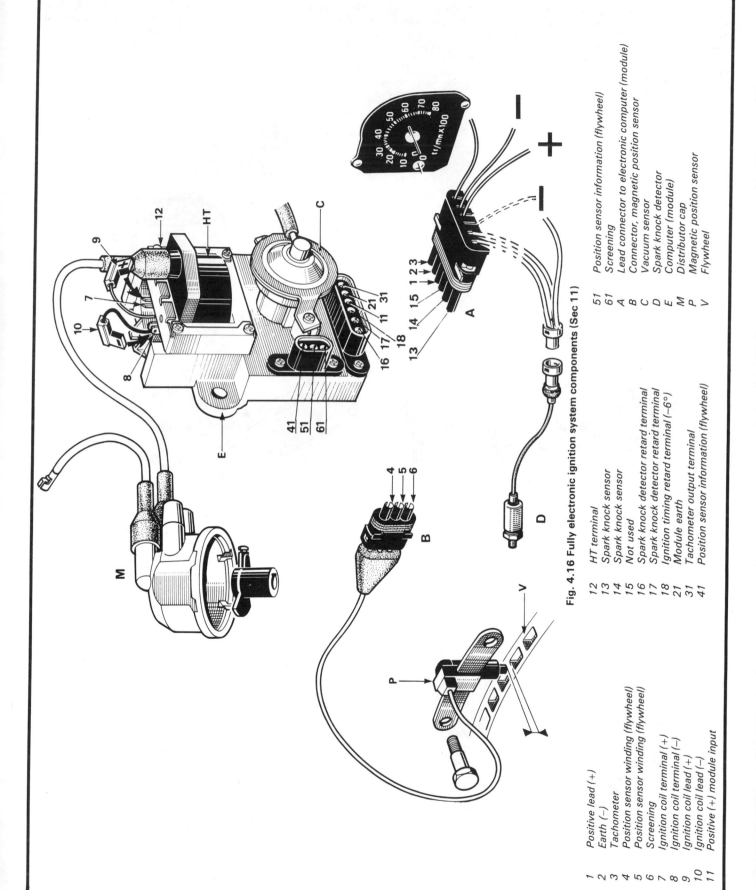

Fig. 4.16 Fully electronic ignition system components (Sec 11)

1   Positive lead (+)
2   Earth (−)
3   Tachometer
4   Position sensor winding (flywheel)
5   Position sensor winding (flywheel)
6   Screening
7   Ignition coil terminal (+)
8   Ignition coil terminal (−)
9   Ignition coil lead (+)
10 Ignition coil lead (−)
11 Positive (+) module input

12 HT terminal
13 Spark knock sensor
14 Spark knock sensor
15 Not used
16 Spark knock detector retard terminal
17 Spark knock detector retard terminal
18 Ignition timing retard terminal (−6°)
21 Module earth
31 Tachometer output terminal
41 Position sensor information (flywheel)

51 Position sensor information (flywheel)
61 Screening
A   Lead connector to electronic computer (module)
B   Connector, magnetic position sensor
C   Vacuum sensor
D   Spark knock detector
E   Computer (module)
M   Distributor cap
P   Magnetic position sensor
V   Flywheel

25 Switch off the ignition and disconnect the HT lead from the coil. Connect an ohmmeter between terminals 7 and 12. If the resistance is not between 2500 and 5500 ohms, renew the coil.

26 Disconnect wires 9 and 10. Connect the ohmmeter between terminals 7 and 8. If the resistance is not between 0.4 and 0.8 ohm, renew the coil.

27 If there is still no HT voltage, renew the module.

28 Run the engine at 3000 rpm then disconnect the vacuum hose at the module. The engine speed should drop. If not, check the hose condition; but if this is good, renew the module.

29 Connect a timing light and run the engine at idling speed. Using a soft metal object tap **near** the spark knock detector repeatedly. Do not tap directly on the detector. While tapping, the timing should retard by 6 degrees. If not, renew the detector.

Chapter 5 Clutch

For modifications, and information applicable to later models, see Supplement at end of manual

Contents

Specifications

Type .... Single dry plate, with diaphragm spring pressure plate, cable-operated

Friction plate diameter .... 181.5 mm (7.15 in)
200.0 mm (7.88 in) or
215.0 mm (8.47 in)

Torque wrench settings

	lbf ft	Nm
Pressure plate	37	50

1 General description

A cable-operated clutch is employed, with an adjustable cable which permits wear to be taken up.

The clutch pedal pivots on the same shaft as the brake pedal. The release arm activates a thrust bearing (clutch release bearing) which bears on the diaphragm spring of the pressure plate. The diaphragm then releases or engages the clutch friction plate which is splined onto the gearbox primary shaft. The clutch friction plate (disc) spins in between the clutch pressure plate and the flywheel face when it is released, and is held there when engaged, to connect the drive from the engine to the transmission unit.

2 Clutch – removal, inspection and refitting

Removal

1 Remove the gearbox, as described in Chapter 6.
2 Mark the position of the clutch cover in relation to the flywheel. Remove the cover bolts and lift the cover away (photo).
3 As the cover is lifted away collect the friction plate (photo).

Inspection

4 Examine the friction plate linings for wear and loose rivets. Check the disc for distortion, cracks, broken hub springs or worn splines in its hub. The surface of the linings may be highly glazed but provided the woven pattern of the friction material can be clearly seen, then the plate is serviceable. Any signs of oil staining will necessitate renewal of the friction plate and investigation and rectification of the oil leak (probably crankshaft rear main bearing and seals) being required.
5 Check the amount of wear which has taken place on the friction linings and, if they are worn level with or within 1.6 mm (0.063 in) of the heads of the securing rivets, the friction plate should be renewed as an assembly. Do not attempt to re-line it yourself as it is rarely successful.
6 Examine the machined faces of the flywheel and the pressure plate and if scored or grooved, renew both components on a factory exchange basis.

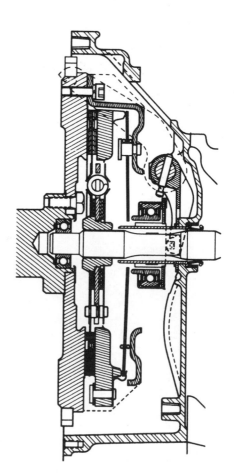

Fig. 5.1 Cross-section of the clutch components (Sec 1)

2.2 Removing the clutch cover bolts

2.13 Aligning the friction plate using an old gearbox primary shaft

2.3 Removing the clutch cover and friction plate

7   Check the segments of the pressure plate diaphragm spring for cracks and renew the assembly if apparent.

8   Where clutch engagement has been fierce, or clutch slip has occurred in spite of the friction plate being in good condition, renew the pressure plate assembly complete.

9   Examine the release bearing and mechanism (see Sections 3 and 4). Renew the bearing as a matter of course unless it is known to be virtually new.

10   Ensure that all frictional surfaces are clean and free from greasy deposits. Clean the contact faces of the flywheel and clutch cover.

Refitting

11   Offer up the friction plate to the flywheel, with the damper plate and springs facing towards the gearbox.

12   Offer up the cover plate assembly, lining up the marks made when dismantling. Refit the cover plate bolts, but leave them just finger tight.

13   Align the centre of the friction plate with the centre of the crankshaft using a proprietary alignment tool, old gearbox primary shaft (photo) or wooden dowel rod. On early models the gearbox input shaft locates in a spigot bearing in the end of the crankshaft, but later models do not have this bearing and the shaft is correspondingly shorter. However, even on the later models, the friction plate must be

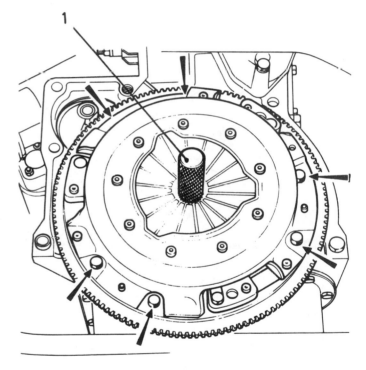

Fig. 5.2 Friction plate alignment using special tool (1) (Sec 2)

Arrows indicate cover plate bolts

centralised to ensure that the gearbox will engage the locating dowels on the cylinder block.

14   Tighten the cover plate bolts progressively, and in a diametrically opposite sequence, to avoid distortion of the cover.

15   **Very lightly** lubricate the release bearing surface on the clutch cover spring.

16   Refit the gearbox to the engine, with reference to Chapter 6.

17   Adjust the clutch cable, as described in Section 5.

3   Clutch release bearing – removal and refitting

1   Remove the gearbox, as described in Chapter 6.

2   On all but 829 and J6R engine models release the spring ends and

3.2A Release the spring ends ...

3.2B ... and withdraw the release bearing

3.2C The release bearing on 829 and J6R engine models

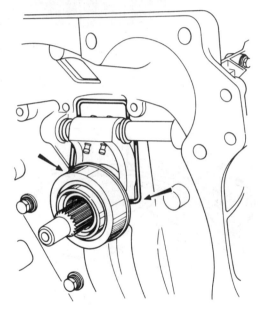
Fig. 5.3 Release bearing spring end location points (Sec 3)

withdraw the release bearing (photos). On 829 and J6R models disconnect the release arm then withdraw the release bearing (photo).
3   To refit, lubricate the location sleeve and the fork/arm bearing surfaces with a suitable grease.
4   Fit the bearing on the sleeve and reconnect the spring or arm, as applicable.
5   Proceed as described in Section 2, paragraphs 15 to 17.

4   Clutch release fork/arm – removal and refitting

1   Proceed as described in Section 3, paragraphs 1 and 2.

829 and JGR engine models
2   Slacken the cable adjustment nut, remove the pushrod and clip, then pull the rubber grommet from the bellhousing aperture (photos).
3   Note how the spring clip on the release arm is attached to the ball pivot, then slide the release arm away and withdraw it.
4   Lubricate the ball pivot with grease then refit the release arm, making sure that the pivot fully enters the recess and is retained by the spring ends.
5   Refit the rubber grommet.
6   Refit the release bearing, with reference to Section 3.

Except 829 and JGR engine models
7   Pull out the pins securing the fork to the shaft, if necessary using an extractor tool obtained from a tool hire agent (photo). A slide hammer with a suitable adaptor to fit on the pins may also be used as an alternative.
8   Pull out the fork shaft, and withdraw the fork and spring.
9   To refit, lubricate the shaft with a suitable grease. Place the fork and spring in position, and insert the shaft together with the rubber seal.
10 Refit the pins, ensuring that dimension D in Fig. 5.5 is as indicated.
11 Refit the release bearing, with reference to Section 3.

5   Clutch cable – adjustment, removal and refitting

Cable adjustment
1   Refer to Fig. 5.7. Maintain hand pressure on lever L in the direction of arrow A, thereby ensuring that the release bearing is in contact with the diaphragm spring.

4.2A Removing the rubber grommet from the release arm on 829 and J6R engine models

4.2B View of the release arm (arrowed) and bellhousing aperture on 829 and J6R engine models

4.7 Clutch release fork on non-829/J6R engine models

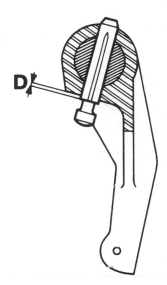

Fig. 5.4 Renault tool EMB 384 for removing the release fork pins (Sec 4)

Fig. 5.5 Release fork pin installation dimension (Sec 4)

D = 1.0 mm (0.04 in)

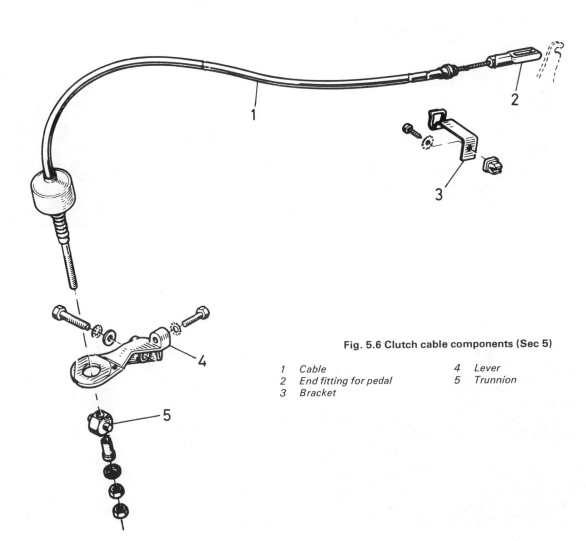

Fig. 5.6 Clutch cable components (Sec 5)

1 Cable
2 End fitting for pedal
3 Bracket
4 Lever
5 Trunnion

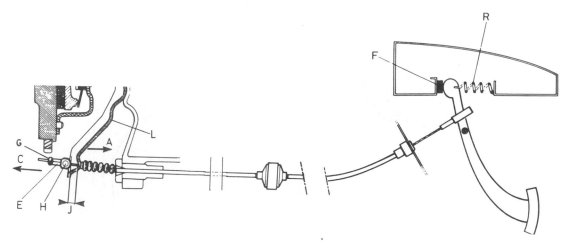

Fig. 5.7 Clutch cable and release mechanism (diagrammatic representation) (Sec 5)

E Adjuster nut   G Adjuster nut locknut   L Clutch housing operating   R Return spring
F Stop pad   H Trunnion   lever   For A, C and J, see text

5.3 Cable adjustment nut on 829 and J6R engine models (arrowed)

5.6B Clutch cable bracket on the valve cover

5.6A Bracket and clip at gearbox end of clutch cable

2   Release locknut G, and screw nut E in or out as necessary until clearance J is 2.5 mm (0.10 in), when the cable is pulled by hand pressure in direction C.

3   Lock nut G against nut E (photo).

Cable removal and refitting

4   Remove the nuts and trunnion from the cable at the gearbox end.

5   Disconnect the cable at the pedal end.

6   Remove the cable from the clips and bracket (photos).

7   To refit, reverse the removal procedure.

8   Adjust the cable as described in paragraphs 1 to 3.

6   Clutch pedal – removal and refitting

1   The clutch and brake pedals operate on a common cross-shaft.

2   To remove the pedals, disconnect the pedal return spring and prise the clips from each end of the shaft.

3   Disconnect the clutch cable and the pushrod from the pedals.

4   Slide off the clutch pedal then tap the shaft from the bracket and withdraw the brake pedal.

5   Refitting is a reversal of removal, but lubricate the shaft with a little grease and finally check the cable adjustment, as described in Section 5.

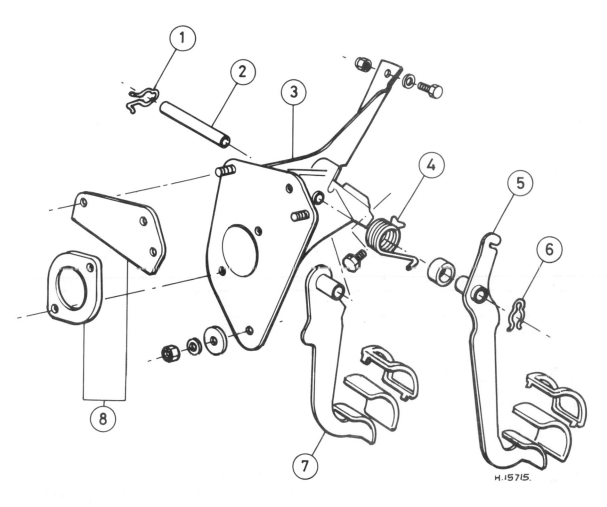

Fig. 5.8 Clutch and brake pedal components (Sec 6)

1	Clip	3	Bracket	5	Clutch pedal	7	Brake pedal
2	Shaft	4	Return spring	6	Clip	8	Gaskets

---

7   Fault diagnosis – clutch

Symptom	Reason(s)
Judder when taking up drive	Loose engine/gearbox mountings or over-flexible mountings Badly worn friction surfaces or friction plate contamination with oil deposit Worn splines in the friction plate hub or on the gearbox input shaft
Clutch drag (or failure to disengage) so that gears cannot be meshed	Clutch actuating cable clearance too great Clutch friction disc sticking because of rust on splines (usually apparent after standing idle for some length of time) Damaged or misaligned pressure plate assembly Incorrect release bearing fitted
Clutch slip – (increase in engine speed does not result in increase in car speed – especially on hills)	Clutch actuating cable clearance from fork too small resulting in partially disengaged clutch at all times Clutch friction surfaces worn out (beyond further adjustment of operating cable) or clutch surfaces oil soaked

Chapter 6 Manual gearbox and final drive

For modifications, and information applicable to later models, see Supplement at end of manual

Contents

Specifications

Type	Four or five forward speeds and reverse; synchromesh on all forward speeds

Codes

Four-speed	352 and NG0
Five-speed	395, NG1 and NG3

Ratios

	352	395	NG0	NG1	NG3
1st	3.82:1	3.82:1	3.82:1 or 4.09:1	3.82:1 or 4.09:1	3.82:1 or 4.09:1
2nd	2.24:1	2.24:1	2.18:1	2.18:1	2.18:1
3rd	1.48:1	1.48:1	1.41:1	1.41:1	1.41:1
4th	0.97:1	1.04:1	0.97:1 or 1.03:1	0.97:1 or 1.03:1	1.03:1 or 0.97:1
5th	–	0.86:1	–	0.86:1 or 0.78:1	0.86:1 or 0.78:1
Reverse	3.08:1	3.08:1	3.08:1 or 3.55:1	3.08:1 or 3.55:1	3.08:1 or 3.55:1
Final drive	3.78:1	3.78:1	3.78:1 or 3.56:1	3.78:1 or 3.56:1 3.45:1 or 4.13:1	3.78:1
Speedometer drive	3.4:1	3.4:1	3.40:1 or 3.33:1 or 3.20:1	3.40:1 or 3.33:1 or 3.20:1 or 3.17:1 or 3.60:1	3.33:1

Setting-up limits

Backlash – crownwheel and pinion	0.12 to 0.25 mm (0.0047 to 0.0099 in)
Preload – differential bearings:	
Re-used bearings	No play, but free to turn
New bearings	7 to 22 lbf ft (10 to 30 Nm)
Differential pinion protrusion (types 352 and 395)	59.0 mm (2.325 in)
Primary shaft endplay (types 352 and NG0)	0.02 to 0.12 mm (0.0008 to 0.005 in)

Torque wrench settings

	lbf ft	Nm
Half-casing bolts:		
7 mm	15 to 19	20 to 26
8 mm	22	30
Rear cover bolts	9	12
Clutch housing bolts:		
8 mm	18	24
10 mm	26	35
Reverse selector bolt	18	24
Speedometer worm/nut	75 to 90	102 to 122
Primary shaft nut (395, NG1 and NG3)	75 to 90	102 to 122
Differential ring nut lock bolt	18	24

1 General description

The gearbox is of four- or five-speed type. The design of both types is similar, with an aluminium gearcase in four sections, namely the clutch housing, the right- and left-hand housings (housing the main gear assemblies and also the differential unit), and the rear cover unit (containing the selector control shaft and selector finger). On the five-speed gearbox, the rear cover also houses the fifth gear and its synchromesh assembly. All forward gears are fitted with synchromesh. Drive to the gears from the flywheel and clutch unit is via the clutch shaft, which is engaged with the primary shaft splines. The clutch shaft passes through the differential compartment. The primary shaft transmits motion via the respective gears to the pinion (secondary) shaft. The reverse idler gear is located on a separate shaft in the rear of the main casing.

Motion is transmitted when a particular gear is engaged; transferring the drive from the primary to the secondary shaft, which in turn drives the differential unit and consequently the driveshafts.

The gear selector forks and shafts are located in the side of the gear casing and are actuated by the selector rod mechanism located in the rear casing. The selector forks are in constant engagement with the synchro sliding hubs which move to and fro accordingly to engage the gear selected.

The speedometer drivegear is attached to the end of the secondary shaft, and this in turn drives the drivegear unit to which the drive cable is attached. Both the speedometer cable and the driven gear unit can be removed with the gearbox in place.

On the five-speed gearbox, work upon the 5th gear and associated parts is feasible with the unit in place in the vehicle, by first removing the rear cover. All other gear assemblies, and the differential unit, are accessible only with the unit removed from the car.

Although the transmission unit is basically simple in operation, certain dismantling, adjustment and reassembly operations require the use of specialised tools. Therefore, if you are contemplating overhauling the gearbox it is essential that you read through the relevant sections concerning your gearbox before starting any work.

Another point to consider is the availability of parts. You will not know what you require until the casing sections are separated. At this stage an assessment should be made of the work required and parts that will be needed. In some instances, certain items are only supplied as complete assemblies, and in many cases the simplest course of

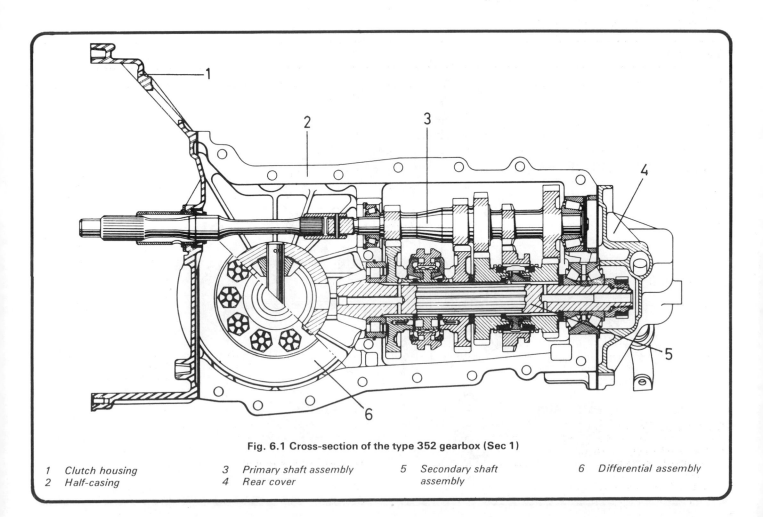

Fig. 6.1 Cross-section of the type 352 gearbox (Sec 1)

1	Clutch housing	3	Primary shaft assembly	5	Secondary shaft assembly	6	Differential assembly
2	Half-casing	4	Rear cover				

NG1   NG3

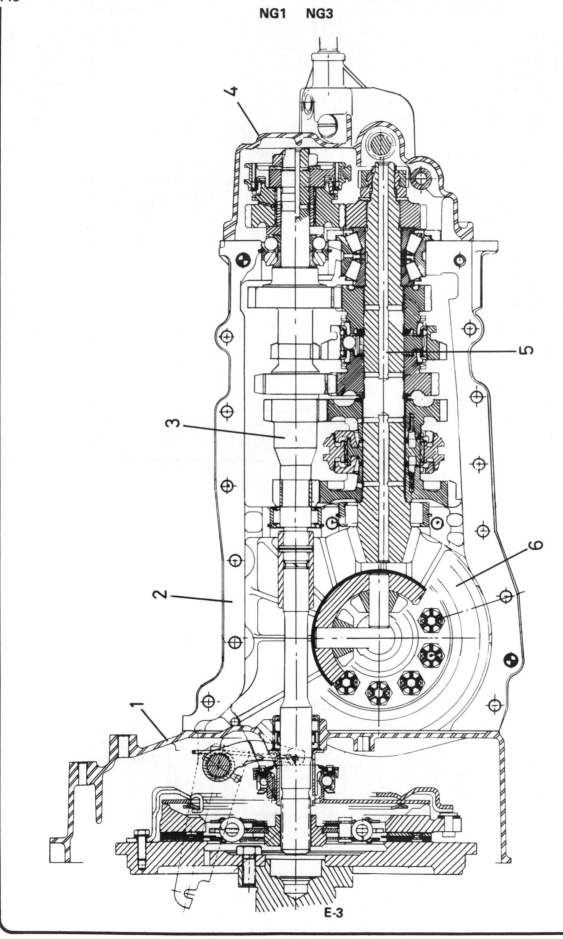

E-3

Fig. 6.2 Cross-section of the type NG1/NG3 gearbox (Sec 1)

1   Clutch housing
2   Half-casing

3   Primary shaft assembly
4   Rear cover

5   Secondary shaft assembly
6   Differential assembly

action is to reassemble the casings and get an exchange unit – usually the most satisfactory and economical solution.

The gearbox is identified by a plate attached under one of the rear end cover bolts (photo). The plate carries details of the type, and also the suffix and fabrication numbers.

1.1 Gearbox identification plate

2 Gearbox – removal and refitting

Note: *The gearbox may be removed either together with the engine or separately; leaving the engine in the car. Refer to Chapter 1 if it is to be removed with the engine.*

1   Disconnect the battery negative lead.
2   Jack up the front of the car and support on axle stands. Apply the handbrake.
3   Remove the starter motor, as described in Chapter 1.
4   Disconnect the wiring from the reversing light switch and emission control switches, as applicable.
5   Disconnect the clutch cable at the lower end, with reference to Chapter 5.
6   Remove the driveshafts, as described in Chapter 8. Alternatively the driveshafts can be disconnected at their inboard ends only by supporting the suspension, removing the inner roll pins, then tilting the stub axle carriers outward after disconnecting the steering tie-rod and upper suspension balljoints.
7   Disconnect the speedometer cable.
8   Disconnect the gearshift linkage from the gearbox (see Section 16) (photo).
9   Unbolt the gearbox front cover.
10 Support the gearbox with a trolley jack, then unscrew the rear mounting nuts and bolts and remove the mounting(s) (photo).
11 Unscrew the engine-to-gearbox bolts, noting the location of the brackets.
12 Lower the jack and withdraw the gearbox with the help of an assistant. Do not allow the gearbox to hang on the input shaft.
13 Refitting is a reversal of removal, but note the following: Lubricate the splines on the input shaft with a little high melting-point grease. Centralise the clutch plate if it has been disturbed, with reference to Chapter 5. Refit the driveshafts, with reference to Chapter 8. Adjust the clutch cable, with reference to Chapter 5.

3 Gearbox (type 352) – dismantling

General

1   Drain the oil and remove the reversing light switch (photo).
2   Remove the clutch release bearing (see Chapter 5).
3   Remove the clutch housing bolts, washers and spring washers, noting the correct positions for the bolts of various lengths (12 bolts).

2.8 Unscrewing the balljoint bolt on the early gear linkage

2.10 Gearbox mounting (two side type)

3.1 Removing the reversing light switch

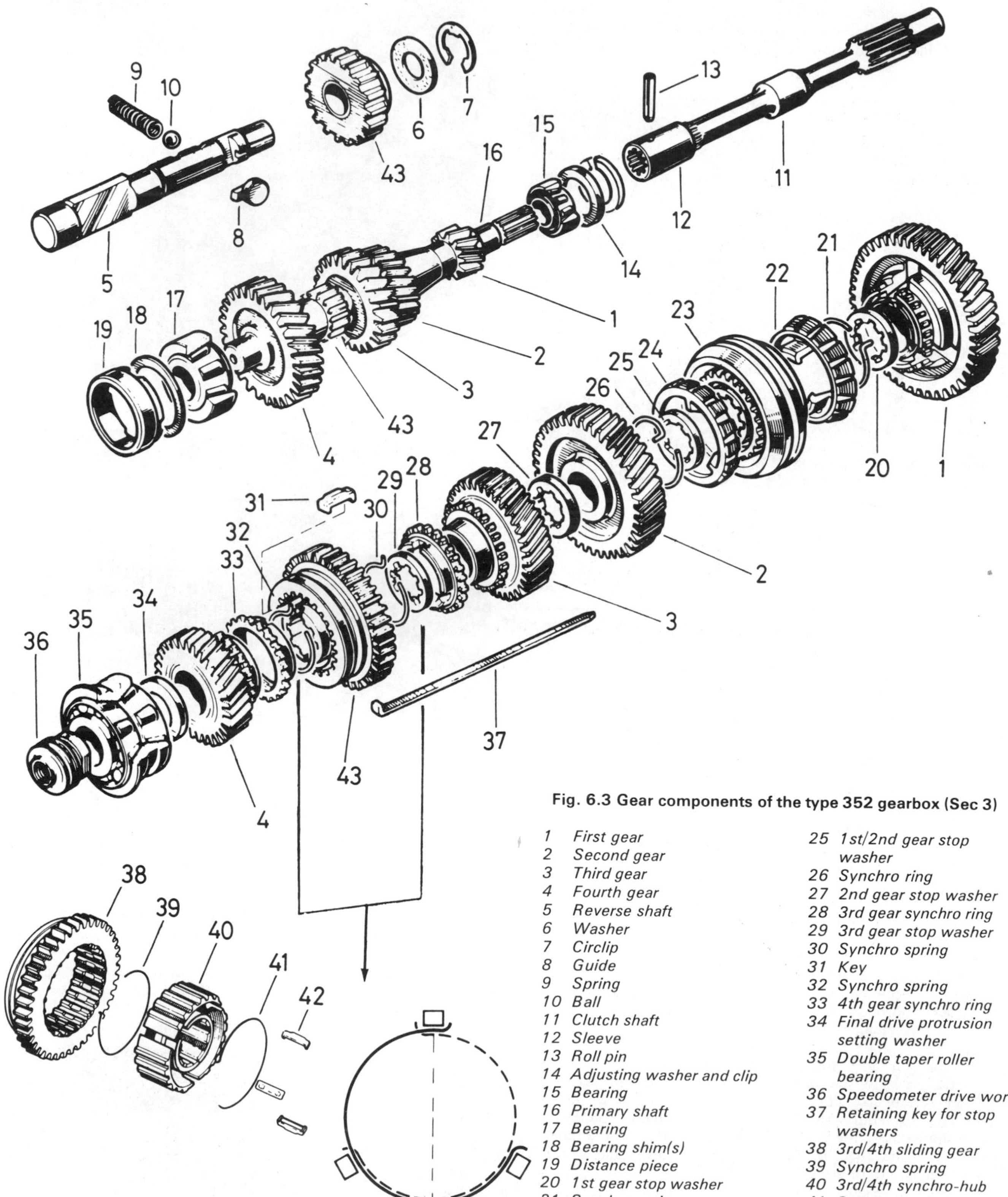

Fig. 6.3 Gear components of the type 352 gearbox (Sec 3)

1   First gear
2   Second gear
3   Third gear
4   Fourth gear
5   Reverse shaft
6   Washer
7   Circlip
8   Guide
9   Spring
10 Ball
11 Clutch shaft
12 Sleeve
13 Roll pin
14 Adjusting washer and clip
15 Bearing
16 Primary shaft
17 Bearing
18 Bearing shim(s)
19 Distance piece
20 1st gear stop washer
21 Synchro spring
22 1st gear synchro ring
23 1st/2nd sliding gear
24 2nd gear synchro ring

25 1st/2nd gear stop
    washer
26 Synchro ring
27 2nd gear stop washer
28 3rd gear synchro ring
29 3rd gear stop washer
30 Synchro spring
31 Key
32 Synchro spring
33 4th gear synchro ring
34 Final drive protrusion
    setting washer
35 Double taper roller
    bearing
36 Speedometer drive worm
37 Retaining key for stop
    washers
38 3rd/4th sliding gear
39 Synchro spring
40 3rd/4th synchro-hub
41 Synchro spring
42 Keys
43 3rd/4th synchro-hub
    and reverse gear
    assembly

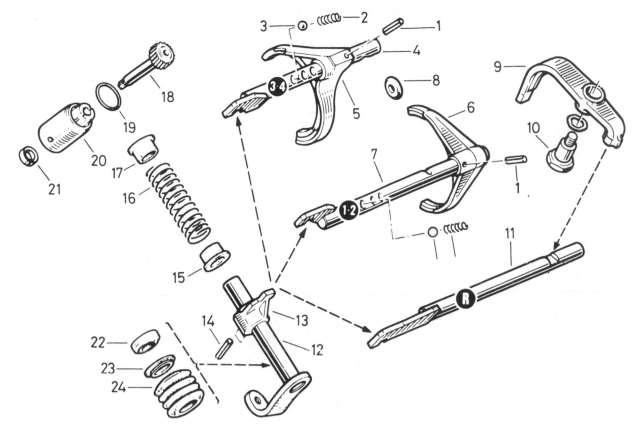

Fig. 6.4 Exploded view of the selector mechanism in the type 352 gearbox (Sec 3)

1	Roll pin	6	1st/2nd gear selector fork
2	Spring	7	1st/2nd gear selector rod
3	Ball	8	Locking disc
4	3rd/4th gear selector rod	9	Reverse selector lever
5	3rd/4th gear selector fork	10	Reverse selector pivot

11	Reverse selector shaft	18	Speedo wheel
12	Control shaft	19	O-ring
13	Selector finger	20	Bush
14	Roll pin	21	Seal
15	Collar	22	Control shaft seal
16	Spring	23	Bellows washer
17	Collar	24	Bellows

4   Remove the clutch housing, and keep the gasket (photo).

5   Remove the 8 bolts securing the rear cover, noting the identification tag under one bolt.

6   Remove the cover, and preserve the gasket (photo).

7   Remove the primary shaft distance piece and bearing shims from under the rear cover (photos).

8   Remove the half casing securing bolts, noting their correct positions.

9   Separate the half-casings, if necessary by gentle use of a soft-headed mallet (photo).

10 Lift out the differential assembly (photo).

11 Lift out the secondary geartrain assembly with the stop peg from the double taper roller bearing cup (photo).

12 Lift out the primary gear shaft assembly (photo).

13 Tap the roll pin from the 3rd/4th gear selector fork, and withdraw the shaft and fork. Catch and keep the ball and spring, and remove the locking disc from between the shafts (photo).

14 With 1st gear selected, take the reverse selector shaft right back to the gearshift control end. Punch out the 1st/2nd selector fork roll pin, remove the shaft and fork, and retain the ball and spring.

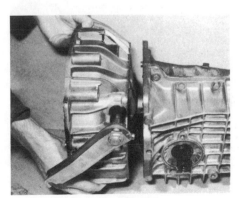

3.4 Removing the clutch housing

3.6 Removing the rear cover

3.7A Primary shaft distance piece

3.7B Primary shaft bearing shim

3.9 Separating the half-casings

3.10 Removing the differential assembly

3.11 Secondary geartrain assembly

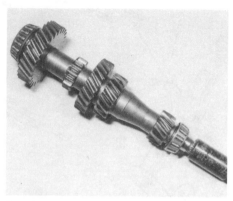
3.12 Primary shaft assembly

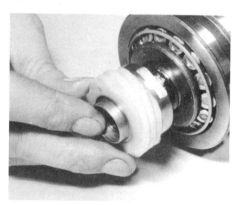
3.13 Selector forks and shafts

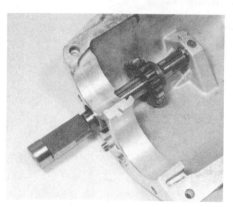
3.16 Removing the reverse gear and shaft

3.18 Primary/clutch shaft sleeve and roll pin

3.20 Removing the speedometer drivegear

3.21A Removing the double taper roller bearing

3.21B Removing the pinion adjusting washer

3.22 Removing the 4th synchro ring

15 Remove the pivot bolt from the reverse selector lever, remove the selector lever, and withdraw the reverse selector shaft.
16 Remove the circlip against the reverse gearwheel, and remove the shaft, gearwheel, washer and sleeve (photo). Recover the ball and spring.

Primary shaft
17 Remove the bearing track rings and associated washers.
18 Support the shaft adequately, and drive out the roll pin, thereby separating the clutch shaft from the primary shaft. Note the spring washer inside the sleeve (photo).
19 Hold the primary shaft in a soft-jawed vice, and pull the bearings from each end of the shaft.

Secondary shaft
20 Hold the shaft by the 1st gear on a soft-jawed vice. Select 1st gear, and unlock the speedometer drivegear using a suitable open-ended spanner. In the absence of such a spanner, we employed a suitable size exhaust clamp on the flats of the gear, gripped and turned by a large open-ended wrench (photo).
21 Withdraw the double taper roller bearing followed by the final drive pinion adjusting washer (photos).
22 Remove the 4th gear and synchromesh ring (photo).
23 Remove the 3rd/4th gear sliding synchromesh unit. Mark the relative position of the gear to the shaft and retain the hub keys.
24 Remove the 3rd/4th synchro-hub by supporting it carefully to prevent damage, and driving the shaft through with a soft-headed mallet.
25 Remove the gearwheel stop washer retaining key (see Fig. 6.5).

3.28 Removing the 1st/2nd sliding gear

3.30 Removing 1st gear

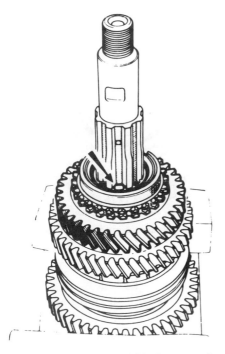

Fig. 6.5 Retaining key for gearwheel stop washers (arrowed) (Sec 3)

26 Remove the 3rd gear stop washer, gear and synchro ring.
27 Remove the 2nd gear stop washer, gear and synchro ring.
28 Mark the position of the 1st/2nd sliding synchro gear in relation to the hub. Remove the gear and stop washer (photo).
29 Remove the 1st/2nd speed synchro-hub, as described in paragraph 24, taking care as this is done not to disturb the front roller bearing outer track.
30 Remove the 1st gear synchro ring, stop washer and gear (photo).
31 The front roller bearing cannot be renewed independently as the inner track is bonded to the final drive pinion. To prevent the rollers and outer track becoming dislodged, fit a suitable retaining clip or clamp over the bearing, as shown in Fig. 6.6.

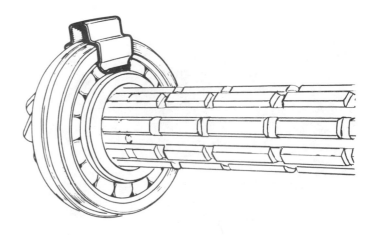

Fig. 6.6 Clip to retain front roller bearing (Sec 3)

Rear cover

32 Tap out the roll pins which secure the control finger, and slide out the shaft. Recover the bushes, spring, finger and bellows (photo).
33 Prise out the shaft oil seal.
34 Remove the speedo drive retaining bolt, and take out the pinion unit and seal.

3.32 Control finger and spring in the rear cover

Differential unit

35 Major dismantling of this unit is not a task for the home mechanic, and it is recommended that the work is either entrusted to a Renault agent, or that an exchange unit be obtained.
36 Renewal of the taper roller bearings is feasible, and these should be drawn from the differential unit using a suitable puller. Hold the unit in a soft-jawed vice, and if necessary remove two diametrically opposed crownwheel holding bolts to permit the legs of the puller to be properly secured.
37 Remove the bearing outer cups from the half gearbox cases, by removing the adjuster rings and seals (after first marking their approximate positions to aid refitting) and then pressing or driving out the cups using a suitable sized piece of tube (photo).

3.37 Differential adjuster rings and seals

4 Gearbox (type 352) – examination and renovation

1 Clean all parts and examine the gears for chipping and obvious wear. Check that all bearings, when cleaned and lightly oiled, are completely smooth in operation.
2 It is advised that all oil seals and gaskets be renewed as a matter of course when the unit is dismantled.
3 Obtain replacements where possible for small items such as roll pins or clips, which may have altered dimensionally when dismantled.

5 Gearbox (type 352) – reassembly

1 With all items properly cleaned, spread them on a clean workbench, using paper or cardboard to provide a grit-free surface.

Secondary shaft

2 Engage the 1st gear synchro spring as shown in Fig. 6.7, ensuring that it contacts the three segments.
3 Slide 1st gear into position on the shaft (against the pinion bearing) and locate the synchro ring. Fit the stop washer and rotate it to align the keyway. A suitable temporary key should now be slid into position down the keyway in the shaft to hold the washer in position during subsequent operations. This 'dummy' key can be fabricated from an old washer retaining key by removing the hooked lug. Ensure that the keyway spline chosen is one with an oil hole, as shown in Fig. 6.8.

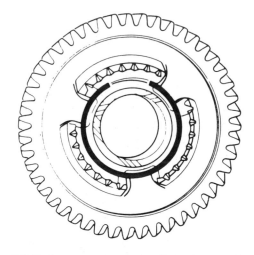

Fig. 6.7 First gear synchro spring fitting location (Sec 5)

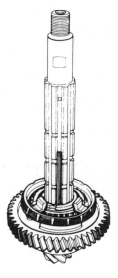

Fig. 6.8 Stop washer 'dummy' key location (Sec 5)

4   Detach the bearing outer race retaining clip.

5   When fitting the 1st/2nd speed synchro-hub, first heat it up to an oven temperature of 120°C (248°F). Leave the hub in the oven at this temperature for about 15 minutes, then assemble it onto the pinion shaft so that an unsplined section is aligned with the dummy key. The matching mark on the hub should be towards the second gear or, if no mark exists, orientation must be as in Fig. 6.9. Press the hub fully into position so that it just comes into contact with the stop washer. As the hub is pressed into position, centralise the synchro ring with the lugs below the stop washer level in order not to damage the spring. Withdraw the dummy key and allow the hub to cool.

6   Next, assemble the synchro-hub sliding gear with the chamfered side facing the 2nd gear and the relative hub match markings in alignment.

7   Locate the stop washer with its splines aligned with those on the shaft (photo).

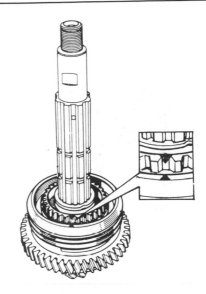

Fig. 6.10 Fitting 1st/2nd synchro unit (Sec 5)

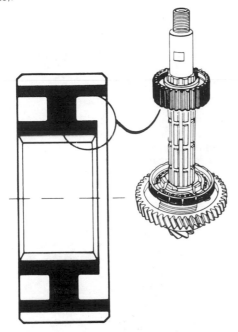

Fig. 6.9 Orientation of 1st/2nd synchro-hub (Sec 5)

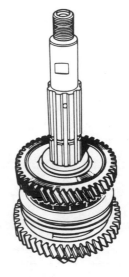

Fig. 6.11 Fitting 2nd gear and stop washer (Sec 5)

5.7 1st/2nd synchro and stop washer

8   Fit the synchro spring to the 2nd gear (in a similar fashion to that for the 1st) and assemble the 2nd gear with synchro ring, as shown in Fig. 6.11. Fit the stop washer and align the splines with those of the shaft (photo).

5.8 Fitting 2nd gear and synchro ring

9   Next, assemble the 3rd gear and synchro ring.
10 Slide the stop washer into position and rotate it to align the splines.
11 Slide the stop washer location key into position down a keyway in the shaft (choose a keyway with an oil hole in it) (photo).

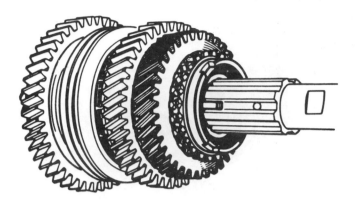

Fig. 6.12 Fitting 3rd gear, synchro ring and stop washer (Sec 5)

5.13 Fitting 4th gear

5.11 3rd gear stop washer and key

12 Press or drive the 3rd/4th synchro-hub into position, so that it is flush against the 3rd gear stop washer. Check when fitting that the notch on the hub is facing the 3rd gear and is aligned with the stop key. The three synchro ring notches must be aligned with the keys.
13 Locate the 4th gear and its synchro ring (photo).
14 Fit the pinion protrusion adjustment washer and double taper roller bearing.
15 Fit the speedometer worm drivegear.
16 Support the shaft assembly vertically in a vice with soft jaws, fastened to the 1st gear. Select the 1st gear to lock the shaft, and tighten the speedometer worm pinion to the specified torque. When tightened, do not lock the nut until the pinion shaft is adjusted on assembly.

Primary shaft
17 Check for cleanliness of the bearings and their mounting areas on the shaft. Support the shaft and fit the bearings at each end using a press, or alternatively use a piece of tube and a hammer. Refit the clutch shaft (reverse of Section 3, paragraph 18).

Final drive pinion protrusion – adjustment
18 The correct positioning of the front face of the final drive pinion in relation to the crown wheel centre is very important (see Fig. 6.13) and must be checked and reset as necessary if the component parts of the secondary shaft have been renewed (other than the bearings which, by virtue of the close limits to which they are manufactured, should not affect the position of the pinion by an acceptable amount).
19 A Renault agent must be requested to carry out this check, as the home mechanic will not have access to the necessary checking tools. The dimension should be corrected, if necessary, by changing the pinion protrusion adjustment washer for another of the appropriate thickness.

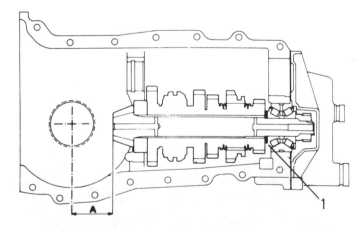

Fig. 6.13 Final drive pinion protrusion adjustment (Sec 5)

A = 59 mm (2.325 in)   1   Adjust washer to suitable thickness

Differential bearings – fitting and adjustment
20 The bearing outer tracks should be carefully pressed or tapped into each half of the gearcase, so that they are slightly below the inner face of the casting.
21 After fitting new bearings, or refitting old ones, place the secondary shaft into the RH half gearcase, fit the differential assembly, and fit the LH half gearcase. Loosely fit the bolts. Fit the rear cover and

gasket, so as to retain the rear secondary shaft bearing in the correct location, and tighten the half-casing bolts in the correct order and to the correct torque figure.

22 Fit the differential ring nuts, but without the oil seals, as they may be damaged by the splines during setting-up. Screw the ring nuts home until they contact the bearing ring tracks.

23 When refitting the old bearings, the differential should be adjusted so that the assembly will revolve smoothly, but without any play. Effect the adjustment by screwing the differential ring nuts in or out as necessary, mark the final positions on the case halves and rings, and remove the rings.

24 When new bearings have been fitted, proceed basically as in paragraph 23. However, in this case a preload is necessary, and the ring nuts should be fitted so that the differential assembly is a little stiff to turn. Check the preload by wrapping a piece of cord round the differential housing, and checking with a spring balance the loading necessary to turn the differential, which should be within the specified limits.

25 If the bearings have not been removed, and providing that the differential ring nuts are marked to ensure correct refitting, then bearing adjustment should not be necessary.

Primary shaft positioning

26 Assemble the bearing rings and adjusting washer to the primary shaft.

27 Fit the primary and secondary shafts into the RH half-casing, and check the steps (R), which must be equal (Fig. 6.16). Correct if necessary by changing the washer (1), using a replacement of the appropriate thickness.

28 Remove the primary and secondary shaft assemblies.

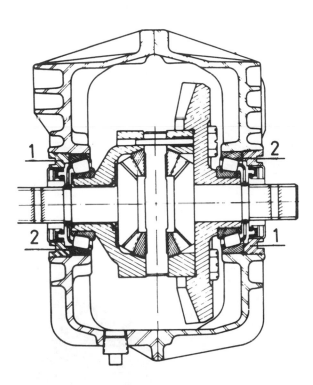

Fig. 6.14 Cross-section of the differential (Sec 5)

1 Ring nuts   2 Bearings

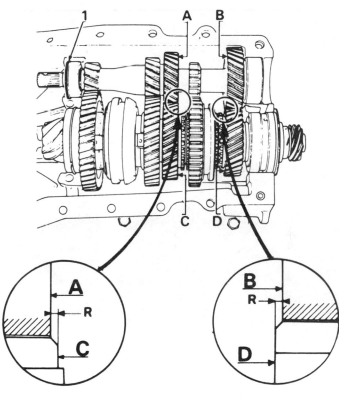

Fig. 6.16 Primary shaft positioning (Sec 5)

1 Adjustment washer

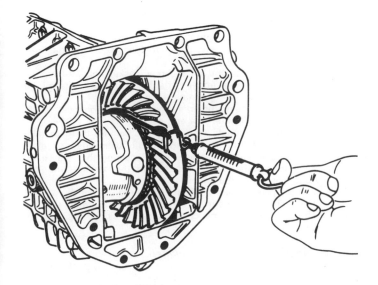

Fig. 6.15 Checking the differential bearing preload (Sec 5)

Roll pin refitting

29 It should be noted that roll pins must always be fitted with the slot towards the rear cover.

Selector forks

30 Slide the reverse gear selector shaft home.

31 Position the reverse gear selector with the end in the slot in the shaft, fit the pivot pin and tighten.

32 Position the 1st/2nd gear spring and ball in the appropriate hole (Fig. 6.17), position the selector fork, slide in the shaft, and roll pin the two together.

33 Position the 3rd/4th gear locking ball and spring and place the locking discs between the shafts. Position the selector fork, slide in the shaft, and roll pin the two together.

Fig. 6.17 Cross-section of the selector shafts in the 352 gearbox (Sec 5)

1　3rd/4th selector shaft and fork
2　1st/2nd selector shaft and fork
3　Reverse selector shaft
4　Reverse selector lever
5　Reverse selector lever pivot
6　Locking disc

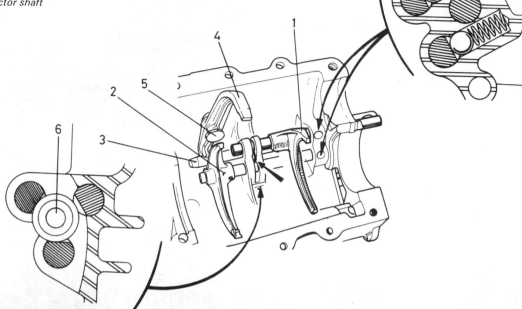

5.34A Reverse gear shaft detent ball

5.34B Reverse gear shaft guide

5.34C Fitting the reverse gear shaft circlip

Reverse gear

34　Position the ball and spring in the LH half gearcase. Start to enter the shaft, position the gearwheel and friction washer (bronze side to gearwheel), fit the guide from inside the bore, and slide the shaft home. Fit the circlip (photos).

Rear cover

35　Fit the oil seal in the cover hole, and position the collars, spring and selector finger internally.
36　Fit the bellows over the shaft, insert the shaft through the case and internal components, and line up the roll pin holes in the shaft and selector finger. Fit new roll pins.

Half-casings

37　Fit the primary shaft, the secondary geartrain and locking peg and differential assembly, into the RH half casing (photo).
38　Smear a non-hardening jointing compound on the half gearcases, offer the LH casing up to the RH casing, and fit the halfcasing bolts without tightening at this stage.
39　Adjust the primary shaft endplay if necessary by fitting the adjusting washers and distance washers, tapping the distance washers lightly to settle the bearings, and fitting the rear cover gasket. Place a straight-edge across the gasket, and measure the clearance between

the distance washer and straight-edge (Fig. 6.19).
40　Change the adjusting washer if the clearance is outside the limits shown. Use as few washers as possible.
41　Smear jointing compound on the rear gasket and offer up the cover, engaging the selector finger in the selector shaft slots. Nip up the securing bolts, without tightening them.
42　Tighten the half-casing bolts in the correct sequence, to the correct torque setting. Tighten the end cover bolts (Fig. 6.20).
43　If the differential ring nuts are still in place, remove them, marking both nuts and gearcase if this has not already been done. Carefully remove the oil seals and fit replacements, ensuring that the seal is flush with the outer surface of the nut. Prise off the external O-ring and fit a new one using only the fingers.
44　Wind a little plastic tape round the splines to protect the oil seal, smear a little jointing compound on the threads of the ring nuts, and screw them home until the marks are correctly aligned. Remove the plastic tape.

Crownwheel and pinion – backlash rechecking

45　Fit a dial gauge to the end of the half-casing with the pointer resting on a crownwheel tooth at the extreme outer edge, but still just on the tooth flank. Check the backlash, which should be within the specified limits (Fig. 6.21).

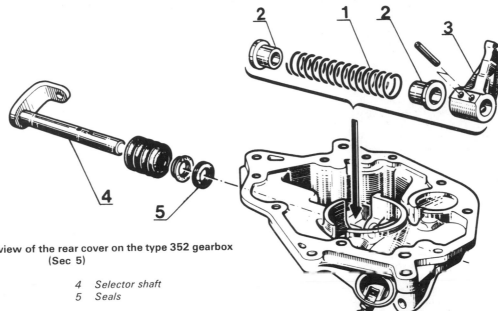

Fig. 6.18 Exploded view of the rear cover on the type 352 gearbox (Sec 5)

1	Spring	4	Selector shaft
2	Bushes	5	Seals
3	Selector finger		

5.37 Right-hand half-casing and gears

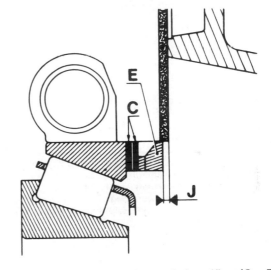

Fig. 6.19 Checking the primary shaft endfloat (Sec 5)

C   Shims   E   Distance piece
J = 0.02 to 0.12 mm (0.0008 to 0.0047 in)

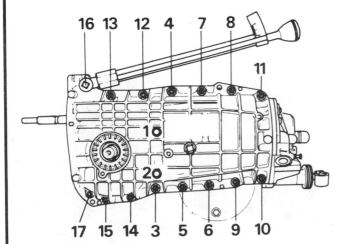

Fig. 6.20 Half-casing bolt tightening sequence on the type 352 gearbox (Sec 5)

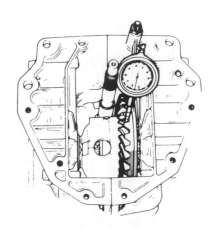

Fig. 6.21 Checking the crownwheel-to-pinion backlash (Sec 5)

46 If backlash is excessive, loosen the ring nut on the differential side a little and screw in that on the crownwheel side by the same amount. If backlash is sufficient, reverse the procedure. Recheck and readjust as necessary.
47 Lock the rings, using the locking plates.

Clutch housing
48 Check the condition of the oil seal, and renew it if there is any doubt about its condition. Carefully drive the seal in using a suitable piece of tube.
49 Wind a little plastic tape onto the splines of the primary shaft to protect the clutch housing oil seal, smear jointing compound on the paper gasket, and fit the gasket and housing. Remove the plastic tape and fit and tighten the housing bolts.
50 Refit the clutch release bearing (see Chapter 5) and the reversing light switch.
51 Fill the unit with oil, but preferably after installation in the vehicle.

6 Rear cover components (type 352) – removal and refitting

1 It is practicable to remove the cover with the gearbox installed for the purpose of changing the selector control shaft oil seal, the selector finger roll pins or the rear cover gasket.
2 Drain the gearbox.
3 Disconnect the speedometer cable.
4 Disconnect the gearchange linkage (see Section 16).
5 Remove the rear cover (see Section 3).
6 Dismantle the rear cover as necessary (see Section 3).
7 Fit new parts as necessary.
8 Check the selector control shaft for any burrs which might damage the new oil seal upon fitting. Remove as necessary, using fine emery cloth.
9 Refitting is the reverse of the removal procedure.

7 TDC pick-up – adjustment

1 If a new pick-up is being fitted, it will automatically be in the correct position by virtue of the three pegs on it. With the pegs touching the flywheel tighten screw (1) (Fig. 6.22).
2 Where an old pick-up with worn pegs is being fitted, first set the pick-up to touch the flywheel, then withdraw it 1.0 mm (0.04 in). Tighten the securing screw.

8 Gearbox (type 395) – dismantling

1 Remove the gearbox and drain the oil.
2 Remove the reversing light switch.
3 Remove the clutch release bearing (see Chapter 5).
4 Unscrew the clutch housing bolts and remove the housing and gasket.
5 At the rear of the unit, remove the 5th speed shaft locking bolt, followed by the spring and ball beneath it (Fig. 6.24).

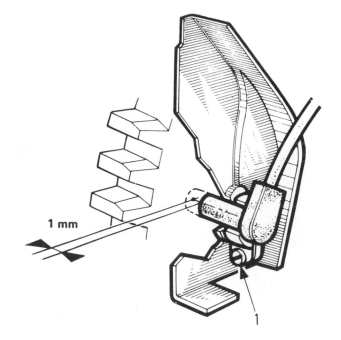

Fig. 6.22 TDC pick-up adjustment (Sec 7)

1   Adjustment screw

6 With neutral selected, remove the bolts from the rear cover. Remove the cover, whilst tilting the selector finger (photo).
7 With 5th and reverse gears selected together, unlock the 5th speed synchro-hub and speedometer drive worm nuts.
8 Select 4th gear.
9 Tap out the roll pin in the 5th gear selector fork, and remove the 5th gear synchro-hub assembly with the fork, the 5th speed gears and the needle bearing and ring.
10 Remove the thrust washer from the secondary shaft, noting that the flanged side is towards the taper roller bearing and the cut-out is located on the 5th speed shaft.
11 Mark the positions of the differential ring nuts, unscrew the locking tabs, and remove the ring nuts. Count and record the number of turns required to unscrew them.
12 Split the casings and remove the geartrains, as described in Section 3, paragraphs 8 to 12.
13 Place the 3rd/4th gear selector shaft in the neutral position, and remove the 5th gear selector shaft. Remove the interlock ball.
14 Proceed as in Section 3, paragraph 13.
15 Remove the reverse selector pivot bolt, remove the selector and pull out the reverse selector shaft (photos).

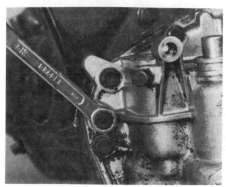

8.6 Removing the rear cover bolts

8.15A Removing the reverse selector pivot bolt

8.15B Pulling out the reverse selector shaft

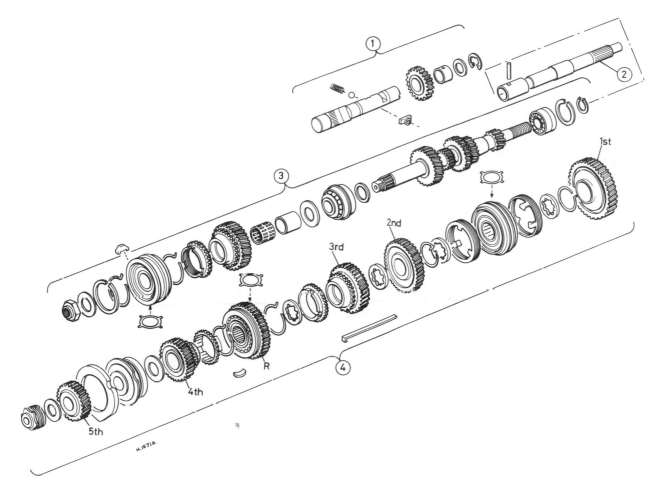

Fig. 6.23 Gear components of the type 395 gearbox (Sec 8)

1   *Reverse gear and shaft*   2   *Clutch shaft*   3   *Primary shaft*   4   *Secondary shaft*

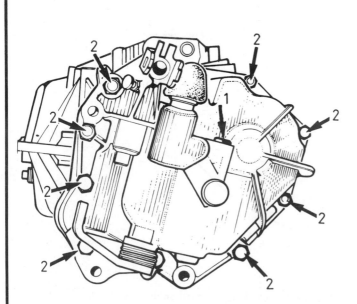

Fig. 6.24 Rear cover bolts on the type 395 gearbox (Sec 8)

1   *5th speed locking bolt*   2   *Rear cover bolts*

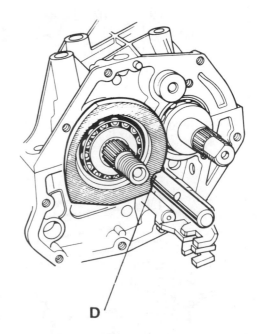

Fig. 6.25 Cut-out (D) on the secondary shaft thrust washer (Sec 8)

Fig. 6.26 Exploded view of the type 395 selector mechanism (Sec 8)

A   Rear cover components   B   Casing components

Fig. 6.27 Rear cover plug (A) and circlip (B) on the type 395
gearbox (Sec 8)

Fig. 6.28 The locking arms (C) on the speedometer gear
(Sec 8)

16 Punch out the roll pin from the 1st/2nd selector fork, remove the shaft and fork, and retain the ball and spring.
17 Remove reverse gear and shaft, as described in Section 3, paragraph 16.
18 If necessary, remove the bearing cups from the half gearbox cases (see Section 3, paragraph 37). Prise out the seals from the differential ring nuts.

Primary shaft

19 Support the shaft adequately and drive out the roll pin to separate the clutch shaft from the primary shaft.
20 Remove the circlip, followed by the bearing outer ring and rollers.
21 Pull the bearings from each end, using a suitable puller. Remove the position adjustment shim.

Secondary shaft

22 Hold the shaft by the 1st gear in a soft-jawed vice, and proceed as described in Section 3, paragraphs 21 to 31.

Differential unit

23 Proceed as described in Section 3, paragraphs 35 to 37.

Rear cover

24 Remove the plug, extract the circlip and withdraw the shaft, bushes and spring after driving out the roll pin.
25 To remove the speedometer gear, use a screwdriver to prise the arms apart then pull out the shaft. Note that the gear must be renewed whenever it is removed.

General

26 The gearbox is now completely dismantled. Reference should be made to Section 4 for the principles of examination and renovation.

9 Gearbox (type 395) – reassembly

Secondary shaft

1   Proceed as described in Section 5, paragraphs 1 to 14 (photo).
2   Support the assembly vertically, by gripping the 1st gear in a soft-jawed vice.
3   Fit the thrust washer, the 5th gear, the wavy washer and speedometer drive worm. Tighten, but do not lock, the worm (see Section 3, paragraph 20).
4   Referring to Fig. 6.29, check the dimension indicated between both the 3rd and 4th speed synchro rings. When checking, the synchro ring must be stuck to the hub cone, and the gear pressed against the hub (photo).

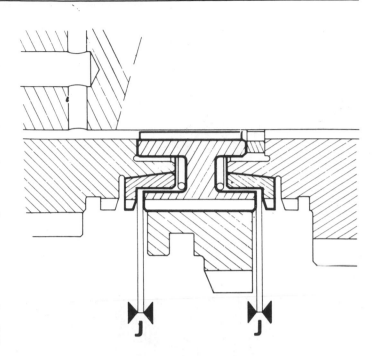

Fig. 6.29 Synchro ring clearance dimensions (Sec 9)

$J = 0.2$ mm (0.008 in)

9.4 Checking the synchro ring wear

Primary shaft

5   Reassemble in reverse of the procedure described in Section 8,, paragraphs 19 to 21.

Final drive pinion protrusion

6   Refer to Section 5, paragraphs 18 and 19.

Differential bearings – fitting and adjustment

7   Proceed as described in Section 5, paragraphs 20 to 25.

Primary shaft positioning

8   Fit the secondary shaft into the RH half gearcase, with the speedometer and worm nut, wavy washer, 5th gear and thrust washer removed.

9.1 Fitting the 1st gear synchro spring

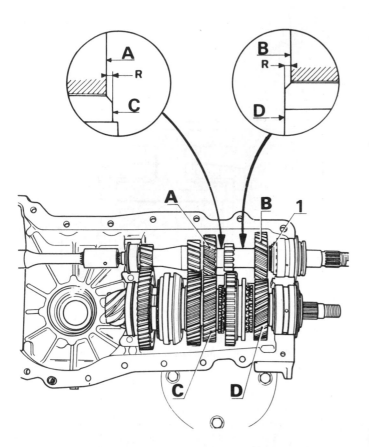

Fig. 6.30 Primary shaft positioning (Sec 9)

1   Adjustment washer

9   Fit the primary shaft and check that steps (R) are equal (Fig. 6.30). If not, adjust by replacing washer (item 1) with a washer of the appropriate thickness.
10   Remove the primary and secondary shaft assemblies.

Selector forks
11   Proceed as described in Section 5 paragraphs 29 to 33 (photos).
12   Fit the 5th speed selector shaft and interlock ball. Select 3rd or 4th gear.

Reverse gear
13   Proceed as described in Section 5, paragraph 34.

Rear cover
14   Insert the speedometer gear shaft through the cover and new gear until the arms lock onto the shaft.
15   Insert the selector shaft, together with the spring and bushes, and fit the circlip.
16   Press the end plug into the casing.

Half casings
17   Proceed as described in Section 5, paragraphs 37 and 38.
18   Tighten the half-casing bolts in the correct order to the specified torque (Fig. 6.31).
19   To the primary shaft, fit the spacer washer, needle bearing with sleeve, and the 5th gear.
20   Assemble together the synchro-hub, sliding gear and fork, and fit them to the primary shaft, followed by the wavy washer and synchro nut.
21   To the secondary shaft, fit the 5th gear, wavy washer and speedometer worm nut.
22   Fit the roll pin to the 5th speed selector fork.
23   Engage both 5th and reverse gears, and tighten the speedo worm

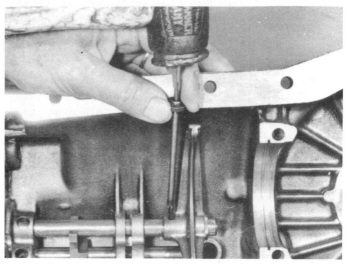

9.11A Driving in 1st/2nd selector fork roll pin

9.11B Tightening the reverse gear selector arm pivot bolt

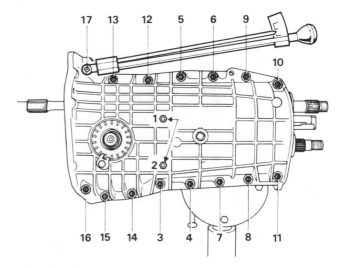

Fig. 6.31 Half-casing bolt tightening sequence on the type 395, NG0, NG1 and NG3 gearboxes (Secs 9 and 13)

nut and primary shaft nuts to the specified torque figures. Lock them both.

24 Referring to Fig. 6.32, push the 5th speed synchro ring hard against the taper and the gear hard against the hub. Check the given dimension.

25 With all gears in neutral, smear the rear cover gasket with jointing compound and fit the cover and gasket with the rocking lever entered into the slot in the shafts. Fit and tighten the cover bolts.

26 Fit the 5th gear locking ball, spring, washer and plug. Use jointing compound on the plug threads.

27 Fit the differential ring nuts, as described in Section 5, paragraphs 43 and 44.

Crownwheel and pinion – backlash checking

28 Proceed as described in Section 5, paragraphs 45 to 47.

Clutch housing

29 Proceed as described in Section 5, paragraphs 48 to 51.

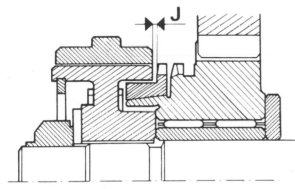

Fig. 6.32 5th synchro ring clearance dimension (Sec 9)

$J = 0.2$ mm (0.008 in)

10 Rear cover components (type 395) – removal and refitting

1 The rear cover can be removed with the gearbox in the car. First raise the car and support on axle stands.

2 Drain the gearbox oil, and remove the gear control linkage and speedometer cable.

3 Proceed as described in paragraphs 5 and 6, Section 8.

4 Dismantle the cover, as described in Section 8, paragraphs 24 and 25.

5 Reassemble as described in Section 9, paragraphs 14 to 16. Ensure that any burrs present on the selector shaft which might damage the new oil seal are removed, using fine emery cloth.

6 Refit all parts in the reverse order of dismantling.

11 Fifth speed synchro (type 395) – removal and refitting

1 The synchro can be removed with the gearbox in the car. First raise the car and support on axle stands.

2 Drain the gearbox oil, and remove the gear control linkage and speedometer cable.

3 Proceed as described in Section 8, paragraphs 5 to 9.

4 When renewing components, note that the hub and sliding gear are matched.

5 To refit; insert the selector fork in the sliding gear. Fit the gear assembled to the primary shaft, fit a new nut, and tighten to the correct torque with 5th and reverse gear engaged. Lock the nut.

6 Fit a new speedo worm nut, tighten to the correct torque, and lock.

7 Fit a new roll pin to the selector fork.

8 Proceed as described in Section 9, paragraphs 24 to 26.

9 Reconnect the control linkage and speedometer cable.

10 Refill the gearbox with oil and lower the car to the ground.

12 Gearbox (types NG0, NG1 and NG3) – dismantling

1 Drain the oil.

2 Unbolt and remove the clutch housing (photos).

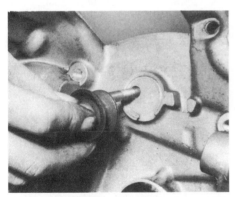

12.2A Removing the clutch release arm pivot bolt

12.2B Inner clutch housing retaining bolts

12.2C Outer clutch housing retaining bolts

12.2D Removing the clutch housing

12.3A Unscrew the 5th selector detent plug ...   12.3B ... and remove the spring

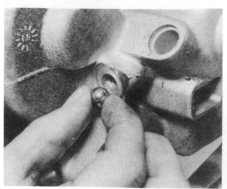

12.3C ... and ball

12.4A Removing the rear casing

12.4B 5th gear components on type NG3 gearbox

3   On NG1 and NG3 types select 3rd or 4th gear to prevent the 5th selector shaft interlock ball falling out. Unscrew the plug and remove the spring and ball for the 5th selector shaft (photos).

4   Unbolt and remove the rear casing. Recover the spacer and shims for the primary shaft bearing on the NG0 type (photos).

5   On NG1 and NG3 types, follow the procedure in Section 8, paragraphs 7 to 10.

6   Split the half-casings with reference to Section 3 paragraphs 8 to 12 (photo).

12.6 Separating the half-casings on type NG3 gearbox

Secondary shaft

7   Grip the shaft in a soft-jawed vice around the 1st gear.

8   Select 1st and unscrew the worm nut. Refer to Section 3, paragraph 20, if necessary.

9   Remove the components with reference to Fig. 6.33. On NG1 and NG3 types a puller will be required to remove the 5th gear.

Primary shaft

10 Drive out the roll pin and separate the clutch shaft from the primary shaft, then remove the small washer.

11 Using a puller, remove the bearings from each end of the shaft as required. Also remove the position adjustment shim.

Differential unit

12 Refer to Section 3, paragraphs 35 to 37.

Reverse shaft

13 Extract the circlip then withdraw the shaft, gear, friction washer and guide.

Gear selector mechanism

14 On the NG0 type, refer to Section 3, paragraphs 13 to 16. On NG1 and NG3 types, refer to Section 8, paragraphs 13 to 18.

Rear cover

15 Refer to Section 8 paragraph 24. Paragraph 25 of the same Section describes the speedometer gear removal on NG1 and NG3 types, but for the NG0 types refer to Section 3 paragraph 34.

16 With the gearbox completely dismantled refer to Section 4 for the examination and renovation procedure.

13 Gearbox (types NG0, NG1 and NG3) – reassembly

Rear cover

1   Press the new oil seal into the cover and reassemble the components in reverse order. To prevent damage to the oil seal, deburr the shaft before inserting it. Smear the threads of the end plug with sealant before tightening it.

Gear selector mechanism

2   Refer to Section 5, paragraphs 29 to 33. On NG1 and NG3 types also refer to Section 9, paragraph 12.

Reverse shaft

3   Refer to Section 5, paragraph 34.

Secondary shaft

4   Refit the components in reverse order, but fit new snap-rings.

5   Fit the synchro-hub with reference to Figs. 6.38 and 6.39. Note that the hubs are free turning on the shaft and it may be necessary to rotate them to find the position where they slide on the easiest.

6   On early NG1 and NG3 types where the 5th gear has full splines, apply locking fluid to the splines before fitting the gear followed by the washer.

7   On later NG1 and NG3 types where the 5th gear has quarter splines, the gear must be pressed on without any locking fluid until the turning torque of the taper bearing in between 11 and 30 lbf ft (15 and 40 Nm). The press loading must be more than 100 kg (220 lb), but less than 1500 kg (3307 lb). Use a spring balance and cord to determine the torque for the bearing preload.

8   Fit the worm nut with locking fluid and tighten to the specified torque with 1st gear engaged.

Primary shaft

9   Press the bearings onto each end of the shaft as required. On early NG1 and NG3 types the 5th synchro-hub must be bonded to the shaft with locking fluid, but on later types the hub is a press fit and must be pressed on with a load of more than 100 kg (280 lb) but less than 1500 kg (3307 lb). Refit the clutch shaft, together with the washer and roll pin.

10 Apply locking fluid to the threads of the end nut before tightening it to the specified torque and locking it.

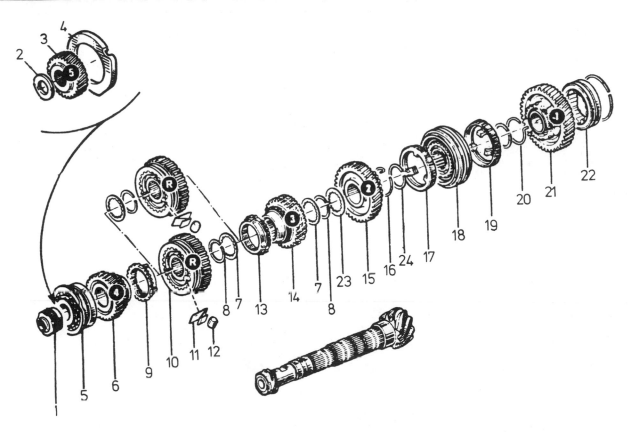

Fig. 6.33 Secondary shaft components for types NG0, NG1 and NG3 gearboxes (Sec 12)

1	Worm/nut	7	Washer	13	Synchro ring	19	Synchro ring
2	Washer	8	Circlip	14	3rd gear	20	Spring
3	5th gear	9	Synchro ring	15	2nd gear	21	1st gear
4	Thrust washer	10	3rd/4th synchro unit	16	Spring	22	Bearing
5	Bearing	11	Spring	17	Synchro ring	23	Washer
6	4th gear	12	Roller	18	1st/2nd synchro unit	24	Circlip

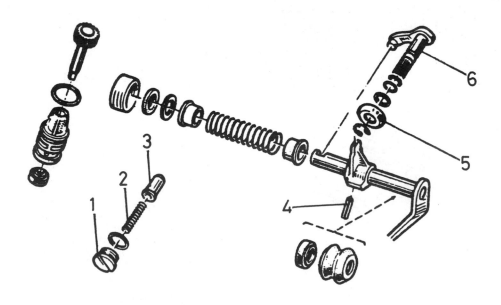

Fig. 6.34 Rear cover components on the type NG0 gearbox (Sec 12)

1	Plug	3	Plunger	5	Seal retainer
2	Spring	4	Roll pin	6	Shaft

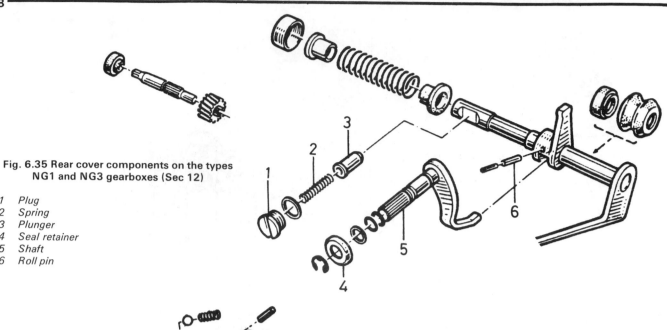

Fig. 6.35 Rear cover components on the types
NG1 and NG3 gearboxes (Sec 12)

1 Plug
2 Spring
3 Plunger
4 Seal retainer
5 Shaft
6 Roll pin

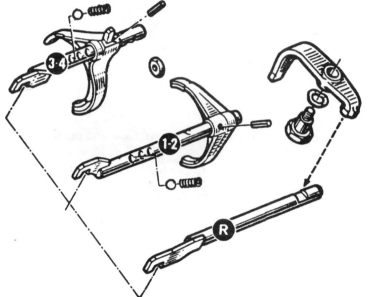

Fig. 6.36 Gear selector components on the type NG0 gearbox (Sec 13)

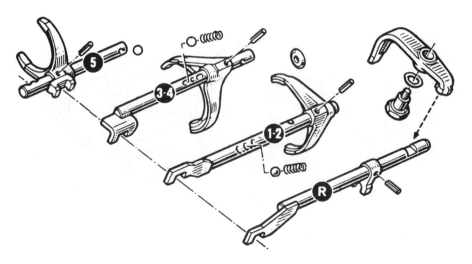

Fig. 6.37 Gear selector components on the types NG1 and NG3 gearboxes (Sec 13)

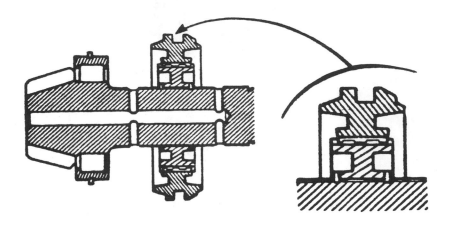

Fig. 6.38 Correct fitting for 1st/2nd synchro hub (Sec 13)

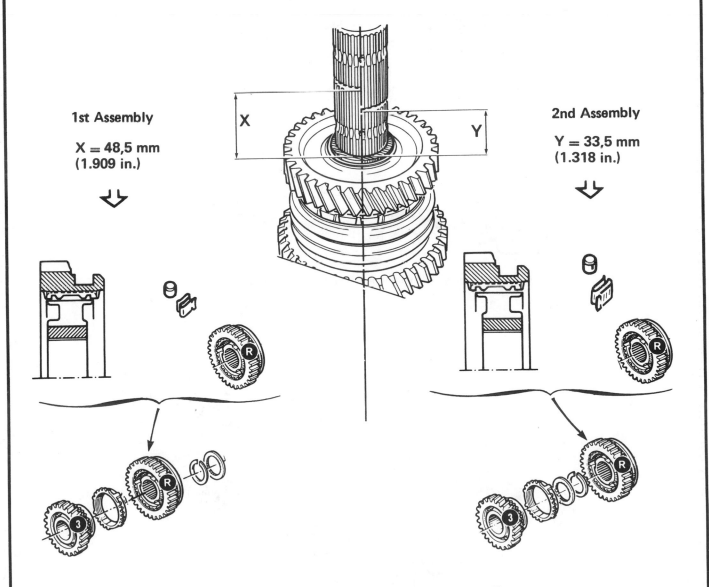

1st Assembly

**X = 48,5 mm
(1.909 in.)**

⇩

2nd Assembly

**Y = 33,5 mm
(1.318 in.)**

⇩

Fig. 6.39 Correct fitting for 3rd/4th synchro-hub (Sec 13)

All the parts are identical, but the two assemblies differ depending on the dimension X or Y

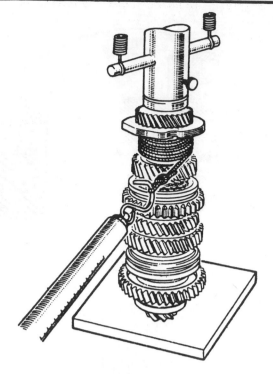

Fig. 6.40 Checking the secondary shaft taper bearing torque (Sec 13)

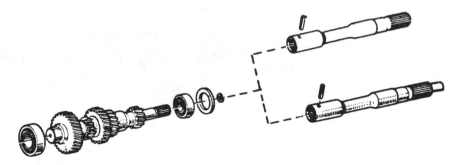

Fig. 6.41 Primary shaft components on the type NG0 gearbox (Sec 13)

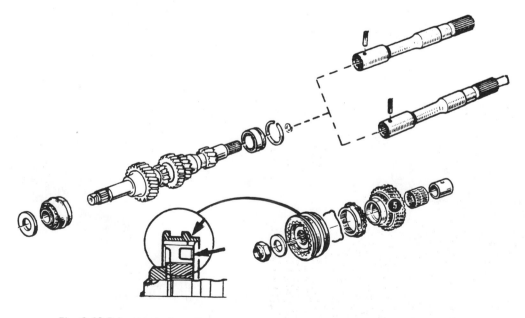

Fig. 6.42 Primary shaft components on type NG1 and NG3 gearboxes (Sec 13)

Differential bearings — fitting and adjustment
11 Refer to Section 5, paragraphs 20 to 25.

Half-casings
12 Proceed as described in Section 5, paragraphs 37 and 38 (photos).
13 Tighten the half-casing bolts in the correct order to the specified torque (Fig. 6.31).
14 Check the crown wheel and pinion backlash, as described in Section 5, paragraphs 45 to 47.
15 On the NG0 type, check and adjust the primary shaft bearing preload, as described in Section 5, paragraphs 39 to 40.
16 Renew the differential oil seals with reference to Section 5, paragraphs 43 and 44. Note the two types of oil seal fitted (Figs. 6.43 and 6.44). and make sure that the correct type is installed.
17 On NG1 and NG3 types, refit the 5th gear components in reverse order.
18 On the NG0 type, refit the primary shaft spacer and shims.
19 Refit the rear casing, together with a new gasket and tighten the bolts.
20 On NG1 and NG3 types insert the 5th selector shaft ball and spring and tighten the plug.
21 Refit the clutch housing, as described in Section 5, paragraphs 40 to 51 (photos).

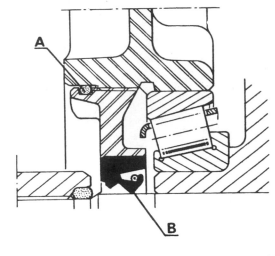

Fig. 6.43 Cross-section of early type differential oil seal (Sec 13)

A   O-ring   B   Oil seal

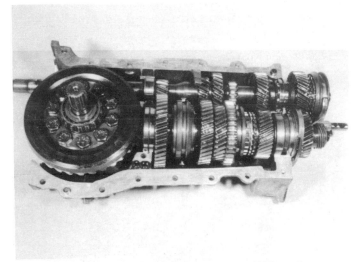

13.12A Right-hand half-casing and gears on type NG3 gearbox

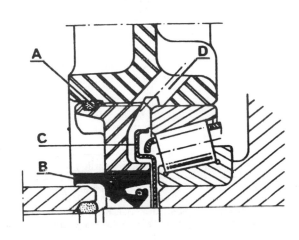

Fig. 6.44 Cross-section of later type differential oil seal (Sec 13)

A   O-ring   C   Deflector
B   Oil seal with front bush   D   Lubrication hole

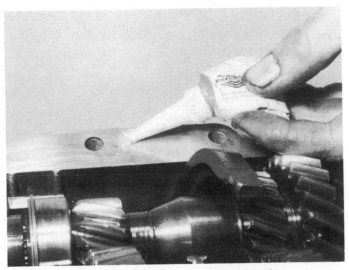

13.12B Applying sealing compound to the casing joint face

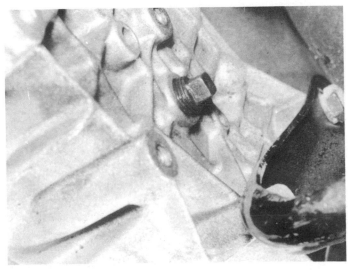

13.21A Gearbox filler plug

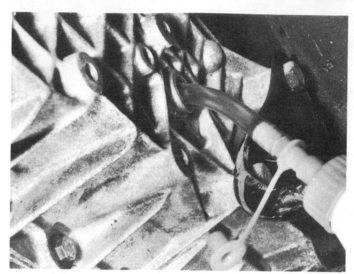

13.21B Topping-up the gearbox oil level

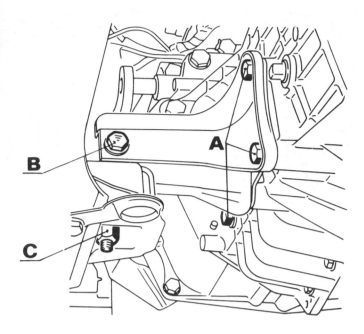

Fig. 6.45 Side gearbox mounting (Sec 15)

A   Bolt to gearbox   C   Nut to rubber pad
B   Bolt to sub-mountings

14 Diffential oil seal – renewal in the car

1   Disconnect the driveshaft at the gearbox, as described in Chapter 8.
2   Mark the position of the ring nut on both nut and casing, take off the locking plate, and unscrew the ring nut. Count and record the number of turns necessary for removal.
3   Remove the old components and fit the new seal and O-ring, as described in Section 5, paragraphs 43 and 44.
4   Refit in the reverse order of the removal procedure.

15 Gearbox mountings – removal and refitting

1   Jack up the front of the car and support on axle stands. Apply the handbrake.
2   Using a trolley jack, support the gearbox.
3   Unbolt the mountings from each side of the gearbox or from the single mounting (photo).
4   Refitting is a reversal of removal.

15.3 Mounting bracket on type NG3 gearbox

16.1 Gear lever and bellows

16 Gearchange mechanism – removal, refitting and adjustment

1   Remove the bellows from the top of the gear lever and remove the console, as applicable (photo).
2   Jack up the car and support on axle stands. Apply the handbrake.
3   Unbolt the gear lever housing from below.
4   On early models unscrew the nuts/bolts from the balljoints and disconnect the linkage from the gearbox.
5   On later models remove the bolt securing the adaptor to the rear of the gearbox, then prise off the clip and disconnect the rod from the ball stud. Note the location of the seal protector (photos).
6   Refitting is a reversal of removal, but adjust the early type as described in paragraphs 7 to 10 or 11 to 15. The gearchange referred to in paragraph 5 requires no adjustment.

16.5A Remove the adaptor bolt and seat ...

16.5B ... and disconnect the gearchange

16.5C Prise off the clip (arrowed) ...

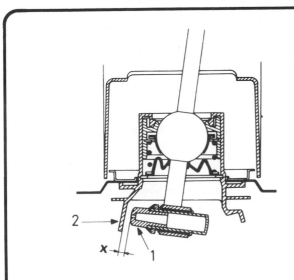

16.5D ... and disconnect the rod

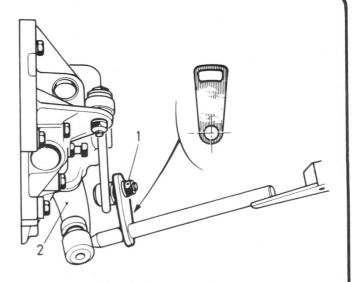

16.5E Seal protector on the selector shaft

First early type

7 Loosen the link bolt.
8 Set lever in the 3rd/4th speed plane.
9 Referring to Fig. 6.46, fit a shim 2.0 mm (0.08 in) thick between lever (1) and housing (2).
10 Tighten the link bolt, and recheck the clearance.

Second early type

11 Select neutral.
12 Referring to Fig. 6.47, unlock nut (1).
13 Set lever (2) in the 3rd/4th speed plane.
14 Proceed as described in paragraph 9.
15 Referring to Fig. 6.47, tighten the nut and recheck the clearance.

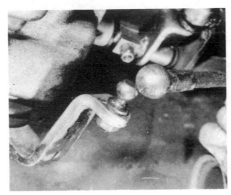

Fig. 6.46 Gearchange adjustment dimension (Sec 16)

1 Lever   2 Housing
X = 2.0 mm (0.08 in)

Fig. 6.47 Gearchange adjustment (second early type) (Sec 16)

1 Nut   2 Lever

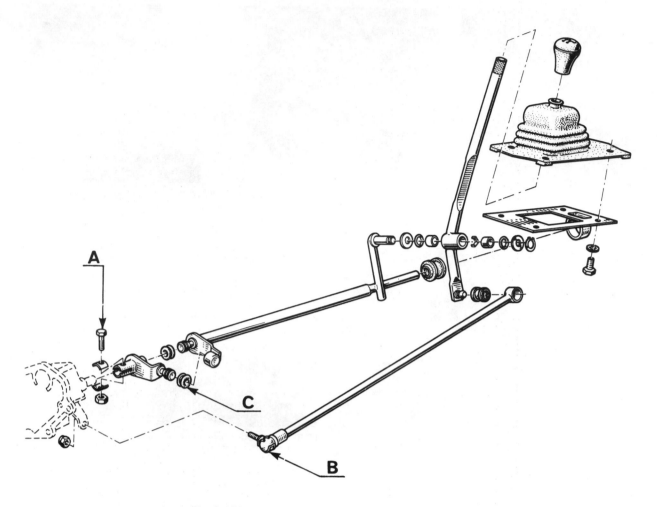

Fig. 6.48 Late type gearchange components (Sec 16)

A   Bolt   B   Clip   C   Rubber bush

---

17 Fault diagnosis – manual gearbox and final drive

Symptom	Reason(s)
Ineffective synchromesh	Worn synchro rings
Jumps out of gear	Weak detent spring Worn selector forks Worn gears Gearchange adjustment incorrect (where applicable)
Noisy operation	Worn bearings or gears
Difficulty in engaging gears	Clutch fault Worn selector components or gearchange Worn synchro units

Chapter 7 Automatic transmission and final drive

For modifications, and information applicable to later models, see Supplement at end of manual

Contents

Specifications

General

Codes	4139-61, 4139-65, MJ1 or MJ3
Type	Computer controlled fully automatic, with three forward speeds and one reverse; epicyclic geartrain with hydraulic control; three element hydraulic torque converter

Ratios (:1):	Final drive	Step down gears	Speedometer drive
Model 1362 (4139-61)	3.56 (9/32)	1.03 (37/38)	2.22 (9/20)
Model 1368 (4139-65)	3.56 (9/32)	1.03 (37/39)	3.00 (6/18)
Model 1362 (MJ1)	3.56 (9/32)	0.96 (26/25)	3.00 (6/18)
Model 1363 (MJ3)	3.56 (9/32)	0.96 (26/25)	3.00 (6/18)

Fluid capacity

Model 1362 (4139-61):	
Total	5.0 litre (8.8 Imp pint, 5.3 US qt)
Service	3.0 litre (5.3 Imp pint, 3.2 US qt)
Model 1368 (4139-65):	
Total	5.0 litre (8.8 Imp pint, 5.3 US qt)
Service	2.5 litre (4.4 Imp pint, 2.6 US qt)
Models 1362 (MJ1) and 1363 (MJ3):	
Total	6.0 litre (10.6 Imp pint, 6.3 US qt)
Service	2.5 litre (4.4 Imp pint, 2.6 US qt)

Torque wrench settings

	lbf ft	Nm
Driveplate to converter	22 to 26	30 to 35
Drain plug	21	28
Selector rod (early models)	12	16

1 General description

The automatic transmission provides fully automatic gearchanging without the use of a clutch. An override system of manual gear selection remains available to the driver.

The transmission consists of three main assemblies, namely the torque converter, the final drive and the gearbox.

The torque converter takes the place of a conventional clutch, transmitting the engine torque smoothly and automatically to the gearbox. Increased torque is provided for starting off.

The gearbox contains an epicyclic geartrain, providing three forward gear ratios and one reverse, and the mechanical, hydraulic and electrical geartrain control elements.

The epicyclic geartrain consists of an assembly of helical gears which provide for different ratios to be obtained, depending upon the

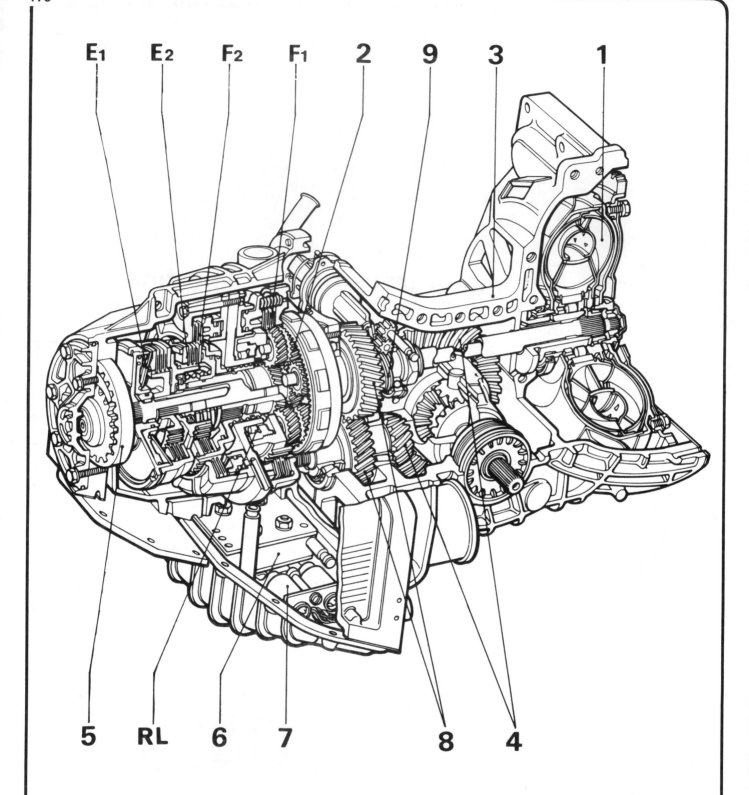

Fig. 7.1 Cutaway view of the type 4139 transmission (Sec 1)

1 Torque converter	4 Crownwheel and pinion	8 Step-down gears	F1 Brake
2 Epicyclic geartrain and its elements	5 Oil pump	9 Governor worm	F2 Brake
3 Differential casing	6 Hydraulic distributor	E1 Clutch	RL Epicyclic geartrain flywheel
	7 Solenoid ball valves	E2 Clutch	

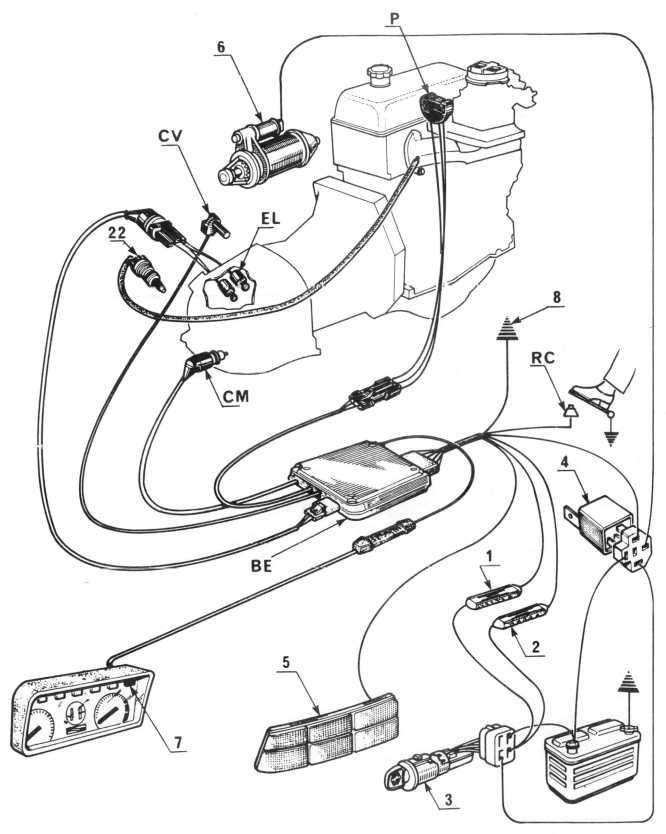

Fig. 7.2 Transmission control components on the types MJ1 and MJ2 transmissions (Sec 1)

1	Reversing light fuse (5A)	5	Reversing lights
2	Supply fuse (1.5A)	6	Starter
3	Starter switch	7	Instrument panel
4	Starter relay		(warning light)
		8	Automatic transmission earth

22	Vacuum capsule	EL	Pilot solenoid valves
BE	Computer module	P	Load potentiometer
CM	Multi-purpose switch	RC	Kick-down switch
CV	Speed sensor		

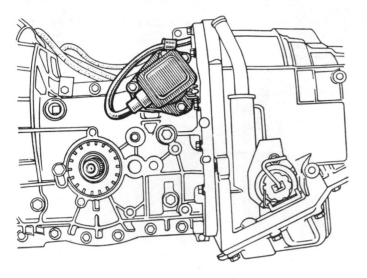

Fig. 7.3 Governor/computer location on the type 4139
transmission (Sec 1)

pressure of the hydraulic feed to the receivers. The gear assembly
consists of 2 sunwheels, 3 pairs of planet wheels joined by a planet
wheel carrier, and an involute gear ring.

A geared oil pump located at the rear of the unit supplies oil at the
required pressures to the converter, the brakes and clutches, and for
gear lubrication.

The hydraulic distributor ensures the regulation of oil pressure to
suit the engine load, and the pressure feed or release to the brakes and
clutches. Ratio changes are affected by the operation of two solenoid
ball valves, instructed by the governor and computer on type 4139
models, or solely by the computer on type MJ1 and MJ3 models.
Circuit pressure is controlled by the capsule and pilot valve, thus
determining pressure to the receiver and controlling gear changing
quality.

A freewheel transmits torque in the same direction as the
roadwheels, but does not permit engine braking in first gear when D
or 2 are selected. The clutches and brakes lock or release the geartrain
components in various way depending upon hydraulic pressure, and
thereby provide the different ratios.

Gearchange instruction is given by the governor and/or computer
unit, the exact moment of change varying according to vehicle speed
and engine torque.

The governor is, in fact, an alternator, and provides power to the
computer, the amount being dependent upon vehicle speed and
engine loading.

The computer supplies electrical pulses to the solenoid ball valves.

The kickdown switch earths one of the computer circuits, causing
instant selection of a lower gear in some circumstances. The switch is
operated by the throttle pedal at the extreme of its travel.

The solenoid ball valves open or close hydraulic passages, to
permit gear changing.

The MJ1 and MJ3 type transmission are fully computerised. There
is no governor, but additionally, a multi-purpose switch, load poten-
tiometer, and speed sensor are fitted.

The selector lever, centrally placed inside the car, has 6 positions
as follows:

P (or park): Transmission in neutral, and the driving wheels
mechanically locked.

R (or reverse): Reverse gear position. When the ignition switch is
on, the ignition lights will automatically illuminate.

N (or neutral): Transmission in neutral.

D (or drive): Gears engage automatically.

2: Second gear hold.

1: First gear hold.

Note that whenever the selector lever is moved between D, P and
R, the vehicle must be stationary, the footbrake applied, and the

accelerator pedal raised. The mechanism must also be unlocked, by
squeezing together the top of the selector lever.

To start the engine, the selector lever must be in either the P or N
positions, for safety reasons. The starter will not function in other
positions.

To move away, place the selector lever in the D position and drive
away on the accelerator pedal.

In special circumstances, such as on very hilly and twisting roads,
the selection of 2 will prevent frequent gear changing, and will provide
engine braking when moving downhill, whilst retaining automatic
changing between 1 and 2. Similarly, if 1 is selected, second and third
gears are not obtainable.

When the vehicle is not required, engage P.

On normal roads, the most economical use is provided by driving
with the selector lever at D, and with light accelerator pressure to give
gearchanges at low engine speeds. Do not use positions 1 or 2.

When driving fast, gearchanging will take place at higher speeds.
To obtain snap acceleration, such as when overtaking, smartly press
the throttle to the floor. This will cause the kickdown switch to
operate, and given an immediate change down to a lower gear.

In cold weather, wait for between $\frac{1}{2}$ and 2 minutes, depending
upon the temperature, before moving the selector lever. This will
prevent stalling of the engine.

The complexity of the automatic transmission unit makes it largely
unsuitable for working upon by the home mehanic, and any problems
arising should be discussed with a Renault agent. Trouble-free running
and long life will only be obtained if the unit is serviced correctly, and
is not abused.

2 Routine maintenance

1   Every 5000 miles (8000 km) check the transmission fluid level
and top up as necessary.
2   Every 30 000 miles (50 000 km) drain the transmission fluid and fill
with new fluid.

3 Automatic transmission fluid – checking, draining and refilling

Checking

1   With the vehicle on level ground, and the selector lever in P, start
the engine and wait for approximately two minutes. This ensures that
the converter is filled.
2   If the dipstick incorporates hot and cold level marks, check that
the level is between the appropriate marks. 'Hot' is defined as after a
drive of at least half an hour, and 'Cold' when starting up or after
changing the transmission fluid.
3   If the dipstick incorporates only one minimum and one maximum
level mark, the transmission must be cold; ie when starting up or after
changing the fluid.
4   Never overfill, or overheating or leakage may occur. Top up via the
dipstick tube, using a clean funnel.
5   When wiping the dipstick, always use a non-fluffy rag.

Draining

6   Always drain when the transmission is hot, to ensure that the
impurities held in suspension in the hot oil are disposed of.
7   Remove the dipstick.
8   Remove the drain plug and allow the oil to drain for as long as
possible. Renew the filter – see Supplement.
9   Refit the drain plug.

Refilling

10 Refill via a funnel, using one that has a filter to trap any impurities
in the oil.
11 With the funnel in the dipstick tube, pour in the specified quantity
of the recommended automatic transmission fluid.
12 Start up, check the level and top up as required.

4 Governor control cable (type 4139) – adjustment

1   Jack up the front of the car and support on axle stands. Apply the
handbrake.

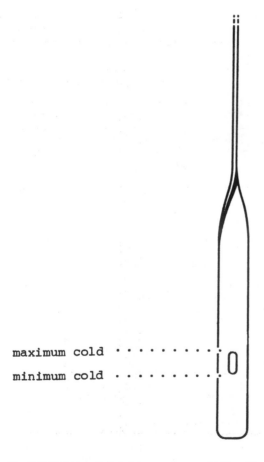

Fig. 7.4 Fluid level dipstick cut-outs – hot and cold (Sec 3)

Type 4139-61

2   Free the locknut (1) and adjust the stop (2) to the mid position (see Fig. 7.6).

3   Depress the throttle pedal fully, and adjust the cable by means of stop (6), until play is just eliminated (see Fig. 7.7).

4   With the throttle pedal fully down, adjust the cable at the governor end to give clearance (J) of 0.3 to 0.5 mm (0.012 to 0.020 in) between the stop peg and the quadrant (see Fig. 7.8).

5   Tighten the locknuts.

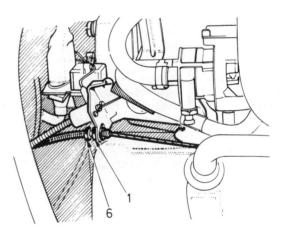

Fig. 7.6 Governor control cable (governor end) (Sec 4)

1 Locknut	3 Adjuster
2 Stop	

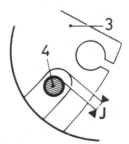

Fig. 7.7 Governor control cable (engine end) (Sec 4)

1   Locknut   6   Stop

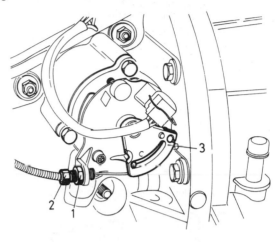

Fig. 7.8 Governor control cable adjustment dimension (J) (Sec 4)

3   Quadrant   4   Stop peg

J = 0.3 to 0.5 mm (0.012 to 0.020 in)

Fig. 7.5 Fluid level dipstick cut-out – cold (Sec 3)

Type 4139-65

6   Adjust the accelerator cable, as described in Chapter 3.
7   Loosen the locknuts at each end of the governor control cable and set the end stops to their midway positions.
8   Have an assistant fully depress the throttle pedal, then adjust the *governor* end stop until the clearance between the quadrant and the stop screw is as shown in Fig. 7.9. Note that the stop screw is preset by the manufacturers and must not be altered.
9   Tighten the locknuts, then check that the inner cable moves approximately 20.0 mm (0.788 in) between the throttle wide open and close positions.

Both types

10   Lower the car to the ground.

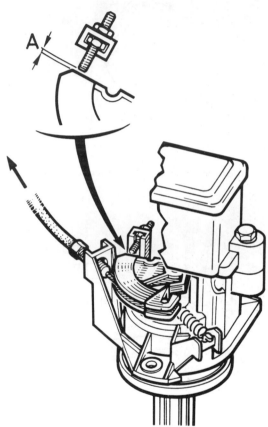

Fig. 7.9 Governor cable adjustment dimension on the type 4139-65 transmission (Sec 4)

A = 0.2 to 0.7 mm (0.008 to 0.028 in)

5   Gear selector lever – removal, refitting and adjustment

Note: *The gear selector mechanism has been modified, as shown in Figs. 7.10, 7.11 and 7.12. Although the adjustment procedure is similar, this Section only describes removal and refitting procedures for early models.*

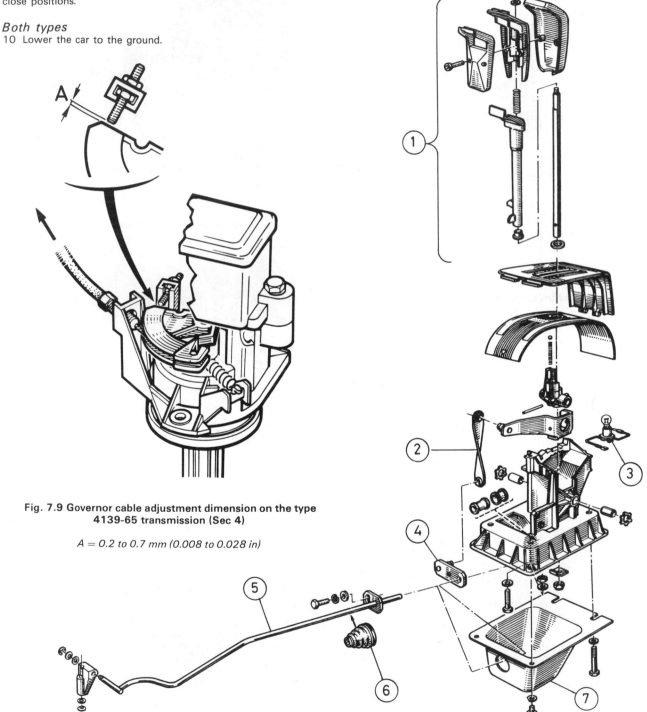

Fig. 7.10 Gear selector components (Sec 5)

1	Lever	3	Bulb	5	Rod	7	Cover
2	Link	4	Arm	6	Boot		

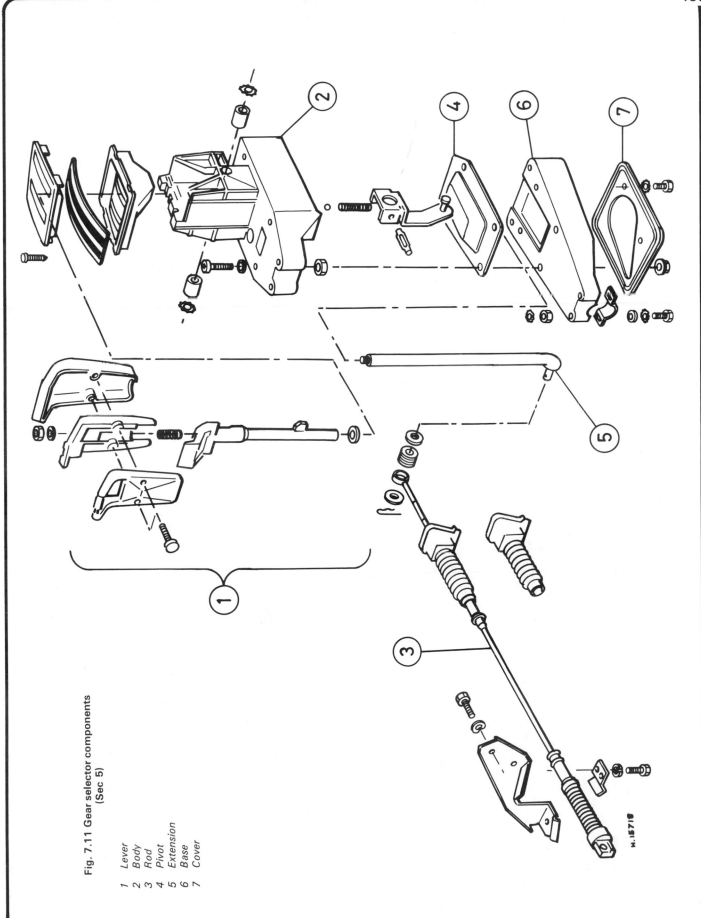

Fig. 7.11 Gear selector components
(Sec 5)

1 Lever
2 Body
3 Rod
4 Pivot
5 Extension
6 Base
7 Cover

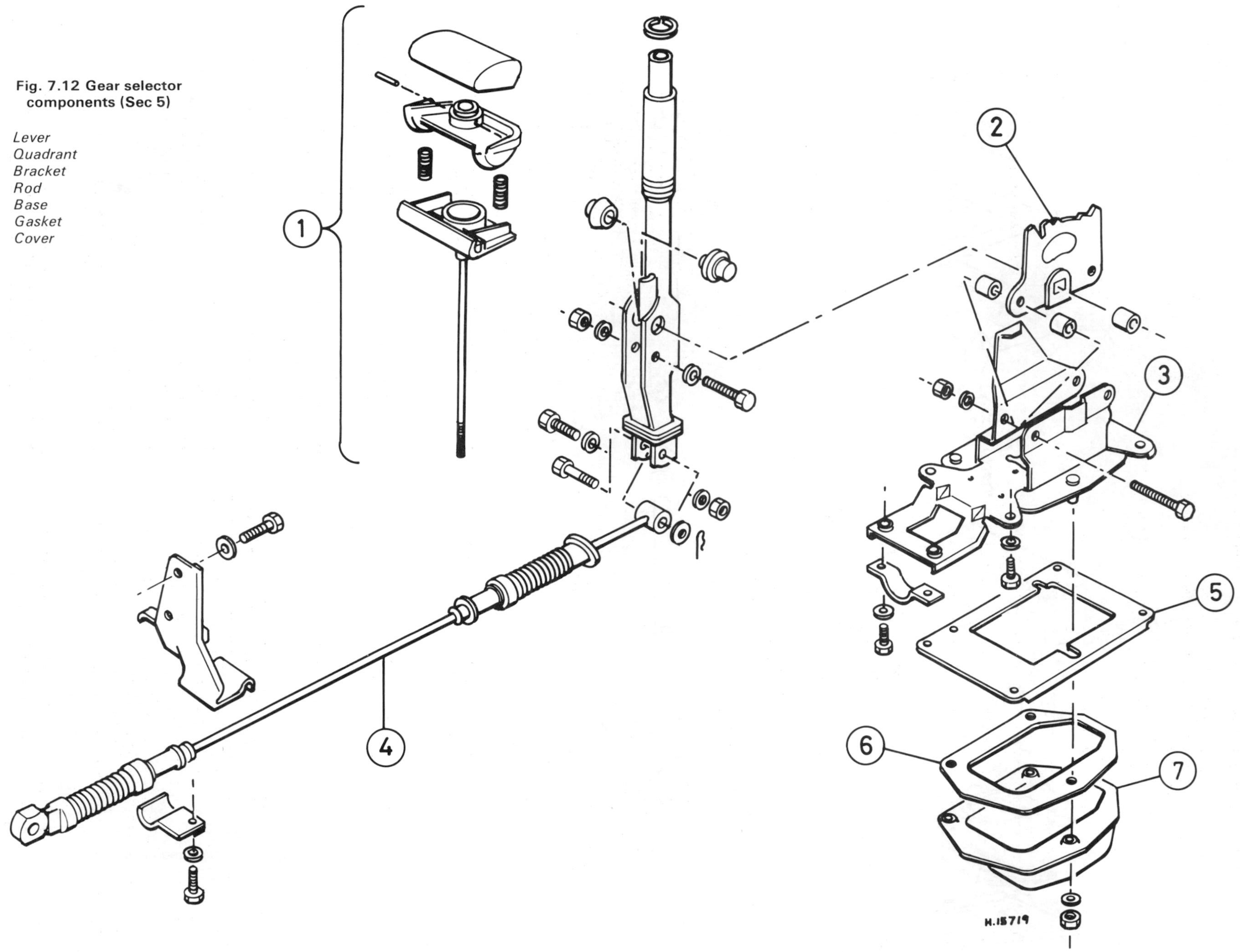

Fig. 7.12 Gear selector
components (Sec 5)

1   Lever
2   Quadrant
3   Bracket
4   Rod
5   Base
6   Gasket
7   Cover

1   Jack up the front of the car and support on axle stands. Apply the handbrake.
2   Position the selector lever in Neutral (N).
3   Working under the car, extract the circlip at the transmission control arm and disconnect the rod.
4   Unbolt the selector lever bottom cover.
5   Unscrew the bolt securing the rear of the rod to the arm, and withdraw the rod.
6   From inside the car slide out the selector lever index plate, then withdraw the selector lever assembly.
7   To refit, check that the transmission lever is set at neutral.
8   Fit the rubber boot on the control rod.
9   Fit the arm to the rod and loosely secure with the bolt.
10 Locate the selector lever assembly in position and insert the rear bolts loosely.
11 Insert the control rod in the bearing at the lever end, and also locate the arm in the link.
12 Connect the control rod to the transmission lever and fit the circlip.

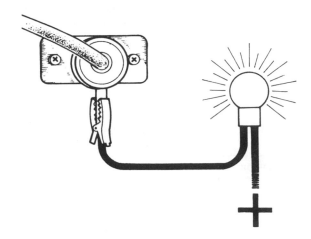

Fig. 7.14 Checking the kickdown switch (Sec 6)

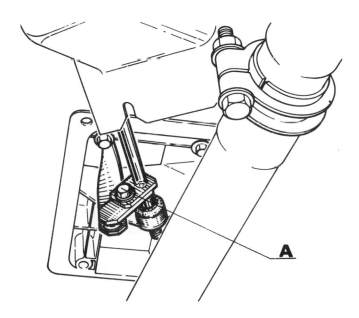

Fig. 7.13 Gear selector adjustment bolt (A) on early models (Sec 5)

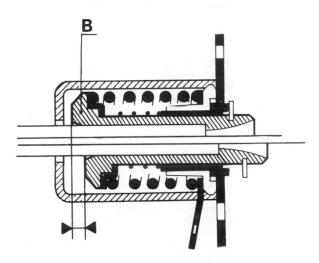

Fig. 7.15 Cross-section of the throttle cable, showing stop sleeve (B) and adjustment dimension (Sec 6)

Adjustment
13 With both the transmission and selector levers set at neutral, tighten the bolt securing the rod to the arm. Where a cable is fitted on later models, tighten the clamp with the shaft and selector lever in the P position.
14 Fit the bottom cover and tighten all the bolts.
15 Lower the car to the ground.

6   Kickdown switch – testing, removal, refitting and adjustment

1   To check the switch operation, connect a 12 volt test bulb between the switch terminal and the battery positive terminal.
2   Press the accelerator hard down. If the bulb lights, the switch is in order.
3   To remove the switch, first remove the accelerator cable (Chapter 3) then disconnect the cable from the switch.
4   Remove the screws and withdraw the switch from the floor.
5   Refitting is a reversal of removal, but adjust the switch as follows:

Adjustment
6   Adjust the throttle cable so that the stop sleeve is compressed by 3.0 to 4.0 mm (0.118 to 0.158 in) with the throttle pedal *fully* depressed (Fig. 7.15).
7   Ensure that the kickdown switch cover is in position.
8   Adjustment of the throttle cable, kickdown switch and governor control cable are inter-related, and should be carried out together.

7   Multi-purpose switch (types MJ1 and MJ3) – renewal

1   The multi-purpose switch is located on the rear of the transmission and it operates the starting circuit, reverse light circuit and solenoid valves according to the position of the selector lever.
2   To renew the switch, the wire to the electronic module must be cut and the new wire connected using connectors supplied with the new switch.
3   Jack up the front of the car and support on axle stands. Apply the handbrake.
4   Disconnect the battery negative lead.
5   Unbolt the old switch then cut the existing wiring to the same length as the wire supplied with the new switch.
6   When there are *seven* wires from the switch, cut the yellow wire flush with the cable sleeve at the casing end.
7   Strip the wires and fit the seals provided to each one. Connect the wires by crimping.
8   Fit the switch to the transmission and tighten the bolt.
9   Connect the battery lead and lower the car to the ground.

8   Speed sensor (types MJ1 and MJ3) – renewal

1   The speed sensor is located on the left-hand side of the transmission. It provides an output signal proportional to the speed of the car.

2   Jack up the car and support on axle stands. Apply the handbrake.
3   Disconnect the battery negative lead.
4   Unscrew the bolt, remove the clamp and withdraw the speed sensor.
5   Cut the existing wire to the same length as the wire supplied with the new sensor.
6   Strip the wires and fit the seals provided to each one. Connect the wires by crimping.

9 Instrument panel warning light (types MJ1 and MJ3) – checking

1   The instrument panel warning light illuminates whenever a fault is detected by the electronic module.
2   To check the warning light, locate the connector on the wire leading from the warning light to the electronic module. Refer to the wiring diagnosis in Chapter 10 if necessary.
3   Separate the connector and connect an earth lead to the warning light wire.
4   Switch on the ignition and check that the warning light is illuminated. If not, the bulb is probably blown and a new one should be fitted; with reference to Chapter 10.
5   Finally reconnect the wires.

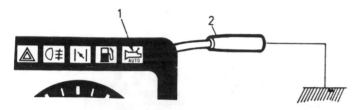

Fig. 7.16 Checking the instrument panel warning light (Sec 9)

1   Warning light   *2   Earth connector*

10 Vacuum capsule (types MJ1 and MJ3) – removal and refitting

1   If the vacuum capsule is not functioning correctly, violent gear changes will occur at low throttle. If this is the case check the vacuum line for leakage which may be indicated by a whistling noise. The capsule is located on the left-hand side of the transmission at the rear.
2   To remove the unit, jack up the front of the car and support on axle stands. Apply the handbrake.
3   Support the transmission with a trolley jack and unbolt the rear mounting.
4   Disconnect the vacuum pipe.
5   Unscrew the bolt, remove the holding bracket and withdraw the vacuum capsule.
6   Refitting is a reversal of removal, but finally check the transmission fluid level with reference to Section 3.

11 Speedometer drive oil seal (types MJ1 and MJ3) – renewal

1   Jack up the rear of the car and support on axle stands. Apply the handbrake.
2   Disconnect the cable and extract the seal, preferably using Renault tool B Vi 905.
3   Clean the seating, press the new seal into position and refit the cable.
4   Lower the car to the ground.

12 Automatic transmission – removal and refitting

1   Disconnect the battery negative lead.
2   Jack up the front of the car and support on axle stands. Apply the handbrake.
3   Remove the starter motor if necessary, with reference to Chapter 10.
4   Disconnect the vacuum capsule hose.

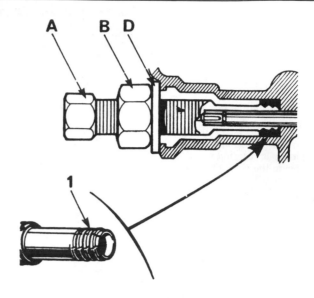

Fig. 7.17 Using the special tool to extract the speedometer drive oil seal (Sec 11)

A   Extractor   *D   Spacer*
B   Nut   *I   Special thread*

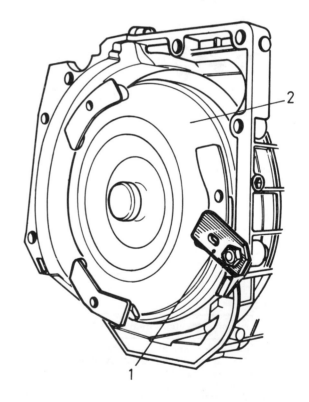

Fig. 7.18 Fitting a metal plate (1) to the transmission in order to retain the torque converter (2) (Sec 12)

5   Disconnect all wiring from the transmission, if necessary identifying each wire for location.
6   Remove the driveshafts, as described in Chapter 8. Alternatively, the driveshafts can be disconnected at their inboard ends only by supporting the suspension, removing the inner roll pins and tilting the stub axle carriers outwards after disconnecting the steering tie-rod and upper suspension balljoints.

7   Remove the selector rod from the transmission, with reference to Section 5.

8   Remove the transmission fluid dipstick tube.

9   Unbolt the transmission front cover and unscrew the bolts securing the torque converter to the driveplate. Turn the engine as required to gain access to each of the three bolts.

10 Unscrew the nut securing the exhaust pipe bracket to the transmission.

11 Support the transmission on a jack, but ensure that the load is properly spread by using a substantial piece of wood of adequate size.

12 Remove the transmission mountings, one at each side-member.

13 Lower the jack and disconnect the speedometer cable and, where applicable, the governor cable.

14 Remove the engine-to-transmission fixing bolts, and carefully lift out the unit with the help of an assistant. Ensure that the converter does not become separated from the remainder of the unit. Keep it in position by bolting a suitable piece of steel through one of the engine-to-transmission bolt holes, thus retaining the converter.

15 Refitting is a reversal of removal, but when assembling the converter to the driveplate, ensure that the boss on the converter which is in line with the timing hole is fitted opposite the sharp angled machined edge on the driveplate (Identified by a paint splash). Tighten the fixing bolts a little at a time and in rotation, ensuring proper location, until the correct torque figure is reached. Refer to Chapter 8 when refitting the driveshafts. Where a TDC sensor is fitted, adjust its position with reference to Fig. 7.19. Adjust the selector lever (Section 5) and, where applicable, the governor cable (Section 4). Fill the transmission, with reference to Section 3.

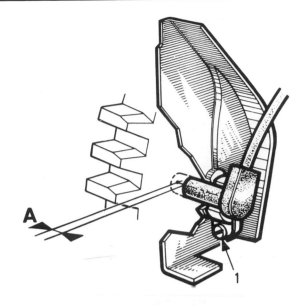

Fig. 7.19 TDC sensor adjustment (Sec 12)

1   Adjustment screw   *A = 1.0 mm (0.04 in)*

---

13 Fault diagnosis – automatic transmission and final drive

Symptom	Reason(s)
Engine stalls	Vacuum leak at capsule
Car moves in N	Incorrect selector lever adjustment
No drive or judder	Incorrect fluid level
Incorrect gear shift speeds	Incorrect cable or kick-down adjustment
Excessive bump on engagement of gear	Idling speed too high

Note: Accurate fault diagnosis by a Renault dealer is only possible with the transmission unit in the car

Chapter 8 Driveshafts

For modifications, and information applicable to later models, see Supplement at end of manual

Contents

1 General description

The driveshafts transmit the drive from the transmission unit to the front roadwheels. Each driveshaft has an inner and outer joint (coupling) to allow for the movement of the front suspension. Splines are provided at each end of the driveshafts for engagement with the front wheel hubs and transmission differential unit. Roll pins retain the driveshafts to the differential shafts and the hub ends are retained with nuts and washers.

The type of driveshaft varies according to model, therefore it is essential to quote model and chassis numbers when obtaining new components.

2 Routine maintenance

Every 40 000 miles (65 000 km) check the driveshaft bellows for damage and splits which would permit water and dirt to enter the joint resulting in early failure. Also check the joints for vibration and knocking noises, particularly on full lock, indicating excessive wear.

3 Driveshaft – removal and refitting

1 Raise the front of the car on stands placed under the bodyframe sidemembers.
2 Place a jack or stand under the front suspension lower wishbone and compress the suspension slightly.
3 Remove the roadwheel.
4 Unscrew the hub nut from the outboard end of the driveshaft (photo). To prevent the hub from rotating while this is being done, have an assistant apply the footbrake or use a long lever between two of the roadwheel studs, but protect the stud threads from damage.
5 Unscrew the retaining nut and then using a suitable balljoint splitter, disconnect the tie-rod from the steering arm.
6 Unbolt the brake caliper with reference to Chapter 9, but do not disconnect the hydraulic hose. Tie the caliper to one side without straining the hose.

7 Disconnect the suspension upper balljoint from the stub axle carrier. Access to this balljoint is very restricted for fitting most types of splitting tool although forked wedges are suitable. If the balljoint has previously been renewed, then the balljoint fixing bolts can be undone to separate the components (see Chapter 11).

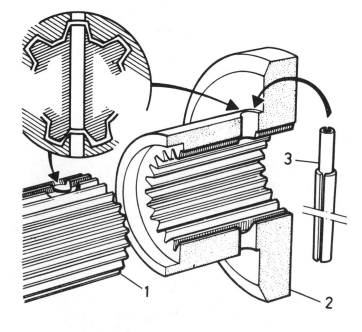

Fig. 8.1 Alignment of the driveshaft and differential shaft (Sec 3)

1   Differential shaft
2   Driveshaft
3   Double roll pin

8 Working under the car, drive out the roll pins from the inboard end of the driveshaft (photos).
9 Carefully pull the top of the stub axle outwards until the driveshaft can be released from the transmission.
10 Support the stub axle carrier and push the driveshaft from the hub. If it is tight use a two- or three-legged extractor to remove it (photo).
11 Refitting is a reversal of removal, but align the roll pin holes at the inner ends before driving in the new roll pins. Double roll pins are used. Grease the splines before fitting the driveshaft. Once the roll pins are fitted, seal their ends with a dab of silicone gasket compound. Tighten the hub and balljoint nuts to the specified torque (photo) – see Chapter 11, Specifications.

4 Rubber bellows (coupling GE 86) – renewal

1 This type of coupling is fitted at the outboard end of all driveshafts. Renewal of the bellows is the only operation which can be carried out, wear in the joint can only be rectified by renewal of the complete shaft.
2 Remove the driveshaft, as described in Section 3.
3 Prise off the retaining spring clip; if necessary using two lengths of metal tubing.
4 Cut off the old bellows and inner rubber retaining ring and wipe away as much grease as possible.

3.4 Removing the driveshaft hub nut

3.8A Driveshaft inner joint roll pin (arrowed)

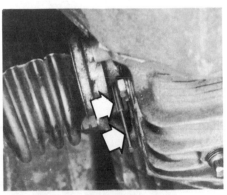
3.8B Removing the inner joint double roll pins (arrowed)

3.10 Removing the driveshaft from the hub

3.11 Tightening the driveshaft hub nut

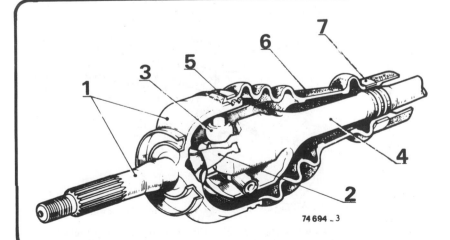

Fig. 8.2 Cutaway view of the GE 86 coupling (Sec 4)

1 Stub axle
2 Star plate retainer
3 Spider
4 Shaft
5 Retaining spring clip
6 Bellows
7 Rubber retaining ring

4.5 Prising up the star plate ends

4.6A Remove the thrust button ...

4.6B ... and thrust spring

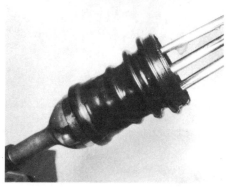

4.9 Using an expander to fit the bellows

4.14 Applying the special grease

4.15 Locating the bellows in the shaft grooves

5   Release the bell shaped section of the driveshaft by prising up the ends of the star plate (photo). Do not distort the star plate ends.

6   Separate the components and extract the thrust button and spring (photos).

7   A special conical expander must be used to fit the new bellows. If the official tool (T. Av 537-02) cannot be borrowed it may be possible to make up a suitable substitute. First grip the driveshaft in a vice fitted with soft metal jaw protectors.

8   Fit the new bellows to the expander tool. Lubricate the inside of the bellows with oil, then clean the hands thoroughly.

9   Using a piece of rag to grip the bellows, pull the bellows over the expander onto the driveshaft (photo). Three or four attempts may be necessary in order gradually to expand the rubber, however, take care not to 'double-fold' the bellows.

10   Fit the spring and thrust button and move the roller cages towards the centre.

11   Position the star plate equidistant between the rollers.

12   Connect the driveshaft yoke to the bell shaped section.

13   Engage the star plate ends in their notches.

14   Spread a pack of special grease (195 g) equally between coupling and bellows (photo).

15   Locate the lips of the bellows both in the shaft and bell shaped section (photo).

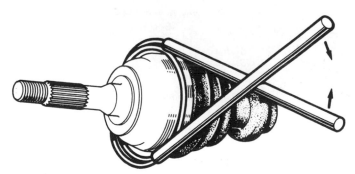

Fig. 8.3 Using two lengths of metal tubing to remove the spring type clip (Sec 4)

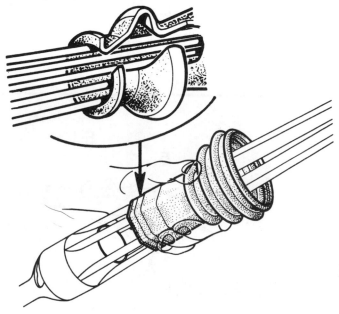

Fig. 8.4 Fitting the new bellows to the expander tool (Sec 4)

16 Temporarily insert a screwdriver between the bellows and shaft in order to release any air pressure.
17 Fit the inner rubber retaining ring and outer retaining clip (photos).
18 Refit the driveshaft, as described in Section 3.

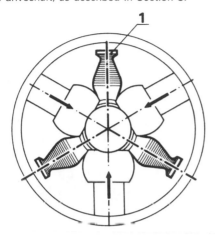

Fig. 8.5 Correct location of the star plate (1) with the roller cages at the centre (Sec 4)

4.17A Bellows inner rubber retaining ring

4.17B Fitted bellows

5 Rubber bellows (constant velocity outer joint) – renewal

1 This joint incorporates six balls, and if the joint is worn excessively the complete driveshaft must be renewed as service items are not obtainable.
2 Remove the driveshaft, as described in Section 3.
3 Prise off the retaining spring clip, if necessary using two lengths of metal tubing.

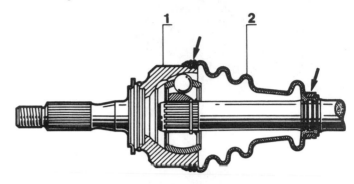

Fig. 8.6 Cross-section of the constant velocity outer joint (Sec 5)

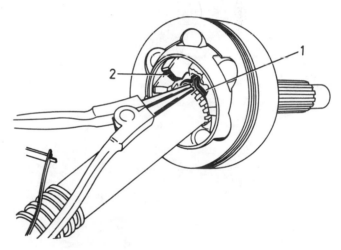

Fig. 8.7 Using circlip pliers to remove the circlip (1) securing the hub (2) to the driveshaft (Sec 5)

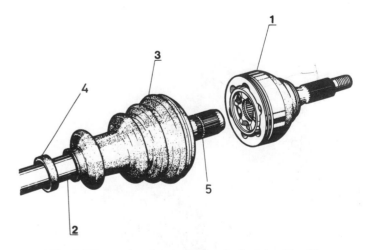

Fig. 8.8 Removing the constant velocity joint (Sec 5)

1 Yoke
2 Shaft
3 Bellows
4 Inner ring
5 Circlip groove

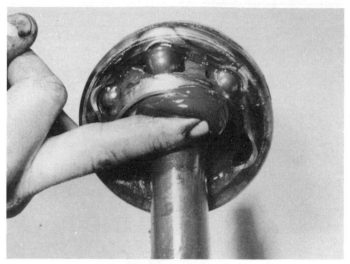

5.8 Applying the special grease

5.9 Locating the bellows on the yoke

5.10A Tightening the inner clip

5.10B Tightening the outer clip

4   Cut off the old bellows and inner rubber retaining ring or clip and wipe away as much grease as possible.

5   Using circlip pliers, open the circlip retaining the hub to the driveshaft and at the same time use a soft-faced mallet to drive the hub from the driveshaft. If necessary grip the driveshaft in a vice.

6   Clean the driveshaft, then locate the new inner ring and bellows on it.

7   Push on the joint until the circlip locates in the groove.

8   Spread a pack of special grease (140 g) equally between the joint and bellows (photo).

9   Locate the lips of the bellows in the grooves on the shaft and bell shaped section (photo).

10 Fit the new inner ring/clip and outer clip (photos).

11 Refit the driveshaft, as described in Section 3.

6   Coupling (type GE 82) – overhaul

1   This type of joint is fitted at the inner end of the driveshaft, and it is possible to renew the bellows, spider and yoke. First remove the driveshaft, as described in Section 3.

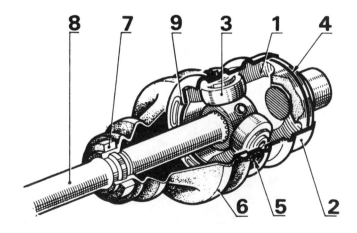

Fig.8.9 Cutaway view of the GE 82 coupling joint (Sec 6)

1	Yoke	6	Bellows
2	Housing	7	Retaining rubber ring
3	Spider	8	Shaft
4	O-ring	9	Locking plate
5	Retaining spring or clip		

2   Prise back the retaining clip from the larger diameter of the bellows.
3   Cut the bellows along its full length, remove it and wipe away as much grease as possible.
4   Using a pair of pliers, prise up the ends of the anti-separation plate.
5   Remove the yoke, taking care not to dismantle the roller cages which are matched components. Tape them if necessary to prevent separation.
6   Press the driveshaft out of the coupling spider.

Bellows or spider renewal
7   Lubricate the driveshaft and slide on the retaining collar and bellows.
8   Push the spider onto the splines and retain by crimping at 120° intervals. The driveshaft should be held in a vice and a punch used to stamp the ends of three splines.
9   Engage the yoke and spider then make up a wedge to the dimensions shown in Fig. 8.13.

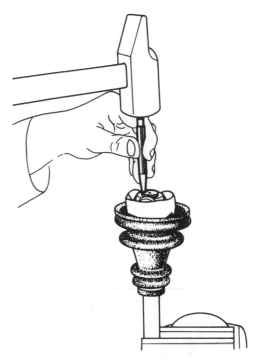

Fig. 8.12 Crimping the spider onto the driveshaft (Sec 6)

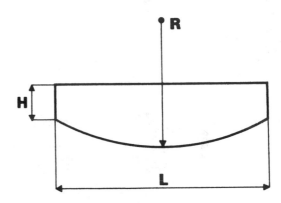

Fig. 8.13 Fitting wedge dimensions (Sec 6)

H = 6 mm (0.24 in)   R = 45 mm (1.77 in)
L = 40 mm (1.58 in)

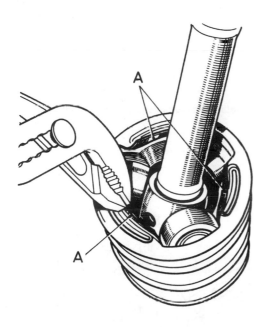

Fig. 8.10 Lifting the anti-separation plate tabs (A) (Sec 6)

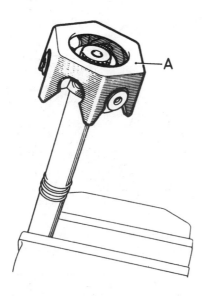

Fig. 8.11 Plastic retainer (A) supplied with the new spider for holding the roller cages on their matched trunnions (Sec 6)

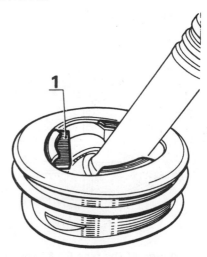

Fig. 8.14 Anti-separation plate wedge (1) in position (Sec 6)

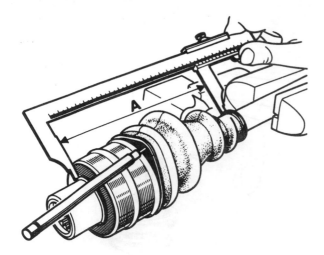

Fig. 8.15 Bellows setting dimension on the type GE 82 coupling
(Sec 6)

$$A = 162 \pm 1 \text{ mm } (6.383 \pm 0.039 \text{ in})$$

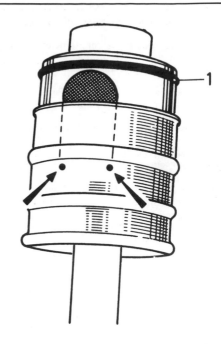

Fig. 8.17 Metal housing bosses aligned with the cut-out (Sec 6)

1   O-ring

10 Insert the wedge between the yoke and the anti-separation plate.
Tap the anti-separation plate into its original position and remove the
temporary wedge.
11 Spread a pack of special grease (150 g) equally between the
bellows and yoke.
12 Locate the lips of the bellows in the grooves on the shaft and yoke
housing, then adjust the coupling to the dimension shown in Fig. 8.15.
13 Temporarily insert a screwdriver between the bellows and shaft in
order to release any air pressure, then fit the retaining clips or spring
as applicable. Refit the driveshaft, with reference to Section 3.

Yoke renewal
14 Lubricate the driveshaft and slide on the retaining collar and
bellows.
15 Locate the yoke metal housing on the driveshaft and push the
spider onto the splines crimping it at 120° intervals. To do this, hold
the driveshaft in a vice and use a punch to stamp the ends of three
splines.
16 Engage the metal housing and yoke so that the two bosses are
aligned with a cut-out as shown in Fig. 8.17. Make sure that the O-ring
is correctly located.
17 Support the metal housing, then tap the yoke fully into position
and hold it; preferably using a press.
18 Crimp the housing onto the yoke using a soft metal drift around
the full circumference.
19 Follow the procedure given in paragraphs 11, 12 and 13.

Fig. 8.18 Crimping the metal housing onto the yoke (Sec 6)

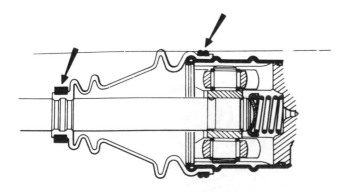

Fig. 8.16 Cross-section of the type GE 82 coupling showing
bellows retaining clips/springs or rubber ring (Sec 6)

7   Rubber bellows (coupling GI 76) – renewal

1   This type of coupling is fitted to the inner end of the driveshaft.
First remove the driveshaft, as described in Section 3.
2   With the driveshaft held in a vice, prise the clips from each end of
the bellows.
3   Cut the full length of the bellows and remove it.
4   Remove the yoke, taking care not to dismantle the roller cages
which are matched components. Tape them if necessary to prevent
separation.
5   Press the driveshaft out of the coupling spider.

6   Lubricate the driveshaft and slide on the retaining collar and bellows.

7   Push the spider onto the splines and retain by crimping at 120° intervals. The driveshaft should be held in a vice and a punch used to stamp the ends of three splines.

8   Spread the pack of special grease equally between the bellows and yoke.

9   Fit the yoke to the spider, then locate the lips of the bellows in the grooves on the shaft and yoke.

10   Fit the large diameter clip and adjust the coupling to the dimension shown in Fig. 8.19.

11   Temporarily insert a screwdriver between the bellows and shaft in order to release any air pressure, then fit the small diameter clip or rubber ring.

12   Refit the driveshaft, with reference to Section 3.

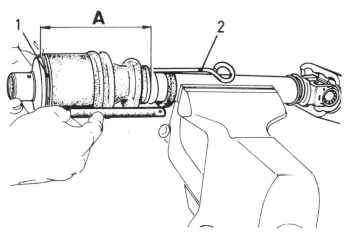

Fig. 8.19 Bellows setting dimension on the type GI 76 coupling (Sec 7)

A = 156 mm (6.141 in)
1   Clip
2   Rod or screwdriver to release air pressure

8   Fault diagnosis – driveshafts

Symptom	Reason(s)
Vibration	Worn joints
	Worn wheel or differential bearings
Noise on taking up drive	Worn driveshaft splines
	Worn joints
	Loose driveshaft nut

Chapter 9 Braking system

For modifications, and information applicable to later models, see Supplement at end of manual

Contents

Specifications

System type ....

Discs front, drums rear (except Turbo) or discs rear (Turbo); vacuum servo-assistance; dual hydraulic circuit split front/rear or diagonally, according to model; self-adjusting rear brakes; rod and cable-operated handbrake on rear brakes; rear pressure limiter; ventilated front discs on all models except 1397 cc.

Front brakes
Discs
Diameter ....

228 mm (8.983 in)
238 mm (9.377 in) or
260 mm (10.244 in)

Thickness:

New ....

10.0 mm (0.394 in)
12.0 mm (0.473 in)
20.0 mm (0.788 in) or
19.7 mm (0.776 in)

Minimum ....

9.0 mm (0.355 in)
11.0 mm (0.433 in)
18.0 mm (0.709 in) or
17.7 mm (0.697 in)

Disc pad thickness (minimum, including backing):
All models except Turbo ....

7.0 mm (0.276 in)

Turbo ....

9.0 mm (0.355 in)

Disc run-out (maximum) ....

0.07 mm (0.003 in) at diameter of 228 mm (8.983 in)

Rear brakes
Drums
Drum internal diameter:

New .... 180.25 mm (7.102 in)
180.5 mm (7.112 in) or
228.5 mm (9.003 in)

After regrinding .... 181.25 mm (7.141 in)
181.5 mm (7.151 in) or
229.5 mm (9.042 in)

Lining minimum thickness .... 0.5 mm (0.020 in) above rivet heads or shoe

Discs
Disc diameter .... 254 mm (10.0 in)
Disc thickness:

New .... 12.0 mm (0.473 in)
Minimum .... 10.5 mm (0.414 in)
Disc pad thickness (minimum, including backing) .... 7.0 mm (0.276 in)

Handbrake
Lever minimum travel .... 12 notches (to allow self-adjusting mechanism to function)

General
Vacuum servo diameter .... 200 mm (7.880 in)
203 mm (7.998 in)
225 mm (8.865 in) or
228 mm (8.983 in)

Brake pressure limiter
	Cut-off pressure
Models 1360 and 1362 (pre 1982):	
Full fuel tank	41 to 45 bar (594 to 652 lbf/in^2)
Half-full tank	38 to 42 bar (551 to 609 lbf/in^2)
Empty tank	35 to 39 bar (507 to 565 lbf/in^2)
Model 1363 (pre 1983):	
Full fuel tank	26 to 30 bar (377 to 435 lbf/in^2)
Half-full tank	23 to 27 bar (333 to 391 lbf/in^2)
Empty tank	20 to 24 bar (290 to 348 lbf/in^2)
Model 1362 (1982 on):	
Full fuel tank	31 to 35 bar (449 to 507 lbf/in^2)
Half-full tank	28 to 32 bar (406 to 464 lbf/in^2)
Empty tank	25 to 29 bar (362 to 420 lbf/in^2)
Models 1361 and 1363 (1983 on):	
Full fuel tank	30 to 34 bar (435 to 493 lbf/in^2)
Half-full tank	27 to 31 bar (391 to 449 lbf/in^2)
Empty tank	23 to 27 bar (333 to 391 lbf/in^2)
Models 1368 and 136A:	
Full fuel tank	26 to 30 bar (377 to 435 lbf/in^2)
Half-full tank	23 to 27 bar (333 to 391 lbf/in^2)
Empty tank	20 to 24 bar (290 to 348 lbf/in^2)
Model 1365:	
Full fuel tank	21 to 25 bar (304 to 362 lbf/in^2)
Half-full tank	18 to 22 bar (261 to 319 lbf/in^2)
Empty tank	15 to 19 bar (217 to 275 lbf/in^2)

Torque wrench settings
	lbf ft	Nm
Bleed screw	4 to 5	5 to 7
Caliper hose	10	14
Hose to rear arm	15	20
Wheel cylinder union	15	20
Master cylinder unions	15	20
Limiter inlet	19	26
Limiter outlet	15	20
Caliper bolt	42	57
Caliper bracket	74	100
Girling guide bolts	26	35

1 General description

The braking system is of dual hydraulic circuit type with discs fitted at the front and either drums or discs at the rear, according to model. The hydraulic circuit is split either between the front and rear wheels or diagonally, again according to model. Each circuit is operated independently so that, in the event of a failure in one circuit, the remaining circuit remains functional. A vacuum servo is fitted to all models to provide assistance to the driver when the footbrake pedal is depressed.

The disc calipers are of single piston type with floating housings. The drum rear brakes incorporate self-adjusting shoes, the automatic mechanism being operated by the footbrake. The handbrake operates on the rear brakes by rod and cable. A brake pressure limiter is incorporated in the rear hydraulic circuit(s) to control the braking

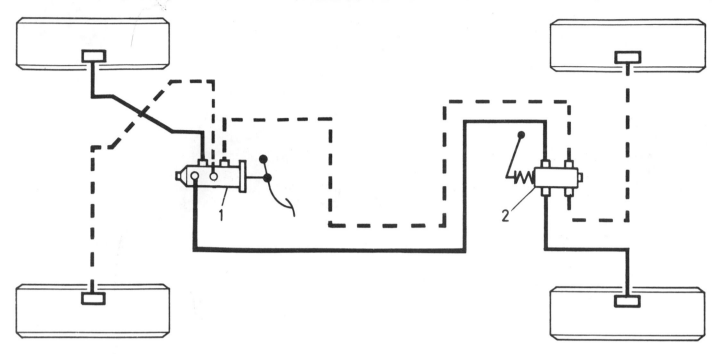

Fig. 9.1 Diagram of the diagonally split dual hydraulic braking circuit (Sec 1)

1   Master cylinder   *2   Brake pressure limiter*

balance between the front and rear brakes according to the load on the rear suspension, preventing lock up of the rear brakes before the front brakes.

2   Routine maintenance

1   At the first 5000 miles (8000 km) and thereafter every 10 000 miles (16 000 km) check the level of hydraulic fluid in the reservoir and top up if necessary. Frequent topping-up will require investigation for fluid leakage.

2   Every 10 000 miles (16 000 km) check the disc pads for wear, and renew them if necessary. Also check the condition of the discs for scoring.

3   Every 40 000 miles (65 000 km) check the rear brake shoe linings for wear and renew them if necessary. At the same time check the operation of the handbrake and adjust the cable.

3   Disc pads (front) – inspection and renewal

1   Apply the handbrake then jack up the front of the car and support on axle stands. Remove the front roadwheels.

2   Check the total width of each disc pad, and if less than the minimum amount given in the Specifications renew all the front pads as a set.

3   To remove the pads, first disconnect the pad wear warning wiring, if applicable (photo).

Bendix type caliper

4   Extract the small clip and tap the retaining key from the top of the caliper (photo).

5   Using a screwdriver, push one of the pads away from the disc to provide a small clearance then pull out and remove the pad. Repeat the procedure on the remaining pad (photos).

6   Brush away the accumulated dust and dirt from the pads and caliper, however, *take care not to inhale it as the lining dust is injurious to health.* Check the piston dust seal and the caliper slide and bellows for damage and renew them if necessary.

7   Using blocks of wood, push the piston into the cylinder until flush.

8   Fit the anti-rattle springs on the new pads. Note that the wear warning wiring must always be located at the top of the pad (see Fig. 9.2).

9   Fit the pads in the caliper bracket, then slide the retaining key into position. If necessary, file a chamfer on the key for ease of fitting.

10   Retain the key by fitting the clip to its inner end.

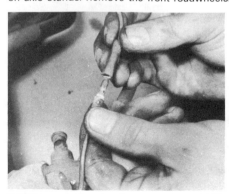

3.3 Disconnecting the disc pad wear warning wiring

3.4 Removing the pad retaining key on the Bendix caliper

3.5A Removing the outer disc pad on the Bendix caliper

3.5B Removing the inner disc pad on the Bendix caliper

3.12 Unscrewing the guide bolts on the Girling caliper

3.13 Removing the Girling caliper

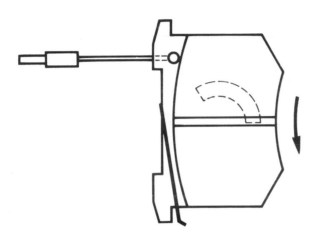

Fig. 9.2 Correct location of the disc pad wear warning wire on the Bendix caliper (Sec 3)

Arrow indicates forward rotation of disc

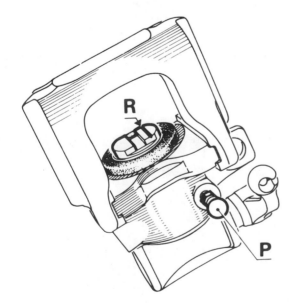

Fig. 9.3 Rear caliper piston groove (R) aligned with the bleed screw (P) (Sec 3)

Girling type caliper

11 Pull the caliper outwards slightly to provide clearance for removing the pads.

12 Unscrew the guide bolts while holding the guides stationary with an open-ended spanner (photo). Note that the bolts should be renewed every time the pads are renewed. Do not unscrew the socket head cap screws.

13 Withdraw the caliper and tie it to one side without straining the hydraulic hose (photo). Alternatively place it on an axle stand.

14 Remove the disc pads and brush away the accumulated dust and dirt *taking care not to inhale it as the lining dust is injurious to health* (photo).

3.14 Removing the inner disc pad on the Girling caliper

15 Check the condition of the brake disc and hydraulic hose and renew them if necessary.

16 Push the piston into the caliper until flush.

17 Locate the new pads on the caliper bracket.

18 Place the caliper over the pads and fit the lower bolt to the guide. Press the top of the caliper and fit the upper bolt. Tighten both bolts to the specified torque while holding the guides stationary.

Bendix and Girling calipers

19 Reconnect the pad wear warning wiring, if applicable.

20 Refit the roadwheels and lower the car to the ground.

21 Depress the brake pedal several times to reset the disc pads.

4   Disc pads (rear) – inspection and renewal

1   Chock the front wheels, jack up the rear of the car, and remove the rear roadwheels.

2   Check the total width of each disc pad, and, if less than the minimum amount given in the Specifications, renew all the rear pads as a set.

3   To remove the pads, first disconnect the handbrake cables from the caliper levers. To do this unscrew the cable compensator nut until the cable ends can be released from the levers.

4   Extract the clips and tap out the sliding keys.

5   Withdraw the caliper and tie it to one side without bending the rigid hydraulic pipe. Alternatively place it on an axle stand.

6   Where applicable disconnect the wear warning wiring.

7   Remove the disc pads and the anti-rattle springs.

8   Brush away the accumulated dust and dirt, *taking care not to inhale it as it is injurious to health.*

9   Using a suitable tool, turn the piston until it is screwed in as far as it will go and further rotation will not make it enter any deeper. This operation will cause the fluid level in the master cylinder reservoir to rise. Anticipate this by syphoning out some fluid.

10   Align the caliper piston so that the line on the piston thrust face is towards the bleed screw.

11   Fit the anti-rattle springs, followed by the disc pads.

12   Connect the wear warning wiring where applicable.

13   Locate the caliper over the pads, then tap in the keys and fit the clips.

14   Reconnect the handbrake cables.

15   Depress the brake pedal several times to reset the disc pads.

16   Adjust the handbrake, as described in Section 17, then refit the roadwheels and lower the car to the ground.

5   Rear brake drum – removal and refitting

1   Chock the front wheels then jack up the rear of the car and support on axle stands. Remove the roadwheel.

2   Release the handbrake.

3   Tap off the grease cap then extract the split pin and remove the nut retainer (photos).

4   Unscrew the stub axle nut and remove the washer (photos).

5   Remove the brake drum, taking care not to drop the outer bearing (photo). If the brake shoes are binding on the drum, back off the handbrake adjustment nut on the compensator then prise out the rubber plug from the backplate and use a screwdriver to push the lever outward so that it releases the shoes. If the outer bearing is tight on the stub axle use a puller on the drum.

6   Brush the accumulated dust from the drum and brake shoes *taking care not to inhale it as it is injurious to health.*

7   Remove the old grease from the hub and bearings.

8   Examine the drum for scoring and excessive wear and, if necessary, renew it or have it reground within the limits given in the Specifications.

9   Grease the bearing and the inside of the hub with a suitable lubricant, using about 20 g (0.75 oz).

10   Fit the drum, position the outer bearing, and fit the washer and nut (photo).

11   Tighten the nut to 22 lbf ft (30 Nm) while rotating the drum, then tap the drum lightly with a mallet (photo).

12   Loosen the nut one eighth to one sixth of a turn then retighten it until the bearing endfloat is just perceptible. If available, use a dial gauge to check that the endfloat is between 0 and 0.03 mm (0 and 0.001 in).

13   Fit the retainer and split pin without moving the nut.

14   Put 10 g (0.25 oz) of a suitable grease in the end cap, and tap it home.

15   Press the brake pedal several times, to settle the brake shoes, then adjust the handbrake (Section 17).

16   Refit the sealing plug to the backplate, then refit the roadwheel and lower the car to the ground.

6   Rear brake shoes – inspection and renewal

1   Remove both rear brake drums, as described in Section 5 (photo).

5.3A Remove the grease cap ...

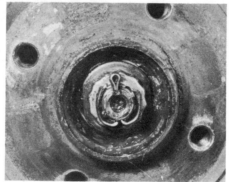

5.3B ... the split pin ...

5.3C ... and the nut retainer

5.4A Remove the stub axle nut ...

5.4B ... and thrust washer

5.5 Removing a rear brake drum

5.10 Fitting the rear hub outer bearing

5.11 Adjusting the rear hub bearings

6.1 View of the Bendix rear brake with the drum removed

2   Check the brake shoe linings for wear, and if any one is worn down to the minimum thickness given in the Specifications, renew all the rear shoes as a set.

Bendix type
3   Place a strong rubber band or flexible wire round the wheel cylinder, to prevent the pistons coming out.
4   Remove the upper return spring.
5   Disconnect the handbrake cable at the internal operating lever (photo).
6   Press the bottom of the shoe steady springs, to release them (photo).
7   Push the toothed lever fully rearward and lift the brake shoes out from the wheel cylinder.
8   Free the link from the front shoe.
9   Move the toothed sector to its original position.
10   Tilt the leading (front) shoe to 90° from the backplate, free the bottom return spring, and remove the shoe.
11   Remove the trailing (rear) shoe. Take the shoes to the bench, prise off the spring clips which hold the handbrake lever, the adjuster lever and the sprung toothed sector to the old shoes. Fit them to the new shoes.
12   Clean the backplate then fit the new shoes as follows: With the lower spring attached to both shoes, offer up the shoes with the front one at 90° to the backplate.

6.5 The handbrake cable attached to the shoe operating lever

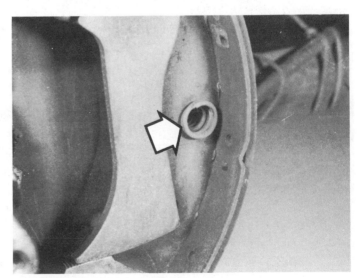

6.6 Shoe steady spring (arrowed)

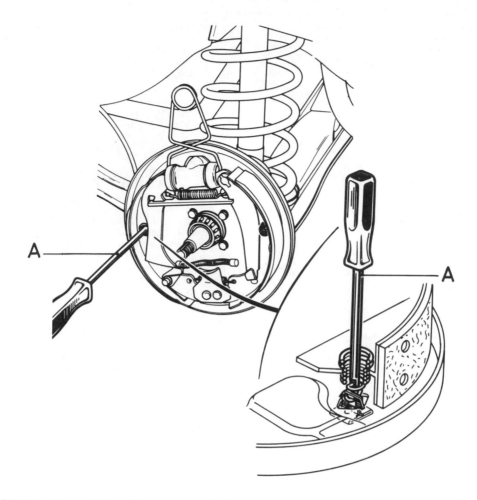

Fig. 9.4 Using the special tool (A) to remove the shoe steady springs on the Bendix rear brakes (Sec 6)

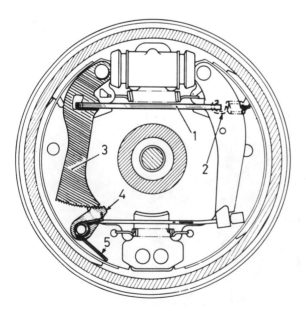

Fig. 9.5 Bendix type rear brake (Sec 6)

1 Link   4 Toothed sector
2 Spring   5 Spring
3 Lever

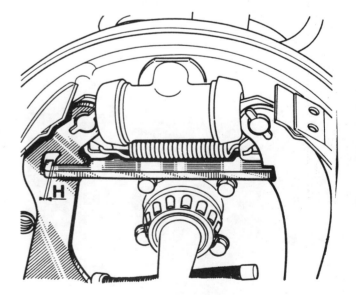

Fig. 9.6 Link clearance on Bendix type rear brake (Sec 6)

H = 1.0 mm (0.039 in)

13 Push the toothed lever fully rearward, and offer up the link, straightening up the shoe as the link is fitted.
14 Reverse the procedure in paragraphs 3 to 6.
15 Check the automatic adjustment by measuring dimension 'A' (see Fig. 9.6), which should be approximately as specified when the handbrake operating lever is resting against the shoe. If the dimension is incorrect, the link spring and both shoe return springs must be renewed.
16 Refit the brake drum as described in Section 5.

Girling type
17 Disconnect the handbrake cable.
18 Remove the top return spring and clip (see Fig. 9.7).
19 Disconnect the spring (3), and remove the lever (4), the spring, and the lever thrust washer.
20 Remove the two steady spring assemblies (6).
21 Place a strong rubber band, or flexible wire, round the wheel cylinder, to prevent the pistons coming out.
22 Remove the link assembly (7).
23 Cross the brake shoes one behind the other, to bring the lower return spring from behind the fulcrum. Remove the shoes and spring, and separate them. Take the shoes to the bench and transfer the handbrake lever to the new shoe, if not already fitted when supplied.
24 Clean the backplate then fit the new shoes. Note the colour coding applied to the adjustable link assembly. That for the LH side of the vehicle has a grey threaded plunger, whilst that for the RH side is coded yellow.
25 Reverse the procedure given in paragraphs 19 to 23.
26 Adjust the link assembly length until the lining diameter is about 178 mm (7 in), by pushing the handbrake operating lever back to the shoe, and turning the ratchet wheel until the required dimension is obtained.
27 Fit the top return spring and clip.
28 Reconnect the handbrake cable.
29 Refit the brake drum as described in Section 5.

7 Disc caliper (front) – removal, overhaul and refitting

1 Remove the disc pads, as described in Section 3, however, on the Girling caliper loosen the hydraulic hose before unscrewing the guide bolts.
2 Remove the brake fluid reservoir filler cap and retighten it onto a piece of polythene in order to reduce the loss of fluid when the caliper is removed. Alternatively use a hose clamp on the caliper hose.

Bendix type
3 Loosen the hydraulic hose.
4 Unscrew the retaining bolts from the stub axle carrier, then unscrew the caliper from the hose.
5 Check the condition of the hose and, if necessary, renew it with reference to Section 13.
6 Remove the dust cover and push out the piston using an air line or foot pump. Place a piece of wood in the caliper opening to prevent damage to the piston.
7 Using a feeler blade or similar tool prise the piston seal from inside the caliper bore.
8 Clean the components in methylated spirit and examine them for excessive wear and damage. Check the piston and bore for scoring. If the components are in good condition obtain a repair kit of rubbers, otherwise renew the caliper. For some models it is possible to obtain a repair kit which includes a new piston.
9 Reassemble the caliper in reverse order using the brake grease provided to lubricate the components.
10 Screw the caliper onto the hydraulic hose, using a new copper washer.
11 Locate the caliper on the stub axle carrier making sure that the hose is not twisted, insert the bolts and tighten them to the specified torque.

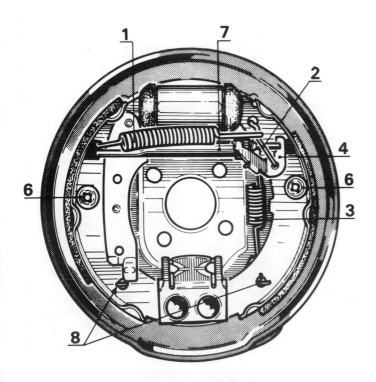

Fig. 9.7 Girling type rear brake (Sec 6)

1	Upper return spring	6	Shoe steady spring assembly
2	Clip		
3	Adjusting lever spring	7	Thrust link
4	Adjusting lever	8	Lower return spring

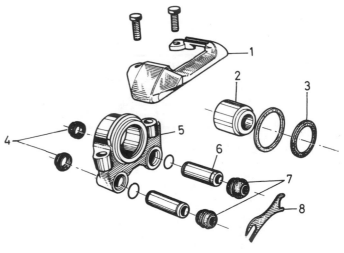

Fig. 9.8 Exploded view of the Bendix front brake caliper (Sec 7)

1	Bracket	5	Housing
2	Piston	6	Guides
3	Dust cover	7	Seals
4	Seals	8	Spacer

Girling type
12 Unscrew the caliper from the hose.
13 Check the condition of the hose and, if necessary, renew it with reference to Section 13.
14 Follow the procedure described in paragraphs 6 to 10, however, it is not possible to obtain repair kits with pistons for any Girling calipers.
15 Check the sliding guides for scoring and excessive wear as the correct operation of the caliper depends on them. If necessary remove

7.15 Girling caliper bracket mounting bolts (arrowed)

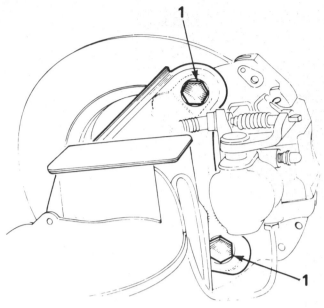

Fig. 9.9 Rear disc caliper bracket retaining bolts (1) (Sec 8)

the guides and dust covers from the bracket and obtain a repair kit. The bracket can also be removed if necessary (photo).

16 Fit new dust covers to the caliper bracket.

17 Lubricate the new guides with the special grease provided with them. Fit them to the caliper bracket. Note that the hexagon guide with a rubber sleeve is fitted to the top of the bracket, opposite the bleed screw, and the steel guide with two flats is fitted at the bottom.

Bendix and Girling types

18 Tighten the hose to the caliper. Remove the hose clamp or polythene and refit the disc pads with reference to Section 3.

19 Bleed the hydraulic circuit, as described in Section 12.

8 Disc caliper (rear) – removal, overhaul and refitting

1 Remove the disc pads, as described in Section 4.

2 Remove the brake fluid reservoir filler cap and retighten it onto a piece of polythene in order to reduce the loss of fluid when the caliper is removed. Alternatively, use a hose clamp on the relevant rear flexible hose.

3 Unscrew the union nut and disconnect the hydraulic pipe from the caliper. Withdraw the caliper. The caliper bracket may also be removed if necessary.

4 Clean away external dirt and then grip the caliper in a vice fitted with soft metal protectors.

5 Pull off the piston dust excluder.

6 Using a suitable tool, unscrew the piston (see Section 4). While the piston is being rotated, apply air pressure from a tyre pump to the port of the caliper to eject the piston.

7 Examine the piston and cylinder bore for scoring or metal-to-metal rubbed areas. If evident, then the piston/cylinder must be renewed as an assembly. This will necessitate separating the cylinder from its carrier using a wedge made to the dimensions shown in Fig. 9.10. Tap the wedge between the carrier legs, then depress the spring-loaded plunger and slide the cylinder out of the carrier. Fit the new cylinder by reversing the procedure (photos).

8 If the piston and cylinder are in good condition, pick the piston seal from its groove using a sharp pointed tool, taking care not to scratch the cylinder bore.

9 Obtain a repair kit which will contain all the renewable items.

10 Clean all components using only hydraulic fluid or methylated spirit.

11 Fit the new piston seal, manipulating it into its groove using the fingers only.

12 Apply clean hydraulic fluid to the piston and cylinder bore and insert the piston squarely using hand pressure.

13 Using a lever in the piston groove turn the piston until it is screwed

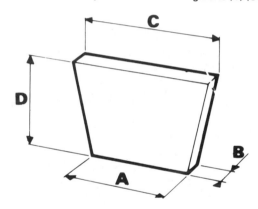

Fig. 9.10 Rear disc caliper leg spreading wedge (Sec 8)

A = 51.5 mm (2.03 in)   C = 56.0 mm (2.21 in)
B = 8.0 mm (0.31 in)   D = 35.0 mm (1.38 in)

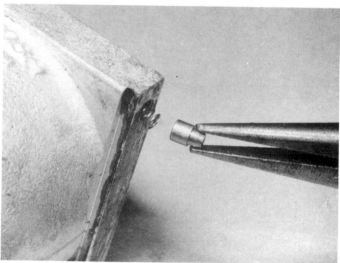

8.7A Fitting the spring-loaded plunger ...

8.7B ... and sliding the cylinder into the carrier

8 Dip all items in clean brake fluid, fit them as illustrated in Fig. 9.11 and check that the parts slide correctly in the cylinder.
9 Refitting is a reversal of removal with reference to Section 5. Finally bleed the hydraulic circuit, as described in Section 12.

9.2 Rear wheel cylinder and return spring with brake drum removed

in as far as it will go and further rotation will not make it enter any deeper.
14 Align the caliper piston so that the line of the piston thrust face is toward the bleed screw. Fit the new dust excluder.
15 Connect the caliper to the hydraulic pipe and tighten the union nut.
16 Remove the hose clamp or polythene and refit the disc pads with reference to Section 4.
17 Bleed the hydraulic system, as described in Section 12.

9 Rear wheel cylinder — removal, overhaul and refitting

1 Remove the brake drum, as described in Section 5.
2 Remove the upper return spring, and pull the brake shoes apart (photo).
3 Remove the brake fluid reservoir filler cap and retighten it onto a piece of polythene in order to reduce the loss of fluid. Alternatively use a hose clamp on the relevant rear flexible hose.
4 Unscrew the union nut and remove the brake pipe from the wheel cylinder (photo). Plug the end of the pipe.
5 Unscrew the bolts and withdraw the wheel cylinder from the backplate.
6 Clean the cylinder externally in methylated spirit, and dismantle it.
7 Examine the pistons and bore, and discard the complete unit if rust or scoring exist. Always use new rubber parts when reassembling. Fit them using the fingers only.

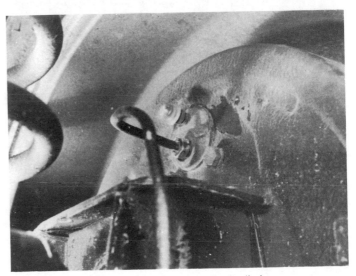
9.4 Hydraulic pipe and union nut on the wheel cylinder

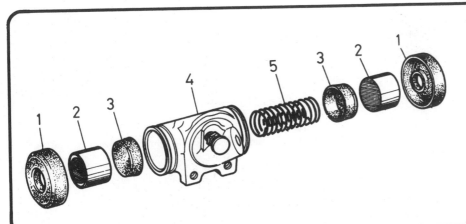

Fig. 9.11 Typical rear wheel cylinder components (Sec 9)

1 Dust seal
2 Pistons
3 Seals
4 Housing/cylinder
5 Spring

10 Brake disc – examination, removal and refitting

1   Remove the disc pads, as described in Section 3 or 4.
2   Unbolt and remove the caliper and/or bracket. On Bendix front brakes tie the caliper to one side without straining the hydraulic hose.
3   Examine both sides of the disc for scoring and excessive wear. Also check the disc for run-out using a dial gauge or metal block and feeler blades, however, do not confuse bearing endfloat with disc run-out. If the disc is worn excessively or if the run-out exceeds the maximum amount given in the Specifications renew the brake disc.
4   Unscrew the disc retaining screws using a Torx key and withdraw the brake disc (photo). If difficulty is experienced with a front disc it may be necessary to slightly loosen the driveshaft nut in order to release the outer cup.
5   Refitting is a reversal of removal with reference to Section 7 or 8, but tighten the bolts and screws to the specified torque. Apply locking fluid to the disc retaining screws before inserting them (photo).

10.4 Removing a front brake disc

10.5 Applying locking fluid to the disc retaining screws

11 Master cylinder – removal, overhaul and refitting

Note: The overhaul procedure in this Section covers Bendix and Teves type master cylinders – overhaul of Bendiberica, DBA and Girling types is similar.

1   Drain the brake fluid reservoir using a syringe taking care not to drop any fluid. Spilled fluid must be washed off the bodywork immediately with cold water otherwise the paintwork will be permanently damaged.
2   Pull the reservoir from the master cylinder and prise out the rubber sealing rings.
3   Unscrew the union nuts and disconnect the hydraulic pipes. If necessary identify them for position.
4   Unscrew the mounting nuts and withdraw the master cylinder from the servo unit.

Bendix type
5   Make up the tool shown in Fig. 9.12, and fit it to the master cylinder to compress the piston assemblies.
6   Grip a 3.5 mm drill in a vice, bring the master cylinder up to it, and enter the drill in the secondary piston roll pin, working via the secondary port. Rotate the cylinder to cause the drill to enter and grip the pin, and pull the cylinder away, leaving the pin on the drill.
7   Repeat the procedure given in paragraph 6 for the primary piston.
8   Remove the special tool and extract the pistons and springs, keeping them identified for position.

Fig. 9.12 Bendix master cylinder overhaul tool and dimensions (Sec 11)

Note: Dimensions in mm. Rod diameter approx 6 mm (0.25 in)

Teves type
9   Mount the cylinder body in a soft-jawed vice.
10   Using a suitable implement, compress the piston and spring assembly. Remove the stop screw, circlip and stop washer.
11   Release the piston/spring assembly carefully, and take the primary piston out.
12   Gently blow out the secondary piston with air from a tyre pump.

Bendix and Teves types
13   Check the surfaces of the pistons and bore for scoring and corrosion and renew the complete unit if necessary. Clean all the components with methylated spirit. If the bore is in good condition obtain a repair kit of pistons and seals.
14   Dip all the new components in new brake fluid and check that all the seals are correctly fitted using only the fingers to manipulate them.

Bendix type
15   Insert the secondary and primary piston assemblies with the roll pin slots aligned with the holes in the ports, then fit the special tool to compress them.
16   Insert the roll pins with their slots facing the mounting end of the cylinder, then remove the special tool.

Teves type
17   Insert the secondary piston assembly followed by the primary piston assembly.
18   Using a screwdriver, depress the primary piston and fit the stop washer, circlip and stop screw. Release the primary piston.

Bendix and Teves types
19   Check the length of the pushrod which is proud of the servo face, and adjust if necessary to give a dimension X as shown in Fig. 9.15.

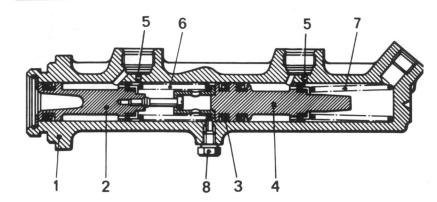

Fig. 9.13 Cross-section of the Teves master
cylinder (Sec 11)

1   Body
2   Primary piston
3   Seal
4   Secondary piston
5   Expansion holes
6   Return spring
7   Return spring
8   Stop screw

20 Refit the cylinder to the servo, and tighten the securing nuts.
21 Reconnect the hydraulic pipes and tighten the union nuts.
22 Refit the rubber sealing rings and press the reservoir fully into them.
23 Refill the system with hydraulic fluid and carry out the bleeding procedure described in Section 12.

12 Hydraulic system – bleeding

1   If the entire system is being bled, the sequence of bleeding should be carried out by starting at the bleed screw furthest from the master cylinder and finishing at the one nearest to it. Unless the pressure bleeding method is being used, do not forget to keep the fluid level in the master cylinder reservoir topped up to prevent air from being drawn into the system which would make any work done worthless.
2   Before commencing operations, check that all system hoses and pipes are in good condition with all unions tight and free from leaks.
3   Take great care not to allow hydraulic fluid to come into contact with the vehicle paintwork as it is an effective paint stripper. Wash off any spilled fluid immediately with cold water.
4   If the system incorporates a vacuum servo, destroy the vacuum by giving several applications of the brake pedal in quick succession.

Bleeding – two-man method
5   Gather together a clean jar and a length of rubber or plastic tubing which will be a tight fit on the brake bleed screws.
6   Engage the help of an assistant.
7   Push one end of the bleed tube onto the first bleed screw and immerse the other end in the jar which should contain enough hydraulic fluid to cover the end of the tube (photos).

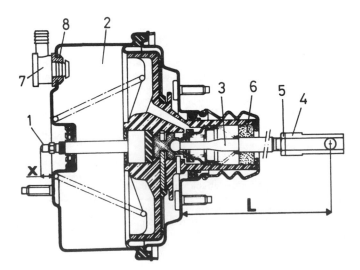

Fig. 9.14 Inserting the roll pins in the Bendix master cylinder
(Sec 11)

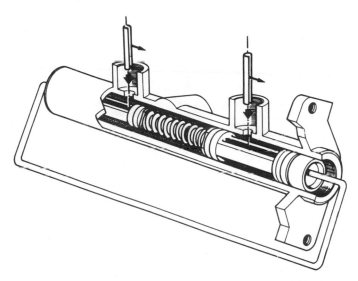

Fig. 9.15 Cross-section of the vacuum servo unit (Secs 11 and 14)

1   Pushrod
2   Servo body
3   Pushrod
4   Clevis
5   Locknut
6   Air filter
7   Check valve
8   Check valve sealing
    grommet
X = 9 mm (0.354 in)
L = 126 mm (4.960 in)
       – UK models
L = 128.5 mm (5.063 in)
       – North American models

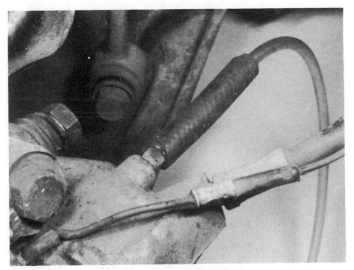

12.7A Fit the brake bleeding tube to the bleed screw ...

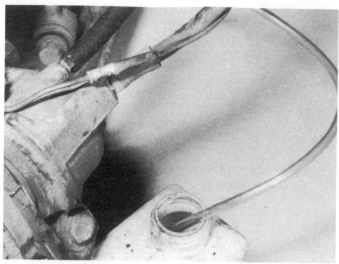

12.7B ... and immerse the other end in a jar

8   Open the bleed screw one half turn and have your assistant depress the brake pedal fully then slowly release it. Tighten the bleed screw at the end of each pedal downstroke to obviate any chance of air or fluid being drawn back into the system.
9   Repeat this operation until clean hydraulic fluid, free from air bubbles, can be seen coming through into the jar.
10 Tighten the bleed screw at the end of a pedal downstroke and remove the bleed tube. Bleed the remaining screws in a similar way.

Bleeding – using one way valve kit
11 There are a number of one-man, one-way brake bleeding kits available from motor accessory shops. It is recommended that one of these kits is used wherever possible as it will greatly simplify the bleeding operation and also reduce the risk of air or fluid being drawn back into the system, quite apart from being able to do the work without the help of an assistant.
12 To use the kit, connect the tube to the bleed screw and open the screw one half turn.
13 Depress the brake pedal fully and slowly release it. The one-way valve in the kit will prevent expelled air from returning at the end of the each pedal downstroke. Repeat this operation several times to be sure of ejecting all air from the system. Some kits include a translucent container which can be positioned so that the air bubbles can be seen being ejected from the system.
14 Tighten the bleed screw, remove the tube and repeat the operations on the remaining brakes.
15 On completion, depress the brake pedal. If it still feels spongy repeat the bleeding operations, as air must still be trapped in the system.

Bleeding – using a pressure bleeding kit
16 These kits are also available from motor accessory shops and are usually operated by air pressure from the spare tyre.
17 By connecting a pressurised container to the master cylinder fluid reservoir, bleeding is then carried out by simply opening each bleed screw in turn and allowing the fluid to run out, rather like turning on a tap, until no air is visible in the expelled fluid.
18 By using this method, the large reserve of hydraulic fluid provides a safeguard against air being drawn into the master cylinder during bleeding which often occurs if the fluid level in the reservoir is not maintained.
19 Pressure bleeding is particularly effective when bleeding difficult systems or when bleeding the complete system at the time of routine fluid renewal.
20 Where a vacuum servo is fitted, it is recommended that the brake pedal is depressed slowly and held down with a wooden strut after opening the first bleed screw.
21 Where a pressure drop indicator is fitted which incorporates a bypass, remember to bleed from the bleed screw on this device.

All methods
22 When bleeding is completed, check and top up the fluid level in the master cylinder reservoir.
23 Check the feel of the brake pedal. If it feels at all spongy, air must still be present in the system and further bleeding is indicated. Failure to bleed satisfactorily after a reasonable repetition of the bleeding operations may be due to worn master cylinder seals.
24 Discard brake fluid which has been expelled. It is almost certain to be contaminated with moisture, air and dirt making it unsuitable for further use. Clean fluid should always be stored in an airtight container as it absorbs moisture readily (hygroscopic) which lowers its boiling point and could affect braking performance under severe conditions.

13 Hydraulic pipes and hoses – general

1   Hydraulic pipes and hoses should be examined periodically, the metal pipes being checked for signs of severe corrosion, and the rubber hoses for cracks. Both should be checked for any signs of chafing (photo).

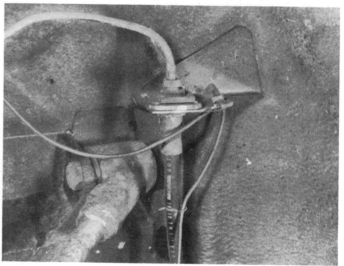

13.1 Front brake pipe and hose on bracket

2   Renew any defective rubber hoses with new parts.
3   Metal pipes can sometimes be purchased complete and ready to fit. Alternatively, it will be necessary to have replacements made by an engineering concern who possess the necessary tools. When ordering, it is advisable to provide the manufacturer with the old pipe as a pattern.
4   Care should be taken to ensure that the correct metric pipe fittings and ends are supplied.

14 Vacuum servo unit – checking, removal and refitting

1   Whilst the braking system will continue to function with an inoperative servo, considerably more pedal pressure will be required. If this is the case, a loss of vacuum may be the cause. To check the unit, depress the brake pedal several times with the engine stopped in order to dissipate the vacuum. Depress the pedal moderately then start the engine. If the pedal drops slightly the servo unit is functioning correctly but, if it remains still, the unit is faulty. If the repairs described in Section 15 are ineffective and the hoses are in good condition, renew the unit.
2   To remove the unit, first remove the master cylinder, as described in Section 11.
3   Disconnect the vacuum hose.
4   Remove the brake pedal clevis pin (photo).
5   Remove the nuts securing the servo to the bulkhead, and then the servo complete with the spacer plate.
6   Check the pushrod dimensions on both sides of the servo, as

14.4 Brake pedal, pushrod and clevis pin

shown in Fig. 9.15, and adjust as necessary by adjusting the pushrod nut or clevis.
7 Refitting is a reversal of removal with reference to Section 11 where necessary.

15 Vacuum servo unit – air filter and check valve renewal

Air filter
1 Using a screwdriver or hooked instrument, prise the old filter from the pushrod end of the servo unit and, if necessary, cut it free.
2 Cut the new filter as shown in Fig. 9.16, locate it over the pushrod and press it into the end of the servo unit.

Check valve
3 Remove the vacuum hose from the servo.
4 Twist the check valve, and pull it out.
5 Examine the rubber seal for damage. Note that a new seal is provided with a new check valve.
6 Refitting is a reversal of removal.

16 Brake pressure limiter – removal, refitting, checking and adjustment

1 To remove the unit, first remove the brake fluid reservoir filler cap and retighten it onto a piece of polythene in order to reduce the loss of fluid.
2 Jack up the rear of the car and support on axle stands. Chock the front wheels.
3 Loosen the flexible hose union(s) at the limiter (photo).

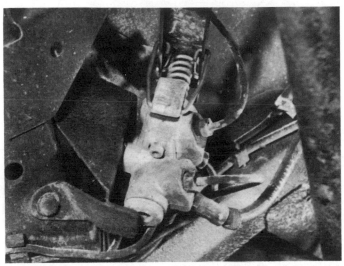

16.3 Brake pressure limiter and hydraulic pipes and hoses

4 Unscrew the union nuts and disconnect the hydraulic pipes.
5 Unscrew the mounting bolts and disconnect the operating rod from the suspension centre arm.
6 Unscrew the unit from the flexible hose(s), then plug the hose(s).
7 Check the hose(s) and renew if necessary. If the hose between the limiter and the three-way union is renewed, also renew the copper washers if their thickness is less than 1.5 mm (0.059 in).
8 Refitting is a reversal of removal, but make sure that the hose is not twisted. Where applicable, unscrew the hose at the three-way union, off-set it one notch, then retighten it. Bleed the hydraulic system, as described in Section 12, then adjust the unit as follows.

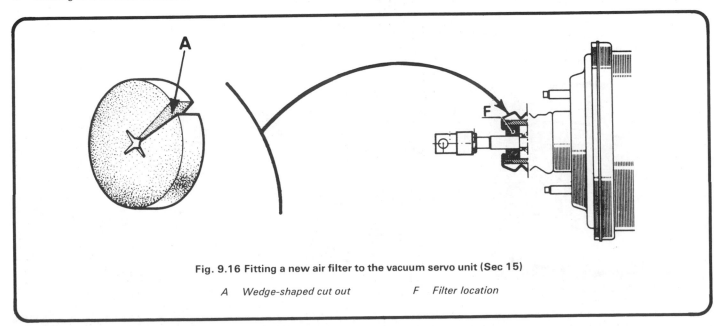

Fig. 9.16 Fitting a new air filter to the vacuum servo unit (Sec 15)

A Wedge-shaped cut out　　　*F Filter location*

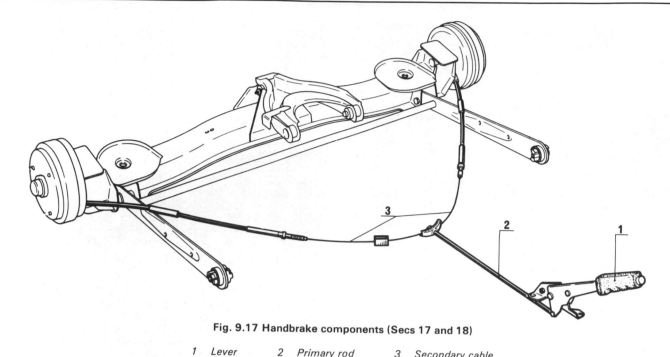

Fig. 9.17 Handbrake components (Secs 17 and 18)

1 Lever   2 Primary rod   3 Secondary cable

9 First ensure that the vehicle is on the ground, with a driver in the driving seat, and the boot empty.

10 Remove a bleed screw from one of the rear wheel cylinders, fit the special pressure gauge (Renault part number FRE 214-02/04) in place of the screw, and bleed the circuit and gauge.

11 Press the pedal several times, and check the cut-off reading given by the gauge. Correct readings are given in the Specifications.

12 Adjust the cut-off pressure if necessary, by screwing the adjusting nut up to increase, or down to decrease.

13 Check the pressure gauge reading several times, and if satisfactory remove the gauge.

14 Bleed the brakes (Section 12).

17 Handbrake – adjustment

1 Correct adjustment is essential, so that the self-adjusting braking system functions normally. Adjustment should be carried out only when work on the linings or on the cables themselves has been carried out.

2 All four wheels must be on the ground (or on a lift).

3 Release the handbrake at the lever.

4 Release the adjuster locknut, and turn the adjusting nut until the cable deflection is approximately 20 mm (0.75 in) in the centre of the cable run (photo).

5 Check that the handbrake lever travel is at least 12 notches.

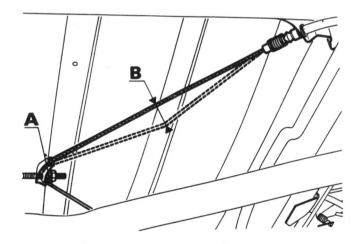

Fig. 9.18 Handbrake adjustment nut (A) and cable deflection (B) (Sec 17)

17.4 Handbrake rod and cable adjuster

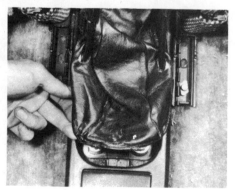

18.1A Lift the gaiter ...

18.1B ... for access to the safety belt anchor bolts

18 Handbrake lever, rod and cable – removal and refitting

Lever

1 Remove both centre safety belt anchor bolts (photos) where applicable.
2 Jack up the rear of the car and support on axle stands. Chock the front wheels then disconnect the handbrake under the car.
3 Disconnect the handbrake warning switch (photo).
4 Remove the lever fixing bolts from the floor, and pull the lever out.
5 To further dismantle, take out the ratchet pin, and the pin in the toothed quadrant.

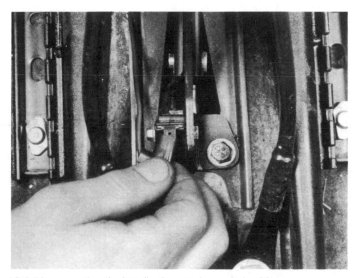

18.3 Disconnecting the handbrake warning switch wiring

6 Unscrew the lever plunger knob, and remove the detail parts beneath it.
7 To refit, assemble the detail items under the plunger knob in the following order: flat washer, rubber washer, flat washer, spring and plunger.
8 Refit the ratchet and toothed quadrant pins.
9 Refit the bellows.
10 Offer the assembly to the floor, bolt in place, and reconnect the handbrake warning light switch.
11 Refit the seat belt anchor bolts.
12 Reposition the bellows, beginning at the front.
13 Reconnect the rod and cable, and adjust the mechanism (see Section 17).

Rod

14 Disconnect the underfloor mechanism at the cable.
15 Remove the lever assembly (see paragraphs 1 to 4) and take out the pin to the underfloor rod.
16 To refit, reverse the removal procedure and adjust the handbrake, as described in Section 17.

Cable

17 Remove the brake drums, as described in Section 5.
18 Place a strong rubber band or flexible wire round the operating cylinder, to prevent the pistons coming out.
19 Remove the upper return spring.
20 Disconnect the handbrake cable at the internal operating lever.
21 Pull the cable stop out of the backplate.
22 Disconnect the cable at the forward end, and pull out the brackets on the chassis.
23 To refit, reverse the procedure given in paragraphs 18 to 22.
24 Refit the brake drums, as described in Section 5.
25 Adjust the cable, as described in Section 17.

19 Footbrake pedal – removal and refitting

Refer to Chapter 5, Section 6, but on automatic transmission models ignore the references to the clutch pedal.

20 Fault diagnosis – braking system

Symptom	Reason(s)
Excessive pedal travel	Air in hydraulic system Failure of one hydraulic circuit Handbrake adjustment incorrect
Uneven braking and pulling to one side	Contaminated linings Seized caliper or wheel cylinder Incorrect tyre pressures Faulty handbrake mechanism
Brake judder	Worn or distorted discs or drums Excessively worn linings Worn suspension balljoints
Brake pedal feels 'spongy'	Air in hydraulic system Worn master cylinder seals
Excessive effort to stop car	Servo unit faulty Excessively worn linings Seized caliper or wheel cylinder Contaminated linings Failure of one hydraulic circuit

Chapter 10 Electrical system

For modifications, and information applicable to later models, see Supplement at end of manual

Contents

Specifications

System type .... 12 volt, negative earth

Battery capacity .... 36, 40, 48, 50, 65 or 70 amp hr

Alternator
Type .... Paris-Rhone, Ducellier, SEV or Motorola
Regulated voltage .... 13.5 to 15.0 volt

Starter motor
Type .... Ducellier, Paris-Rhone or Bosch pre-engaged

Fuses*

Number	Rating (amps)	Circuit
1	8	Flasher unit and, on UK models, stop-light switch
2 (UK)	5	Windscreen wiper 'park'
2 (North America)	–	Not used
3 (UK)	–	Not used
3 (North America)	5	Stop-light switch
4 (UK)	–	Not used
4 (North America)	5	Windscreen wiper 'park'
5 (UK)	–	Not used
5 (North America)	5	Radio and washer/wipers
6 (UK)	8	Cigar lighter, interior lights
6 (North America)	8	Cigar lighter, interior lights, key warning buzzer and tailgate light
7	–	Not used
8 (UK)	16	Wiper/washer combination switch
8 (North America)	–	Not used
9 (UK)	–	Not used
9 (north America)	16	Rear window defroster switch
10 (UK)	5	Console illumination, left-hand side and rear lights
10 (North America)	5	Left-hand side markers
11	10	Left-hand window
12 (UK)	5	Right-hand side and rear lights
12 (North America)	5	Right-hand side markers
13	10	Right-hand window
14	5	Instrument panel
15 (UK)	16	Reversing light switch
15 (North America)	5	Reversing light and intermittent wipers
16	1.5	Automatic transmission
17 (UK)	17	Heater or air conditioning fan rheostat
17 (North America)	–	Not used
18 (UK)	16	Rear window defroster switch
18 (North America)	16	Heater, air conditioning, sunroof and rear window wiper
19 (North America)	–	Not used

* This table is for early models – minor changes have taken place on later models

Bulbs

	Wattage
Headlight (UK)	H4 or 45/40
Sidelight (UK)	4
Turn/parking (North America)	21/5
Direction indicator (UK)	21
Stop/tail	21/5
Tail	5
Reversing light	21
Foglight (rear)	21
Side marker (North America)	5
Number plate	5

1 General description

The electrical system is of 12 volt negative earth type. The major components consist of a battery, an alternator for charging purposes, and a starter motor.

Where components are connected into the electrical system, the greatest care should be taken to see that correct polarities are observed. Failure to observe this precaution may result in irreparable damage to the items concerned.

Although repair procedures are given in this Chapter it may well be more economical to renew worn components as complete units.

2 Routine maintenance

1 Every 5000 miles (8000 km) check the battery electrolyte level and top up as necessary. At the same interval check all the driving and warning lights for operation and renew bulbs where necessary.
2 Every 10 000 miles (16 000 km) check the headlight beam alignment and adjust as necessary. Also check the alternator drivebelt tension and adjust as necessary.

3 Battery – removal and refitting

1 The battery is located in the engine compartment on the right-hand side for RHD models and the left-hand side for LHD models (photo). On North American turbo models it is located in the luggage compartment.

3.1 Battery location on RHD models

2 Disconnect the negative terminal followed by the positive terminal. **Never** disconnect the battery with the engine running.
3 Unscrew the clamp bolt or nuts and lift the battery from the platform, taking care not to spill any electrolyte on the bodywork (photo).
4 Refitting is a reversal of removal, however, do not over-tighten the clamp bolt or nuts.

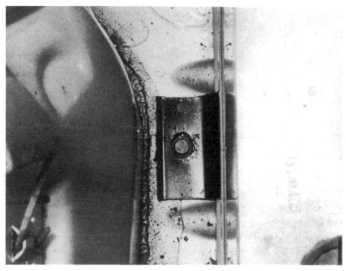

3.3 Battery clamp

4 Battery – maintenance

1 At the intervals given in Section 2 top up the electrolyte level so that the plates are just covered. Do not overfill, and use only distilled water.
2 Keep the battery top clean.
3 Keep the battery terminals and connections clean, and greased with petroleum jelly.
4 When charging the battery from an external source, do not use any naked lights in the vicinity, as the danger of an explosion caused by igniting of the battery gases is a very real one. Charging from an external source, at a low rate, can be advisable during the winter time when battery loading can be very heavy.

5 Alternator – special precautions

1 The alternator generates alternating current, which is then rectified by diodes into direct current. Very little attention is required.
2 Apart from brush renewal, any work required on the alternator should be left to a properly qualified auto-electrician, as should the location of defects in the charging system.
3 Certain precautions must be taken to prevent damage to the alternator system, as follows:

(a) *Always disconnect the battery before removing the alternator*
(b) *When the alternator is running, the connections must always be properly made, ie the positive terminal connected to the battery, and the alternator and battery negative terminals earthed*
(c) *Never disconnect the battery or the regulator when the alternator is running*
(d) *Ensure that the regulator earth connection is always properly made, when running*
(e) *Disconnect the battery and alternator wiring before using electric-arc welding equipment to repair any part of the car*
(f) *Disconnect the battery before charging it*

6 Alternator – removal and refitting

1   Disconnect the battery negative lead.
2   For better access to the lower bolts, jack up the front of the car and support on axle stands. Apply the handbrake, and remove the splash panels.
3   Loosen the mounting and adjustment bolts, swivel the alternator towards the engine and remove the drivebelt from the pulley (photo).

6.3 Rear view of the alternator (ohc engine)

4   Remove the mounting and adjustment bolts, disconnect the wiring, and withdraw the alternator from the engine. On certain models the mounting bracket must first be unbolted from the cylinder block.
5   Refitting is a reversal of removal, but adjust the drivebelt tension, as described in Chapter 2.

7 Alternator brushes – renewal

1   Where necessary remove the alternator.

Paris-Rhone and Ducellier
2   Remove the rear cover.
3   Disconnect the wiring then unbolt the voltage regulator, together with the brush holder.

SEV
4   Remove the rear cover.
5   Disconnect the diode bridge wire.
6   Unbolt the regulator.
7   Note the location of the wires, then unsolder them from the brush holder.

Motorola
8   Remove the regulator screws, then disconnect the wires after noting their locations.
9   Remove the screws and withdraw the brush holder.

All types
10   Wipe clean the slip rings with a fuel-moistened cloth – if they are very dirty use fine glasspaper then wipe clean with the cloth.
11   Fit the new brushes using a reversal of the removal procedure.

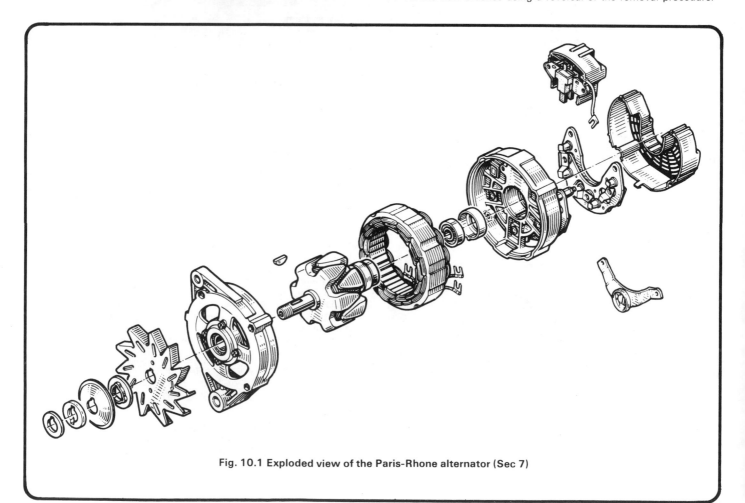

Fig. 10.1 Exploded view of the Paris-Rhone alternator (Sec 7)

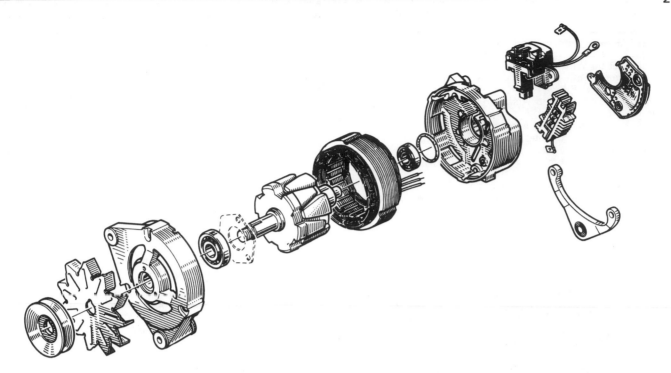

Fig. 10.2 Exploded view of the Ducellier alternator (Sec 7)

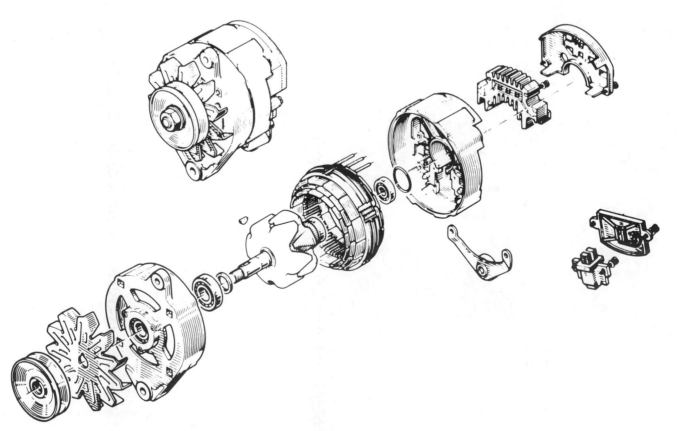

Fig. 10.3 Exploded view of the Motorola alternator (Sec 7)

8 Starter motor – removal and refitting

1   Disconnect the battery negative lead.
2   Remove the air cleaner and ducting with reference to Chapter 3 where necessary.
3   Where applicable on North American models remove the catalytic converter and starter shield.
4   Unscrew the mounting nuts securing the starter to the transmission bellhousing. Note that the bolt heads are fitted with locktabs (photo).
5   Unbolt the starter from the bracket(s) on the cylinder block and recover the spacers (photo).
6   Withdraw the starter from the engine.
7   Refitting is a reversal of removal, but tighten the transmission bellhousing bolts *before* the bracket bolt(s).

8.4 Starter motor bolts

8.5 Starter motor mounting brackets

9 Starter motor – overhaul

Ducellier
1   Remove the motor rear shield.
2   Remove the armature end bolt.
3   Remove the terminal.

4   Remove the rear bearing.
5   Take off the motor body.
6   Remove the solenoid securing body.
7   Remove the bearing pin from the solenoid-to-pinion fork.
8   Remove the armature and solenoid.
9   Examine the commutator condition, and if necessary either have it skimmed by a specialist and the segments undercut, or fit a replacement.
10 Examine the brushes and the pinion assembly, and change them if necessary.
Pinion assembly
11 With the armature removed, tap the stop collar with a suitable-sized piece of tube, thereby freeing the clip (Fig. 10.5).
12 Remove the pinion assembly.
13 Fit the replacement pinion.
14 Fit the circlip, and push the stop collar over it.
15 Reassemble the motor, and adjust the fork position, as described in paragraphs 20 to 22.
Brushes
16 With the starter body removed, unsolder the brushes and solder new brushes in their place (Fig. 10.6).
Solenoid
17 With the body and armature removed, take out the solenoid.
18 Remove the bolt securing the fork to the solenoid core, and remove the fork.
19 To reassemble, secure the fork to the solenoid by refitting and fully tightening the bolt.
20 Refit the solenoid (see paragraph 24) and adjust the assembly fork by first removing the plug at the solenoid front end.
21 Ensure that minimal clearance exists between the bolt and adjusting nut, and that the pinion assembly is resting against the armature.
22 Push the solenoid bolt fully inwards, and check the clearance between the pinion and stop collar, which should be as shown in Fig. 10.7. Turn the adjusting nut as necessary to obtain the correct clearances (Fig. 10.4).
General
23 To reassemble, first lubricate the starter front bush.
24 Fit the armature and solenoid into the starter nose, replace and tighten the solenoid securing nuts, and refit the fork pin.
25 Fit the commutator and washers, first the steel washer and then the fibre one.
26 Oil the rear bush.
27 Refit the body.
28 Refit the rear bearing, the spring, and the washer, noting the slots. Fit and tighten the fixing bolt.
29 Refit the shield.

Paris-Rhone
30 Disconnect the field wire.
31 Remove the clip (where fitted), the rear bearing and the body, noting washer arrangements.
32 Remove the pinion operating fork pin.
33 Remove the solenoid securing nuts.
34 Remove the armature and solenoid.
35 Overhaul the pinion assembly, as described in paragraphs 11 to 14.
36 Reassemble the motor, and adjust the fork position by first removing the solenoid cap.
37 Connect the solenoid to a battery to energise it, and check that the clearance between the pinion and the stop is as shown in Fig. 10.9.
38 To correct the clearance, turn the adjusting screw (1) as necessary (Fig. 10.10).
39 Renew the brushes with reference to paragraph 16.
Solenoid
40 Disconnect the lead, and remove the solenoid securing nuts.
41 Withdraw the solenoid, noting the spring and seal.
42 To refit, reverse the removal procedure.
General
43 To reassemble the starter, follow paragraphs 23 to 27, but note the different washer build-up.
44 Refit the remaining items in the reverse order to removal.

Bosch
45 Disconnect the leads from the solenoid terminals and remove the solenoid securing screws.

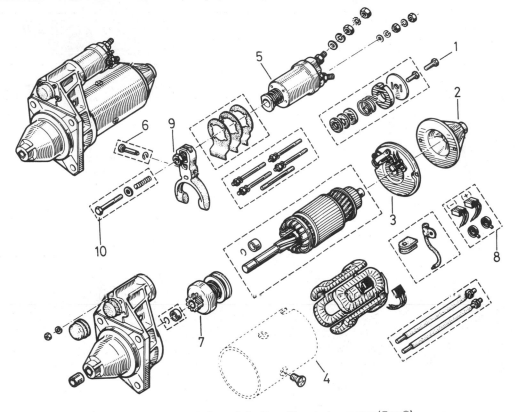

Fig. 10.4 Exploded view of the Ducellier starter motor (Sec 9)

1	Armature end bolt
2	Cap
3	Rear bearing
4	Motor body
5	Solenoid
6	Solenoid fork bearing pin
7	Pinion assembly
8	Brushes
9	Adjusting nut, solenoid
10	Bolt, solenoid

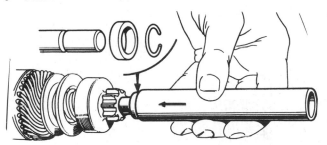

Fig. 10.5 Removing the pinion assembly (Sec 9)

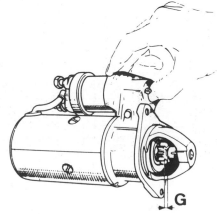

Fig. 10.7 Checking the pinion-to-stop collar clearance (Sec 9)

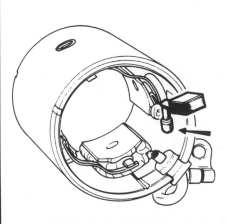

Fig. 10.6 Starter motor brush soldering points (Sec 9)

G = 0.5 to 1.5 mm (0.02 to 0.06 in)

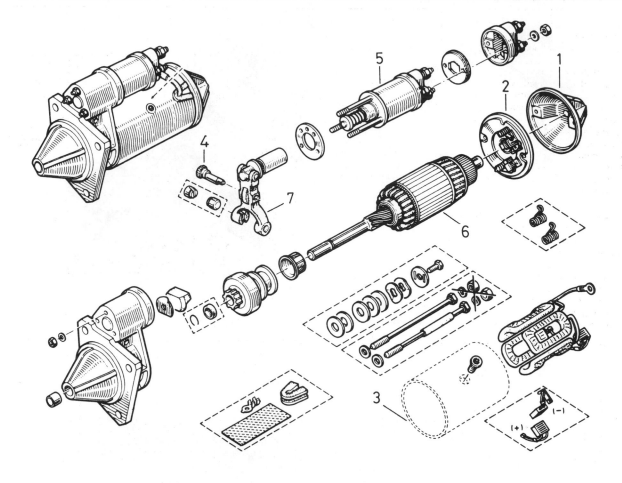

Fig. 10.8 Exploded view of the Paris-Rhone starter motor (Sec 9)

1	Cap	3	Body	5	Solenoid	7	Fork
2	Bearing plate	4	Fork bearing pin	6	Armature		

1 Cap
2 Bearing plate
3 Body
4 Fork bearing pin
5 Solenoid
6 Armature
7 Fork

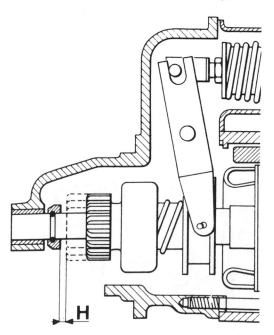

Fig. 10.9 Pinion-to-stop ring clearance with solenoid energised (Sec 9)

H = 1.5 mm (0.06 in)

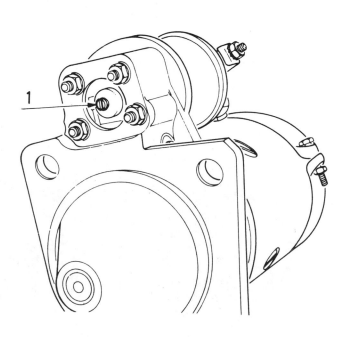

Fig. 10.10 Adjusting screw (1) for pinion-to-stop clearance (Sec 9)

46 Lift the rear end of the solenoid slightly and unhook its front end from the engagement lever.
47 Remove the armature shaft end cap, U-washer, spacers and gasket.
48 Remove the two tie-bolts and remove the commutator end cover.
49 Using a hooked piece of wire, lift the brushes from their holders, unscrew the brush holder plate and extract the fibre and steel washers.
50 Renew the brushes by soldering if they have worn to 5.0 mm (0.20 in) or less.
51 If the starter drive is to be renewed, pull off the drive housing; retaining the rubber and steel washers.
52 Using a piece of tubing, drive the stop ring towards the pinion gear, extract the snap-ring, and pull off the stop ring and pinion.
53 Reassemble in reverse order, using a puller to locate the stop ring over the snap-ring.

10 Fuses and relays – general

1 The fusebox is located under the facia and the cover simply unclips (photo).
2 Whenever a fuse is being renewed, refit one of the correct type and rating. If using one of the spare fuses supplied in the fusebox, do not forget to obtain a replacement at the earliest opportunity.
3 The respective fuse circuit layouts are shown in the accompanying diagrams (Figs. 10.11 and 10.12).

10.1 Fusebox location

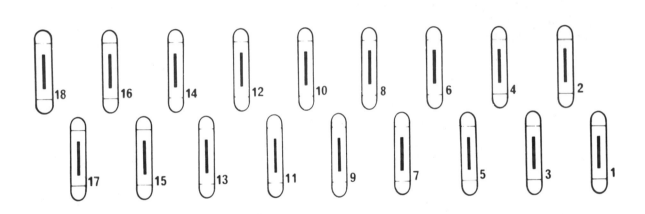

Fig. 10.11 Fuse numbering on early models (Sec 10)

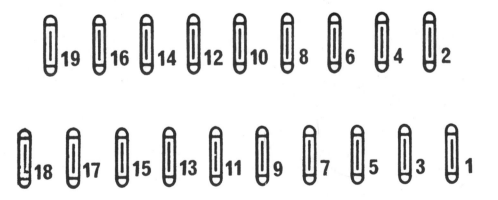

Fig. 10.12 Fuse numbering on later models (Sec 10)

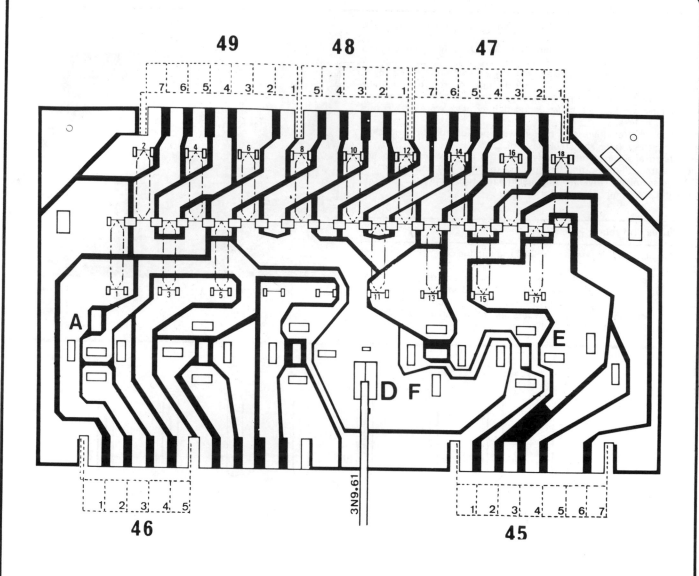

Fig. 10.13 Printed circuit and relay locations on UK models (Sec 10)

Connector 45
1 Earth
2 + after ignition switch
3 + after ignition switch
4 Not used
5 Heating-ventilating fan motor rheostat +
6 Not used
7 Not used

Connector 46
1 Flasher unit fuse +
2 Stop-lights switch and radio +
3 Direction indicators tell-tale
4 Direction indicators switch +
5 Not used

Connector 47
1 Rear screen demister switch +
2 Reversing lights +
3 Automatic transmission +
4 RH window switch +
5 Instrument panel +
6 LH window switch +
7 Sidelight/interior light fuses +

Connector 48
1 RH side and rear lights and identification illumination
2 Not used
3 LH side and tail lights and instrument panel illumination
4 Not used
5 Windscreen wiper +

Connector 49
1 Not used
2 Interior light, cigar lighter +
3 + before luggage compartment switch
4 Not used
5 Not used
6 Windscreen wiper 'park' +
7 Windscreen wiper 'park' fuse +

Units
A Flasher unit
D Feed to plate
E Relay after ignition switch
F Window winder relay

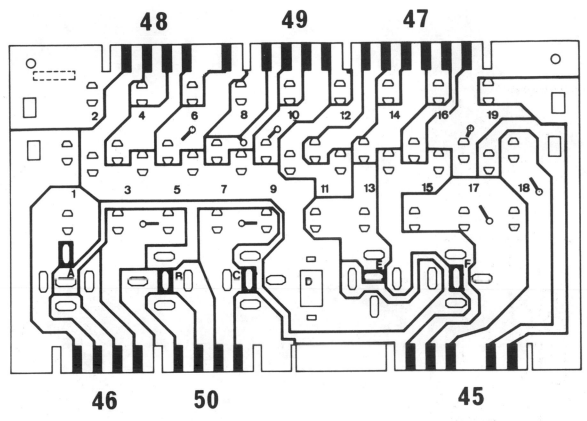

Fig. 10.14 Printed circuit and relay locations on North American models (Sec 10)

Connector 45
1 Earth
2 + after ignition
3 + after ignition
4 Sunroof/rear windshield
5 Heater
6 Not used
7 Not used

Connector 46
1 Flasher unit
2 Not used
3 Turn signal indicator light
4 Turn signal switch
5 + Accessory

Connector 47
1 Not used
2 + Reversing light/intermittent wipers
3 Automatic transaxle
4 Power window (right)
5 + instrument panel
6 Power window (left)
7 + parking lights fuse

Connector 48
1 Accessories radio/washer-wipers
2 Cigar lighter/dome/clock

3 Key warning buzzer/trunk light
4 Stop-lights
5 Wiper parking position
6 Not used
7 Not used

Connector 49
1 Right side markers
2 Rear window defroster switch
3 Left side markers
4 Not used
5 Not used

Connector 50
1 Not used
2 Dead wire
3 Not used
4 Not used
5 Rear window relay feed

Components
A Flasher unit
B Not used
C Rear window relay
D Current feed
E Power window relay
F Relay after ignition

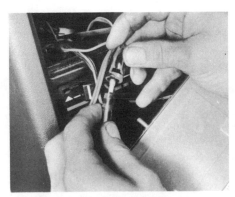

10.4 Removing the in-line radio fuse

10.5A Fuse board and relays

10.5B Removing a relay

4 The fuse for the radio is of the in-line type and is located behind the radio (photo).
5 The relays are located behind the fuses and are accessible by removing two screws and withdrawing the fusebox panel. The relays

are a press fit in the printed circuit board (photos). Relay locations are shown in Figs. 10.13 and 10.14.
6 Additional relays are located in the rear window wiper enclosure and on the engine compartment front panel (photos).

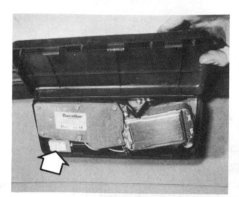

10.6A Rear window wiper motor and relay (arrowed)

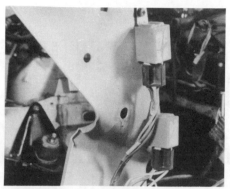

10.6B Relays located on the engine compartment front panel

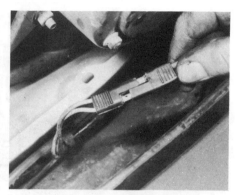

11.3 Disconnecting the headlight wiring

11.5A Headlight unit upper nut (arrowed)

11.5B Headlight unit outer mounting bolt (arrowed)

11.5C Headlight unit inner mounting bolt (arrowed)

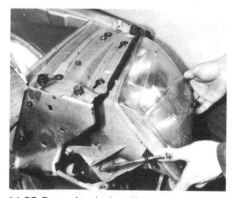

11.5D Removing the headlight unit

11.5E Front view of the headlight unit

11.5F Side view of the headlight unit, showing the wiper motor

11 Headlight units – removal and refitting

1   Disconnect the battery negative lead.

UK models

2   Unhook the inner spring and remove the direction indicator light.
3   Disconnect the headlight wiring and, where fitted, the wiring to the headlight wiper motor, and also the wiper arm (photo).
4   Remove the front grille (Chapter 12).
5   Unscrew the mounting nuts and bolts, and withdraw the headlight unit, together with the wiper motor where fitted (photos).

North American models

6   Remove the headlight bezel upper screws and unhook the inner spring. Withdraw the bezel and disconnect the wiring for the parking/direction indicator light.
7   Disconnect the headlight wiring then unscrew the upper and lower screws and withdraw the headlight sealed beam unit.

All models

8   Refitting is a reversal of removal, but check and adjust the beam alignment, as described in Section 13.

12 Rear light units – removal and refitting

1   Disconnect the battery negative lead.
2   Remove the inner trim plastic cover.
3   Disconnect the wiring.

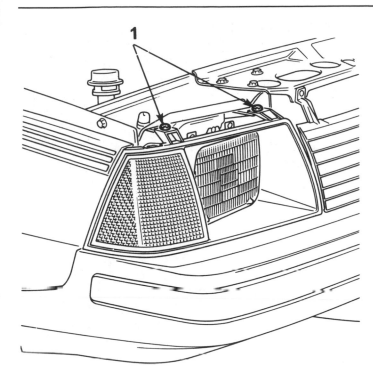

Fig. 10.15 Headlight bezel upper screws on North American models (Sec 11)

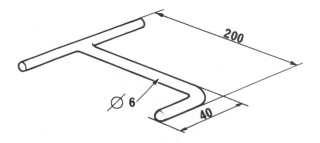

Fig. 10.17 Rear light unit removal tool (Sec 12)

Measurements in mm

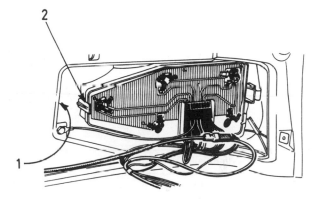

Fig. 10.18 Rear light unit retaining clip location (1) and bulb holder tab (2) (Sec 12)

13 Headlights – beam alignment

1 A proper optical instrument is required to obtain correct alignment. In an emergency, however, proceed as follows:
2 Position the car on level ground, tyres correctly inflated, approximately 5.0 metres (16 feet) in front of and, at right-angles to, a wall or garage door.
3 Make marks corresponding to the headlight centres then switch on the main beams.
4 Adjust each headlight using the knobs or screws shown in Fig. 10.19. Note on UK models the screw in the centre of the height

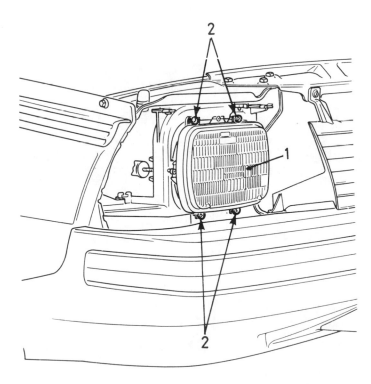

Fig. 10.16 North American headlight sealed beam unit (1) and retaining screws (2) (Sec 11)

4 Prise the plastic tabs outward and withdraw the bulb holder.
5 Using a tool made up as shown in Fig. 10.17 engage the hook in the unit retaining clip and pull it inwards, then press the clip and withdraw the rear light unit.
6 Refitting is a reversal of removal, using the tool to pull out the clip.

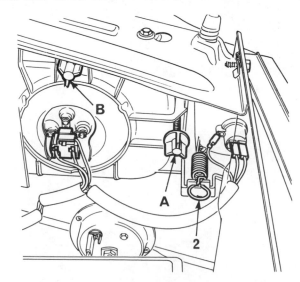

Fig. 10.19 Headlight horizontal (A) and vertical (B) adjustment knobs on North American models (Sec 13)

2   *Bezel retaining spring*

13.4A Headlight horizontal adjustment screw (arrowed)

13.4B Headlight vertical adjustment screw/knob

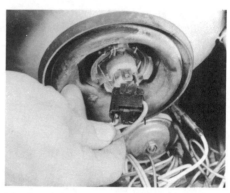

14.1 Pull off the wiring connector ...

adjusting knob should be used for the initial setting with the knob in a central position. The knob can then be adjusted according to the load being carried – turning it clockwise lowers the beam, and vice versa (photos).

14 Lamp bulbs – renewal

Headlight (UK models)
1   Pull off the rear wiring connector (photo).
2   To remove the halogen bulb, release the clips and extract the bulb (photos).
3   To remove the conventional bulb prise back the clips and extract the bulb.

Sidelight (UK models)
4   Pull the bulb holder from the headlight, then depress and twist the bulb to remove it (photos).

Front direction indicator light (UK models)
5   Release the rear spring and withdraw the unit (photos).
6   Turn the bulb holder a quarter turn and extract it from the light unit, then depress and twist the bulb to remove it (photos).
7   When refitting the light unit make sure that the lugs are correctly located.

Parking/turn signal light (North American models)
8   Remove the headlight bezel upper screws and unhook the inner spring. Withdraw the bezel and disconnect the wiring.

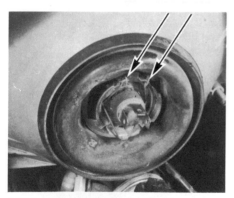

14.2A ... release the clips (arrowed) ...

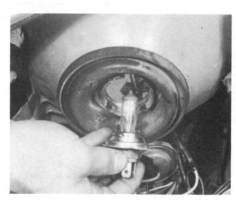

14.2B ... and extract the headlight bulb

14.4A Pull out the sidelight bulb holder ...

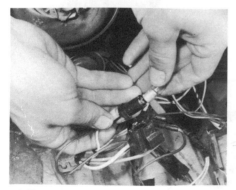

14.4B ... and remove the bulb

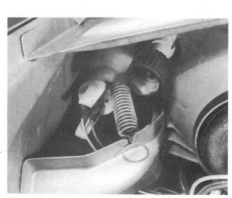

14.5A Release the spring ...

14.5B ... and withdraw the front direction indicator light

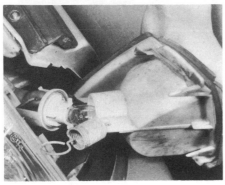

14.6A Remove the front direction indicator bulb holder ...

14.6B ... and remove the bulb

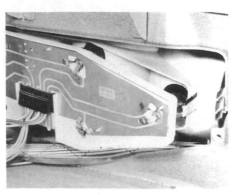

14.12 Removing the rear light bulb holder

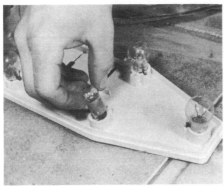

14.13 Removing a rear light bulb

14.16A Prise up the rear number plate light ...

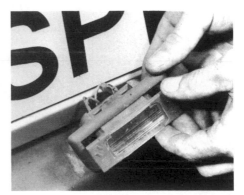

14.16B ... extract the lens ...

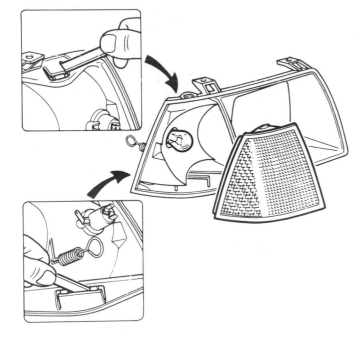

Fig. 10.20 Removing the parking/turn signal bulb on North American models (Sec 14)

9   Prise back the upper and lower plastic lugs and remove the light lens.
10   Depress and twist the bulb to remove it.

Rear light
11   Remove the inner trim plastic cover.
12   Prise the plastic tabs outwards and withdraw the bulb holder (photo).
13   Depress and twist the bulb to remove it (photo).

Side marker light (North American models)
14   Remove the screws and pull out the unit.
15   Twist out the bulb holder then pull out the bulb.

Number plate light (UK models)
16   Prise the light from the bumper, then push the plastic clips apart and extract the lens cover (photos).
17   Remove the festoon type bulb from the spring contacts (photo).

Interior lights
18   Prise out the light unit, then remove the festoon type bulb from the spring contacts (photos).

Front foglights/driving lights
19   Remove the screws and withdraw the lower cover (photos).
20   Remove the screws at the sides of the lens and withdraw the light unit (photos).
21   Disconnect the wiring, release the clip and extract the bulb holder (photos).
22   Unclip and remove the bulb.

Instrument panel warning light
23   Remove the instrument panel, as described in Section 15.
24   Twist the bulb holder a quarter turn to remove it then pull out the bulb (photos).

All light fittings
25   Refitting is a reversal of removal.

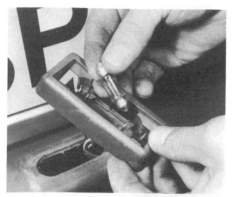

14.17 ... and remove the festoon type bulb

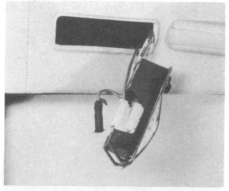

14.18A Removing the front interior light

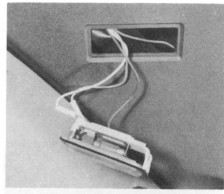

14.18B Removing the rear interior light

14.19A Remove the front foglight cover screws ...

14.19B ... and withdraw the cover

14.20A Remove the side screws ...

14.20B ... and withdraw the light unit

14.21A Disconnect the wiring and clip ...

14.21B ... and extract the bulb holder

14.24A Removing an instrument panel warning light, type A ...

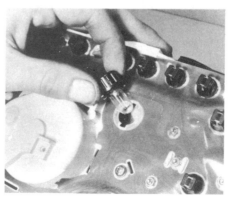

14.24B ... and type B

15.2 Removing the instrument panel surround switch cover

15.3A Remove the screws (arrowed) ...

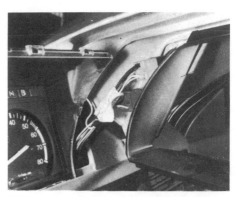

15.3B ... and withdraw the surround

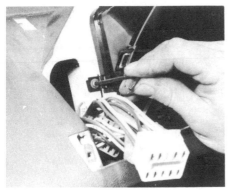

15.4 Removing the support plate screws

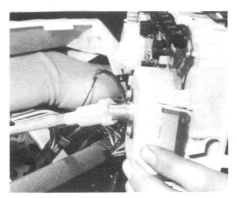

15.5A Disconnecting the speedometer cable

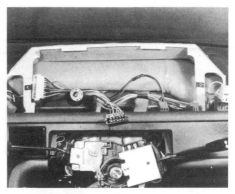

15.5B Instrument panel aperture, showing speedometer cable and wiring connectors

15.5C Front view of the instrument panel

15.5D Rear view of the instrument panel

15 Instrument panel – removal and refitting

1   Disconnect the battery negative lead.
2   Pull the switch covers from the bottom corners of the panel surround (photo).
3   Remove the cross-head screws and withdraw the surround sufficiently to disconnect the switch wiring (photos). Although not essential, the steering wheel can be removed to provide better access (refer to Chapter 11).
4   Unscrew the Torx screws and remove the support plate (photo).
5   Depress the upper retaining clips and withdraw the instrument panel until the speedometer cable and wiring can be disconnected (photos).
6   Refitting is a reversal of removal, but make sure that the speedometer cable is fully connected.

16 Ignition switch – removal and refitting

1   Disconnect the battery negative lead.
2   Remove the steering wheel, as described in Chapter 11.
3   Remove the screws and withdraw the steering column shrouds (photos).
4   Disconnect the wiring plug.
5   Turn the ignition key to position '1' (Fig. 10.21).
6   Unscrew the retaining screw then depress the pin with a suitable pointed instrument and push out the switch.
7   To renew the steering lock stop on the switch, remove the key to release the latch, then remove the two rear bracket screws and slide the switch rearwards. Apply locking fluid to the screws during reassembly.
8   Refitting is a reversal of removal.

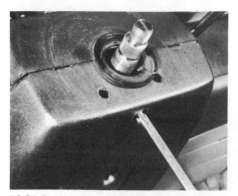

16.3A Remove the screws ...

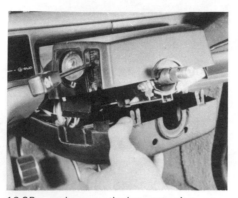

16.3B ... and remove the lower steering column shroud ...

16.3C ... and upper shroud

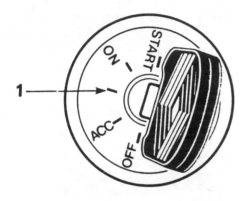

Fig. 10.21 The 'garage' position (1) for the ignition key (Sec 16)

17 Combination switches – removal and refitting

1   Disconnect the battery negative lead.
2   Remove the steering wheel, as described in Chapter 11.
3   Remove the screws and withdraw the steering column shrouds (photo).
4   Disconnect the wiring plugs.
5   Unbolt and remove the switch assembly.
6   To remove the light switch from the assembly use a soft metal drift 3.8 mm (0.15 in) in diameter to drive out the connecting pin, while supporting the assembly with a length of tubing approximately 8.0 mm (0.315 in) in diameter. On some models the switches may be bolted to a bracket.
7   Refitting is a reversal of removal.

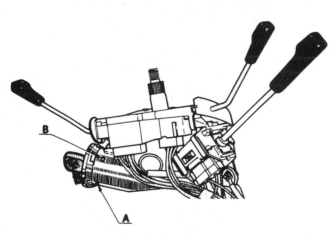

Fig. 10.22 Ignition switch retaining screw (A) and pin (B) locations (Sec 16)

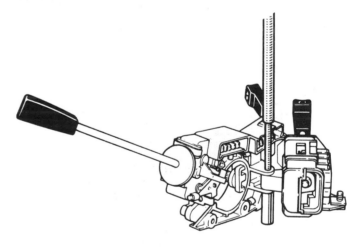

Fig. 10.24 Separating the light switch from the assembly (Sec 17)

18 Switches – removal and refitting

1   Disconnect the battery negative lead.

Facia switch

2   Pull off the cover, where applicable.
3   Prise the switch from the instrument panel surround and disconnect the wiring plug.
4   Where applicable extract the bulb from the rear of the switch (photo).
5   Refitting is a reversal of removal.

Courtesy light switch

6   Prise the switch from the door pillar (photo).
7   Disconnect the wiring, making sure that it does not fall into the pillar.
8   Refitting is a reversal of removal.

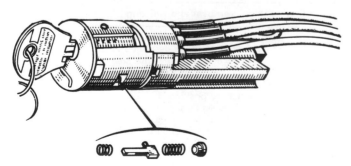

Fig. 10.23 Ignition switch, showing steering lock stop (Sec 16)

17.3 View of the combination switches with the steering column shrouds removed

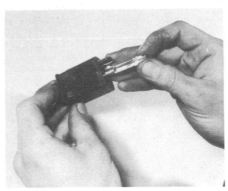

18.4 Removing a bulb from a facia switch

18.6 Removing a courtesy light switch

19 Rear window wiper motor – removal and refitting

1 Disconnect the battery negative lead.
2 Remove the wiper blade and arm (Section 23).
3 Unscrew the mounting nuts, noting the location of the spacers.
4 Withdraw the assembly and disconnect the wiring.
5 Refitting is a reversal of removal, but do not overtighten the mounting nuts.

20 Electric window motor and reduction gear – removal and refitting

1 Remove the window regulator, as described in Chapter 12.
2 Remove the screw and nut and pull the motor from the reduction gear.

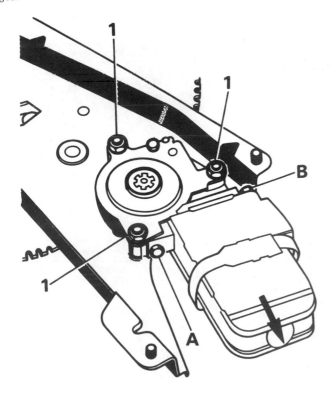

Fig. 10.25 Electric window motor and reduction gear (Sec 20)

A Screw
B Nut
1 Reduction gear mounting bolts

3 The motor is sealed and cannot be repaired; however, it can be tested by connecting it to a 12 volt supply. The motor should run in both directions by reversing the supply leads.
4 Unbolt the reduction gear from the regulator.
5 Refitting is a reversal of removal.

21 Windscreen wiper motor and linkage – removal and refitting

1 Disconnect the battery negative lead.
2 Remove the wiper blades and arms (Section 22).
3 Unscrew the spindle nuts and remove the spacers and lever.
4 Disconnect the wiring plug.
5 Unbolt the earth lead and unscrew the mounting bolt near the motor (photo).

21.5 Windscreen wiper motor showing lower mounting bolt (arrowed)

6 Push the spindles through the valance, then withdraw the assembly from the left-hand side of the bulkhead.
7 Unscrew the nut and disconnect the link from the motor driveshaft.
8 Unbolt the motor from the linkage.
9 If necessary, the spindles can be renewed separately. To renew the SEV type unscrew the bolts and disconnect the spindle from the linkage – the Bosch type is secured with rivets which must be renewed.
10 Refitting is a reversal of removal, but check that both links are aligned with each other when the motor is in the 'parked' position.

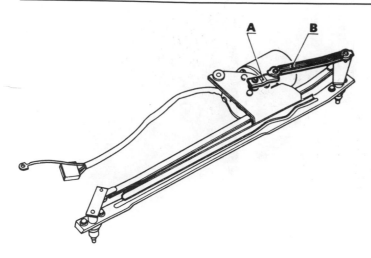

Fig. 10.26 Windscreen wiper linkage links (A and B) aligned in the 'parked' position (Sec 21)

22 Windscreen wiper blade and arm – removal and refitting

1   With the wipers in the 'parked' position note the location of the blades for reference when refitting the arms.
2   To remove a wiper blade, first swivel the arm from the windscreen, then depress the plastic tab beneath the centre and withdraw the blade from the slot in the end of the arm (photos).
3   To remove a wiper arm, lift the spindle cover, unscrew the nut and pull the arm from the tapered spindle. Where applicable pull the extra arm from the second spindle (photos).

4   Refitting is a reversal of removal, but refit the wiper arm so that the wiper blade is in its previously noted position.

23 Rear window wiper blade and arm – removal and refitting

Follow the procedure given in Section 22; however, there is no spindle cover or additional arm.

24 Headlight wiper blade and arm – removal and refitting

1   To remove a wiper blade, swivel the arm out then disconnect the blade.
2   To remove a wiper arm, lift the spindle cover, unscrew the nut, pull off the arm and disconnect the washer tube (photos).
3   Refitting is a reversal of removal, but with the motor in the 'parked' position refit the arm so that the wiper blade is at the bottom of the headlight.

25 Windscreen washer pump – removal and refitting

UK models
1   Disconnect the battery negative lead.
2   Disconnect the wiring and tube.
3   Unscrew the cap and withdraw the pump assembly.
4   Refitting is a reversal of removal.

North American models
5   Remove the battery (Section 3) except on turbo models.
6   Lift out the windscreen washer bottle and disconnect the wiring and tube.
7   Remove the pump from the bottle.
8   Refitting is a reversal of removal, but check that the seal is seated correctly.

22.2A Depress the tab (arrowed) ...

22.2B ... and remove the wiper blade in the direction of the arrow

22.3A Windscreen wiper arm retaining nut

22.3B Disconnecting the additional wiper arm

24.2A Removing a headlight wiper arm

24.2B Disconnecting the washer tube

26.4 Engine oil level sensor on the ohc engine

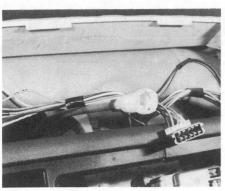

27.1 View of the speedometer cable with the instrument panel removed

27.3A Extract the plastic retaining pin ...

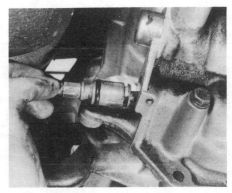

27.3B ... and withdraw the speedometer cable ferrule

28.1 Air horns fitted to R1363 models

26 Engine oil level sensor – removal and refitting

1   Disconnect the battery negative lead.
2   Where necessary remove the engine splash guard panels.
3   Disconnect the wiring.
4   Unscrew the sensor (ohv engines) or unbolt the clamp and remove the sensor from the cylinder block (ohc engines) (photo).
5   Refitting is a reversal of removal.

27 Speedometer cable – removal and refitting

1   Remove the instrument panel, as described in Section 15 (photo).
2   Jack up the front of the car and support on axle stands. Apply the handbrake.
3   Disconnect the cable from the transmission by extracting the retaining pin and withdrawing the ferrule (photos).
4   On certain North American models a service interval box is inserted in the upper part of the cable and there are two cable sections. Disconnect the cables from the box as required.
5   Withdraw the cable through the bulkhead after prising out the grommet.
6   Refitting is a reversal of removal.

28 Horn – removal and refitting

1   Either a resonator horn or air horns are fitted according to model (photo). First remove the left-hand headlight unit on the front grille, as applicable.
2   With the battery disconnected, disconnect the wiring and unbolt the horn bracket.
3   On the air horn type the pump and horns can be unbolted from the bracket if necessary.
4   Refitting is a reversal of removal.

29 Remote door lock control – general

1   Some models are equipped with the PLIP remote door lock control comprising a key ring transmitter and a facia-mounted receiver which operates the central locking system.
2   The system operates by an infra-red ray which transmits a coded signal to the receiver.
3   The transmitter uses three 1.5 volt batteries.
4   No repair is possible, but if new units are required the code must be quoted. The code is stamped on the printed circuit chip of the transmitter and either the front or interior of the receiver.

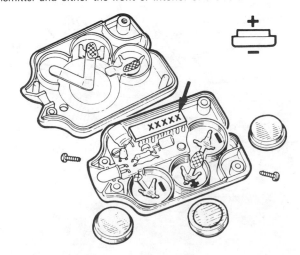

Fig. 10.27 Remote door lock control transmitter (Sec 29)

Arrow shows code location

30.4 Unscrew the retaining nuts ...

30.5 ... and remove the radio surround

30.7 Rear of the radio, showing the wiring and aerial connections

30 Radio – removal and refitting

1   Disconnect the battery negative lead.
2   Remove the console side panels with reference to Chapter 12.
3   Pull off the control knobs.
4   Unscrew the circular retaining nuts using long-nosed pliers if necessary (photo).
5   Remove the surround (photo).
6   Unscrew the rear mounting nut, where fitted.
7   Disconnect the wiring and aerial (photo).
8   Withdraw the radio from the facia.
9   Refitting is a reversal of removal.

31 Central door locking system – general

1   The system provides for simultaneous locking of the four doors, either from outside by turning the key in either front door, or from inside by pressing the door-locking switch on the central console.

2   A red tell-tale on each door, when visible, indicates that the doors are locked.
3   An electrical circuit, consisting of an inertia switch and a thermal cut-out, causes all the doors to become unlocked in the event of an impact of more than 9 mph (15 kph) occurring. Very light impacts will not cause this to happen.
4   The inertia switch can be reset by depressing the resetting button, in the event of an accidental unlocking situation occurring. The cut-out prevents the inertia switch circuit remaining live too long, and is reset by pressing the cut-out button below the steering wheel.
5   The lock is operated by a ferrite plunger located between two coils (Fig. 10.29).

32 Mobile radio equipment – interference-free installation

Aerials – selection and fitting

The choice of aerials is now very wide. It should be realised that the quality has a profound effect on radio performance, and a poor, inefficient aerial can make suppression difficult.

A wing-mounted aerial is regarded as probably the most efficient for signal collection, but a roof aerial is usually better for suppression purposes because it is away from most interference fields. Stick-on wire aerials are available for attachment to the inside of the windscreen, but are not always free from the interference field of the engine and some accessories.

Motorised automatic aerials rise when the equipment is switched on and retract at switch-off. They require more fitting space and supply leads, and can be a source of trouble.

There is no merit in choosing a very long aerial as, for example, the type about three metres in length which hooks or clips on to the rear of the car, since part of this aerial will inevitably be located in an interference field. For VHF/FM radios the best length of aerial is about one metre. Active aerials have a transistor amplifier mounted at the base and this serves to boost the received signal. The aerial rod is sometimes rather shorter than normal passive types.

A large loss of signal can occur in the aerial feeder cable, especially over the Very High Frequency (VHF) bands. The design of feeder cable is invariably in the co-axial form, ie a centre conductor surrounded by a flexible copper braid forming the outer (earth) conductor. Between the inner and outer conductors is an insulator material which can be in solid or stranded form. Apart from insulation, its purpose is to maintain the correct spacing and concentricity. Loss of signal occurs in this insulator, the loss usually being greater in a poor quality cable. The quality of cable used is reflected in the price of the aerial with the attached feeder cable.

The capacitance of the feeder should be within the range 65 to 75 picofarads (pF) approximately (95 to 100 pF for Japanese and American equipment), otherwise the adjustment of the car radio aerial trimmer may not be possible. An extension cable is necessary for a long run between aerial and receiver. If this adds capacitance in excess of the above limits, a connector containing a series capacitor will be required, or an extension which is labelled as 'capacity-compensated'.

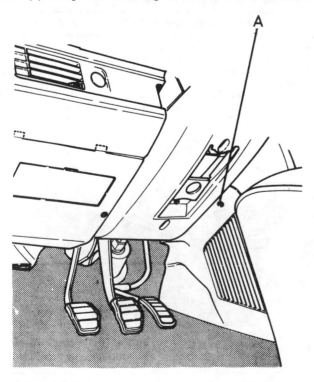

Fig. 10.28 Central door locking system reset button location (A) (Sec 31)

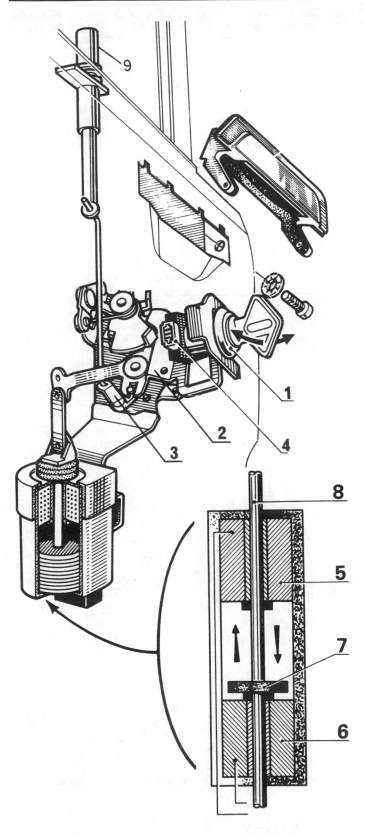

Fitting the aerial will normally involve making 22 mm diameter hole in the bodywork, but read the instructions that come with the aerial kit. Once the hole position has been selected, use a centre punch to guide the drill. Use sticky masking tape around the area for this helps with marking out and drill location, and gives protection to the paintwork should the drill slip. Three methods of making the hole are in use:

(a) Use a hole saw in the electric drill. This is, in effect, a circular hacksaw blade wrapped round a former with a centre pilot drill.

(b) Use a tank cutter which also has cutting teeth, but is made to shear the metal by tightening with an Allen key.

(c) The hard way of drilling out the circle is using a small drill, say 3 mm, so that the holes overlap. The centre metal drops out and the hole is finished with round and half-round files.

Whichever method is used, the burr is removed from the body metal and paint removed from the underside. The aerial is fitted tightly ensuring that the earth fixing, usually a serrated washer, ring or clamp, is making a solid connection. *This earth connection is important in reducing interference.* Cover any bare metal with primer paint and topcoat, and follow by underseal if desired.

Aerial feeder cable routing should avoid the engine compartment and areas where stress might occur, eg under the carpet where feet will be located. Roof aerials require that the headlining be pulled back and that a path is available down the door pillar. It is wise to check with the vehicle dealer whether roof aerial fitting is recommended.

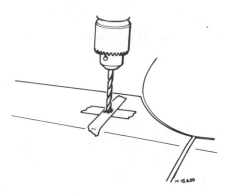

Fig. 10.30 Drilling the bodywork for aerial mounting (Sec 32)

Loudspeakers

Speakers should be matched to the output stage of the equipment, particularly as regards the recommended impedance. Power transistors used for driving speakers are sensitive to the loading placed on them.

Before choosing a mounting position for speakers, check whether the vehicle manufacturer has provided a location for them. Generally door-mounted speakers give good stereophonic reproduction, but not all doors are able to accept them. The next best position is the rear parcel shelf, and in this case speaker apertures can be cut into the shelf, or pod units may be mounted.

For door mounting, first remove the trim, which is often held on by 'poppers' or press studs, and then select a suitable gap in the inside door assembly. Check that the speaker would not obstruct glass or winder mechanism by winding the window up and down. A template is often provided for marking out the trim panel hole, and then the four fixing holes must be drilled through. Mark out with chalk and cut cleanly with a sharp knife or keyhole saw. Speaker leads are then threaded through the door and door pillar, if necessary drilling 10 mm diameter holes. Fit grommets in the holes and connect to the radio or tape unit correctly. Do not omit a waterproofing cover, usually supplied with door speakers. If the speaker has to be fixed into the metal of the door itself, use self-tapping screws, and if the fixing is to the door trim use self-tapping screws and flat spire nuts.

Rear shelf mounting is somewhat simpler but it is necessary to find gaps in the metalwork underneath the parcel shelf. However, remember that the speakers should be as far apart as possible to give

Fig. 10.29 Central door locking system components (Sec 31)

1	Lock barrel	6	Unlocking coil
2	Door lever	7	Ferrite plunger
3	Unlocking lever	8	Rod
4	Changeover switch	9	Indicator button
5	Locking coil		

a good stereo effect. Pod-mounted speakers can be screwed into position through the parcel shelf material, but it is worth testing for the best position. Sometimes good results are found by reflecting sound off the rear window.

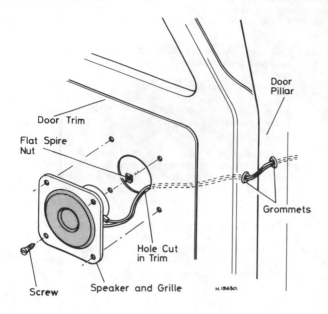

Fig. 10.31 Door-mounted speaker installation (Sec 32)

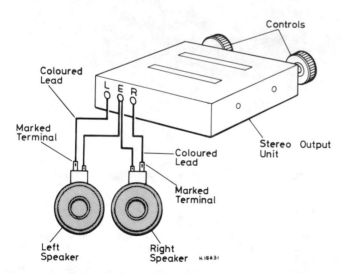

Fig. 10.32 Speaker connections must be correctly made as shown (Sec 32)

Unit installation

Many vehicles have a dash panel aperture to take a radio/audio unit, a recognised international standard being 189.5 mm x 60 mm. Alternatively a console may be a feature of the car interior design and this, mounted below the dashboard, gives more room. If neither facility is available a unit may be mounted on the underside of the parcel shelf; these are frequently non-metallic and an earth wire from the case to a good earth point is necessary. A three-sided cover in the form of a cradle is obtainable from car radio dealers and this gives a professional appearance to the installation; in this case choose a position where the controls can be reached by a driver with his seat belt on.

Installation of the radio/audio unit is basically the same in all cases, and consists of offering it into the aperture after removal of the knobs (*not* push buttons) and the trim plate. In some cases a special mounting plate is required to which the unit is attached. It is worthwhile supporting the rear end in cases where sag or strain may

occur, and it is usually possible to use a length of perforated metal strip attached between the unit and a good support point nearby. In general it is recommended that tape equipment should be installed at or nearly horizontal.

Connections to the aerial socket are simply by the standard plug terminating the aerial downlead or its extension cable. Speakers for a stereo system must be matched and correctly connected, as outlined previously.

Note: *While all work is carried out on the power side, it is wise to disconnect the battery earth lead.* Before connection is made to the vehicle electrical system, check that the polarity of the unit is correct. Most vehicles use a negative earth system, but radio/audio units often have a reversible plug to convert the set to either + or − earth. *Incorrect connection may cause serious damage.*

The power lead is often permanently connected inside the unit and terminates with one half of an in-line fuse carrier. The other half is fitted with a suitable fuse (3 or 5 amperes) and a wire which should go to a power point in the electrical system. This may be the accessory terminal on the ignition switch, giving the advantage of power feed with ignition or with the ignition key at the 'accessory' position. Power to the unit stops when the ignition key is removed. Alternatively, the lead may be taken to a live point at the fusebox with the consequence of having to remember to switch off at the unit before leaving the vehicle.

Before switching on for initial test, be sure that the speaker connections have been made, for running without load can damage the output transistors. Switch on next and tune through the bands to ensure that all sections are working, and check the tape unit if applicable. The aerial trimmer should be adjusted to give the strongest reception on a weak signal in the medium wave band, at say 200 metres.

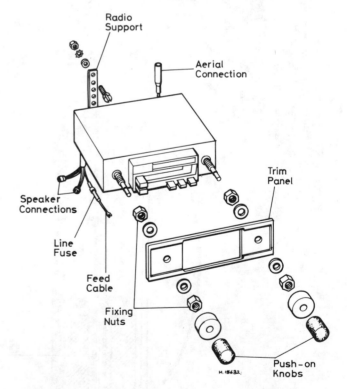

Fig. 10.33 Mounting component details for radio/cassette unit (Sec 32)

Interference

In general, when electric current changes abruptly, unwanted electrical noise is produced. The motor vehicle is filled with electrical devices which change electric current rapidly, the most obvious being the ignition system.

When the spark plugs operate, the sudden pulse of spark current causes the associated wiring to radiate. Since early radio transmitters used sparks as a basis of operation, it is not surprising that the car radio will pick up ignition spark noise unless steps are taken to reduce it to acceptable levels.

Interference reaches the car radio in two ways:

(a) by conduction through the wiring.
(b) by radiation to the receiving aerial.

Initial checks presuppose that the bonnet is down and fastened, the radio unit has a good earth connection (not through the aerial downlead outer), no fluorescent tubes are working near the car, the aerial trimmer has been adjusted, and the vehicle is in a position to receive radio signals, ie not in a metal-clad building.

Switch on the radio and tune it to the middle of the medium wave (MW) band off-station with the volume (gain) control set fairly high. Switch on the ignition (but do not start the engine) and wait to see if irregular clicks or hash noise occurs. Tapping the facia panel may also produce the effects. If so, this will be due to the voltage stabiliser, which is an on-off thermal switch to control instrument voltage. It is located usually on the back of the instrument panel, often attached to the speedometer. Correction is by attachment of a capacitor and, if still troublesome, chokes in the supply wires.

Switch on the engine and listen for interference on the MW band. Depending on the type of interference, the indications are as follows.

A harsh crackle that drops out abruptly at low engine speed or when the headlights are switched on is probably due to a voltage regulator.

A whine varying with engine speed is due to the dynamo or alternator. Try temporarily taking off the fan belt — if the noise goes this is confirmation.

Regular ticking or crackle that varies in rate with the engine speed is due to the ignition system. With this trouble in particular and others in general, check to see if the noise is entering the receiver from the wiring or by radiation. To do this, pull out the aerial plug, (preferably shorting out the input socket or connecting a 62 pF capacitor across it). If the noise disappears it is coming in through the aerial and is radiation noise. If the noise persists it is reaching the receiver through the wiring and is said to be line-borne.

Interference from wipers, washers, heater blowers, turn-indicators, stop lamps, etc is usually taken to the receiver by wiring, and simple treatment using capacitors and possibly chokes will solve the problem. Switch on each one in turn (wet the screen first for running wipers!) and listen for possible interference with the aerial plug in place and again when removed.

Electric petrol pumps are now finding application again and give rise to an irregular clicking, often giving a burst of clicks when the ignition is on but the engine has not yet been started. It is also possible to receive whining or crackling from the pump.

Note that if most of the vehicle accessories are found to be creating interference all together, the probability is that poor aerial earthing is to blame.

Component terminal markings

Throughout the following sub-sections reference will be found to various terminal markings. These will vary depending on the manufacturer of the relevant component. If terminal markings differ from those mentioned, reference should be made to the following table, where the most commonly encountered variations are listed.

Alternator	Alternator terminal (thick lead)	Exciting winding terminal
DIN/Bosch	B+	DF
Delco Remy	+	EXC
Ducellier	+	EXC
Ford (US)	+	DF
Lucas	+	F
Marelli	+B	F

Ignition coil	Ignition switch terminal	Contact breaker terminal
DIN/Bosch	15	1
Delco Remy	+	−
Ducellier	BAT	RUP
Ford (US)	B/+	CB/−
Lucas	SW/+	−
Marelli	BAT/+B	D

Voltage regulator	Voltage input terminal	Exciting winding terminal
DIN/Bosch	B+/D+	DF
Delco Remy	BAT/+	EXC
Ducellier	BOB/BAT	EXC
Ford (US)	BAT	DF
Lucas	+/A	F
Marelli		F

Suppression methods — ignition

Suppressed HT cables are supplied as original equipment by manufacturers and will meet regulations as far as interference to neighbouring equipment is concerned. It is illegal to remove such suppression unless an alternative is provided, and this may take the form of resistive spark plug caps in conjunction with plain copper HT cable. For VHF purposes, these and 'in-line' resistors may not be effective, and resistive HT cable is preferred. Check that suppressed cables are actually fitted by observing cable identity lettering, or measuring with an ohmmeter — the value of each plug lead should be 5000 to 10 000 ohms.

A 1 microfarad capacitor connected from the LT supply side of the ignition coil to a good nearby earth point will complete basic ignition interference treatment. NEVER fit a capacitor to the coil terminal to the contact breaker — the result would be burnt out points in a short time.

If ignition noise persists despite the treatment above, the following sequence should be followed:

(a) Check the earthing of the ignition coil; remove paint from fixing clamp.
(b) If this does not work, lift the bonnet. Should there be no change in interference level, this may indicate that the bonnet is not electrically connected to the car body. Use a proprietary braided strap across a bonnet hinge ensuring a first class electrical connection. If, however, lifting the bonnet increases the interference, then fit resistive HT cables of a higher ohms-per-metre value.
(c) If all these measures fail, it is probable that re-radiation from metallic components is taking place. Using a braided strap between metallic points, go round the vehicle systematically — try the following: engine to body, exhaust system to body, front suspension to engine and to body, steering column to body (especially French and Italian cars), gear lever to engine and to body (again especially French and Italian cars), Bowden cable to body, metal parcel shelf to body. When an offending component is located it should be bonded with the strap permanently.
(d) As a next step, the fitting of distributor suppressors to each lead at the distributor end may help.
(e) Beyond this point is involved the possible screening of the distributor and fitting resistive spark plugs, but such advanced treatment is not usually required for vehicles with entertainment equipment.

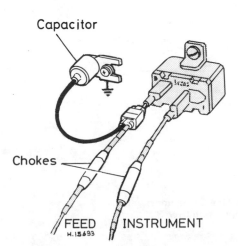

Capacitor

Chokes

FEED   INSTRUMENT
H.15693

Fig. 10.34 Voltage stabiliser interference suppression (Sec 32)

Electronic ignition systems have built-in suppression components, but this does not relieve the need for using suppressed HT leads. In some cases it is permitted to connect a capacitor on the low tension supply side of the ignition coil, but not in every case. Makers' instructions should be followed carefully, otherwise damage to the ignition semiconductors may result.

Suppression methods – generators

For older vehicles with dynamos a 1 microfarad capacitor from the D (larger) terminal to earth will usually cure dynamo whine. Alternators should be fitted with a 3 microfarad capacitor from the B+ main output terminal (thick cable) to earth. Additional suppression may be obtained by the use of a filter in the supply line to the radio receiver.

It is most important that:

(a) *Capacitors are never connected to the field terminals of either a dynamo or alternator.*

(b) *Alternators must not be run without connection to the battery.*

Suppression methods – voltage regulators

Voltage regulators used with DC dynamos should be suppressed by connecting a 1 microfarad capacitor from the control box D terminal to earth.

Alternator regulators come in three types:

(a) *Vibrating contact regulators separate from the alternator. Used extensively on continental vehicles.*

(b) *Electronic regulators separate from the alternator.*

(c) *Electronic regulators built-in to the alternator.*

In case (a) interference may be generated on the AM and FM (VHF) bands. For some cars a replacement suppressed regulator is available. Filter boxes may be used with non-suppressed regulators. But if not available, then for AM equipment a 2 microfarad or 3 microfarad capacitor may be mounted at the voltage terminal marked D+ or B+ of the regulator. FM bands may be treated by a feed-through capacitor of 2 or 3 microfarad.

Electronic voltage regulators are not always troublesome, but where necessary, a 1 microfarad capacitor from the regulator + terminal will help.

Integral electronic voltage regulators do not normally generate much interference, but when encountered this is in combination with alternator noise. A 1 microfarad or 2 microfarad capacitor from the warning lamp (IND) terminal to earth for Lucas ACR alternators and Femsa, Delco and Bosch equivalents should cure the problem.

Suppression methods – other equipment

Wiper motors – Connect the wiper body to earth with a bonding strap. For all motors use a 7 ampere choke assembly inserted in the leads to the motor.

Heater motors – Fit 7 ampere line chokes in both leads, assisted if necessary by a 1 microfarad capacitor to earth from both leads.

Electronic tachometer – The tachometer is a possible source of ignition noise – check by disconnecting at the ignition coil CB terminal. It usually feeds from ignition coil LT pulses at the contact breaker terminal. A 3 ampere line choke should be fitted in the tachometer lead at the coil CB terminal.

Horn – A capacitor and choke combination is effective if the horn is directly connected to the 12 volt supply. The use of a relay is an alternative remedy, as this will reduce the length of the interference-carrying leads.

Electrostatic noise – Characteristics are erratic crackling at the receiver, with disappearance of symptoms in wet weather. Often shocks may be given when touching bodywork. Part of the problem is the build-up of static electricity in non-driven wheels and the acquisition of charge on the body shell. It is possible to fit spring-loaded contacts at the wheels to give good conduction between the rotary wheel parts and the vehicle frame. Changing a tyre sometimes helps – because of tyres' varying resistances. In difficult cases a trailing flex which touches the ground will cure the problem. If this is not acceptable it is worth trying conductive paint on the tyre walls.

Fuel pump – Suppression requires a 1 microfarad capacitor between the supply wire to the pump and a nearby earth point. If this is insufficient a 7 ampere line choke connected in the supply wire near the pump is required.

Fluorescent tubes – Vehicles used for camping/caravanning frequently have fluorescent tube lighting. These tubes require a relatively high voltage for operation and this is provided by an inverter (a form of oscillator) which steps up the vehicle supply voltage. This can give rise to serious interference to radio reception, and the tubes themselves can contribute to this interference by the pulsating nature of the lamp discharge. In such situations it is important to mount the aerial as far away from a fluorescent tube as possible. The interference problem may be alleviated by screening the tube with fine wire turns spaced an inch (25 cm) apart and earthed to the chassis. Suitable chokes should be fitted in both supply wires close to the inverter.

Radio/cassette case breakthrough

Magnetic radiation from dashboard wiring may be sufficiently intense to break through the metal case of the radio/cassette player. Often this is due to a particular cable routed too close and shows up

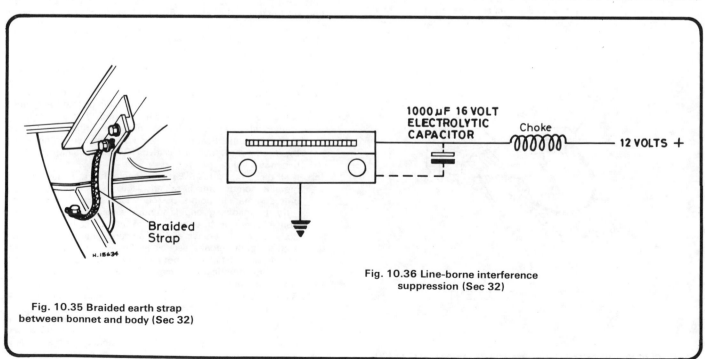

1000 μF 16 VOLT ELECTROLYTIC CAPACITOR

Choke

12 VOLTS +

Braided Strap

H.15634

Fig. 10.36 Line-borne interference suppression (Sec 32)

Fig. 10.35 Braided earth strap between bonnet and body (Sec 32)

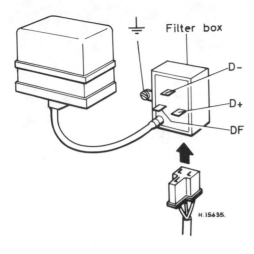

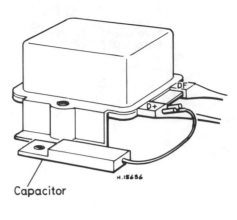

Fig. 10.37 Typical filter box for vibrating contact voltage regulator (alternator equipment) (Sec 32)

Fig. 10.38 Suppression of AM interference by vibrating contact voltage regulator (alternator equipment) (Sec 32)

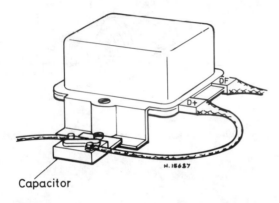

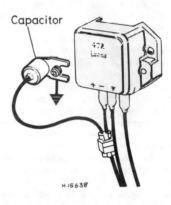

Fig. 10.39 Suppression of FM interference by vibrating contact voltage regulator (alternator equipment) (Sec 32)

Fig. 10.40 Electronic voltage regulator suppression (Sec 32)

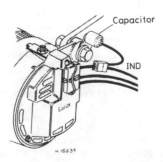

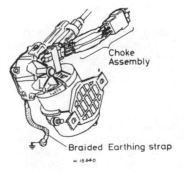

Fig. 10.41 Suppression of interference from electronic voltage regulator when integral with alternator (Sec 32)

Fig. 10.42 Wiper motor suppression (Sec 32)

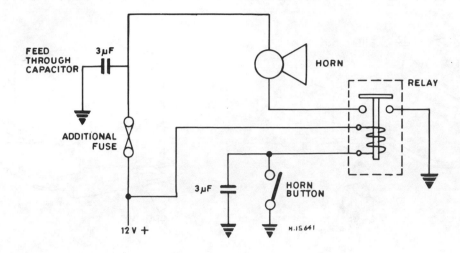

Fig. 10.43 Use of spring contacts at interface (Sec 32)

as ignition interference on AM and cassette play and/or alternator whine on cassette play.

The first point to check is that the clips and/or screws are fixing all parts of the radio/cassette case together properly. Assuming good earthing of the case, see if it is possible to re-route the offending cable – the chances of this are not good, however, in most cars.

Next release the radio/cassette player and locate it in different positions with temporary leads. If a point of low interference is found, then if possible fix the equipment in that area. This also confirms that local radiation is causing the trouble. If re-location is not feasible, fit the radio/cassette player back in the original position.

Alternator interference on cassette play is now caused by radiation from the main charging cable which goes from the battery to the output terminal of the alternator, usually via the + terminal of the starter motor relay. In some vehicles this cable is routed under the dashboard, so the solution is to provide a direct cable route. Detach the original cable from the alternator output terminal and make up a new cable of at least 6 mm² cross-sectional area to go from alternator to battery with the shortest possible route. *Remember – do not run the engine with the alternator disconnected from the battery.*

Ignition breakthrough on AM and/or cassette play can be a difficult problem. It is worth wrapping earthed foil round the offending cable run near the equipment, or making up a deflector plate well screwed down to a good earth. Another possibility is the use of a suitable relay to switch on the ignition coil. The relay should be mounted close to the ignition coil; with this arrangement the ignition coil primary current is not taken into the dashboard area and does not flow through the ignition switch. A suitable diode should be used since it is possible that at ignition switch-off the output from the warning lamp alternator terminal could hold the relay on.

Connectors for suppression components

Capacitors are usually supplied with tags on the end of the lead, while the capacitor body has a flange with a slot or hole to fit under a nut or screw with washer.

Connections to feed wires are best achieved by self-stripping connectors. These connectors employ a blade which, when squeezed down by pliers, cuts through cable insulation and makes connection to the copper conductors beneath.

Chokes sometimes come with bullet snap-in connectors fitted to the wires, and also with just bare copper wire. With connectors, suitable female cable connectors may be purchased from an auto-accessory shop together with any extra connectors required for the cable ends after being cut for the choke insertion. For chokes with bare wires, similar connectors may be employed together with insulation sleeving as required.

VHF/FM broadcasts

Reception of VHF/FM in an automobile is more prone to problems than the medium and long wavebands. Medium/long wave transmitters are capable of covering considerable distances, but VHF

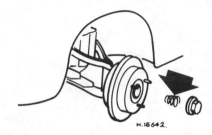

Fig. 10.44 Use of spring contacts at wheels (Sec 32)

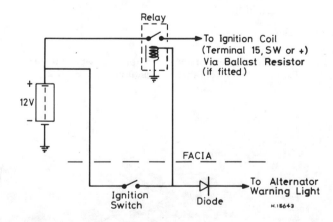

Fig. 10.45 Use of ignition coil relay to suppress case breakthrough (Sec 32)

transmitters are restricted to line of sight, meaning ranges of 10 to 50 miles, depending upon the terrain, the effects of buildings and the transmitter power.

Because of the limited range it is necessary to retune on a long journey, and it may be better for those habitually travelling long distances or living in areas of poor provision of transmitters to use an AM radio working on medium/long wavebands.

When conditions are poor, interference can arise, and some of the suppression devices described previously fall off in performance at very high frequencies unless specifically designed for the VHF band.

Available suppression devices include reactive HT cable, resistive distributor caps, screened plug caps, screened leads and resistive spark plugs.

For VHF/FM receiver installation the following points should be particularly noted:

(a) Earthing of the receiver chassis and the aerial mounting is important. Use a separate earthing wire at the radio, and scrape paint away at the aerial mounting.

(b) If possible, use a good quality roof aerial to obtain maximum height and distance from interference generating devices on the vehicle.

(c) Use of a high quality aerial downlead is important, since losses in cheap cable can be significant.

(d) The polarisation of FM transmissions may be horizontal, vertical, circular or slanted. Because of this the optimum mounting angle is at 45° to the vehicle roof.

Citizens' Band radio (CB)

In the UK, CB transmitter/receivers work within the 27 MHz and 934 MHz bands, using the FM mode. At present interest is concentrated on 27 MHz where the design and manufacture of equipment is less difficult. Maximum transmitted power is 4 watts, and 40 channels spaced 10 kHz apart within the range 27.60125 to 27.99125 MHz are available.

Aerials are the key to effective transmission and reception. Regulations limit the aerial length to 1.65 metres including the loading coil and any associated circuitry, so tuning the aerial is necessary to obtain optimum results. The choice of a CB aerial is dependent on whether it is to be permanently installed or removable, and the performance will hinge on correct tuning and the location point on the vehicle. Common practice is to clip the aerial to the roof gutter or to employ wing mounting where the aerial can be rapidly unscrewed. An alternative is to use the boot rim to render the aerial theftproof, but a popular solution is to use the 'magmount' — a type of mounting having a strong magnetic base clamping to the vehicle at any point, usually the roof.

Aerial location determines the signal distribution for both transmission and reception, but it is wise to choose a point away from the engine compartment to minimise interference from vehicle electrical equipment.

The aerial is subject to considerable wind and acceleration forces. Cheaper units will whip backwards and forwards and in so doing will alter the relationship with the metal surface of the vehicle with which it forms a ground plane aerial system. The radiation pattern will change correspondingly, giving rise to break-up of both incoming and outgoing signals.

Interference problems on the vehicle carrying CB equipment fall into two categories:

(a) Interference to nearby TV and radio receivers when transmitting.

(b) Interference to CB set reception due to electrical equipment on the vehicle.

Problems of break-through to TV and radio are not frequent, but can be difficult to solve. Mostly trouble is not detected or reported because the vehicle is moving and the symptoms rapidly disappear at the TV/radio receiver, but when the CB set is used as a base station any trouble with nearby receivers will soon result in a complaint.

It must not be assumed by the CB operator that his equipment is faultless, for much depends upon the design. Harmonics (that is, multiples) of 27 MHz may be transmitted unknowingly and these can fall into other user's bands. Where trouble of this nature occurs, low pass filters in the aerial or supply leads can help, and should be fitted in base station aerials as a matter of course. In stubborn cases it may be necessary to call for assistance from the licensing authority, or, if possible, to have the equipment checked by the manufacturers.

Interference received on the CB set from the vehicle equipment is, fortunately, not usually a severe problem. The precautions outlined previously for radio/cassette units apply, but there are some extra points worth noting.

It is common practice to use a slide-mount on CB equipment enabling the set to be easily removed for use as a base station, for example. Care must be taken that the slide mount fittings are properly earthed and that first class connection occurs between the set and slide-mount.

Vehicle manufacturers in the UK are required to provide suppression of electrical equipment to cover 40 to 250 MHz to protect TV and VHF radio bands. Such suppression appears to be adequately effective at 27 MHz, but suppression of individual items such as alternators/dynamos, clocks, stabilisers, flashers, wiper motors, etc, may still be necessary. The suppression capacitors and chokes available from auto-electrical suppliers for entertainment receivers will usually give the required results with CB equipment.

Other vehicle radio transmitters

Besides CB radio already mentioned, a considerable increase in the use of transceivers (ie combined transmitter and receiver units) has taken place in the last decade. Previously this type of equipment was fitted mainly to military, fire, ambulance and police vehicles, but a large business radio and radio telephone usage has developed.

Generally the suppression techniques described previously will suffice, with only a few difficult cases arising. Suppression is carried out to satisfy the 'receive mode', but care must be taken to use heavy duty chokes in the equipment supply cables since the loading on 'transmit' is relatively high.

33 Fault diagnosis – electrical system

Symptom	Reason(s)
Starter fails to turn engine	Battery discharged Battery defective internally Battery terminal leads loose or earth lead not securely attached to body Loose or broken connections in starter motor circuit Starter motor solenoid faulty Starter brushes badly worn, sticking, or brush wires loose Commutator dirty, worn or burnt Starter motor armature faulty Field coils earthed Gear selector lever not engaged in P or N (automatic transmission)
Starter turns engine very slowly	Battery in discharged condition Starter brushes badly worn, sticking or brush wires loose Loose wires in starter motor circuit
Starter motor noisy or excessively rough engagement	Pinion or flywheel gear teeth broken or worn Starter motor retaining bolts loose

Symptom	Reason(s)
Battery will not hold charge for more than a few days	Battery defective internally
	Electrolyte level too low or electrolyte too weak due to leakage
	Plate separators no longer fully effective
	Battery plates severely sulphated
	Drivebelt slipping
	Battery terminal connections loose or corroded
	Alternator not charging
	Short in circuit causing continual battery drain
	Regulator unit not working correctly
Ignition light fails to go out, battery runs flat in a few days	Drivebelt loose and slipping or broken
	Alternator brushes worn, sticking, broken or dirty
	Alternator brush springs weak or broken
	Internal fault in alternator
Instrument readings increase with engine speed	Voltage stabilizer faulty

Horn(s)

Horn operates all the time	Horn push either earthed or stuck down
	Horn cable to horn push earthed
Horn fails to operate	Cable or cable connection loose, broken or disconnected
	Horn has an internal fault
Horn emits intermittent or unsatisfactory noise	Cable connections loose

Lights

Lights do not come on	If engine not running, battery discharged
	Wire connections loose, disconnected or broken
	Light switch shorting or otherwise faulty
Lights come on but fade out	If engine not running, battery discharged
	Connections loose or corroded
Lights work erratically – flashing on and off especially over bumps	Battery terminals or earth connection loose
	Lights not earthing properly
	Contacts in light switch faulty

Wipers

Wiper motor fails to work	Blown fuse
	Wire connections loose, disconnected or broken
	Brushes badly worn
	Armature worn or faulty
	Field coils faulty
Wiper motor works very slowly and takes excessive current	Commutator dirty, greasy or burnt
	Armature bearings dirty or unaligned
	Armature badly worn or faulty
Wiper motor works slowly and takes little current	Brushes badly worn
	Commutator dirty, greasy or burnt
	Armature badly worn or faulty
Wiper motor works, but wiper blades remain static	Wiper motor gearbox parts badly worn
	Faulty linkage

Example:

Or as shown in the diagram on the right:
Unit 40 (L.H. door pillar switch) with
wire 214 - N - 2 - 41 connected to Unit 41.

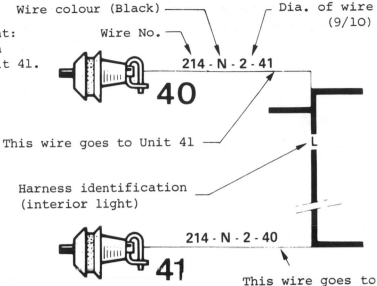

Wire 214 is seen again connected to
Unit 41 (R.H. door pillar switch) but
this time it is numbered:
214 - N - 2 - 40.

Fig. 10.46 Key to using the wiring diagrams

*Each wire is identified by a number followed by a letter(s) indicating its colour, a number giving its diameter
and finally a number giving the unit destination*

Colour code

B	Blue	J	Yellow	R	Red
Bc	White	M	Maroon	S	Pink
Be	Beige	N	Black	V	Green
C	Clear	Or	Orange	Vi	Violet
G	Grey				

Wire diameters

No	mm
1	0.7
2	0.9
3	1.0
4	1.2
5	1.6
6	2.0
7	2.5
8	3.0
9	4.5
10	5.0
11	7.0
12	8.0

Unit locations

*Some of the wiring diagrams are arranged in a grid system. The grid location of the various components
is given in the diagram key, where applicable, after the component description.*

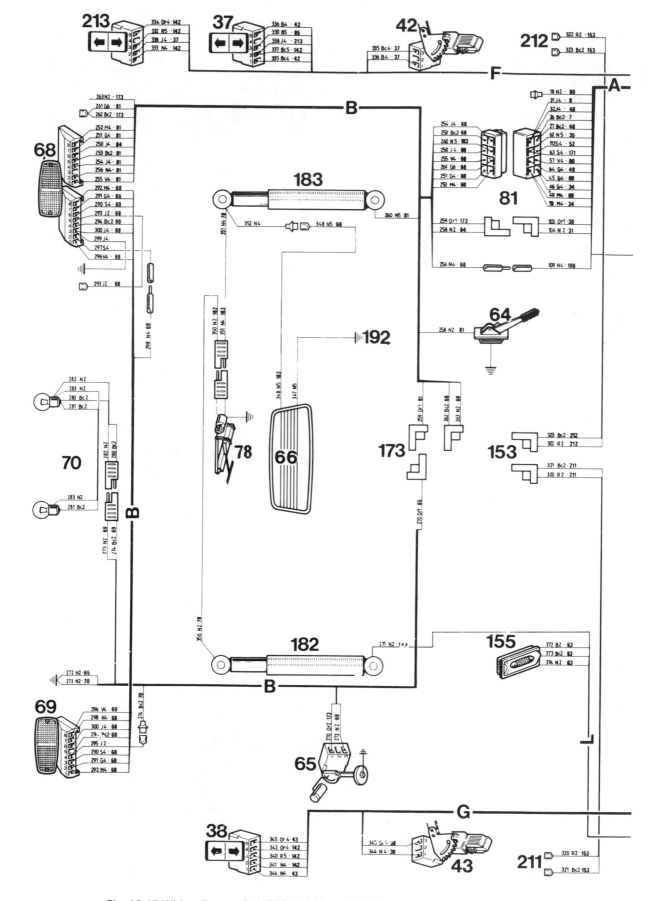

Fig. 10.47 Wiring diagram for 1980 R1360 and R1362 models, and 1981 R1362 models

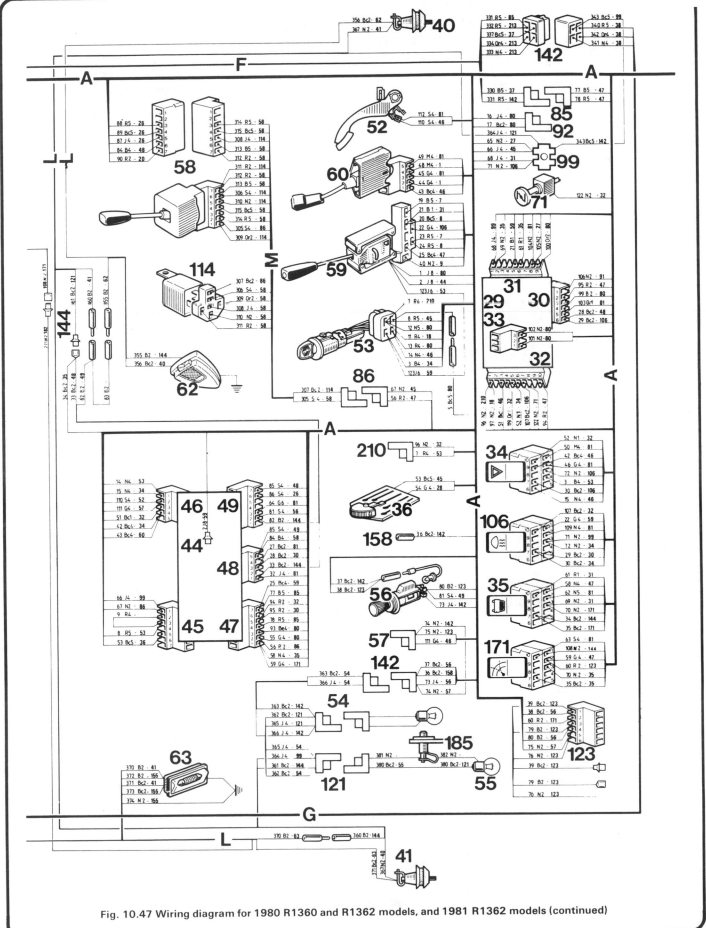

Fig. 10.47 Wiring diagram for 1980 R1360 and R1362 models, and 1981 R1362 models (continued)

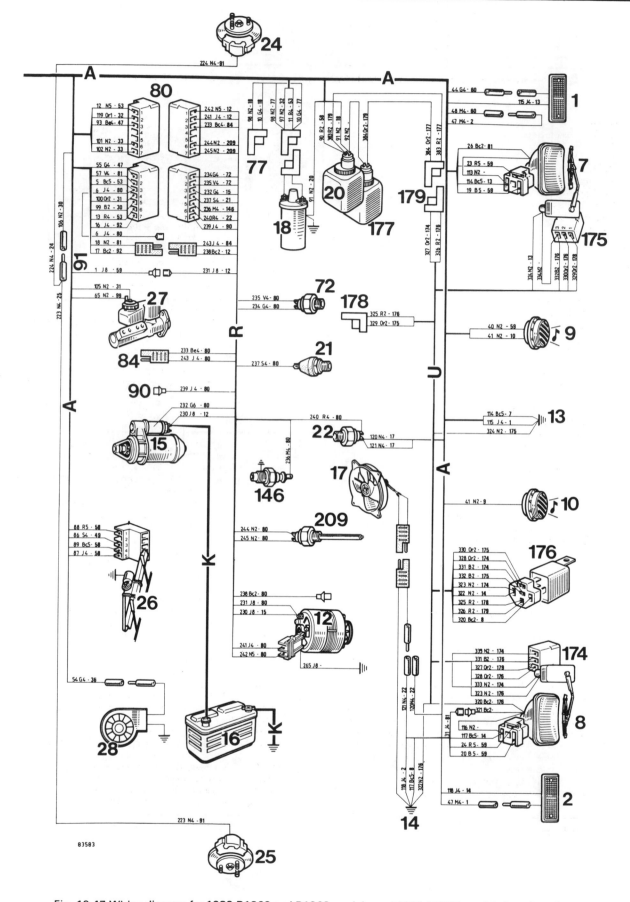

Fig. 10.47 Wiring diagram for 1980 R1360 and R1362 models, and 1981 R1362 models (continued)

Key to wiring diagram for 1980 R1360 and R1362 models, and 1981 R1362 models

Harnesses

A   Engine front
B   Rear
F   LH window winder
G   RH window winder
K   Starter
L   Interior light – door switches
M   Windscreen wiper
R   Engine
U   Headlights

Units

1   LH front direction indicator
2   RH front direction indicator
7   LH headlight
8   RH headlight
9   LH horn
10   RH horn
12   Alternator
13   LH side earth
14   RH side earth
15   Starter
16   Battery
17   Engine cooling fan motor
18   Ignition coil
20   Electric windscreen washer pump
21   Oil pressure switch
22   Thermal switch on radiator
24   LH front brake
25   RH front brake
26   Windscreen wiper plate
27   Brake master cylinder
28   Heating-ventilating fan motor
29   Instrument panel
30   Connector No 1 – instrument panel
31   Connector No 2 – instrument panel
32   Connector No 3 – instrument panel
33   Connector No 4 – instrument panel
34   "Hazard" warning lights switch
35   Rear screen demister switch
36   Heating-ventilating fan motor rheostat
37   LH window switch
38   RH window switch
40   LH door pillar switch
41   RH door pillar switch
42   LH window
43   RH window
44   Accessories plate
45   Junction block – front harness to accessories plate
46   Junction block – front harness to accessories plate
47   Junction block – front harness to accessories plate
48   Junction block – front harness to accessories plate
49   Junction block – front harness to accessories plate
52   Stop-lights switch
53   Ignition-starter anti-theft switch
54   Heating-ventilating control panel illumination
55   Glove compartment light
56   Cigar lighter
57   Radio feed

Units

58   Windscreen wiper-washer switch
59   Combination lighting switch
60   Direction indicators switch
62   LH interior light
63   RH interior light
64   Handbrake "On" warning light switch
65   Fuel gauge tank unit
66   Rear screen demister
68   LH rear light assembly
69   RH rear light assembly
70   Number plate lights
71   Choke "On" warning light
72   Reversing lights switch
77   Wire junction – diagnostic socket
78   Rear screen wiper motor
80   Junction block – front harness to engine harness
81   Junction block – front harness to rear harness
84   Junction block – front harness to auto-transmission harness
85   Junction block – window winder harness
86   Junction block – time switch relay
90   Wire junction – air conditioning el. magnetic clutch
91   Wire junction – brake pad wear warning light
92   Wire junction – optional air conditioning
99   Dashboard earth
106 Rear foglight switch
114 Windscreen wiper time switch
121 Junction block – glove compartment light
123 Clock
142 Wire junction – window winder harness and interior light harness
143 Wire junction – main lighting switch harness
144 Wire junction – interior lights harness
146 Thermal switch
153 Loudspeaker wire
155 Rear interior light
158 Auto-transmission selector gate light
171 Rear screen wiper switch
173 Wire junction – fuel tank gauge unit
174 RH headlight wiper-washer motor
175 LH headlight wiper-washer switch
176 Headlight washer-wipers time switch relay
177 Headlight washers pump
178 Headlight washers pump (RHD)
179 Wire junction – windscreen washer-headlight washers pump
182 Tailgate RH counterbalance
183 Tailgate LH counterbalance
185 Glove compartment light switch
192 Tailgate earth
209 Engine oil indicator sensor
210 Junction block – engine front harness to electronic ignition harness
211 Loudspeaker in RH rear panel
212 Loudspeaker in LH rear panel
213 LH window switch on passenger's side

Not all items are fitted to all models

For the colour code and other information, see Fig. 10.46

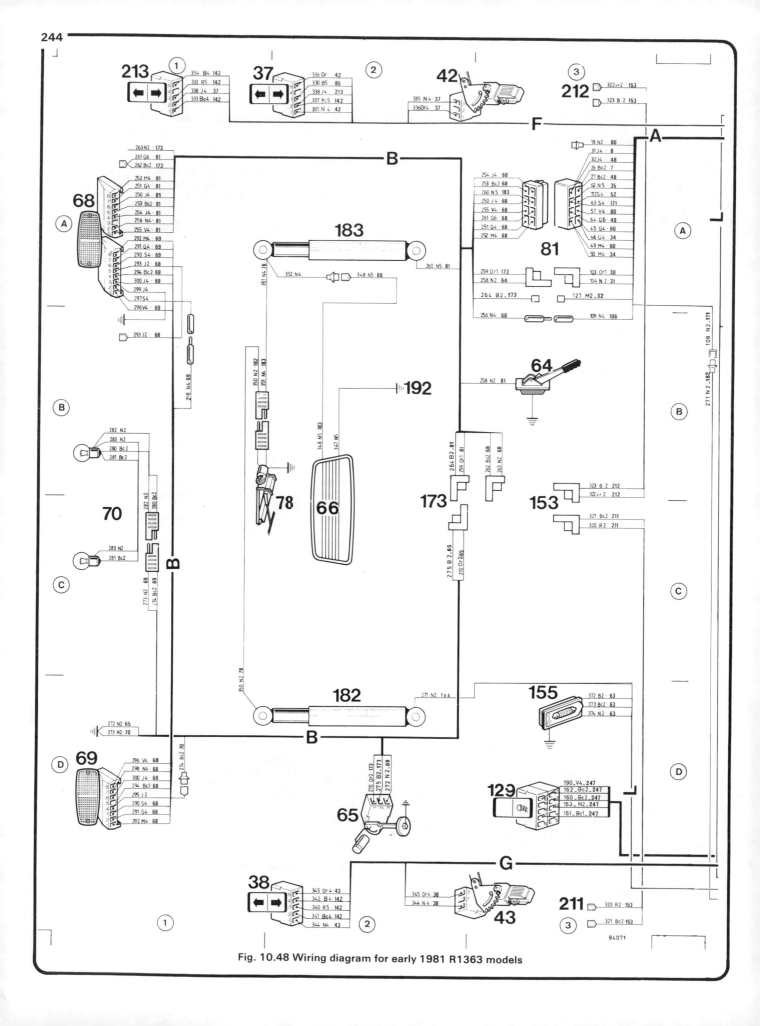

Fig. 10.48 Wiring diagram for early 1981 R1363 models

244

84071

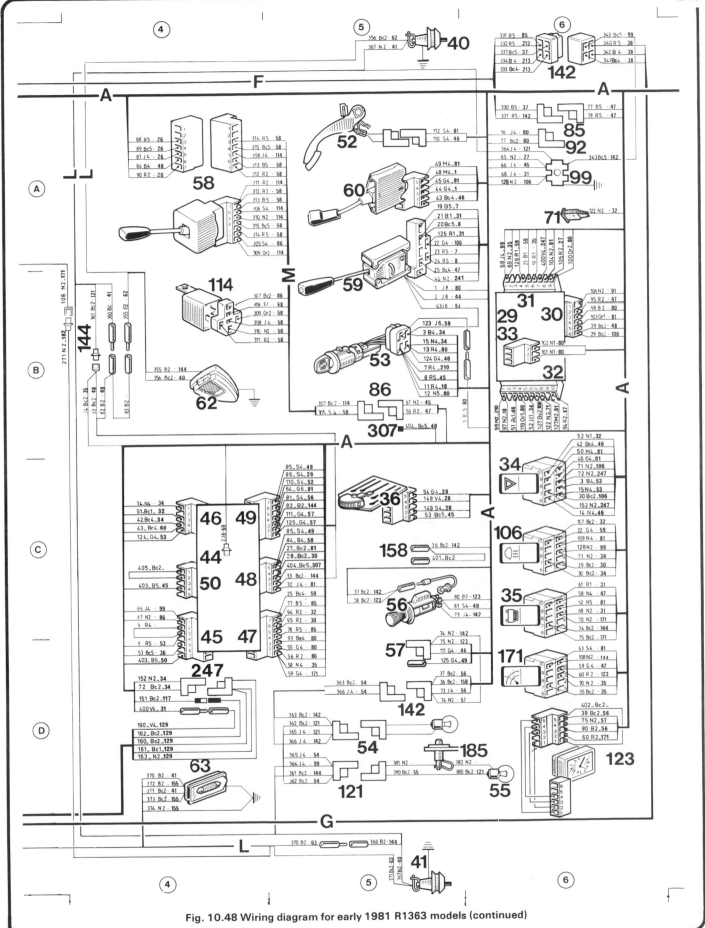

Fig. 10.48 Wiring diagram for early 1981 R1363 models (continued)

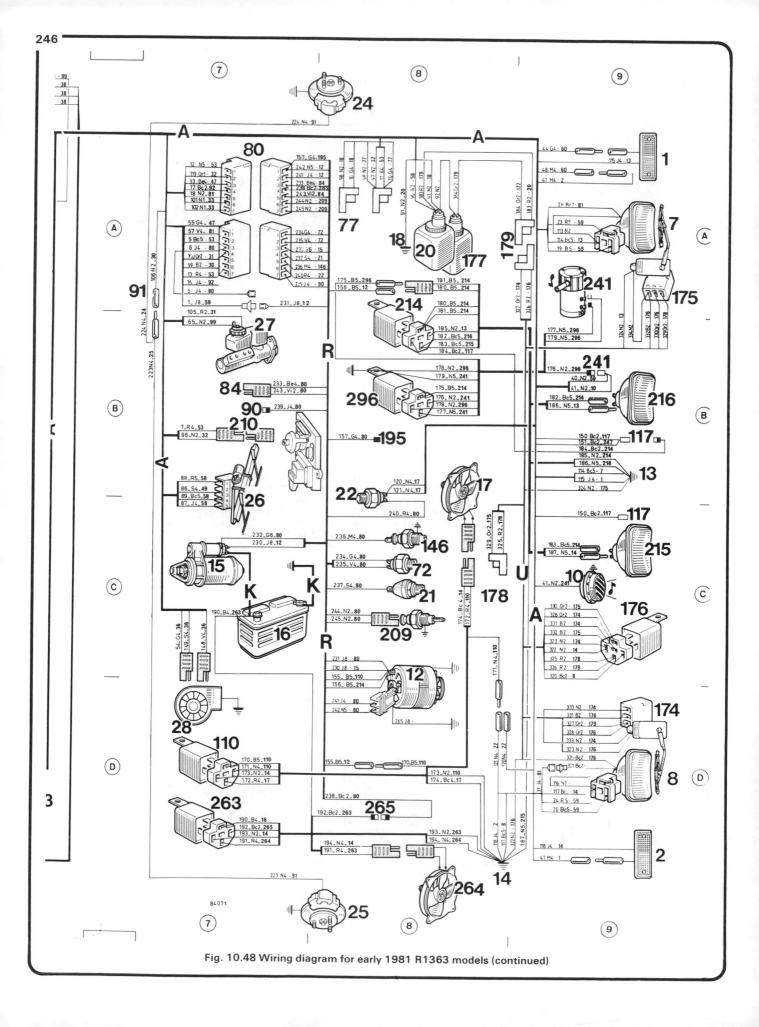

Fig. 10.48 Wiring diagram for early 1981 R1363 models (continued)

Key to wiring diagram for early 1981 R1363 models

Harnesses

A   Engine front
B   Rear
F   LH window winder
G   RH window winder
K   Starter
L   Interior lights – door pillar switches
M   Windscreen wiper
R   Engine
U   Headlights

Units

1	LH sidelight and direction indicator	A-9
2	RH sidelight and direction indicator	D-9
7	LH headlight	A-9
8	RH headlight	D-9
10	RH horn	C-9
12	Alternator	C-8
13	LH earth	B-9
14	RH earth	D-8
15	Starter	C-7
16	Battery	C-7
17	Engine cooling fan motor	B-8
18	Ignition coil	A-8
20	Windscreen washer pump	A-8
21	Oil pressure switch	C-8
22	Thermal switch on radiator	B-8
24	LH front brake	A-8
25	RH front brake	D-8
26	Windscreen wiper plate	C-7
27	Master cylinder	R-7
28	Heating-ventilating fan motor	D-7
29	Instrument panel	B-6
30	Connector No 1 – instrument panel	B-6
31	Connector No 2 – instrument panel	B-6
32	Connector No 3 – instrument panel	B-6
33	Connector No 4 – instrument panel	B-6
34	"Hazard" warning light switch	C-6
35	Rear screen demister switch	C-6
36	Heating-ventilating fan resistance	C-5
37	LH front door window switch	A-1
38	RH front door window switch	D-1
40	LH front door pillar switch	A-5
41	RH front door pillar switch	D-5
42	LH window winder	A-2
43	RH window winder	D-3
44	Accessories plate	C-4
45	Junction block – front harness and accessories plate	D-4
46	Junction block – front harness and accessories plate	C-4
47	Junction block – front harness and accessories plate	D-4
48	Junction block – front harness and accessories plate	C-4
49	Junction block – front harness and accessories plate	C-4
50	Junction block – front harness and accessories plate	C-4
52	Stop-lights switch	A-5
53	Ignition-starter-anti-theft switch	B-5
54	Heater controls illumination	D-5
55	Glove compartment light	D-6
56	Cigar lighter	C-5
57	Feed to car radio	D-5
58	Windscreen wiper-washer switch	A-4
59	Lighting switch	B-5
60	Direction indicators switch	A-5
62	LH interior light	B-4
63	RH interior light	D-4
64	Handbrake "On" warning light switch	B-3
65	Fuel gauge tank unit	D-2
66	Rear screen demister	C-2
68	LH rear light assembly	A-1

69	RH rear light assembly	D-1
70	Number plate light	C-1
71	Choke "On" warning light	A-6
72	Reversing lights switch	C-8
77	Wire junction – diagnostic socket	A-8
78	Rear screen wiper mirror	C-2
80	Junction block – front and engine harnesses	A-7
81	Junction block – front and rear harnesses	A-3
84	Junction block – automatic transmission harness	B-7
85	Junction block – window winder harnesses	A-6
86	Junction block – time switch relay wires	B-5
90	Wire junction – air conditioning el. mag. clutch	B-7
91	Wire junction – brake pad wear warning light wires	A-7
92	Wire junction – air conditioning (optional)	A-6
99	Dashboard earth	A-6
106	Rear foglight switch	C-6
110	Engine cooling fan motor relay	D-7
114	Windscreen wiper time switch	B-4
117	Wire junction – front foglight	B-9
121	Junction block – glove compartment light	D-5
123	Clock	D-6
129	Rear foglight switch	D-3
142	Wire junction – window winder and interior light	A-6
143	Wire junction – main lighting switch harness	D-5
144	Wire junction – interior light harness	B-4
146	Thermal switch	C-8
153	Car radio loudspeaker wire	C-3
155	Rear interior light	D-3
158	Auto-transmission selector illumination	C-5
171	Rear screen wiper-washer switch	D-6
173	Wire junction – fuel tank harness	C-2
174	LH headlight wiper motor	D-9
175	RH headlight wiper motor	A-9
176	Headlight wiper-washers time switch	C-9
177	Headlight washers pump	A-8
178	Headlight washers pump (RHD)	C-8
179	Wire junction – windscreen-headlight washer pump	A-8
182	RH tailgate counterbalance	D-2
183	LH tailgate counterbalance	A-2
185	Glove compartment light switch	D-6
192	Tailgate earth	B-2
195	Idle cut-out	B-8
209	Engine oil indicator sensor	C-8
210	Junction block – engine front and integral electronic ignition harness	B-7
211	RH rear loudspeaker	D-3
212	LH rear loudspeaker	A-3
213	LH window switch for passenger's side (LHD)	A-1
214	Front foglights relay	A-8
215	RH front foglight	B-9
216	LH front foglight	B-9
241	Air horn compressor	A-9 and B-9
247	Wire junction – additional driving lights switch	D-4
263	Auxiliary fan motor relay	D-7
264	Auxiliary fan motor	D-8
265	Junction – auxiliary fan motor harness	D-8
296	Air horn compressor relay	B-8
307	Junction – sunroof motor harness	B-5

For the colour code and other information see Fig. 10.46

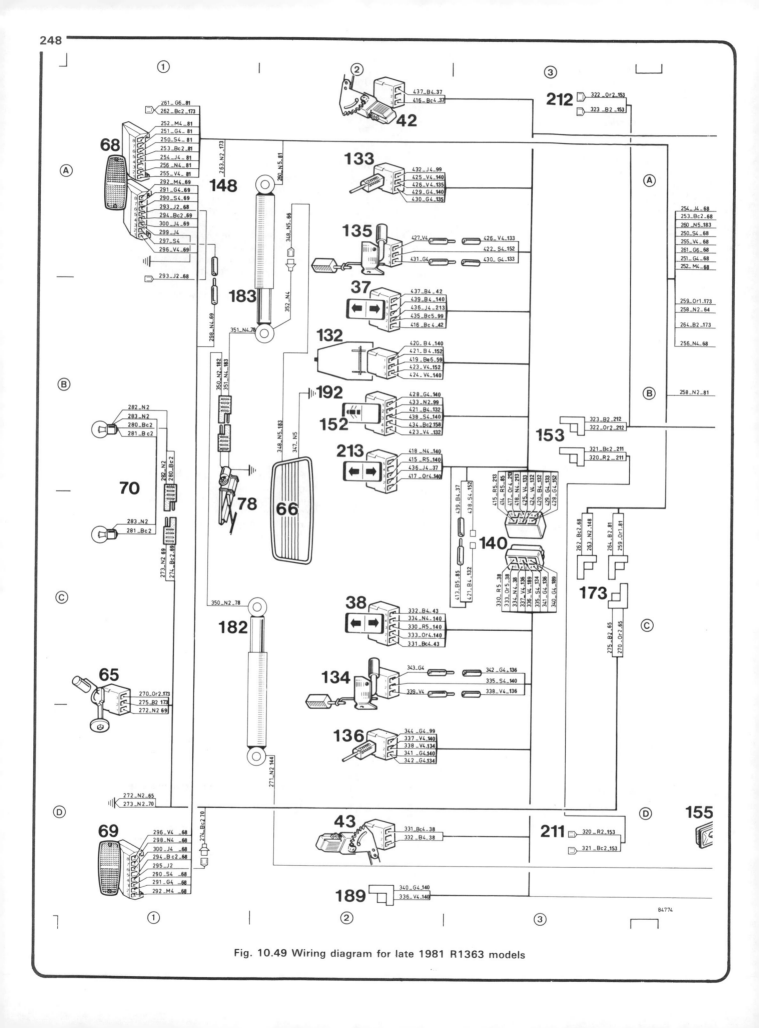

Fig. 10.49 Wiring diagram for late 1981 R1363 models

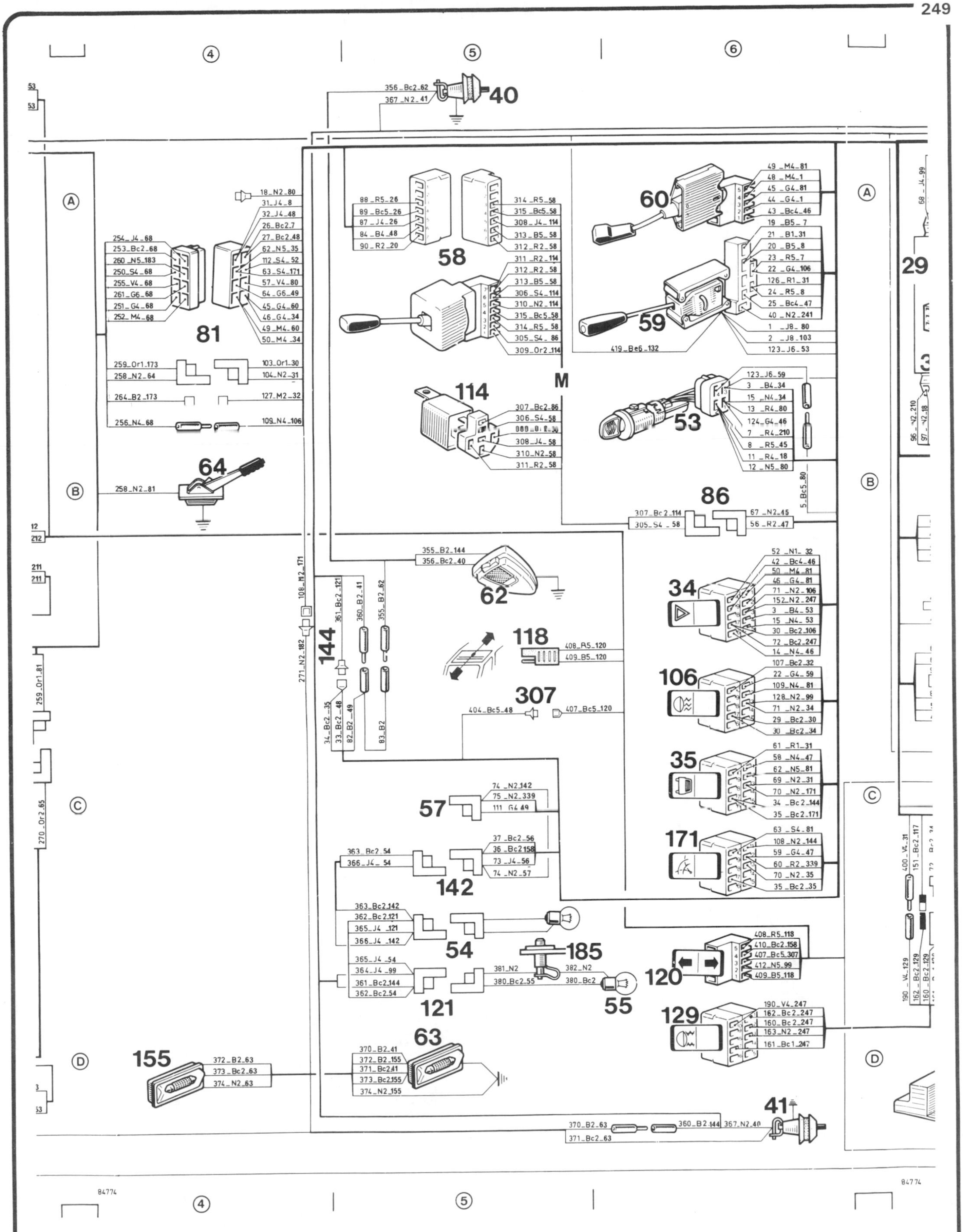

356_Bc2_62
367_N2_41
40

4 **5** **6**

53
53

18_N2_80
31_J4_8
32_J4_48
26_Bc2_7
27_Bc2_48
62_N5_35
112_S4_52
63_S4_171
57_V4_80
64_G6_49
45_G4_60
46_G4_34
49_M4_60
50_M4_34

254_J4_68
253_Bc2_68
260_N5_183
250_S4_68
255_V4_68
261_G6_68
251_G4_68
252_M4_68

81

A

88_R5_26
89_Bc5_26
87_J4_26
84_B4_48
90_R2_20

314_R5_58
315_Bc5_58
308_J4_114
313_B5_58
312_R2_58

58

311_R2_114
312_R2_58
313_B5_58
306_S4_114
310_N2_114
315_Bc5_58
305_S4_86
309_Or2_114

M

49_M4_81
48_M4_1
45_G4_81
44_G4_1
43_Bc4_46
19_B5_7

60

21_B1_31
20_B5_8
23_R5_7
22_G4_106
126_R1_31
24_R5_8
25_Bc4_47
40_N2_241

59

419_Be6_132

1_J8_80
2_J8_103
123_J6_53

A

68_J4_99

29

96_N2_210
97_N2_18

259_Or1_173
258_N2_64

264_B2_173

256_N4_68

103_Or1_30
104_N2_31

127_M2_32

109_N4_106

307_Bc2_86
306_S4_58
308_J4_58
310_N2_58
311_R2_58

114

123_J6_59
3_B4_34
15_N4_34
13_R4_80
124_G4_46
7_R4_210
8_R5_45
11_R4_18
12_N5_80

53

5_Bc5_80

B

258_N2_81

64

86
307_Bc2_114
305_S4_58

67_N2_45
56_R2_47

B

12
212

211
211

355_B2_144
356_Bc2_40

62

52_N1_32
42_Bc4_46
50_M4_81
46_G4_81
71_N2_106
152_N2_247
3_B4_53
15_N4_53
30_Bc2_106
72_Bc2_247
14_N4_46

34

361_Bc2_121
360_B2_41
355_B2_82

106_M2_171
271_N2_182

144

118
408_R5_120
409_B5_120

107_Bc2_32
22_G4_59
109_N4_81
128_N2_99
71_N2_48
29_Bc2_30
30_Bc2_34

106

259_Or1_81

34_Bc2_35
33_Bc2_48
82_B2_49

83_B2

307
404_Bc5_48
407_Bc5_120

61_R1_31
58_N4_47
62_N5_81
69_N2_31
70_N2_171
34_Bc2_144
35_Bc2_171

35

270_Or2_65

C

74_N2_142
75_N2_339
111_G4_49

57

63_S4_81
108_N2_144
59_G4_47
60_R2_339
70_N2_35
35_Bc2_35

171

C

363_Bc2_54
366_J4_54

37_Bc2_56
36_Bc2_158
73_J4_56
74_N2_57

142

400_V4_31
151_Bc2_117

363_Bc2_142
362_Bc2_121
365_J4_121
366_J4_142

54

185
381_N2
380_Bc2_55

382_N2
380_Bc2

408_R5_118
410_Bc2_158
407_Bc5_307
412_N5_99
409_B5_118

120

190_V4_129
162_Bc2_129
160_Bc2_129

365_J4_54
364_J4_99
361_Bc2_144
362_Bc2_54

121

55

190_V4_247
162_Bc2_247
160_Bc2_247
163_N2_247
161_Bc1_247

129

155
372_B2_63
373_Bc2_63
374_N2_63

63
372_B2_155
371_Bc2_41
373_Bc2_155
374_N2_155

D

3
53

41
370_B2_63
371_Bc2_63

360_B2_144 367_N2_40

D

84774

4 **5**

84774

Fig. 10.49 Wiring diagram for late 1981 R1363 models (continued)

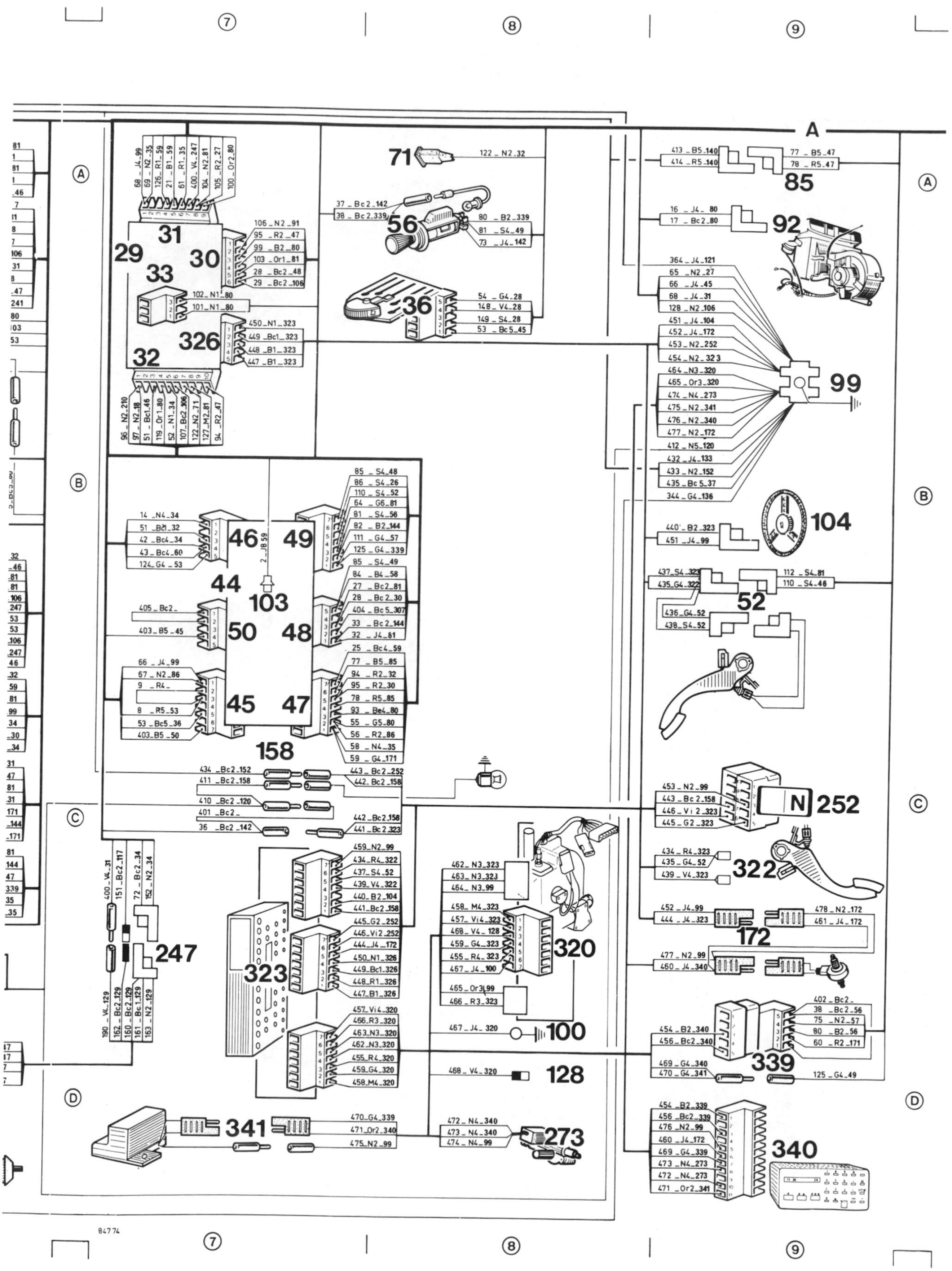

Fig. 10.49 Wiring diagram for late 1981 R1363 models (continued)

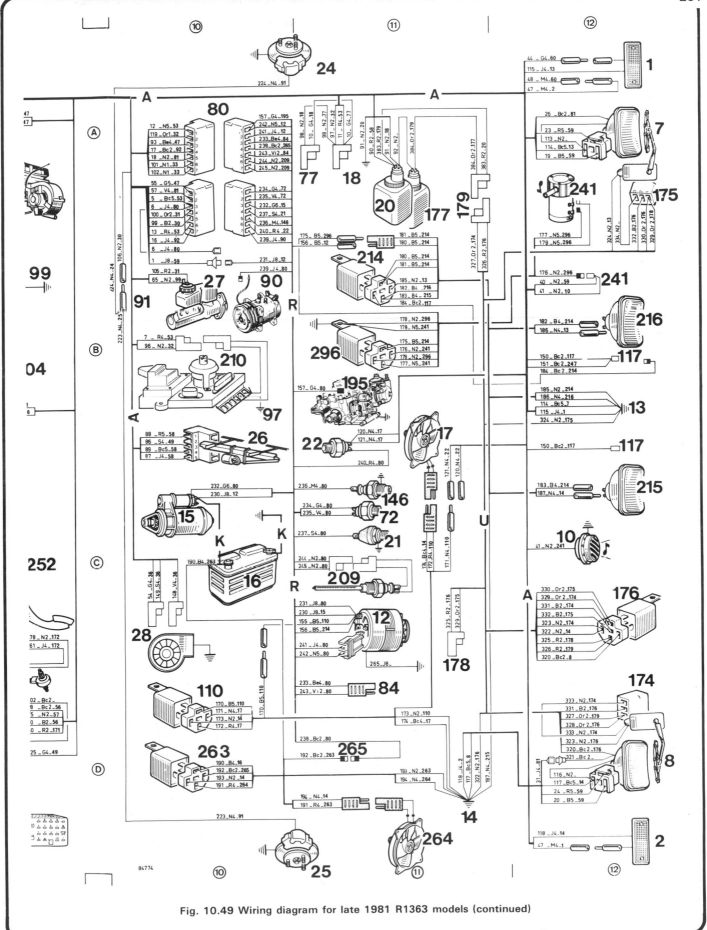

Fig. 10.49 Wiring diagram for late 1981 R1363 models (continued)

Key to wiring diagram for late 1981 R1363 models

Harnesses

A   Engine front
M   Windscreen wiper
R   Engine
U   Headlights

Units

1	LH direction indicator	A-12
2	RH direction indicator	D-12
7	LH headlight	A-12
8	RH headlight	D-12
10	RH horn	C-12
12	Alternator	C-11
13	LH earth	B-12
14	RH earth	D-11
15	Starter	C-10
16	Battery	C-10
17	Engine cooling fan motor	B-11
18	Ignition coil (not used)	A-11
20	Windscreen washer pump	A-11
21	Oil pressure switch	C-11
22	Thermal switch on radiator	B-11
24	LH front brake	A-11
25	RH front brake	D-11
26	Windscreen wiper plate	B-10
27	Master cylinder	B-10
28	Heating-ventilation fan motor	C-10
29	Instrument panel	A-7
30	Connector No 1 – instrument panel	A-7
31	Connector No 2 – instrument panel	A-7
32	Connector No 3 – instrument panel	B-7
33	Connector No 4 – instrument panel	A-7
34	"Hazard" warning lights switch	B-5
35	Rear screen demister switch	C-6
36	Heating-ventilating fan rheostat	A-8
37	LH front door window switch	A-2
38	RH front door window switch	C-2
40	LH front door pillar switch	A-5
41	RH front door pillar switch	D-6
42	LH window winder	A-2
43	RH window winder	D-2
44	Accessories plate	B-7
45	Junction block – front harness and accessories plate	C-7
46	Junction block – front harness and accessories plate	B-7
47	Junction block – front harness and accessories plate	C-7
48	Junction block – front harness and accessories plate	B-7
49	Junction block – front harness and accessories plate	B-7
50	Junction block – front harness and accessories plate	B-7
52	Stop-lights switch	B-9
53	Ignition-starter-anti-theft switch	B-6
54	Heater controls illumination	D-5
55	Glove compartment light	D-6
56	Cigar lighter	A-8
57	Feed to car radio	C-5
58	Windscreen wiper-washer switch	A-5
59	Lighting switch	A-6
60	Direction indicators switch	A-6
62	LH interior light	B-5
63	RH interior light	D-5
64	Handbrake	B-4
65	Fuel gauge tank unit	C-1
66	Rear screen demister	C-2
68	LH rear light assembly	A-1
69	RH rear light assembly	D-1
70	Number plate lights	B-1
71	Choke "On" warning light	A-8
72	Reversing lights switch	C-11
77	Wire junction – diagnostic socket	A-11
78	Rear screen wiper motor	C-1
80	Junction block – front and engine harnesses	A-10
81	Junction block – front and rear harnesses	A-4
84	Junction block – automatic transmission harness	D-11
85	Junction block – window winder harnesses	A-9
86	Junction block time switch relay wires	B-6

Units

90	Wire junction – air conditioning el. mag. clutch	B-10
91	Wire junction – Brake pad wear warning light wires	B-10
92	Wire junction – air conditioning (optional)	A-9
99	Dashboard earth	B-9
100	Scuttle gusset earth	D-8
103	Feed to accessories plate	B-7
104	Junction with steering wheel tracks	B-9
106	Rear foglight switch	C-6
110	Engine cooling fan motor relay	D-10
114	Windscreen wiper time switch	B-5
117	Wire junction – front foglights	C-12-B-12
118	Sunroof motor	C-5
120	Sunroof switch	D-6
121	Junction block – glove compartment light	D-5
128	Kickdown switch	D-8
129	Rear foglight switch	D-6
132	Inertia switch	B-2
133	LH door lock switch	A-2
134	RH door lock switch	C-2
135	LH door servo	A-2
136	RH door servo	D-2
140	Harness junction – electromagnetic door locks	B-3
142	Wire junction – window winder and interior light	C-5
144	Wire junction – interior light harness	C-4
146	Thermal switch	C-11
148	Tailgate fixed contact	A-1
152	Electro-magnetic locks centre switch	B-2
153	Car radio loudspeaker wire	B-3
155	Rear interior light	D-4
158	Auto-transmission selector illumination	C-7
171	Rear screen wiper-washer switch	C-6
172	Signal generator	C-9
173	Wire junction – fuel tank harness	C-3
174	RH headlight wiper motor	D-12
175	LH headlight wiper motor	A-12
176	Headlight wiper-washers time switch	C-12
177	Headlight washers pump	A-11
178	Headlight washers pump (RHD)	D-11
179	Wire junction – windscreen headlight washer pump	A-11
182	RH tailgate counterbalance	C-1
183	LH tailgate counterbalance	A-1
185	Glove compartment light switch	D-5
189	Fuel filler flap lock servo	D-2
192	Tailgate earth	B-2
195	Idle cut-out	B-11
209	Engine oil indicator sensor	C-11
210	Junction block – engine front and Integral Electronic Ignition (AEI) harnesses	B-10
211	RH rear loudspeaker	D-3
212	LH rear loudspeaker	A-3
213	LH window switch for passenger's side (LHD)	A-2
214	Front foglights relay	B-11
215	RH front foglight	C-12
216	LH front foglight	B-12
241	Air horn compressor	A-12-B-12
247	Wire junction – additional driving lights switch	D-7
252	"Normalur" Cruise Control switch	C-9
263	Auxiliary fan motor relay	D-10
264	Auxiliary fan motor	D-11
265	Junction – auxiliary fan motor harness	D-11
273	Flowmeter	B-11
296	Air horn compressor relay	B-11
307	Junction – sunroof motor harness	C-5
320	"Normalur" Cruise Control servo motor	D-8
322	Declutching switch	C-9
323	"Normalur" Cruise Control computer	D-7
326	Harness junction – "Normalur" Cruise Control and air conditioning	B-7
339	Wire junction – Driving Aid	D-9
340	Driving Aid computer	D-9
341	Temperature sensor	

For the colour code and other information see Fig. 10.46

Key to wiring diagram for 1982 R1362 models

Harnesses

A	Engine	
B	Rear	
F	LH window	
G	RH window	
L	Interior light	
R	Engine	

Units

1	LH sidelight and/or direction indicator	D-9
2	RH sidelight and/or direction indicator	A-9
7	LH headlight	D-9
8	RH headlight	A-9
9	LH horn	B-9
10	RH horn	C-9
12	Alternator	D-8
13	LH front earth	B-9
14	RH front earth	C-9
15	Starter	D-8
16	Battery	C-8
17	Engine cooling fan motor	C-9
20	Windscreen washer pump	B-8
21	Oil pressure switch	B-7
22	Thermal switch on radiator	A-8
24	LH front brake	A-7
25	RH front brake	D-7
26	Windscreen wiper motor	D-7
27	Nivocode or ICP (brake pressure drop indicator)	D-7
28	Heating-ventilating fan motor	C-7
29	Instrument panel	B-6
30	Connector No 1 – instrument panel	A-6
31	Connector No 2 – instrument panel	B-6
32	Connector No 3 – instrument panel	B-6
33	Connector No 4 – instrument panel	B-6
34	"Hazard" warning lights switch	C-6
35	Rear screen demister switch	C-6
36	Heating-ventilating fan motor rheostat or resistance	D-4
37	LH window switch	A-3
38	RH window switch	D-3
40	LH front door pillar switch	A-6
41	RH front door pillar switch	D-6
42	LH window motor	A-3
43	RH window motor	D-3
44	Accessories plate or fusebox	B-4
45	Junction block – front harness – accessories plate	B-4
46	Junction block – front harness – accessories plate	C-4
47	Junction block – front harness – accessories plate	B-4
48	Junction block – front harness – accessories plate	C-4
49	Junction block – front harness – accessories plate	B-4
52	Stop-lights switch	D-4
53	Ignition-starter-anti-theft switch	B-4
54	Heater controls illumination	D-5
55	Glove compartment illumination	D-5
56	Cigar lighter	B-5
57	Feed to car radio	D-5
58	Windscreen wiper-washer switch	A-4
59	Lighting and direction indicators switch	B-5
60	Direction indicators switch or connector	A-5
62	Front interior light	A-6
63	RH interior light	D-6

Units

64	Handbrake switch	C-3
65	Fuel gauge tank unit (bottom)	D-2
66	Rear screen demister	C-2
68	LH rearlight assembly	A-1
69	RH rearlight assembly	D-1
70	Number plate lights	C-1
71	Choke "On" warning light	D-6
73	Rearlight assembly earth	B-1
80	Junction block – front and engine harnesses	A-7
81	Junction block – front and rear harnesses	A-2
84	Junction block – front and auto transmission harnesses	B-8
85	Junction block – window or electro-magnetic lock harnesses	B-3
86	Junction block – windscreen wiper time switch relay	A-5
90	Wire junction – air conditioning compressor	B-7
91	Wire junction – brake pad wear warning light	D-8
92	Wire junction – air conditioning motor	C-8
97	Bodyshell earth	C-8
99	Dashboard earth	C-5
101	Fuel tank mounting earth	C-2
103	Feed to accessories plate	C-4
106	Rear foglight switch	C-5
114	Windscreen wiper time switch relay	A-4
117	Wire junction – front foglights	B-9
123	Clock	D-5
124	Automatic transmission	B-8
128	Kickdown switch	B-8
130	Automatic transmission earth	A-8
142	Wire junction – windows/interior light wiring	B-3
144	Wire junction – interior light	A-6
146	Temperature switch or thermal switch	B-7
155	Rear or LH rear interior	D-3
158	Automatic transmission selector illumination	C-4
171	Rear screen wiper-washer switch	C-6
173	Wire junction – fuel tank wiring	D-2
174	RH headlight wiper motor	D-9
175	LH headlight wiper motor	A-9
176	Headlight wipers time switch relay	C-9
177	Headlight washers pump	B-8
178	Headlight washers pump (RHD)	B-9
179	Wire junction – windscreen washer/headlight washers pump	B-9
182	Tailgate RH counterbalance	C-2
183	Tailgate LH counterbalance	B-2
185	Glove compartment light switch	D-6
186	Wire junction – electric pump	D-5
204	Starter relay	B-3
209	Oil level indicator sensor	C-7
210	Wire junction – AEI (ignition) wiring	C-7
213	LH window switch for driver's side (LHD)	A-3
247	Wire junction – auxiliary lights switch	C-5
276	Engine earth	C-9
307	Wire junction – sunroof wiring	C-5
313	Wire junction – Econometer wiring (engine)	D-9
321	AEI ignition module	C-8

For the colour code and other information see Fig. 10.46

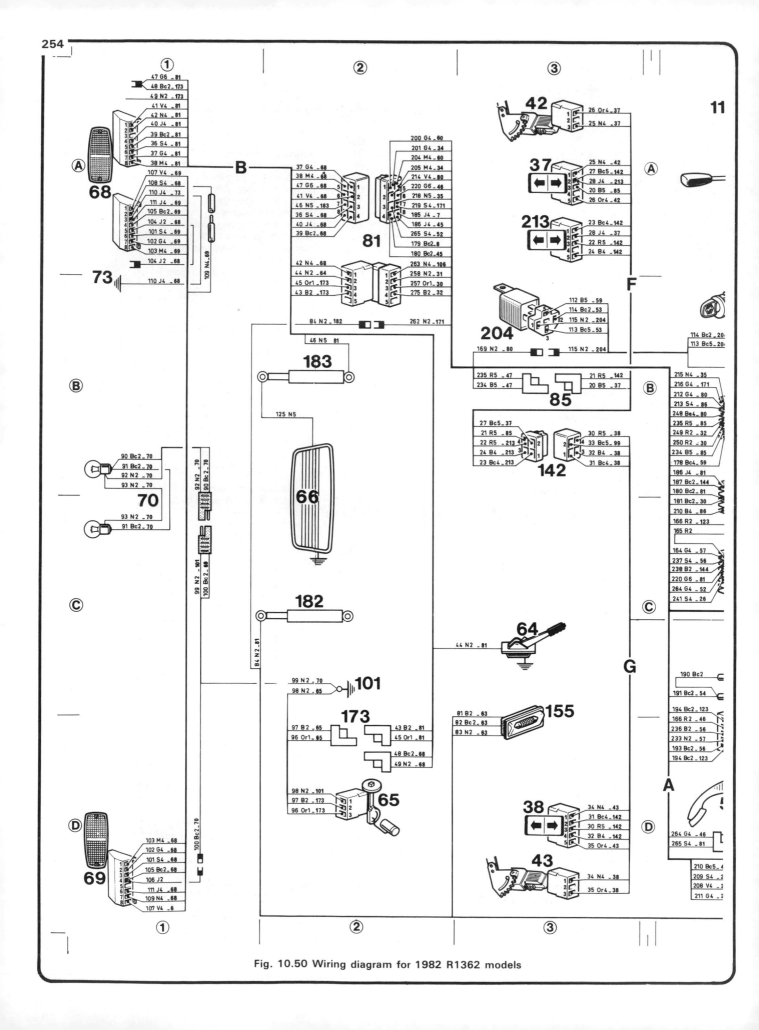

Fig. 10.50 Wiring diagram for 1982 R1362 models

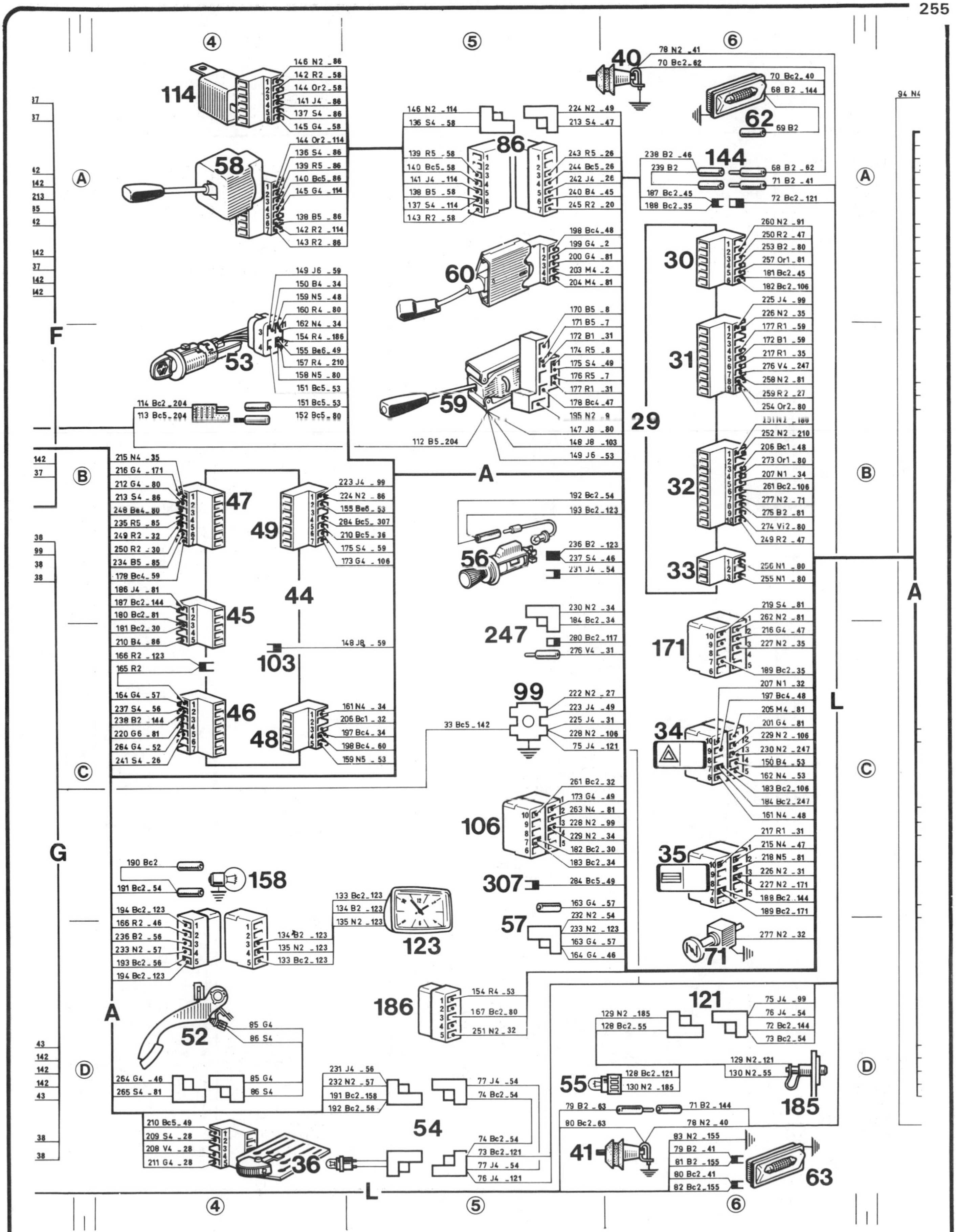

Fig. 10.50 Wiring diagram for 1982 R1362 models (continued)

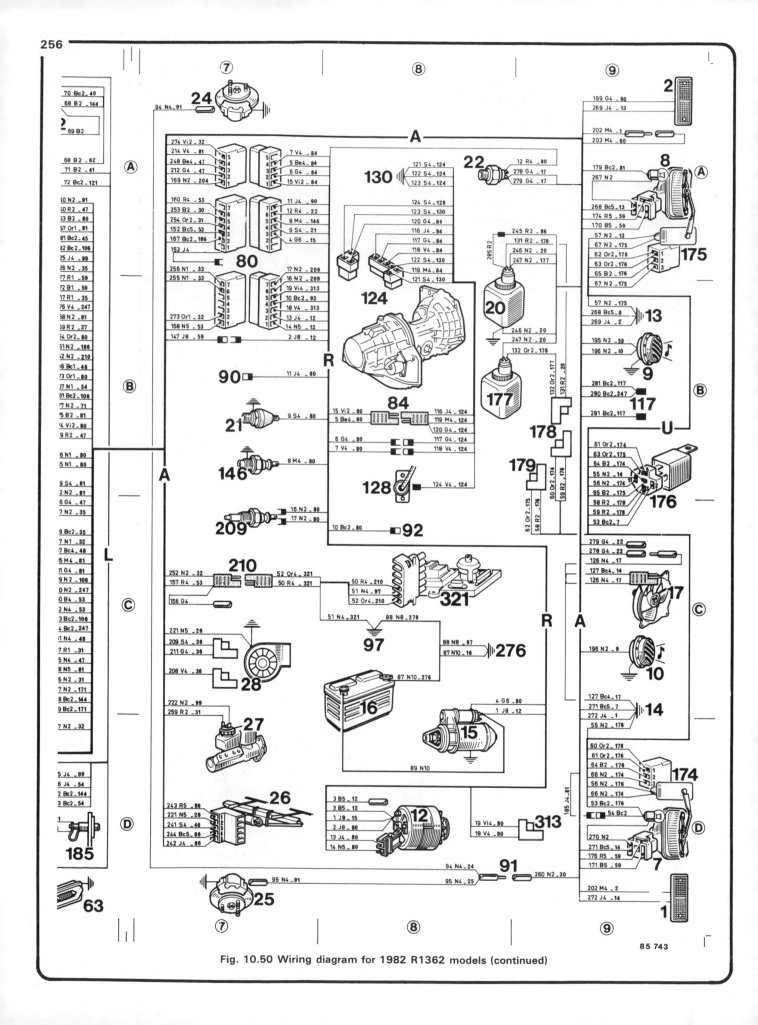

Fig. 10.50 Wiring diagram for 1982 R1362 models (continued)

85 743

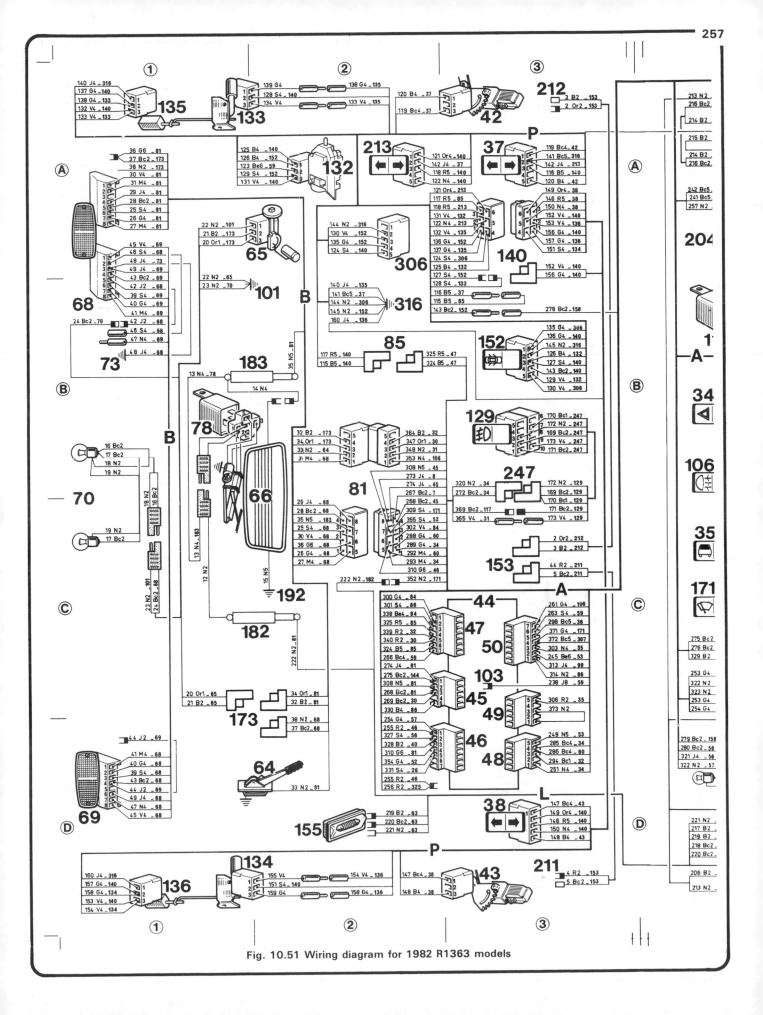

Fig. 10.51 Wiring diagram for 1982 R1363 models

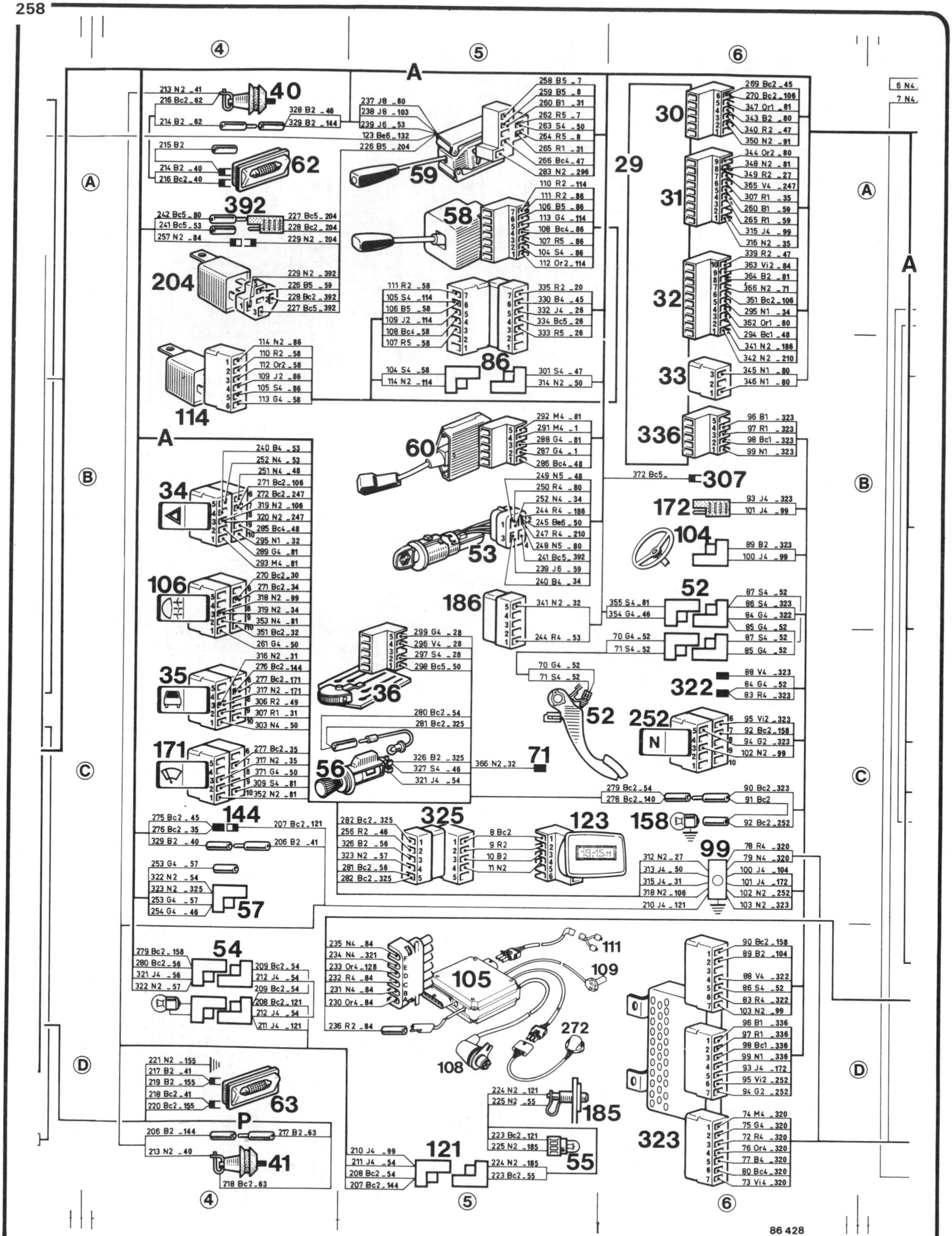

Fig. 10.51 Wiring diagram for 1982 R1363 models (continued)

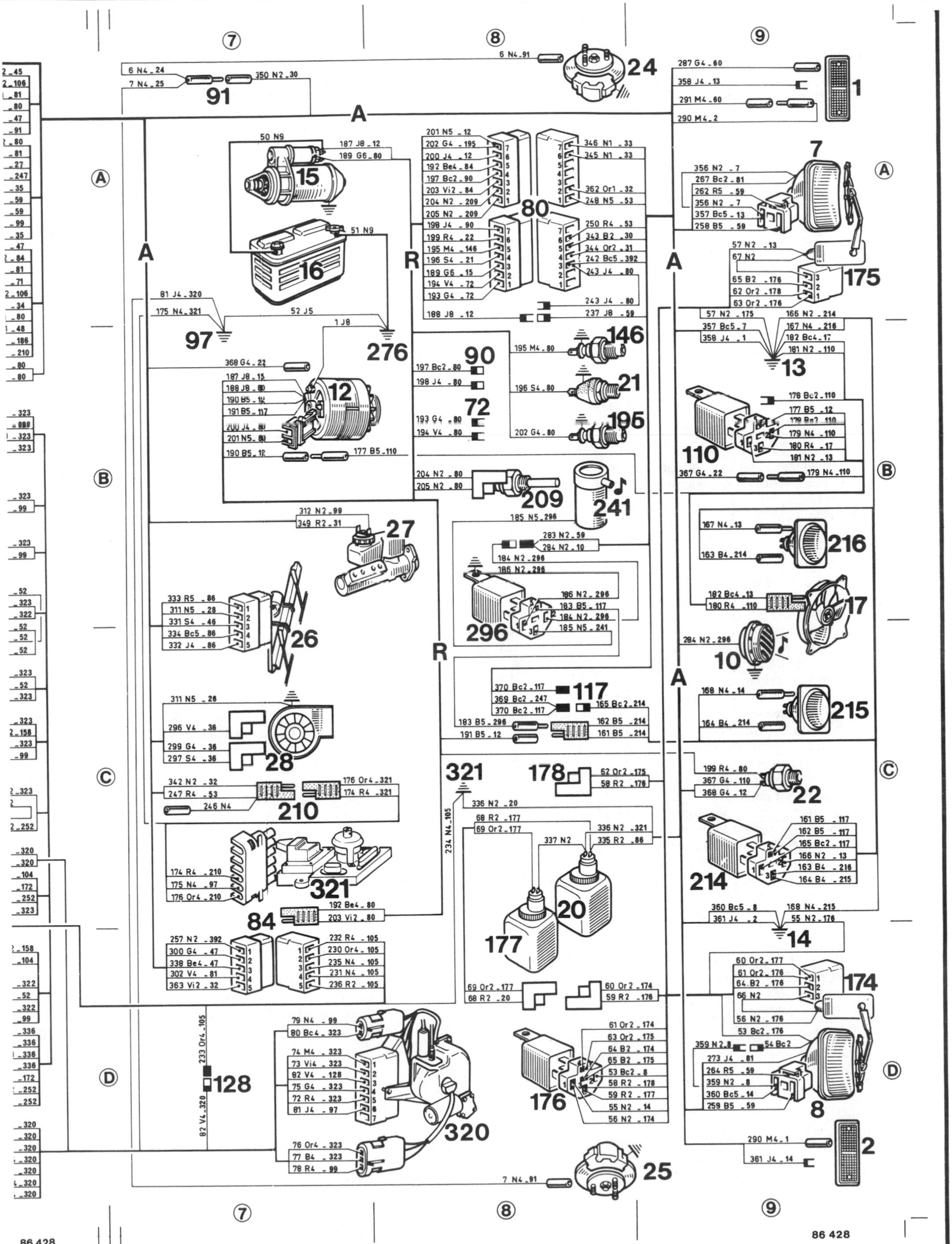

⑦　　　⑧　6 N4 .91　　　⑨

6 N4 .24
7 N4 .25
350 N2 .30
91

287 G4 .60
358 J4 .13
291 M4 .60
290 M4 .2
1

24

2 .45
2 .106
1 .81
.80
.47
.91
2 .80
.81
.27
.247
.35
.59
.59
.99
.35
.47
2 .84
.81
.71
2 .106
.34
.80
.48
.186
.210
.80
.80

Ⓐ

A

50 N9
187 J8 .12
189 G6 .80
15

201 N5 .12
202 G4 .195
200 J4 .12
192 Be4 .84
197 Bc2 .90
203 Vi2 .84
204 N2 .209
205 N2 .209
80
198 J4 .90
199 R4 .22
195 M4 .146
196 S4 .21
189 G6 .15
194 V4 .72
193 G4 .72
188 J8 .12

346 N1 .33
345 N1 .33
362 Or1 .32
248 N5 .53
250 R4 .53
343 B2 .30
344 Or2 .31
242 Bc5 .392
243 J4 .80
243 J4 .80
237 J8 .59

356 N2 .7
267 Bc2 .81
262 R5 .59
356 N2 .7
357 Bc5 .13
258 B5 .59
7

57 N2 .13
67 N2
65 B2 .176
62 Or2 .178
63 Or2 .176
175

Ⓐ

A

51 N9
16

R

57 N2 .175
357 Bc5 .7
358 J4 .1
166 N2 .214
167 N4 .216
182 Bc4 .17
181 N2 .110
13

81 J4 .320
175 N4 .321
97

52 J5

1 J8
276

368 G4 .22
187 J8 .15
188 J8 .80
190 B5 .1½
191 B5 .117
200 J4 .12
201 N5 .8½
190 B5 .12
12

177 B5 .110

195 M4 .80
146

90
197 Bc2 .80
198 J4 .80

196 S4 .80
21

72
193 G4 .80
194 V4 .80

202 G4 .80
195

178 Bc2 .110
177 B5 .12
179 Bn2 .110
179 N4 .110
180 R4 .17
181 N2 .13
110
367 G4 .22
179 N4 .110

Ⓑ

204 N2 .80
205 N2 .80
209

241

185 N5 .296

167 N4 .13
163 B4 .214
216

Ⓑ

2 .323
1 .880
.323

.323
.99

.323
.99

.52
.323
.322
.52
.52

312 N2 .99
349 R2 .31
27

283 N2 .59
284 N2 .10
184 N2 .296
186 N2 .296
186 N2 .296
183 B5 .117
184 N2 .296
185 N5 .241
296

182 Bc4 .13
180 R4 .110
17

284 N2 .296
10

.323
.52
.323

.323
2 .158
.323
.99

333 R5 .86
311 N5 .28
331 S4 .46
334 Bc5 .86
332 J4 .86
26

R

370 Bc2 .117
369 Bc2 .247
370 Bc2 .117
165 Bc2 .214
183 B5 .296
191 B5 .12
162 B5 .214
161 B5 .214
117

168 N4 .14
164 B4 .214
215

Ⓒ

311 N5 .28
296 V4 .36
299 G4 .36
297 S4 .36
28

321

178
62 Or2 .175
58 R2 .176

199 R4 .80
367 G4 .110
368 G4 .12
22

Ⓒ

2 .323
.252

2 .252

.320
.320
.104
.172
.252
.323

342 N2 .32
247 R4 .53
246 N4
176 Or4 .321
174 R4 .321
210

336 N2 .20
68 R2 .177
69 Or2 .177

337 N2
336 N2 .321
335 R2 .86

161 B5 .117
162 B5 .117
165 Bc2 .117
166 N2 .13
163 B4 .216
164 B4 .215
214

234 N4 .105

174 R4 .210
175 N4 .97
176 Or4 .210
321

20

177

2 .158
.104
.322
.52
.322
.99
.336
.336
.336
.336
.172
.252
.252

192 Be4 .80
203 Vi2 .80
84
257 N2 .392
300 G4 .47
338 Be4 .47
302 V4 .81
363 Vi2 .32
232 R4 .105
230 Or4 .105
235 N4 .105
231 N4 .105
236 R2 .105

69 Or2 .177
68 R2 .20
60 Or2 .174
59 R2 .176

360 Bc5 .8
361 J4 .2
168 N4 .215
55 N2 .176
14

60 Or2 .177
61 Or2 .176
64 B2 .176
66 N2
56 N2 .176
53 Bc2 .176
174

.320
.320
.320
.320

233 Or4 .105

79 N4 .99
80 Bc4 .323
74 M4 .99
73 Vi4 .323
82 V4 .128
75 G4 .323
72 R4 .323
81 J4 .97
320

Ⓓ

82 V4 .320
128

61 Or2 .174
63 Or2 .175
64 B2 .174
65 B2 .174
53 Bc2 .8
58 R2 .178
59 R2 .177
55 N2 .14
56 N2 .174
176

359 N2 .8
54 Bc2
273 J4 .81
264 R5 .59
359 N2 .8
360 Bc5 .14
259 B5 .59
8

Ⓓ

.320
.320
.320
.320
.320
.320

76 Or4 .323
77 B4 .323
78 R4 .99

7 N4 .91
25

290 M4 .1
361 J4 .14
2

⑦　　　⑧　　　⑨

86 428　　　86 428

Fig. 10.51 Wiring diagram for 1982 R1363 models (continued)

Key to wiring diagram for 1982 R1363 models

Harnesses

A   Front
B   Rear
P   Door locks
R   Engine

Units

1	LH sidelight and/or direction indicator	A-9
2	RH sidelight and/or direction indicator	D-9
7	LH headlight	A-9
8	RH headlight	D-9
10	RH horn	C-9
12	Alternator	B-7
13	LH front earth	B-9
14	RH front earth	D-9
15	Starter	A-7
16	Battery	A-7
17	Engine cooling fan motor	B-9
20	Windscreen washer pump	C-8
21	Oil pressure switch	B-8
22	Thermal switch on radiator	C-9
24	LH front brake	A-9
25	RH front brake	D-9
26	Windscreen wiper motor	C-7
27	Nivocode or ICP (brake pressure drop indicator)	B-8
28	Heating-ventilating fan motor	C-7
29	Instrument panel	A-6
30	Connector No 1 – instrument panel	A-6
31	Connector No 2 – instrument panel	A-6
32	Connector No 3 – instrument panel	A-6
33	Connector No 4 – instrument panel	B-6
34	"Hazard" warning lights switch	B-4
35	Rear screen demister switch	C-4
36	Heating-ventilating fan motor rheostat or resistance	C-5
37	LH window switch	A-3
38	RH window switch	D-3
40	LH front door pillar switch	A-4
41	RH front door pillar switch	D-4
42	LH window motor	A-3

Units

43	RH window motor	D-3
44	Accessories plate or fusebox	C-3
45	Junction block – front harness accessories plate	C-3
46	Junction block – front harness accessories plate	D-3
47	Junction block – front harness accessories plate	C-3
48	Junction block – front harness accessories plate	D-3
49	Junction block – front harness accessories plate	D-3
50	Junction block – front harness accessories plate	C-3
52	Stop-lights switch	C-6, B-6
53	Ignition-starter-anti-theft switch	B-5
54	Heater controls illumination	D-4
55	Glove compartment illumination	D-5
56	Cigar lighter	C-5
57	Feed to car radio	C-4
58	Windscreen wiper-washer switch	A-5
59	Lighting and direction indicators switch	A-5
60	Direction indicators switch or connector	B-5
62	LH or front centre interior light	A4
63	RH interior light	D-4
64	Handbrake switch	D-2
65	Fuel gauge tank unit	A-2
66	Rear screen demister	C-2
68	LH rearlight assembly	B-1
69	RH rearlight assembly	D-1
70	Number plate lights	C-1
71	Choke "On" warning light	C-5
72	Reversing lights switch	B-8
73	Rear light assembly earth	B-1
78	Rear screen wiper motor	B-1
80	Junction block – front and rear harnesses	A-8
81	Junction block – front and rear harnesses	C-2
84	Junction block – front and auto transmission harnesses	C-7

Key to wiring diagram for 1982 R1363 models (continued)

Units		
85	Junction block – window or electro-magnetic lock harnesses	C-2
86	Junction block – windscreen wiper timer relay	B-5
90	Wire junction – air conditioning compressor	B-8
91	Wire junction – brake pad wear warning light	A-7
97	Bodyshell earth	B-7
99	Dashboard earth	C-6
101	Fuel tank mounting earth	B-2
103	Feed to accessories plate	C-3
104	Junction – steering wheel tracks	B-6
105	Automatic transmission computer	D-5
106	Rear foglight switch	B-4
108	Multi-function switch	D-5
109	Speed sensor	D-5
110	Engine cooling fan motor relay	B-9
111	Solenoid valves 1 and 2	D-5
114	Windscreen wiper timer relay	B-4
117	Wire junction – front foglights	C-8
121	Junction – glove compartment light	D-5
123	Clock	C-5
128	Kickdown switch	D-7
129	Front foglights switch	B-3
132	Inertia switch	A-2
133	LH front door lock switch	A-2
134	RH front door lock switch	D-2
135	LH front door lock solenoid	A-1
136	RH front door lock solenoid	D-1
140	Junction – electro-magnetic door lock harness	A-3
144	Wire junction – interior light	C-4
146	Temperature or thermal switch	B-8
152	Electro-magnetic locks central switch	B-3
153	Radio speaker wires	C-3
155	Rear or LH rear interior light	D-2
158	Automatic transmission selector illumination	C-6
171	Rear screen wiper/washer switch	C-4
172	Impulse generator	B-6

Units		
173	Wire junction – fuel tank wiring	C-1
174	RH headlight wiper motor	D-9
175	LH headlight wiper motor	A-9
176	Headlight wipers time relay	D-8
177	Headlight washers pump	D-8
178	Headlight washers pump (RHD)	C-8
182	Tailgate RH counterbalance	C-2
183	Tailgate LH counterbalance	B-2
185	Glove compartment light switch	D-5
186	Wire junction – electric pump	B-5
192	Tailgate earth	C-2
195	Idle cut-out	B-8
204	Starter relay	A-4
209	Oil level indicator sensor	B-8
210	Wire junction – AEI ignition wiring	C-7
211	Speaker in RH rear panel	D-3
212	Speaker in LH rear panel	A-3
213	LH window switch for driver's side (RHD)	A-2
214	Front foglights relay	C-9
215	RH front foglight	C-9
216	LH front foglight	D-9
241	Air horns compressor	B-8
247	Wire junction – additional driving lights switch	B-3
252	Normalur switch	C-6
272	Butterfly spindle switch	D-5
276	Engine earth	B-8
296	Air horns compressor relay	C-8
306	'PLIP' remote control sensor (infra-red door unlocking)	A-2
307	Wire junction – sunroof	B-6
316	Console earth	B-2
320	Normalur servo motor	D-8
321	AEI ignition module	C-8 & C-7
322	Declutching switch	C-6
323	Normalur computer	D-6
325	Junction – clock wiring	C-5
336	Connector No 5 – instrument panel	B-6
392	Wire junction – starter relay	A-4

For the colour code and other information see Fig. 10.46

Key to wiring diagram (typical) for all 1983 and 1984 models

Units

1   LH sidelight and/or direction indicator
2   RH sidelight and/or direction indicator
7   LH headlight
8   RH headlight
9   LH horn
10 RH horn
12 Alternator
13 LH earth
14 RH earth
15 Starter
16 Battery
17 Engine cooling fan motor
20 Windscreen washer pump
21 Oil pressure switch
22 Fan motor No 1 activating thermal switch
23 Cooling temperature warning thermal switch
24 LH front brake
25 RH front brake
26 Windscreen wiper motor
27 Nivocode or ICP (pressure drop indicator)
28 Heating-ventilating fan motor
29 Instrument panel
30 Connector No 1 – instrument panel
31 Connector No 2 – instrument panel
32 Connector No 3 – instrument panel
33 Connector No 4 – instrument panel
34 'Hazard' warning lights switch
35 Rear screen demister switch
36 Heating/ventilating fan motor rheostat or resistances
37 LH window switch
38 RH window switch
40 LH front door pillar switch
41 RH front door pillar switch
42 LH window motor
43 RH window motor
44 Accessories plate or fusebox
45 Junction block – front harness – accessories plate
46 Junction block – front harness – accessories plate
47 Junction block – front harness – accessories plate
48 Junction block – front harness – accessories plate
49 Junction block – front harness – accessories plate
52 Stop-lights switch
53 Ignition-starter-anti-theft switch
54 Heating/ventilating controls illumination
55 Glove compartment light
56 Cigar lighter
57 Feed to car radio
58 Windscreen wiper/washer switch
59 Lighting and direction indicators switch
60 Direction indicator switch or connector
61 Feed terminal before ignition-starter switch
62 LH or front centre interior light
63 RH interior light
64 Handbrake 'On' warning light switch
65 Fuel gauge tank unit
66 Rear screen demister
68 LH rear light assembly
69 RH rear light assembly
70 Number plate lights
71 Choke 'On' warning light
72 Reversing lights switch
73 Rear light assemblies earth
78 Rear screen wiper motor
80 Junction block – engine harness
84 Junction block – gearbox/automatic transmission harness
90 Air conditioning compressor
97 Bodyshell earth

Units

99 Dashboard earth
103 Feed to accessories plate
105 Automatic transmission computer
106 Rear foglight switch
108 Multi-function switch
109 Speed sensor
110 Engine cooling fan motor relay
111 Solenoid valves 1 and 2
114 Windscreen wiper timer relay
118 Sunroof motor
120 Sunroof switch
121 Junction – glove compartment light
123 Clock
128 Kickdown switch
129 Front foglights switch
132 Inertia switch
133 LH front door lock switch
134 RH front door lock switch
135 LH front door solenoid
136 RH front door solenoid
140 Junction No 1 – door locking – unlocking harness
146 Temperature or thermal switch
150 LH front door speaker
151 RH front door speaker
152 Central door locking switch
153 Radio speaker wires
155 Rear or LH rear interior light
158 Automatic transmission selector illumination
164 Electric fuel pump
171 Rear screen wiper/washer switch
174 RH headlight wiper motor
175 LH headlight wiper motor
176 Headlight wipers timer relay
177 Headlight washers pump
182 Tailgate RH counterbalance
183 Tailgate LH counterbalance
185 Glove compartment light switch
186 Junction – electric pump harness
187 Speedometer relay (fuel pump)
192 Tailgate earth
194 Junction No 1 – cold air blower
195 Idling cut-out
204 Starter relay
207 Anti-stall solenoid valve
209 Oil level indicator sensor
210 Junction – AEI ignition harness
213 LH window switch for passenger's side (LHD)
214 Relay No 1 – additional driving lights
215 RH front foglight
216 LH front foglight
217 LH mirror control (LHD)
241 Horn compressor
262 Heating and air conditioning control panel
263 Additional cooling fan motor relay
264 Additional cooling fan motor
272 Throttle spindle switch
274 Wire junction No 1
276 Engine earth
286 Wire junction No 2
289 Wire junction No 3
290 Wire junction No 4
291 Pinking detector
293 Junction – windscreen wiper wiring
296 Horn compressor relay
307 Wire junction – sunroof harness
308 Junction No 2 – rear harness
316 Console earth
318 Boost pressure gauge illumination

Key to wiring diagram (typical) for all 1983 and 1984 models (continued)

Units
319 Ignition cut-out relay
321 AEI ignition module
342 Headlight washer solenoid valve
360 Idling switch
378 Air conditioning high pressure sensor
383 Ignition cut-out pressure switch
386 Intercooler fan motor
390 Intercooler fan motor pressure switch
392 Junction – starter relay harness
415 Junction – front foglights harness

Units
418 Door opening relay
419 Door closing relay
420 RH mirror control
421 Junction No 2 – door locking-unlocking harness
422 Junction No 3 – door locking-unlocking harness
438 Wire junction No 5
439 Wire junction No 6
456 Junction – engine cooling fan harness
477 Junction – headlight wiper/washers intermediate
485 Junction – fuel filler flap solenoid wiring

Not all items are fitted to all models. For the colour code and other information see Fig. 10.46

Note: *Depending on the function required and the vehicle concerned, the circuit number with the information is given below.*

	All types	847 Engine (1360)	A6M Engine (1362)	J6R Engine (1363)	A5L (1365)
AEI ignition	–	2	2	2	3
Air conditioning	1	–	–	–	–
Automatic transmission	3	–	–	–	–
Boost pressure gauge illumination	1	–	–	–	–
Brake pad wear warning light	4	–	–	–	–
Charging circuit	–	9	9	11	10
Choke	4	–	–	–	–
Clock	2	–	–	–	–
Cigar lighter	2	–	–	–	–
Coolant temperature warning light switch	–	–	–	11	10
Cooling fan motor	–	1	9	11	10
Direction indicators	6	–	–	–	–
Door locks	5	–	–	–	–
Electric fuel pump	–	–	–	–	3
Front foglights	7	–	–	–	–
Fuel gauge	4	–	–	–	–
Handbrake	4	–	–	–	–
Headlight dipped beams	6	–	–	–	–
Headlight main beams	6	–	–	–	–
Headlight wipers/washers	8	–	–	–	–
Heating/ventilating	8	–	–	–	–
Horn	–	1	1	8	1
Identification plates and switches illumination	2	–	–	–	–
Idle cut-out	–	–	–	11	–
Interior lights	4	–	–	–	–
Nivocode (brake pressure drop)	4	–	–	–	–
Oil level indicator	–	–	9	11	10
Oil pressure switch	–	9	9	11	10
Radio feed	2	–	–	–	–
Rear foglight	7	–	–	–	–
Rear screen demister	7	–	–	–	–
Rear screen wiper/washer	7	–	–	–	–
Rear view mirror – electric	5	–	–	–	–
Reversing lights	7	–	–	–	–
Sidelights	6	–	–	–	–
Speakers	2	–	–	–	–
Starter	–	9	9	11	10
Stop-lights	7	–	–	–	–
Sunroof	4	–	–	–	–
Thermal switch	–	11	9	11	10
Window winders	5	–	–	–	–
Windscreen washer/wiper	1	–	–	–	–
Windscreen wiper with timer	8	–	–	–	–

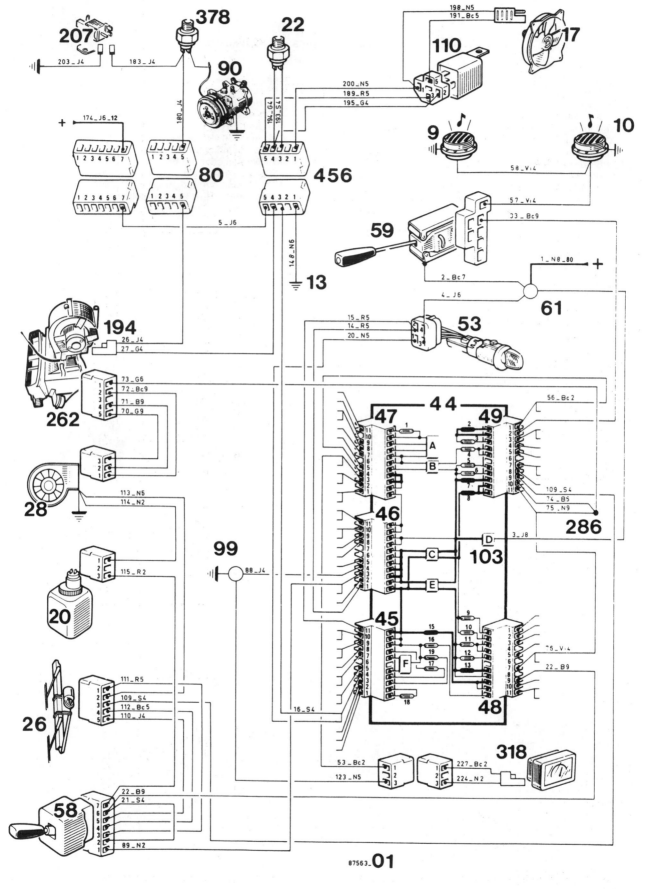

87563_**01**

Fig. 10.52 Wiring diagram (typical) for all 1983 and 1984 models – circuit 1

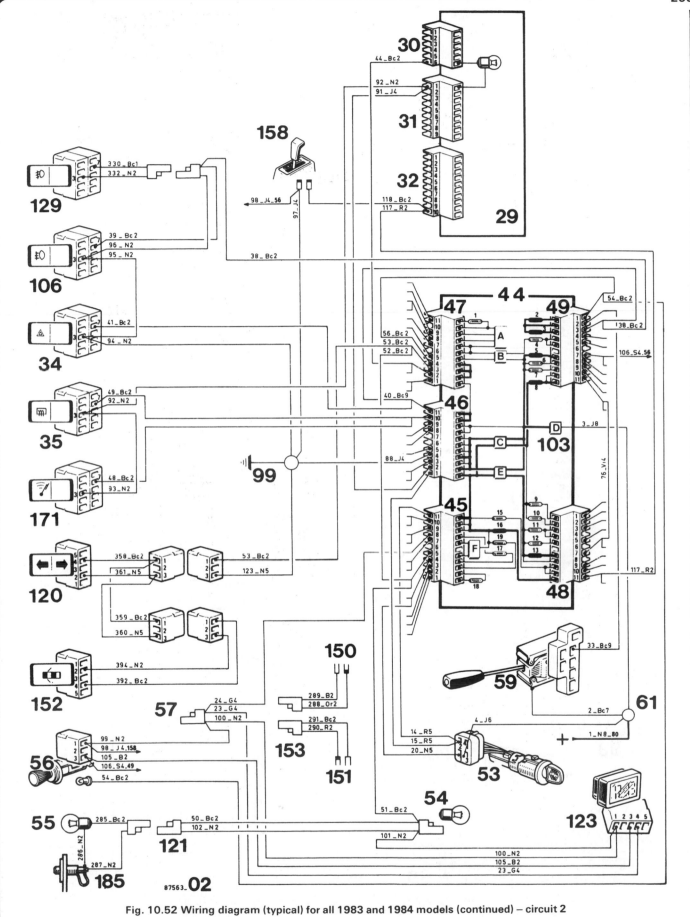

Fig. 10.52 Wiring diagram (typical) for all 1983 and 1984 models (continued) – circuit 2

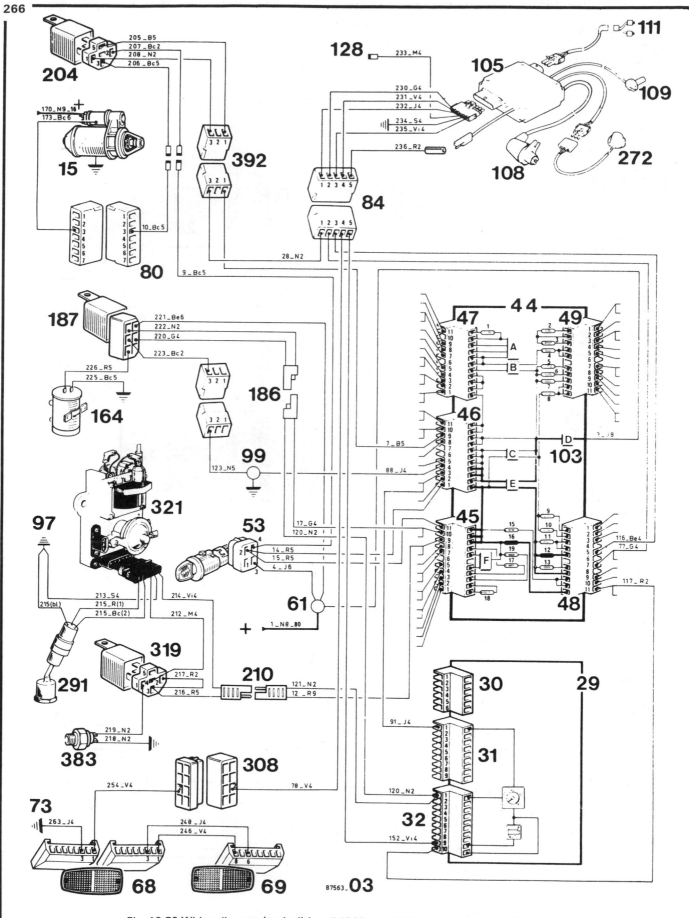

Fig. 10.52 Wiring diagram (typical) for all 1983 and 1984 models (continued) – circuit 3

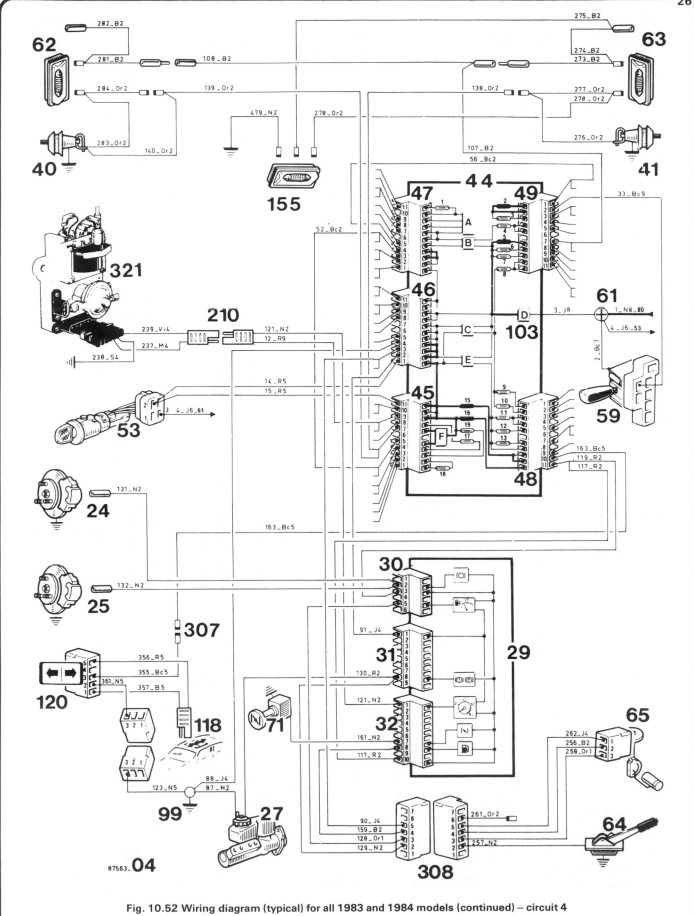

Fig. 10.52 Wiring diagram (typical) for all 1983 and 1984 models (continued) – circuit 4

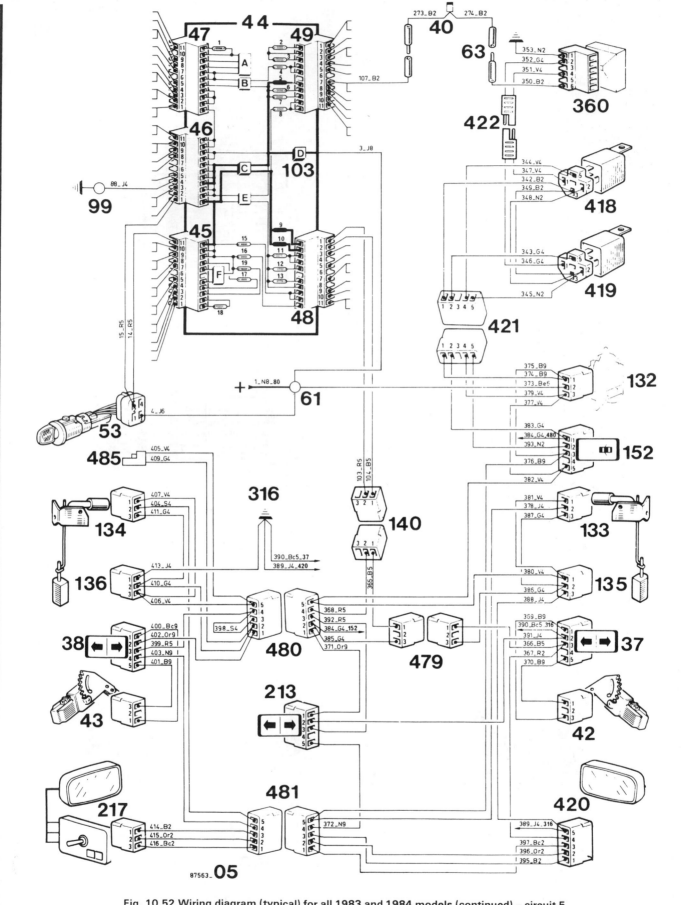

87563 **05**

Fig. 10.52 Wiring diagram (typical) for all 1983 and 1984 models (continued) – circuit 5

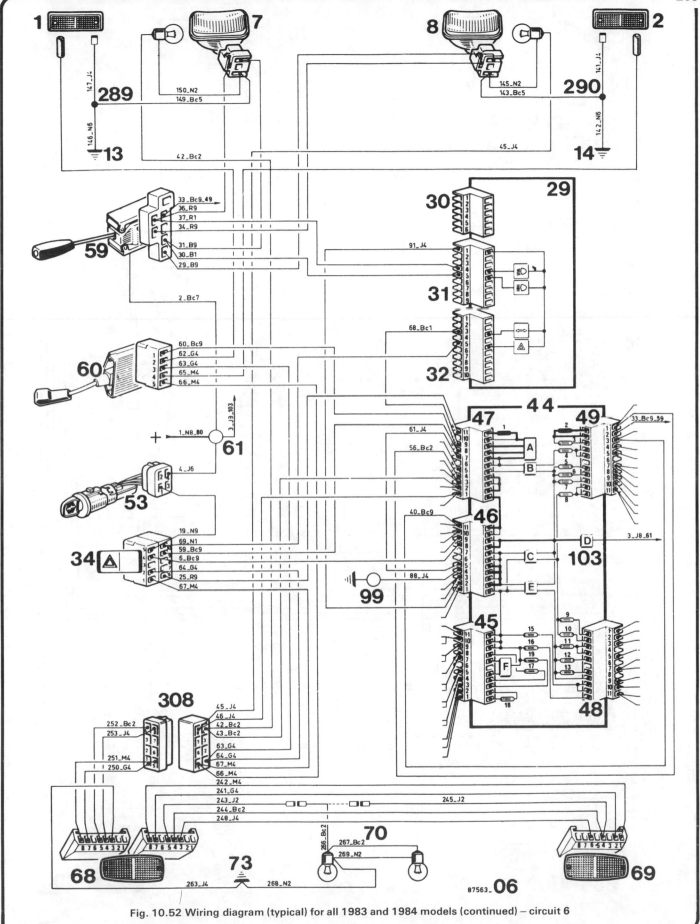

Fig. 10.52 Wiring diagram (typical) for all 1983 and 1984 models (continued) – circuit 6

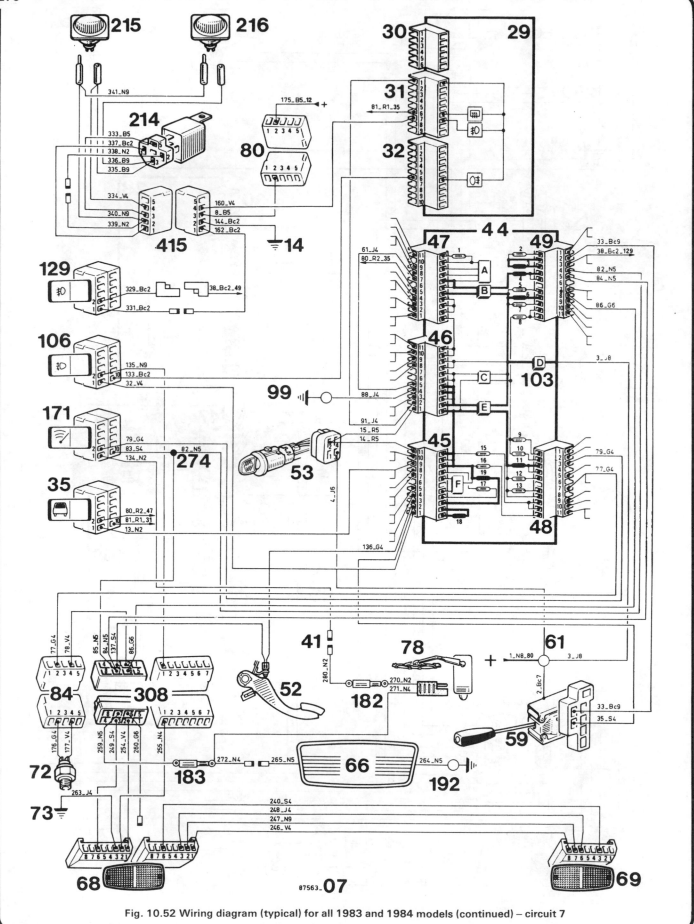

Fig. 10.52 Wiring diagram (typical) for all 1983 and 1984 models (continued) – circuit 7

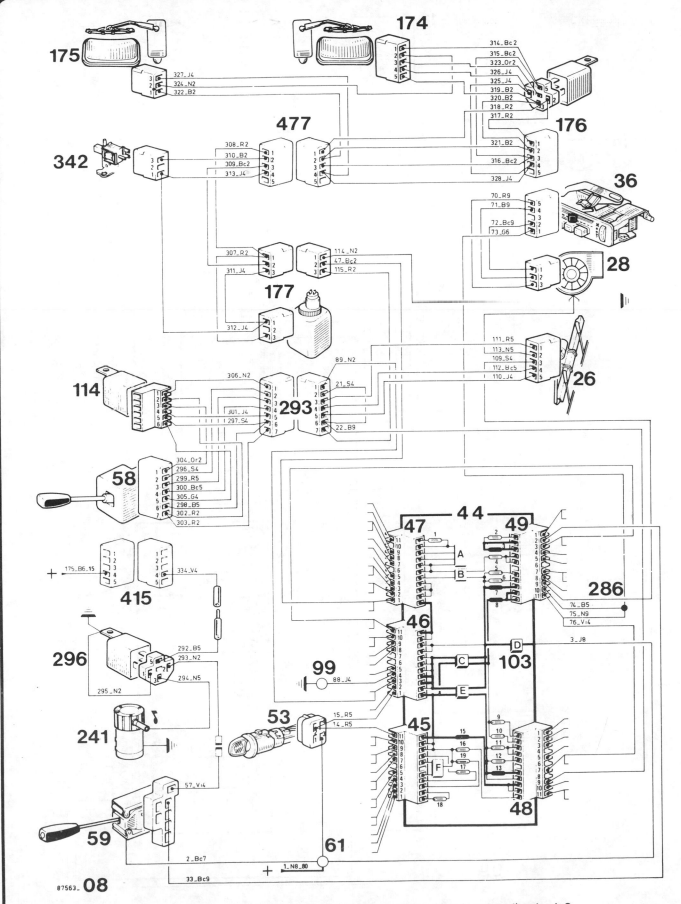

Fig. 10.52 Wiring diagram (typical) for all 1983 and 1984 models (continued) – circuit 8

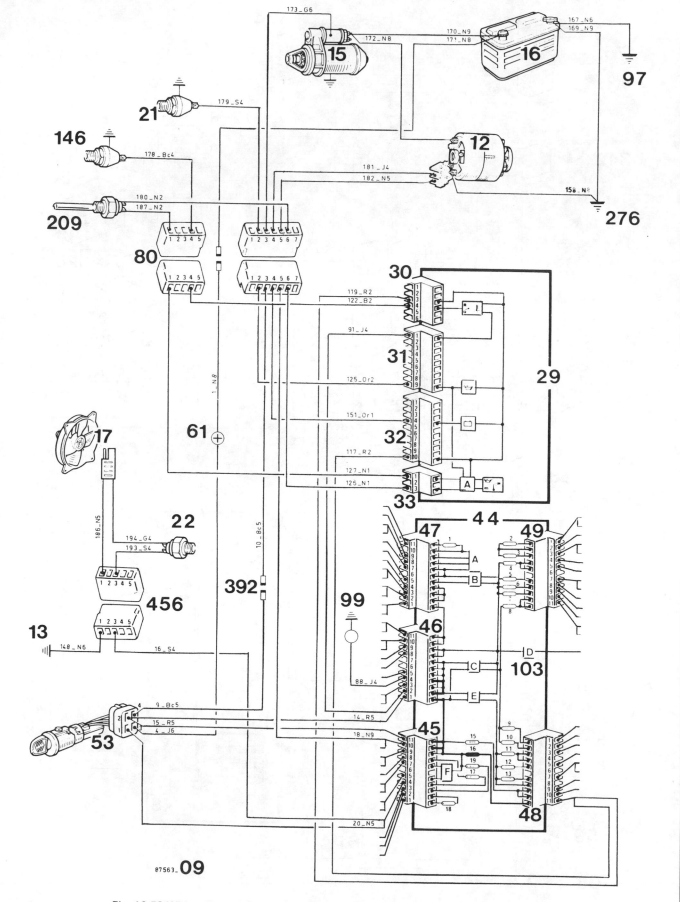

87563_**09**

Fig. 10.52 Wiring diagram (typical) for all 1983 and 1984 models (continued) – circuit 9

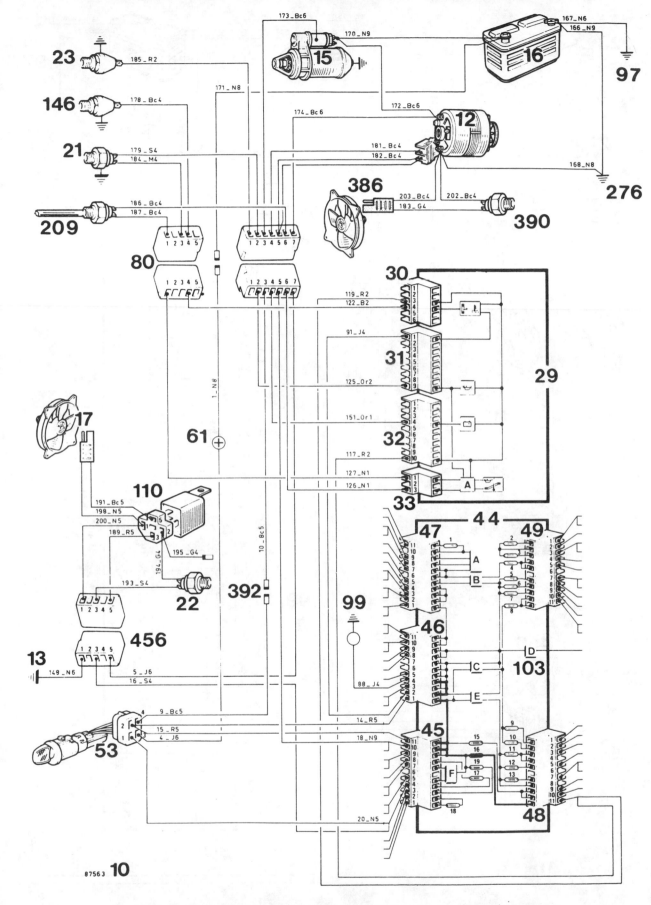

Fig. 10.52 Wiring diagram (typical) for all 1983 and 1984 models (continued) – circuit 10

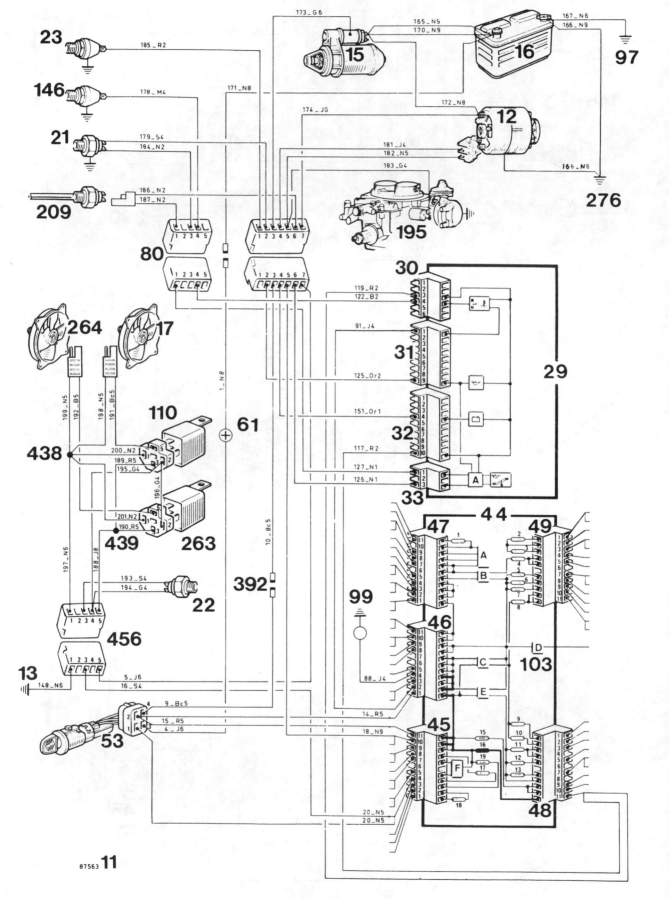

Fig. 10.52 Wiring diagram (typical) for all 1983 and 1984 models (continued) – circuit 11

Chapter 11 Suspension and steering

For modifications, and information applicable to later models, see Supplement at end of manual

Contents

Specifications

Front suspension
Type .... Independent, upper and lower control arms, coil springs and telescopic shock absorbers, anti-roll bar

Front wheel alignment
Camber angle, unladen .... 0° ± 30′ (maximum difference between each side : 1°)
King pin inclination, unladen .... 13° ± 30′ (maximum difference between each side : 1°)
Castor angle (refer to Section 31):

	Manual steering	Power steering
UK models:		
H5-H2 = 35 mm (1.38 in)	2°	3°
H5-H2 = 55 mm (2.17 in)	1° 30′ ± 30′	2° 30′ ± 30′
H5-H2 = 70 mm (2.76 in)	1°	2°
H5-H2 = 90 mm (3.54 in)	0° 30′	1° 30′

Note: Maximum difference between each side : 1°
North American models:
    H5-H2 = 20 mm (0.79 in) ....
    H5-H2 = 35 mm (1.38 in) ....
    H5-H2 = 55 mm (2.17 in) ....
    H5-H2 = 70 mm (2.76 in) ....
Note: Maximum difference between each side 1°
Toe-out, unladen ....

Power steering
3° 30' ± 30'
3° ± 30'
2° 30' ± 30'
2° ± 30'

1 ± 1 mm (0.04 ± 0.04 in), equivalent to 0° 10' ± 10'

Rear suspension
Type ....

Trailing beam, upper centre arm, lower side arms, coil springs and telescopic shock absorbers, anti-roll bar

Rear wheel alignment
Camber angle, unladen ....
Toe-out, unladen ....

0° to 0° 30'
0 to 1.5 mm (0 to 0.06 in), equivalent to 0° to 15'

Steering
Type ....

Rack and pinion, steering column with retractable safety shaft

Wheels
Type ....
Size ....

Steel or light alloy
5½ B13 FH42, 5 B13 FH42, 5½ J14 FH42, or 5 B13 FH46

Tyres
Size ....

155 SR 13, 175/70 HR 13, 165 SR 13, 175/70 HR 13, 185/65 HR 14, 185/70 SR 13 or 165/70 HR 365

Pressure — bar (lbf/in^2)	Front	Rear
UK models:		
TL, GTL	1.8 (26)	2.0 (29)
TS, GTS, TX and GTX	2.0 (29)	2.2 (32)
Automatic transmission models	2.1 (30)	2.2 (32)
North American models:		
1368, 136A	1.9 (28)	2.2 (32)

Note: For motorway or fully laden use, increase pressures by 0.1 bar (1.5 lbf/in^2)

Torque wrench settings

	lbf ft	Nm
Front suspension		
Shock absorber bottom locknut	44	60
Castor tie-rod rear nut	59	80
Lower arm pivot	66	90
Upper arm pivot	66	90
Anti-roll bar link	59	80
Upper balljoint	47	64
Lower balljoint	47	64
Wheel bearing retainer	11	15
Driveshaft nuts	185	250
Roadwheel nuts	59	80
Shock absorber top nuts	11	15
Shock absorber bottom mounting pin	59	80
Rear suspension		
Side arm front mounting	25	34
Side arm rear mounting	29	39
Backplate	25	34
Centre arm front mounting	59	80
Centre arm rear mounting pivot	29	40
Centre arm rear mounting clamp	11	15
Shock absorber top nuts	11	15
Shock absorber bottom nut	22	30
Anti-roll bar (separate)	25	34
Steering		
Tie-rod end nut	29	39

1 General description

The front suspension is of independent type; incorporating upper and lower control arms with the telescopic shock absorbers and coil springs mounted over the upper arm. The stub axle carrier is connected to the arms by balljoints, and the suspension mountings are of rubber. An anti-roll bar is fitted forward of the suspension.

The rear suspension incorporates side arms and a trailing rear axle beam with an upper centre arm pivoting on the underbody. The coil springs and telescopic shock absorbers are located at each end of the axle beam, and the suspension mountings are of rubber. An anti-roll bar is fitted between the lower side arms.

The steering is of rack and pinion type and incorporates a retractable safety shaft. Power steering is fitted to certain models.

Fig. 11.1 Exploded view of the front suspension (Sec 1)

1	Coil spring	10	Stub axle carrier
2	Shock absorber top mounting components	11	Bush
		12	Lower arm
3	Seat	13	Bearing retainer
4	Upper arm pivot pin	14	Locknut
5	Upper arm	15	Shock absorber lower mounting
6	Lower arm pivot pin		
7	Shock absorber	16	Hub
8	Castor tie-rod	17	Disc
9	Spacer		

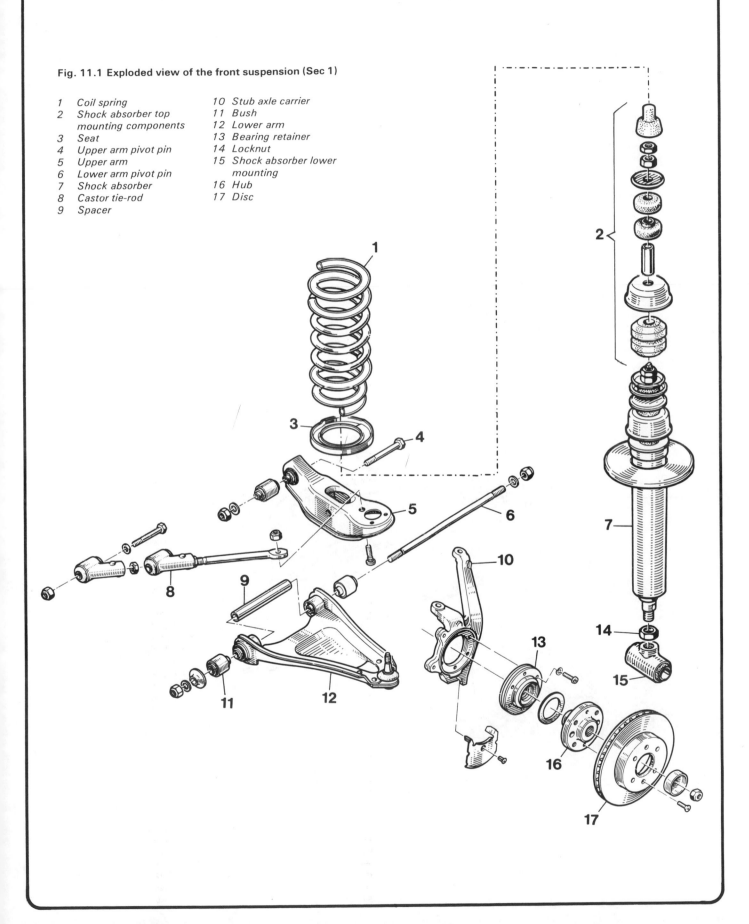

Fig. 11.2 Exploded view of the rear suspension (Sec 1)

1   Shock absorber upper
    mounting components
2   Shock absorber
3   Coil spring
4   Rear axle beam
5   Side arm
6   Pivot pin
7   Anti-roll bar
8   Centre arm
9   Clamp
10 Bush

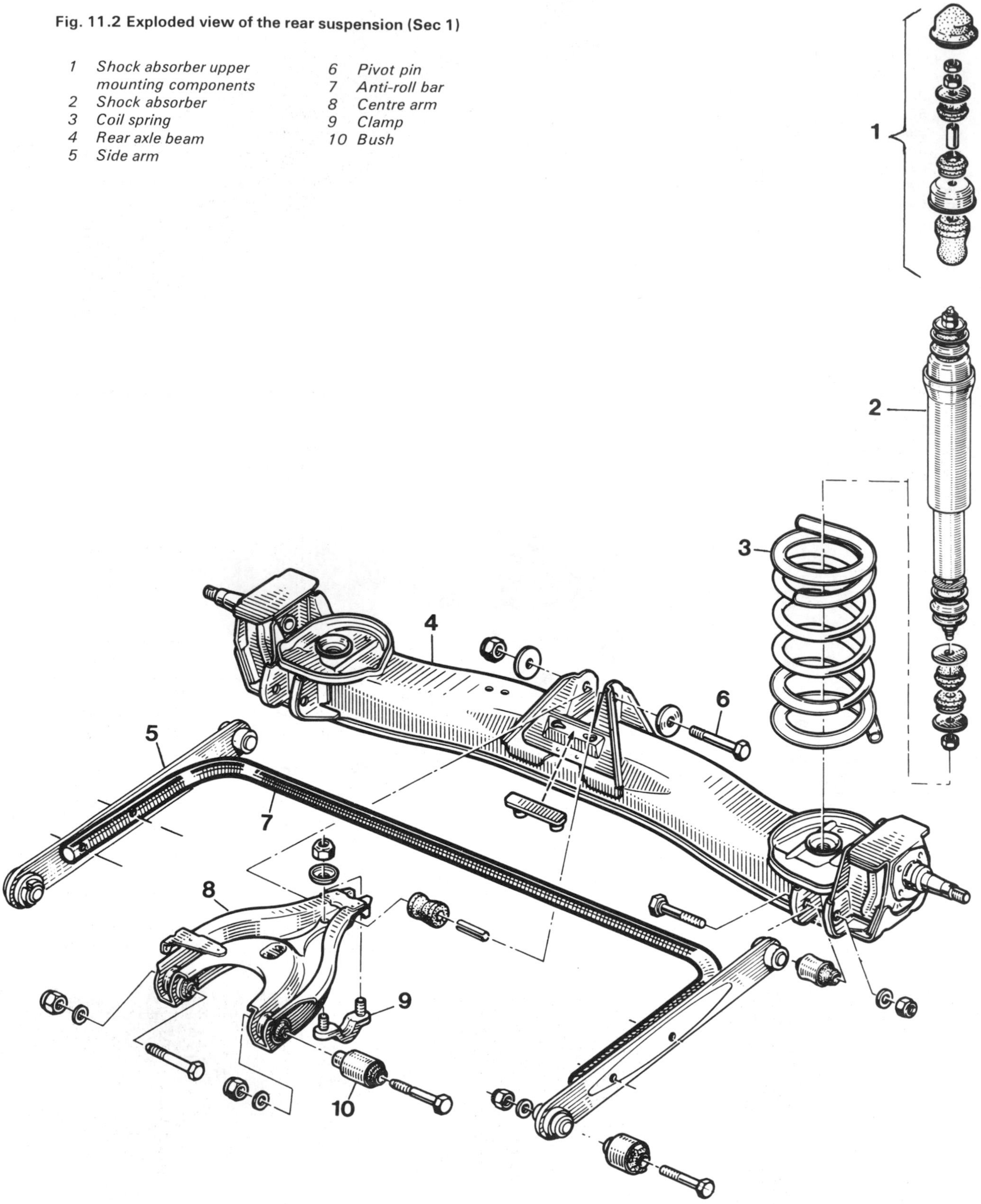

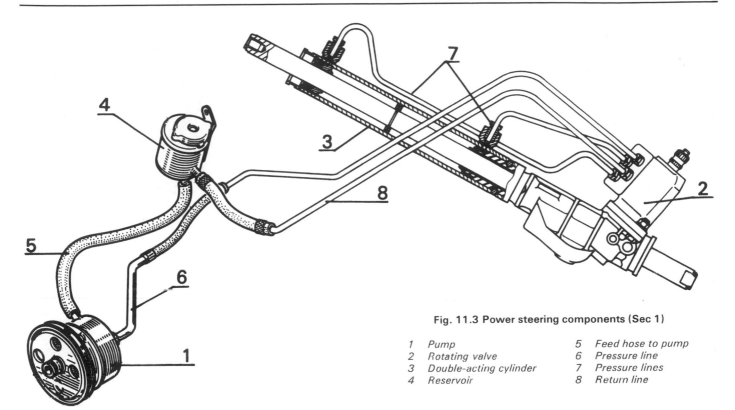

Fig. 11.3 Power steering components (Sec 1)

1	Pump	5	Feed hose to pump
2	Rotating valve	6	Pressure line
3	Double-acting cylinder	7	Pressure lines
4	Reservoir	8	Return line

2 Routine maintenance

1 Every 5000 miles (8000 km) check the tyres for pressure and visually inspect them for wear and damage.
2 Every 10 000 miles (16 000 km) grease the steering linkages and, where applicable, top up the power steering fluid. Also check and tighten the driveshaft nuts.
3 Every 40 000 miles (64 000 km) check all suspension components for wear and damage.

3 Front anti-roll bar – removal and refitting

1 Jack up the front of the car and support on axle stands. Apply the handbrake.
2 Remove the engine splash panels.
3 Remove the nuts securing the clamps to the side-members.
4 Remove the nuts securing the links to the upper arm (photo).
5 Withdraw the bar and links (photo).
6 Examine all parts, and renew as necessary.
7 Offer up and refit the anti-roll bar and associated parts, but do not tighten the fixings.

8 With the wheels on the ground, load the vehicle to the kerbside weight.
9 Tighten the anti-roll bar fixings to the specified torque figures (photo).

4 Front stub axle carrier – removal and refitting

1 If available, fit the spacer tool T AV 509-01 between the lower suspension arm inner pivot and the shock absorber bottom mounting.
2 Jack up the front of the car and support on axle stands. Apply the handbrake and remove the roadwheel.
3 Remove the brake disc, as described in Chapter 9.
4 Using a suitable bar across the wheel studs to prevent the hub from turning, preferably one with holes to accept two of the wheel studs, unscrew the driveshaft nut. This nut is very tight. Retain the nut and thrust washer.
5 Using a Torx key through the holes in the hub flange unscrew the bearing retainer bolts.
6 Withdraw the hub and bearing assembly at the same time pushing the driveshaft inward through the hub.
7 Unscrew the nuts from the stub axle carrier balljoints and steering tie-rod end joint, and use a separator tool to release the joints.

3.4 Front anti-roll bar link

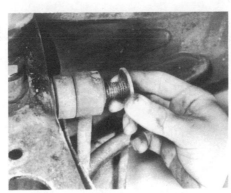

3.5 Removing the front anti-roll bar link

3.9 Tightening the front anti-roll bar link nut

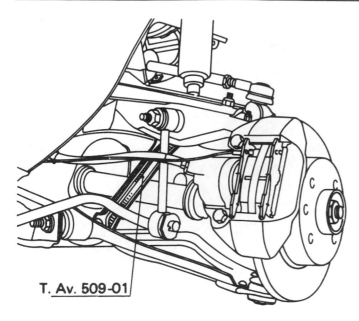

Fig. 11.4 Front suspension spacer tool in position (Sec 4)

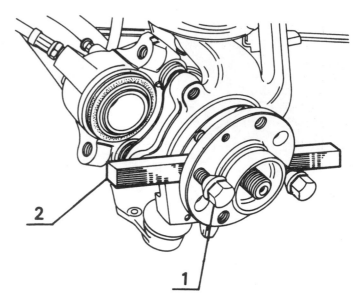

Fig. 11.5 Using two wheel studs (1) and two metal bars (2) to withdraw the front hub (Sec 5)

8   Withdraw the stub axle carrier.
9   Refitting is a reversal of removal, but tighten the nuts and bolts to the specified torque. If the roadwheel design incorporates a central opening, tighten the driveshaft nut with the wheels on the ground.

5   Front wheel bearing – renewal

1   If the roadwheel design incorporates a central opening, loosen the driveshaft nut with the wheels on the ground while an assistant depresses the footbrake pedal.
2   Jack up the front of the car and support on axle stands. Apply the handbrake and remove the roadwheel.
3   Remove the brake disc, as described in Chapter 9.
4   Unscrew the driveshaft nut, if necessary, using a bar across two inserted wheel studs. Remove the thrust washer.
5   Using two square-section metal bars (see Fig. 11.5) tighten two wheel studs onto the bars evenly to pull the hub out of the bearing. Make sure that the driveshaft is not pulled out if the splines are tight.
6   Unscrew the bearing retainer bolts using a Torx key and withdraw the bearing from the stub axle carrier. The inner race will probably drop onto the driveshaft.
7   Using a suitable puller remove the outer race from the hub.
8   Clean all the components and check them for damage and wear. The bearing must be renewed if the races and balls are pitted and worn.

9   To fit the new bearing first use a metal tube to drive the outer race onto the hub.
10   Locate the inner race on the driveshaft and fit the bearing to the stub axle carrier. Insert and tighten the bolts to the specified torque.
11   Apply grease to the bearing and seal, then use a wooden mallet to tap the hub into the bearing and onto the driveshaft splines. When the threads are visible, fit the thrust washer and nut.
12   Tighten the driveshaft nut to the specified torque while holding the hub stationary.
13   Refit the brake disc, with reference to Chapter 9, then lower the car to the ground.

6   Front suspension upper arm – removal and refitting

1   Jack up the front of the car and support on axle stands. Apply the handbrake and remove the roadwheel.
2   Loosen the shock absorber bottom locknut (photo).
3   Remove the fixing securing the castor tie-rod to the arm (photo).
4   Remove the fixing securing the anti-roll bar link to the arm (photos).
5   Remove the balljoint nut at the stub axle carrier, and free the taper using a suitable extractor.
6   Remove the arm pivot pin (photo).
7   Raise the arm, and unscrew the lower shock absorber mounting (photo). Remove the arm.

6.2 Loosening the front shock absorber bottom locknut

6.3 Removing the castor tie-rod from the front suspension upper arm

6.4A Disconnect the link ...

6.4B ... and push out the shock absorber mounting pin

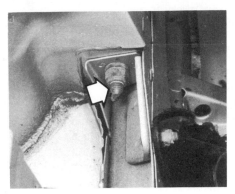

6.6 Front suspension upper arm inner pivot pin (arrowed) viewed from the engine compartment

6.7 Removing the front shock absorber lower mounting

8   Position the arm, and screw on the shock absorber lower mounting.
9   Position the balljoint pin in the stub axle carrier, and loosely refit the nut.
10 Refit, but do not tighten the upper arm pivot pin.
11 Similarly, refit the shock absorber lowering mounting pin, after smearing with a suitable grease.
12 Reconnect, but do not tighten, the castor tie-rod.
13 Tighten the balljoint nut to the specified torque.
14 Loosely refit the anti-roll bar link.
15 Using a trolley jack under the lower suspension arm, take the weight of the car, then tighten the pivot pin nut, shock absorber mounting nut, castor tie-rod nut, and anti roll bar link nut to the specified torque.
16 Refit the roadwheel and lower the car to the ground.

7   Front suspension upper balljoint – renewal

1   Jack up the front of the car and support on axle stands. Apply the handbrake and remove the roadwheel.
2   Unscrew the upper balljoint nut and separate the stub axle carrier using a separator tool if necessary.
3   Unscrew the castor tie-rod nut and balljoint nuts from the upper arm, and withdraw the balljoint (photo).
4   Fit the new balljoint using a reversal of the removal procedure, but tighten the nuts to the specified torques and check the front wheel alignment angles.

8   Front suspension upper arm bushes – renewal

1   Remove the arm, as described in Section 6.
2   Mount the arm in a vice and drive out the bush using a metal tube having an exterior diameter of 26.0 mm (1.024 in). Alternatively use

a larger metal tube, a long bolt and washers to pull out the bush.
3   Clean the bore in the arm then press in the new bush until central.
4   Refit the arm with reference to Section 6.

9   Front suspension lower arm – removal and refitting

1   Jack up the front of the car and support on axle stands. Apply the handbrake and remove the roadwheel.
2   Unscrew the lower balljoint nut until it contacts the driveshaft outer joint. If the joint can be released by levering the arm downward, remove the nut completely. Alternatively use the nut as an extractor by unscrewing it against the driveshaft, however, the nut must be renewed with this method. Another alternative is to unbolt the balljoint from the upper arm, remove the driveshaft and use a conventional balljoint separator (photo).
3   Unscrew the rear inner nut and remove the pivot pin, then withdraw the lower arm (photo). Note the location of the castor adjustment shim – it is at the front of the arm on manual steering models and at the rear on power steering models.
4   To refit the arm, lubricate the pivot pin with grease, position the arm and insert the pin from the front, making sure that the castor shim is correctly located. Fit the rear nut loosely.
5   Insert the balljoint in the stub axle carrier, fit the nut and tighten it to the specified torque.
6   Refit the roadwheel and lower the car to the ground, then tighten the pivot pin nut to the specified torque with the weight of the car on the suspension.

10 Front suspension lower balljoint – renewal

1   Remove the lower arm, as described in Section 9.
2   Drill out the rivet heads or, alternatively, use a sharp cold chisel to remove them.
3   Punch out the rivet stems and remove the old balljoint.

7.3 Removing the front suspension upper balljoint

9.2 Front suspension lower arm and balljoint

9.3 Front suspension lower arm inner pivot pin and rear nut

4   Clean the outer end of the arm and fit the new balljoint to the bottom surface of the arm, inserting the bolts from below. Tighten the nuts.
5   Refit the lower arm with reference to Section 9 and finally check the front wheel alignment angles.

11 Front suspension lower arm bushes – renewal

1   Remove the arm, as described in Section 9.
2   Mount the arm in a vice and drive out one of the bushes using a metal tube having an exterior diameter of 31.0 mm (1.220 in). Alternatively use a larger metal tube, a long bolt and washers to pull out the bush.
3   Clean the arm, then press in the new bush until the dimension shown in Fig. 11.6 is achieved. Alternatively note the external

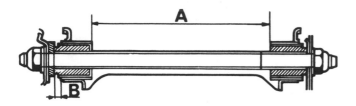

Fig. 11.6 Front suspension lower arm bush fitting dimensions (Sec 11)

A = 181.0 mm (7.131 in)   B = External dimension
                                          (see Sec 11)

dimension 'B' of the old bush and fit the new bush in the same position.
4   Fit the remaining bush using the procedure described in paragraphs 2 and 3.
5   Refit the arm with reference to Section 9.

12 Front shock absorber – removal and refitting

1   The front shock absorber can be removed alone without the coil spring (Method 1) or together with the coil spring (Method 2).

Method 1

2   Preferably employ Renault tool Sus 864 with the base bracket sitting astride the top arm pin and the remainder of the tool disposed as indicated in Fig. 11.7. Alternatively, a suitable proprietary spring clamp system may be employed. *Great care should be taken during this operation, as serious injury may be sustained to the person if a spring should slip from the clamps.*
3   Raise the relevant side of the vehicle, place it on a stand, and remove the roadwheel.
4   With a jack under the lower balljoint, raise the body until it lifts off the stand.
5   Fit and make secure the spring clamping tool (see paragraph 2).
6   Loosen the shock absorber lower mounting pin.
7   Loosen the shock absorber lower locknut.
8   Unscrew the shock absorber top mounting nuts (photo).
9   Lower the jack.
10 Remove the shock absorber by unscrewing it.
11 Push down on the top arm, and take the shock absorber out.
12 To refit, place the shock absorber inside the spring.
13 Screw the shock absorber fully home in the lower mounting.
14 Pull the shock absorber top through the wing, ensuring that the mounting components are correctly refitted. Do not tighten yet.
15 Raise the suspension by means of a jack placed under the lower balljoint, and carefully remove the spring compressor clamps.
16 With the weight of the car on the suspension, tighten the shock absorber mounting pin nut, lower locknut, and top mounting nuts.
17 Refit the roadwheel and lower the car to the ground.

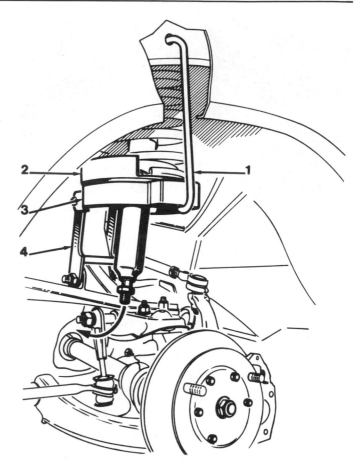

Fig. 11.7 Using tool Sus 864 to remove the front shock absorber (Sec 12)

1   Hook   3   Pivoting base
2   Cup   4   Bracket

12.8 Front shock absorber top mounting nuts

Method 2

18 Proceed as in paragraphs 3 and 4.
19 Fit either Renault tool Sus 863 or a similar three-jaw spring compressor tool, with the 3 jaws hooked on the last but one coil from the top. Careful use of conventional spring compressors is also

12.19 Spring compressors fitted to the front coil spring

possible (photo). Tighten each nut gradually until the spring pressure is contained by the clamps. *Make sure the compressor is secure.*

20 Disconnect the shock absorber at the top by removing the nuts.

21 Loosen the nut on the shock absorber lower mounting pin.

22 Lower the jack until the coil spring is free from the upper cup.

23 Loosen the lower locknut while holding the shock absorber stationary.

24 Unscrew the shock absorber, and withdraw it with the spring and tool combined.

25 Before fitting a new shock absorber mount it vertically in a vice and operate the rod several times over its full stroke to expel any trapped air.

26 To refit, locate the assembly on the upper mounting, screw the shock absorber tightly into the lower mounting and then unscrew it one complete turn.

27 Pull the shock absorber rod through the top mounting, making sure that the rubbers and cups are correctly positioned, then fit the top nut. Tighten the top nut and fit the locknut.

28 Tighten the lower locknut.

29 Raise the front of the car with a trolley jack beneath the lower balljoint and remove the coil spring compressor.

30 Tighten the lower mounting pin nut.

31 Refit the roadwheel and lower the car to the ground.

13 Front coil spring – removal and refitting

1 Remove the front shock absorber, as described in Section 12 using Method 2.

2 Lift the coil spring, together with the compressor tool, from the shock absorber.

3 Special tools, Sus 594 and Sus 594.02, shown in Fig. 11.8 or similar, are necessary to allow the spring to be safely decompressed. **Do not** use makeshift methods. Fit the tool, tighten to permit the spring clamps to be released, and then unscrew the tool to decompress the spring.

4 Refitting is a reversal of removal, with reference to Section 12, but make sure that the bottom end of the spring locates in the stopped end of the bottom cup.

14 Rear anti-roll bar – removal and refitting

1 Chock the front wheels then jack up the rear of the car and support on axle stands placed under the body.

2 Remove the clips retaining the handbrake cables to the side arms and anti-roll bar, as applicable.

3 On models with the anti-roll bar welded to the side arms, unbolt

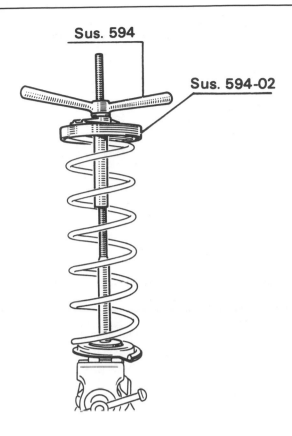

Sus. 594

Sus. 594-02

Fig. 11.8 Using the special tools to release the coil spring (Sec 13)

the complete anti-roll bar/side arm assembly from the underbody and rear axle and withdraw the assembly from the car.

4 On models with a separate anti-roll bar, unbolt the anti-roll bar from the side arms and withdraw it (photo). If the bar is to be refitted, identify it side for side.

5 Refitting is a reversal of removal, but where applicable lubricate the side arm bolts with a little grease. Fully tighten all bolts only when the full weight of the car is on the suspension.

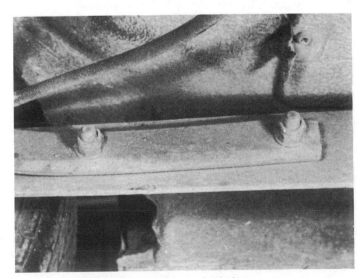

14.4 Rear anti-roll bar (separate) mounting bolts

15 Rear axle assembly – removal and refitting

1   Chock the front wheels then jack up the rear of the car and support on axle stands placed under the body. Remove the roadwheels.
2   Release the shock absorbers at the lower mountings, and push them upwards as far as possible.
3   Disconnect the flexible brake hose(s), running between the 3-way union and brake limiting valve, at one end only. Plug the open ends.
4   Pull the axle down, and withdraw the springs.
5   Disconnect the handbrake cables at the adjuster and remove them from the retaining plates, or refer to Chapter 9 and disconnect them from the drums.
6   Support the axle on a jack.
7   Disconnect the brake limiting valve at the centre arm.
8   Remove the nuts, and then the pivot pins, from both the centre arm-to-chassis points, and from the side arms at the axle beam.
9   Remove the axle beam.
10 To refit, offer up the axle beam on a jack.
11 Lubricate the centre and side arm pivot pins with a suitable grease and refit them, together with their nuts. Do not tighten.
12 Locate the two springs in the axle beam.
13 Pull down the shock absorbers and tighten the bottom mountings.
14 Reconnect the limiter to the centre arm.
15 Reconnect the brake hose(s).
16 Reconnect the handbrake cable(s).
17 Refit the roadwheels and lower the car to the ground.
18 With the weight of the car on the suspension tighten the pivot pin nuts.
19 Refer to Chapter 9 and bleed the brake hydraulic circuit and adjust the limiting valve and handbrake.

16 Rear wheel bearings and hub – removal and refitting

Drum brakes

1   Remove the drum, as described in Chapter 9.
2   Prise the oil seal from the inside of the drum/hub.
3   Using a suitable puller, extract the inner race and deflector from the stub axle.
4   Drive the outer races from the drum/hub using a soft metal drift.
5   Remove all the grease from the drum/hub and wash with paraffin. Check the bearings and stub axle for wear and damage and renew as necessary. Note that the complete rear axle beam must be renewed if the stub axle is damaged.

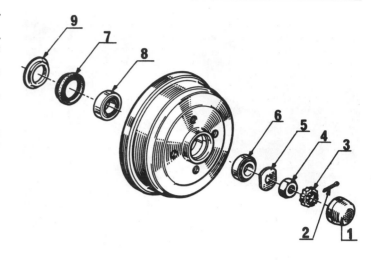

Fig. 11.9 Exploded view of the rear wheel bearings and hub on drum brake models (Sec 16)

1	Cap	6	Outer bearing
2	Split pin	7	Oil seal
3	Retainer	8	Inner bearing
4	Nut	9	Deflector
5	Thrust washer		

6   To refit, drive the outer races into the drum/hub using a metal tube.
7   Drive the deflector and inner race into the stub axle.
8   Press the new oil seal into the drum/hub using a block of wood.
9   Refit the drum and adjust the bearings, as described in Chapter 9.

Disc brakes

10 Remove the disc, as described in Chapter 9.
11 Remove the hub cap, using a puller if necessary.
12 Unscrew the nut and remove the washer.
13 Using a puller if necessary, pull the hub and bearings from the stub axle.

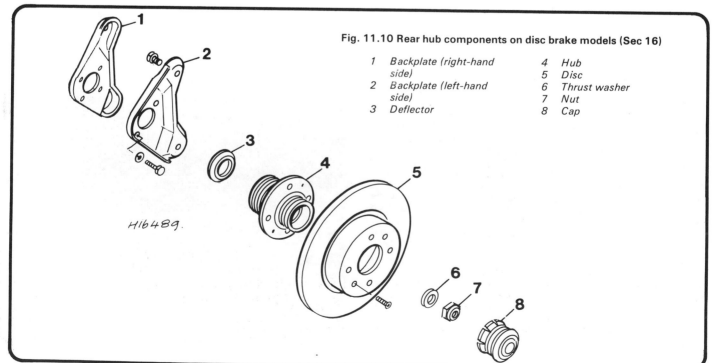

Fig. 11.10 Rear hub components on disc brake models (Sec 16)

1	Backplate (right-hand side)	4	Hub
2	Backplate (left-hand side)	5	Disc
3	Deflector	6	Thrust washer
		7	Nut
		8	Cap

H16489.

14 Pull the deflector from the stub axle using a puller.
15 Remove the bearings and seal, and examine the components as described for drum brakes, however, Renault do not appear to supply replacement bearings. If alternative bearings cannot be obtained from a motor factor, the complete hub must be renewed.
16 To refit, drive the deflector onto the stub axle using a metal tube, and similarly fit the hub and bearings.
17 Fit the washer and nut, and tighten the nut.
18 Grease the bearings and tap the hub cap into place.
19 Refit the disc, as described in Chapter 9.

17 Rear suspension centre arm – removal and refitting

1 Chock the front wheels then jack up the rear of the car and support on axle stands.
2 Disconnect the brake pressure limiter operating rod from the arm.
3 Unscrew the nuts from the clamp at the rear of the arm (photo).
4 Unscrew the nuts from the front pivot bolts.
5 Remove the clamp and pivot bolts, then withdraw the centre arm.
6 Refitting is a reversal of removal, but lightly grease the pivot bolts, and delay fully tightening all the nuts until the weight of the car is on the suspension. Finally adjust the brake pressure limiter, as described in Chapter 9.

17.3 Rear suspension centre arm rear clamp

18 Rear suspension centre arm bushes – renewal

1 Remove the centre arm, as described in Section 17.
2 Mount the arm in a vice and drive out one bush using a metal tube having an exterior diameter of 31.5 mm (1.240 in) and an inside diameter of 26.0 mm (1.024 in). Alternatively use a larger metal tube, a long bolt and washers to pull out the bush.
3 Clean the bore in the arm then lightly grease the new bush and press it into the arm so that the dimension shown in Fig. 11.11 is achieved. Alternatively note the external dimension 'C' of the old bush and fit the new bush in the same position.
4 Fit the remaining bush using the procedure described in paragraphs 2 and 3.
5 Refit the centre arm, with reference to Section 17.

19 Rear suspension side arm – removal and refitting

Note: *On models where the side arms are welded to the anti-roll bar, remove the anti-roll bar, as described in Section 14. This Section describes removal of the separate type side arm.*

1 Jack up the rear of the car and support on axle stands then unbolt the anti-roll bar from the side arm.
2 Unbolt the side arm from the underbody and rear axle, and withdraw it (photo).

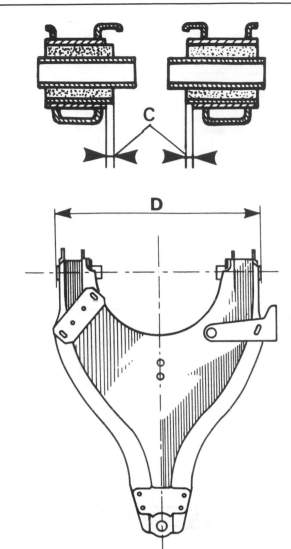

Fig. 11.11 Rear suspension centre arm bush fitting dimensions (Sec 18)

C   *External dimension (see Sec 18)*   *D = 243 mm (9.574 in)*

19.2 Rear suspension side arm front mounting

3   Refitting is a reversal of removal, but lubricate the side arm bolts with a little grease, and fully tighten all the bolts only when the full weight of the car is on the suspension.

20 Rear suspension side arm bushes – renewal

1   Remove the side arm, as described in Section 19.
2   Mount the arm in a vice and drive out the bush using a metal tube having an exterior diameter of 41.5 mm (1.634 in) and an inside diameter of 33.5 mm (1.319 in). Alternatively use a larger metal tube, a long bolt and washers to pull out the bush. On models where the side arms are welded to the anti-roll bar, fit each bush one at a time.
3   Clean the bore in the arm, then lightly grease the new bush and press it into the arm. On separate side arms locate the bush centrally, but on the side arm/anti-roll bar assembly the dimension shown in Fig. 11.12 must be maintained. Also note that the bush slots must be vertical, as shown in Fig. 11.13.
4   Refit the side arm with reference to Section 19.

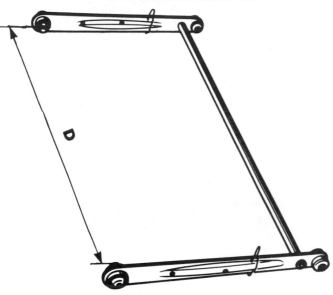

Fig. 11.12 Rear suspension side arm bush fitting dimension (Sec 20)

$D = 959\ mm\ (37.78\ in)$

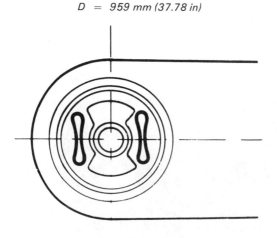

Fig. 11.13 Correct fitted position of side arm bush (Sec 20)

21 Rear shock absorber – removal and refitting

1   Open the tailgate and fold the rear seat backrest forward.
2   Pull the trim cover away and pull the rubber cap from the top of the shock absorber (photos).

21.2A Remove the trim cover ...

21.2B ... and pull the cap from the top of the rear shock absorber

3   Unscrew the shock absorber upper mounting locknut and mounting nut.
4   Jack up the rear of the car and support with axle stands beneath the underbody. Chock the front wheels. Remove the rear roadwheel.
5   Unscrew the shock absorber lower mounting nut and compress the shock absorber by hand.
6   Unclip the rear brake flexible hose(s) at the rear axle, but do not disconnect the hose from the rigid pipe.
7   Press the axle beam down sufficiently to withdraw the shock absorber, together with the coil spring. Recover the spacers and rubbers, noting their positions.
8   Before fitting a new shock absorber, mount it vertically in a vice and operate the rod several times over its full stroke to expel any trapped air.
9   To refit, locate the spacers and rubbers on the shock absorber in their correct positions.
10   Press down the axle beam and fit the shock absorber and coil spring, making sure that the spring locates in the stopped end of the bottom cup.
11   Insert the shock absorber through the top mounting, fit the rubbers and spacers then tighten the nuts.
12   Pull the shock absorber down, fit the bottom mounting rubbers and spacers and tighten the nuts.

13   Reconnect the brake flexible hose(s).
14   Lower the car to the ground, refit the cap and trim cover, and lift the rear seat backrest.

22 Rear coil spring – removal and refitting

1   Jack up the rear of the car and support with axle stands beneath the underbody. Chock the front wheels. Remove the rear roadwheel.
2   Unscrew the shock absorber lower mounting nut and compress the shock absorber by hand.
3   Unclip the rear brake flexible hose(s) at the rear axle, but do not disconnect the hose from the rigid pipe.
4   Press the axle beam down sufficiently to withdraw the coil spring (photo).
5   Refitting is a reversal of removal, but make sure that the shock absorber rubbers and spacers are correctly positioned, and tighten the nut to the specified torque.

23 Steering wheel – removal and refitting

1   Remove the screws and withdraw the steering column shrouds from the combination switches.
2   Pull the centre pad from the steering wheel (photo).
3   Hold the steering wheel stationary, then unscrew the retaining nut (photo).
4   Mark the steering wheel hub in relation to the inner column.
5   Pull the steering wheel from the inner column splines using a suitable extractor tool.
6   Refitting is a reversal of removal, but lock the nut after tightening it by centre punching the edge of the inner column. With the front wheels in the straight-ahead position, the steering wheel must be central.

24 Steering inner column and bushes – removal and refitting

1   Disconnect the battery negative lead.
2   Remove the steering wheel, as described in Section 23.
3   Remove the combination switch, as described in Chapter 10.
4   Extract the top bush circlip from the column.
5   Remove the bottom cover then unscrew and remove the clamp bolt from the universal joint/coupling at the bottom of the inner column. Mark the column and shaft in relation to each other.
6   Temporarily refit the steering wheel to the inner column with the nut loose. With the steering lock released, pull the steering wheel and inner column upward until the top bush comes out, then push it downward until the bottom bush is pushed out.
7   Clean the components and examine them for wear and damage.
8   To refit, grease the lower bush and drive it into the bottom of the outer column with a metal tube. Make sure that it is located between the indents.
9   With the inner column in position and the steering wheel removed, drive the top bush into the outer column and refit the circlip.
10   Engage the inner column with the universal joint then insert and tighten the clamp bolt.
11   Refit the combination switch (Chapter 10) and steering wheel (Section 23).
12   Reconnect the battery negative lead.

25 Retractable steering shaft – removal, checking and refitting

1   Disconnect the battery negative lead.
2   Remove the screws and withdraw the steering column lower cover.
3   Mark the shaft in relation to the inner column and steering gear pinion.

22.4 Rear coil spring

23.2 Removing the steering wheel centre pad

23.3 The steering wheel retaining nut

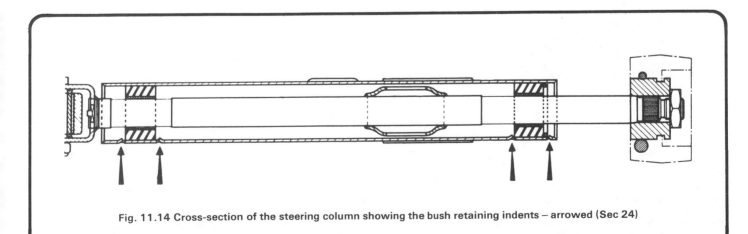

Fig. 11.14 Cross-section of the steering column showing the bush retaining indents – arrowed (Sec 24)

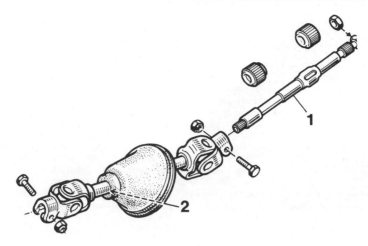

Fig. 11.15 Retractable steering shaft (Sec 25)

1   Column   2   Retractable shaft

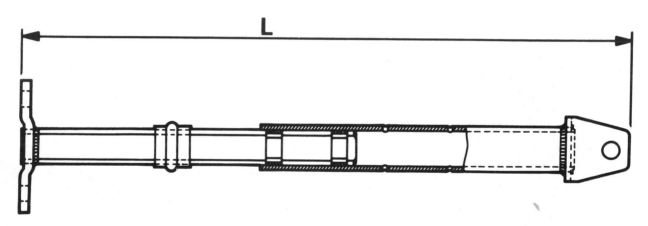

Fig. 11.16 Checking dimension for the flexible coupling type retractable steering shaft (Sec 25)

$$L = 327.7 \; {}^{+1}_{-0} \; mm \, (12.911 \; {}^{+0.039}_{-0} \; in)$$

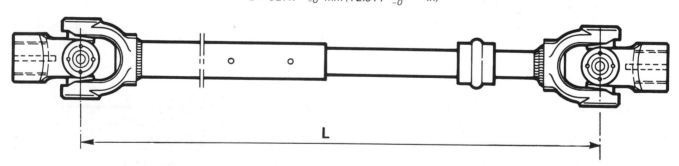

Fig. 11.17 Checking dimension for the universal joint type retractable steering shaft (Sec 25)

$$L = 247.0 \pm 1 \; mm \, (9.732 \pm 0.039 \; in)$$

4   Unscrew and remove the clamp bolts from the universal joints or flexible couplings, as applicable.
5   Unbolt the rubber grommet from the bulkhead and withdraw the shaft.
6   Measure the length of the shaft, and renew it if not as shown in Figs. 11.16 or 11.17.
7   Refitting is a reversal of removal, but do not tighten any of the clamp bolts until the shaft is in position loosely. **Note:** Where flexible couplings are fitted, with the front wheels in the straight-ahead position, one of the upper joint bolt heads must be facing upward.

26 Steering column (adjustable) – adjustment

1   Remove the steering wheel, as described in Section 23.
2   Remove the screws and withdraw the steering column lower cover (photo).
3   Loosen the outer column upper mounting locknut and nut.
4   Move the outer column to its lowest position then locate the adjusting lever in the position shown in Fig. 11.18. Tighten the upper mounting nut and locknut without moving the column or lever.

26.2 Adjustable steering column lever and lower cover

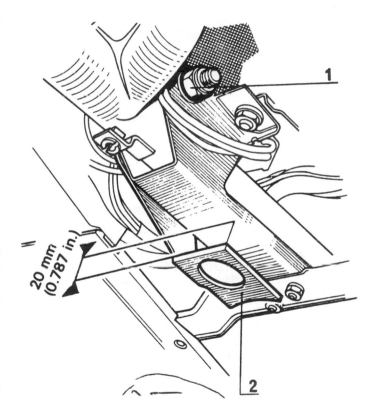

Fig. 11.18 Adjustable steering column setting dimension (Sec 26)

1   *Mounting bolt*   2   *Lever*

5   Refit the lower cover and check the lever for operation. It may be necessary to make some final adjustments.
6   Refit the steering wheel with reference to Section 23.

27 Steering gear – removal and refitting

1   Jack up the front of the car and support on axle stands. Apply the handbrake.
2   Remove the roadwheels then unscrew the nuts from the tie-rod

ends and use a balljoint separator tool to free the tie-rods from the steering arms on the stub axle carriers.
3   Working in the engine compartment, unscrew and remove the clamp bolt securing the retractable steering shaft joint/coupling to the steering gear. Mark the joint/coupling in relation to the pinion.
4   On power steering models, fix hose clamps to the two hoses from the hydraulic fluid reservoir then disconnect the hoses from the steering gear and plug them.
5   Unscrew the mounting bolts/nuts, then withdraw the steering gear through the side aperture.
6   If a new steering gear is to be fitted, the tie-rod ends must be transferred to the new unit, with reference to Section 29.
7   Refitting is a reversal of removal, but tighten the bolts and nuts to the specified torque and check the front wheel toe-out, as described in Section 31.

28 Steering gear – overhaul

Dismantling of the steering gear by the average owner is not advised, and, in the event of wear, a replacement unit should be fitted or the advice of a Renault agent sought.

29 Tie-rod (track rod) end balljoint – removal and refitting

1   Raise the front of the vehicle and remove the roadwheels.
2   Hold the tie-rod with an open-ended spanner, and release the tie-rod locking nut.
3   Remove the ball-pin locking nut.
4   Use a suitable balljoint extractor to free the joint taper from the stub axle carrier (photo). Alternatively, use a pair of hammers, one each side of the tapered hole in the stub axle carrier, and use carefully-directed blows to shock the taper free.

29.4 Using a balljoint extractor to release the tie-rod end balljoint

5   Hold the tie-rod, and unscrew the balljoint, noting the number of turns required to remove it for refitting purposes.
6   To refit, reverse the removal procedure, refitting the balljoint the correct number of turns. Tighten the locknut.
7   On completion, have the toe-out checked, preferably by a Renault agent with the correct equipment.

30 Power steering pump – removal and refitting

1   Fit a hose clamp to the hose from the reservoir to the pump.
2   Position a container beneath the pump then disconnect both hoses. Identify each hose for position.

30.3A Front view of the power steering pump

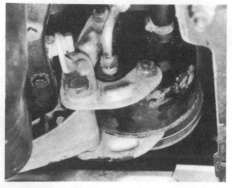

30.3B Rear view of the power steering pump

30.5A Checking the drivebelt tension

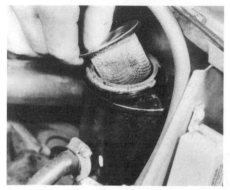

30.5B Power steering reservoir fluid strainer

30.5C Topping-up the power steering fluid reservoir

30.5D Fitting the power steering fluid reservoir cap

3   Loosen the pivot and adjustment bolts, swivel the pump toward the engine, and slip the drivebelt from the pump pulley (photos).
4   Remove the pivot and adjustment bolts, then withdraw the pump from the engine.
5   Refitting is a reversal of removal, but tension the drivebelt so that it deflects between 5.5 and 6.5 mm (0.220 and 0.260 in) midway between the two pulleys under firm thumb pressure. The tension should be rechecked after running the engine for ten minutes. Bleed the hydraulic circuit by first filling the reservoir, turning the steering slowly from lock to lock and topping-up again. Repeat the process with the engine idling, and finally top up the reservoir so that the fluid just covers the bottom of the strainer. Refit the cap (photos).

31 Wheel alignment – checking and adjustment

1   Accurate front wheel alignment is essential to provide good steering and roadholding characteristics and to ensure even and slow tyre wear.
2   It is preferable that any checking or adjustment of the steering and suspension angles is carried out by your dealer using special setting equipment, but for information purposes the following details are given:
Wheel alignment consists of four factors:
Camber
3   This is the angle at which the roadwheels are set from the vertical when viewed from the front of the vehicle. Camber is regarded as positive when the roadwheels are tilted outwards at the top. The angle is not adjustable on the models covered by this manual.
Steering axis (kingpin) inclination
4   This is the angle, when viewed from the front of the vehicle, between the vertical and an imaginary line drawn between the upper and lower suspension arm balljoints. The angle is not adjustable.
Castor
5   This is the angle between the steering axis and a vertical line when viewed from each side of the vehicle. Positive castor is indicated when

the steering axis is inclined towards the rear of the vehicle at its upper end. On certain models castor is adjustable by varying the length of the tie-rods which are connected to the suspension upper arm (photo).
Toe
6   This is the amount by which the distance between the front inside edges of the roadwheel rims differs from that between the inside edges at the rear of the wheel. If the distance between the rims at the front of the wheel is less than that at the rear, then the roadwheels are said to toe-in. If the distance is greater the wheels toe-out.
7   With the arrival of tracking gauges on the retail market it is now

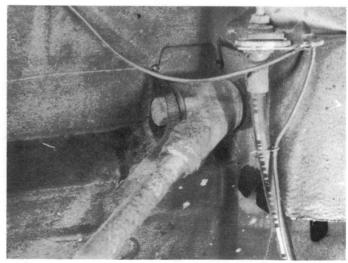

31.5 Castor tie-rod and front mounting

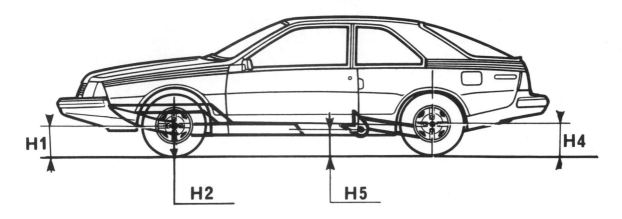

Fig. 11.19 Castor angle check loading points (Sec 31)

possible for the home mechanic to check and adjust the front wheel toe provided the following essential requirements are observed:

(a) *Car on a level floor*
(b) *Tyres correctly inflated*
(c) *Suspension bushes and steering balljoints unworn*
(d) *Hub bearings unworn*

8   When checking the castor angle the car must be loaded so that the height dimensions are as given in the Specifications and Fig. 11.19. For the remaining checks the car must be at kerbside weight and with the tyres correctly inflated.
9   To check the front wheel toe-out setting, position the car on level ground with the wheels straight-ahead, then roll the car back 4 metres (12 ft) and forward again to settle the suspension.
10 Using a wheel alignment gauge, check that the front wheel toe-out dimension is as given in the Specifications.
11 If adjustment is necessary, loosen the tie-rod end locknuts on both tie-rods and turn each tie-rod by equal amounts until the alignment is correct; then tighten the locknuts. Note that one complete turn of the

tie-rod is equal to 3 mm (0.118 in) movement. The tie-rod ends on each tie-rod must be at the identical position – to check this measure the dimension from the shoulder to the tie-rod end centre on each side.

32 Roadwheels and tyres – general

1   Clean the insides of the roadwheels whenever they are removed and, where applicable, remove any rust and repaint them.
2   At the same time remove any flints or stones which may have become embedded in the tyres. Examine the tyres for damage and splits, and, where the depth of tread is almost down to the legal minimum, renew them.
3   The wheels should be rebalanced halfway through the life of the tyres to compensate for loss of rubber.
4   Check and adjust the tyre pressures regularly and make sure that the dust caps are correctly fitted. Remember also to check the spare tyre.

33 Fault diagnosis – suspension and steering

Symptom	Reason(s)
Excessive play in steering	Worn steering gear Worn tie-rod end balljoints Worn suspension arm balljoints
Wanders or pulls to one side	Incorrect wheel alignment Worn tie-rod end balljoints Worn suspension arm balljoints Uneven tyre pressures
Heavy or stiff steering	Incorrect wheel alignment Low tyre pressures Lack of lubricant in steering gear Seized suspension or tie-rod end balljoint Faulty servo pump, broken drivebelt, or low fluid level (power steering models)
Wheel wobble and vibration	Wheels out of balance Wheels damaged Worn shock absorbers Worn wheel bearings Worn suspension or tie-rod end balljoint
Excessive tyre wear	Incorrect wheel alignment Worn shock absorbers Incorrect tyre pressures Wheels out of balance

Chapter 12 Bodywork and fittings

For modifications, and information applicable to later models, see Supplement at end of manual

Contents

1 General description

The bodywork is of all-steel monocoque construction, the integral components being spot welded together. In addition to the normal hinged body panels, the front wings are removable, being bolted into position.

Apart from the normal cleaning, maintenance and minor body repairs, there is little that the DIY owner can do in the event of structural defects caused by collision damage or possibly rust. This Chapter is therefore devoted to the normal maintenance, removal and refitting of those parts of the vehicle body and associate components that are readily dismantled.

Although the underbody is given a protective coating when new, it is still likely to suffer from corrosion in certain exposed areas or where road dirt deposits can congeal. Light corrosion can be treated as described in Section 4, but severe rusting of a structural area in the underbody must be repaired by your Renault dealer or competent vehicle body repair shop.

2 Maintenance – bodywork and underframe

1   The general condition of a vehicle's bodywork is the one thing that significantly affects its value. Maintenance is easy but needs to be regular. Neglect, particularly after minor damage, can lead quickly to further deterioration and costly repair bills. It is important also to keep watch on those parts of the vehicle not immediately visible, for instance the underside, inside all the wheel arches and the lower part of the engine compartment.

2   The basic maintenance routine for the bodywork is washing – preferably with a lot of water, from a hose. This will remove all the loose solids which may have stuck to the vehicle. It is important to flush these off in such a way as to prevent grit from scratching the finish. The wheel arches and underframe need washing in the same way to remove any accumulated mud which will retain moisture and tend to encourage rust. Paradoxically enough, the best time to clean the underframe and wheel arches is in wet weather when the mud is thoroughly wet and soft. In very wet weather the underframe is usually cleaned of large accumulations automatically and this is a good time for inspection.

3   Periodically, it is a good idea to have the whole of the underframe of the vehicle steam cleaned, engine compartment included, so that a thorough inspection can be carried out to see what minor repairs and renovations are necessary. Steam cleaning is available at many garages and is necessary for removal of the accumulation of oily grime which sometimes is allowed to become thick in certain areas. If steam cleaning facilities are not available, there are one or two excellent grease solvents available which can be brush applied. The dirt can then be simply hosed off.

4   After washing paintwork, wipe off with a chamois leather to give an unspotted clear finish. A coat of clear protective wax polish will give added protection against chemical pollutants in the air. If the

paintwork sheen has dulled or oxidised, use a cleaner/polisher combination to restore the brilliance of the shine. This requires a little effort, but such dulling is usually caused because regular washing has been neglected. Care needs to be taken with metallic paintwork, as special non-abrasive cleaner/polisher is required to avoid damage to the finish. Always check that the door and ventilator opening drain holes and pipes are completely clear so that water can be drained out (photo). Bright work should be treated in the same way as paintwork. Windscreens and windows can be kept clear of the smeary film which often appears by the use of a proprietary glass cleaner. Never use any form of wax or other body or chromium polish on glass.

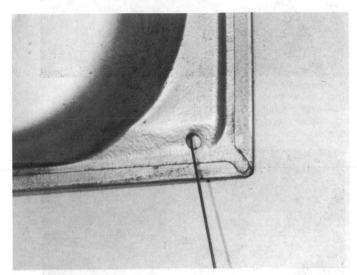

2.4 Clearing a door drain hole

3 Maintenance — upholstery and carpets

Mats and carpets should be brushed or vacuum cleaned regularly to keep them free of grit. If they are badly stained remove them from the vehicle for scrubbing or sponging and make quite sure they are dry before refitting. Seats and interior trim panels can be kept clean by wiping with a damp cloth. If they do become stained (which can be more apparent on light coloured upholstery) use a little liquid detergent and a soft nail brush to scour the grime out of the grain of the material. Do not forget to keep the headlining clean in the same way as the upholstery. When using liquid cleaners inside the vehicle do not over-wet the surfaces being cleaned. Excessive damp could get into the seams and padded interior causing stains, offensive odours or even rot. If the inside of the vehicle gets wet accidentally it is worthwhile taking some trouble to dry it out properly, particularly where carpets are involved. *Do not leave oil or electric heaters inside the vehicle for this purpose.*

4 Minor body damage — repair

The photographic sequences on pages 294 and 295 illustrate the operations detailed in the following sub-sections.

Repair of minor scratches in bodywork

If the scratch is very superficial, and does not penetrate to the metal of the bodywork, repair is very simple. Lightly rub the area of the scratch with a paintwork renovator, or a very fine cutting paste, to remove loose paint from the scratch and to clear the surrounding bodywork of wax polish. Rinse the area with clean water.

Apply touch-up paint to the scratch using a fine paint brush; continue to apply fine layers of paint until the surface of the paint in the scratch is level with the surrounding paintwork. Allow the new paint at least two weeks to harden: then blend it into the surrounding paintwork by rubbing the scratch area with a paintwork renovator or a very fine cutting paste. Finally, apply wax polish.

Where the scratch has penetrated right through to the metal of the

bodywork, causing the metal to rust, a different repair technique is required. Remove any loose rust from the bottom of the scratch with a penknife, then apply rust inhibiting paint to prevent the formation of rust in the future. Using a rubber or nylon applicator fill the scratch with bodystopper paste. If required, this paste can be mixed with cellulose thinners to provide a very thin paste which is ideal for filling narrow scratches. Before the stopper-paste in the scratch hardens, wrap a piece of smooth cotton rag around the top of a finger. Dip the finger in cellulose thinners and then quickly sweep it across the surface of the stopper-paste in the scratch; this will ensure that the surface of the stopper-paste is slightly hollowed. The scratch can now be painted over as described earlier in this Section.

Repair of dents in bodywork

When deep denting of the vehicle's bodywork has taken place, the first task is to pull the dent out, until the affected bodywork almost attains its original shape. There is little point in trying to restore the original shape completely, as the metal in the damaged area will have stretched on impact and cannot be reshaped fully to its original contour. It is better to bring the level of the dent up to a point which is about $\frac{1}{8}$ in (3 mm) below the level of the surrounding bodywork. In cases where the dent is very shallow anyway, it is not worth trying to pull it out at all. If the underside of the dent is accessible, it can be hammered out gently from behind, using a mallet with a wooden or plastic head. Whilst doing this, hold a suitable block of wood firmly against the outside of the panel to absorb the impact from the hammer blows and thus prevent a large area of the bodywork from being 'belled-out'.

Should the dent be in a section of the bodywork which has a double skin or some other factor making it inaccessible from behind, a different technique is called for. Drill several small holes through the metal inside the area — particularly in the deeper section. Then screw long self-tapping screws into the holes just sufficiently for them to gain a good purchase in the metal. Now the dent can be pulled out by pulling on the protruding heads of the screws with a pair of pliers.

The next stage of the repair is the removal of the paint from the damaged area, and from an inch or so of the surrounding 'sound' bodywork. This is accomplished most easily by using a wire brush or abrasive pad on a power drill, although it can be done just as effectively by hand using sheets of abrasive paper. To complete the preparation for filling, score the surface of the bare metal with a screwdriver or the tang of a file, or alternatively, drill small holes in the affected area. This will provide a really good 'key' for the filler paste.

To complete the repair see the Section on filling and re-spraying.

Repair of rust holes or gashes in bodywork

Remove all paint from the affected area and from an inch or so of the surrounding 'sound' bodywork, using an abrasive pad or a wire brush on a power drill. If these are not available a few sheets of abrasive paper will do the job just as effectively. With the paint removed you will be able to gauge the severity of the corrosion and therefore decide whether to renew the whole panel (if this is possible) or to repair the affected area. New body panels are not as expensive as most people think and it is often quicker and more satisfactory to fit a new panel than to attempt to repair large areas of corrosion.

Remove all fittings from the affected area except those which will act as a guide to the original shape of the damaged bodywork (eg headlamp shells etc). Then, using tin snips or a hacksaw blade, remove all loose metal and any other metal badly affected by corrosion. Hammer the edges of the hole inwards in order to create a slight depression for the filler paste.

Wire brush the affected area to remove the powdery rust from the surface of the remaining metal. Paint the affected area with rust inhibiting paint; if the back of the rusted area is accessible treat this also.

Before filling can take place it will be necessary to block the hole in some way. This can be achieved by the use of aluminium or plastic mesh, or aluminium tape.

Aluminium or plastic mesh is probably the best material to use for a large hole. Cut a piece to the approximate size and shape of the hole to be filled, then position it in the hole so that its edges are below the level of the surrounding bodywork. It can be retained in position by several blobs of filler paste around its periphery.

Aluminium tape should be used for small or very narrow holes. Pull a piece off the roll and trim it to the approximate size and shape required, then pull off the backing paper (if used) and stick the tape

This sequence of photographs deals with the repair of the dent and paintwork damage shown in this photo. The procedure will be similar for the repair of a hole. It should be noted that the procedures given here are simplified — more explicit instructions will be found in the text

In the case of a dent the first job — after removing surrounding trim — is to hammer out the dent where access is possible. This will minimise filling. Here, the large dent having been hammered out, the damaged area is being made slightly concave

Now all paint must be removed from the damaged area, by rubbing with coarse abrasive paper. Alternatively, a wire brush or abrasive pad can be used in a power drill. Where the repair area meets good paintwork, the edge of the paintwork should be 'feathered', using a finer grade of abrasive paper

In the case of a hole caused by rusting, all damaged sheet-metal should be cut away before proceeding to this stage. Here, the damaged area is being treated with rust remover and inhibitor before being filled

Mix the body filler according to its manufacturer's instructions. In the case of corrosion damage, it will be necessary to block off any large holes before filling — this can be done with aluminium or plastic mesh, or aluminium tape. Make sure the area is absolutely clean before ...

... applying the filler. Filler should be applied with a flexible applicator, as shown, for best results; the wooden spatula being used for confined areas. Apply thin layers of filler at 20-minute intervals, until the surface of the filler is slightly proud of the surrounding bodywork

Initial shaping can be done with a Surform plane or Dreadnought file. Then, using progressively finer grades of wet-and-dry paper, wrapped around a sanding block, and copious amounts of clean water, rub down the filler until really smooth and flat. Again, feather the edges of adjoining paintwork

The whole repair area can now be sprayed or brush-painted with primer. If spraying, ensure adjoining areas are protected from over-spray. Note that at least one inch of the surrounding sound paintwork should be coated with primer. Primer has a 'thick' consistency, so will find small imperfections

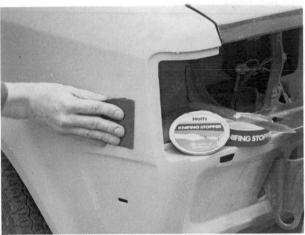

Again, using plenty of water, rub down the primer with a fine grade wet-and-dry paper (400 grade is probably best) until it is really smooth and well blended into the surrounding paintwork. Any remaining imperfections can now be filled by carefully applied knifing stopper paste

When the stopper has hardened, rub down the repair area again before applying the final coat of primer. Before rubbing down this last coat of primer, ensure the repair area is blemish-free — use more stopper if necessary. To ensure that the surface of the primer is really smooth use some finishing compound

The top coat can now be applied. When working out of doors, pick a dry, warm and wind-free day. Ensure surrounding areas are protected from over-spray. Agitate the aerosol thoroughly, then spray the centre of the repair area, working outwards with a circular motion. Apply the paint as several thin coats

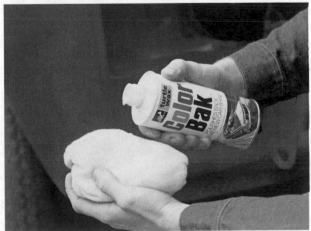

After a period of about two weeks, which the paint needs to harden fully, the surface of the repaired area can be 'cut' with a mild cutting compound prior to wax polishing. When carrying out bodywork repairs, remember that the quality of the finished job is proportional to the time and effort expended

over the hole; it can be overlapped if the thickness of one piece is insufficient. Burnish down the edges of the tape with the handle of a screwdriver or similar, to ensure that the tape is securely attached to the metal underneath.

Bodywork repairs – filling and re-spraying

Before using this Section, see the Sections on dent, deep scratch, rust holes and gash repairs.

Many types of bodyfiller are available, but generally speaking those proprietary kits which contain a tin of filler paste and a tube of resin hardener are best for this type of repair. A wide, flexible plastic or nylon applicator will be found invaluable for imparting a smooth and well contoured finish to the surface of the filler.

Mix up a little filler on a clean piece of card or board – measure the hardener carefully (follow the maker's instructions on the pack) otherwise the filler will set too rapidly or too slowly.

Using the applicator apply the filler paste to the prepared area; draw the applicator across the surface of the filler to achieve the correct contour and to level the filler surface. As soon as a contour that approximates to the correct one is achieved, stop working the paste – if you carry on too long the paste will become sticky and begin to 'pick up' on the applicator. Continue to add thin layers of filler paste at twenty-minute intervals until the level of the filler is just proud of the surrounding bodywork.

Once the filler has hardened, excess can be removed using a metal plane or file. From then on, progressively finer grades of abrasive paper should be used, starting with a 40 grade production paper and finishing with 400 grade wet-and-dry paper. Always wrap the abrasive paper around a flat rubber, cork, or wooden block – otherwise the surface of the filler will not be completely flat. During the smoothing of the filler surface the wet-and-dry paper should be periodically rinsed in water. This will ensure that a very smooth finish is imparted to the filler at the final stage.

At this stage the 'dent' should be surrounded by a ring of bare metal, which in turn should be encircled by the finely 'feathered' edge of the good paintwork. Rinse the repair area with clean water, until all of the dust produced by the rubbing-down operation has gone.

Spray the whole repair area with a light coat of primer – this will show up any imperfections in the surface of the filler. Repair these imperfections with fresh filler paste or bodystopper, and once more smooth the surface with abrasive paper. If bodystopper is used, it can be mixed with cellulose thinners to form a really thin paste which is ideal for filling small holes. Repeat this spray and repair procedure until you are satisfied that the surface of the filler, and the feathered edge of the paintwork are perfect. Clean the repair area with clean water and allow to dry fully.

The repair area is now ready for final spraying. Paint spraying must be carried out in a warm, dry, windless and dust free atmosphere. This condition can be created artificially if you have access to a large indoor working area, but if you are forced to work in the open, you will have to pick your day very carefully. If you are working indoors, dousing the floor in the work area with water will help to settle the dust which would otherwise be in the atmosphere. If the repair area is confined to one body panel, mask off the surrounding panels; this will help to minimise the effects of a slight mis-match in paint colours. Bodywork fittings (eg chrome strips, door handles etc) will also need to be masked off. Use genuine masking tape and several thicknesses of newspaper for the masking operations.

Before commencing to spray, agitate the aerosol can thoroughly, then spray a test area (an old tin, or similar) until the technique is mastered. Cover the repair area with a thick coat of primer; the thickness should be built up using several thin layers of paint rather than one thick one. Using 400 grade wet-and-dry paper, rub down the surface of the primer until it is really smooth. While doing this, the work area should be thoroughly doused with water, and the wet-and-dry paper periodically rinsed in water. Allow to dry before spraying on more paint.

Spray on the top coat, again building up the thickness by using several thin layers of paint. Start spraying in the centre of the repair area and then, using a circular motion, work outwards until the whole repair area and about 2 inches of the surrounding original paintwork is covered. Remove all masking material 10 to 15 minutes after spraying on the final coat of paint.

Allow the new paint at least two weeks to harden, then, using a paintwork renovator or a very fine cutting paste, blend the edges of the paint into the existing paintwork. Finally, apply wax polish.

5 Major body damage – repair

The principle of construction of these vehicles is such that great care must be taken when making cuts, or when renewing major members, in order to preserve the basic safety characteristics of the structure. In addition, the heating of certain areas is not advisable.

In view of the specialised knowledge necessary for this work, and of the alignment jigs and special tools frequently required, the owner is advised to consult a specialist body repairer or Renault dealer.

6 Routine maintenance

1 Every 10 000 miles (16 000 km) check the underbody, wheel arches, sills and door lower edges for corrosion and damage, and repair as necessary.
2 Lubricate the door, tailgate and bonnet hinges with a little oil and check the locks for correct operation and adjustment.

7 Bonnet – removal, refitting and adjustment

1 Open the bonnet and have an assistant hold it.
2 Pencil round the bracket locations on the bonnet, then unscrew the bolts.
3 Disconnect the screen washer pipe and withdraw the bonnet.
4 If necessary, unscrew the pivot bolts and remove the hinge brackets from the body.
5 Refitting is a reversal of removal, but if necessary adjust the bonnet within the slots in the brackets so that it is central in the body aperture. The front height of the bonnet can be adjusted using a screwdriver in the rubber stops, but it may then be necessary to adjust the striker and safety catch, with reference to Section 8.

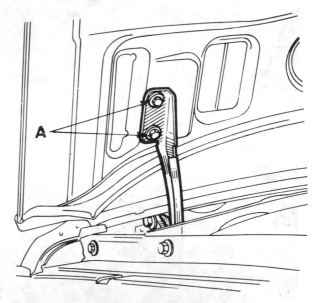

Fig. 12.1 Bonnet hinge bolts (A) (Sec 7)

8 Bonnet lock and cable – removal, refitting and adjustment

1 Open the bonnet and unhook the lock return spring.
2 Unbolt and remove the radiator top mounting.
3 Unscrew the lock mounting bolts.
4 Carefully lever the radiator top forward, then withdraw the lock.
5 Release the end of the cable from the bracket and remove the collar.
6 Release the cable from the clips in the engine compartment.
7 Working inside the car, unbolt the lever then pull the cable through the bulkhead into the car.
8 If required unbolt the striker from the bonnet.

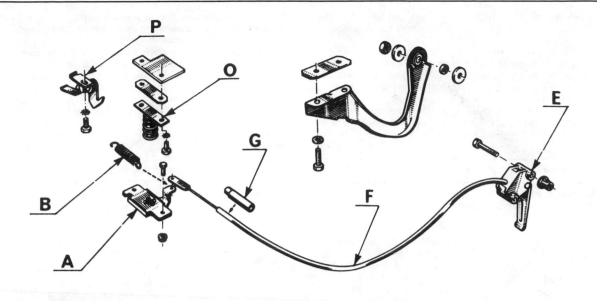

Fig. 12.2 Bonnet lock components (Sec 8)

A	Lock	E	Release lever	G	Collar	P	Safety catch
B	Return spring	F	Cable	O	Striker		

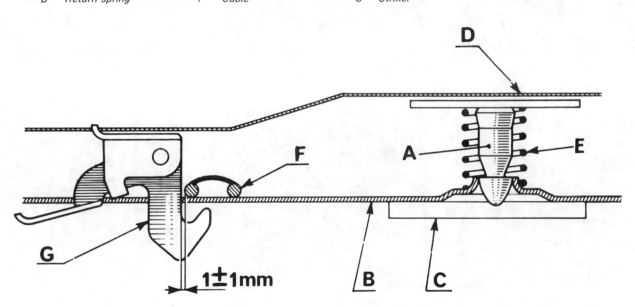

Fig. 12.3 Bonnet striker and catch components showing striker clearance (Sec 8)

A	Striker pin	C	Lock	E	Spring	G	Safety catch
B	Crossmember	D	Bonnet	F	Pin		

9   Refitting is a reversal of removal, but adjust the striker and safety catch as follows:

10   Remove the safety catch and check that the striker enters the lock centrally. If necessary loosen the striker bolts and adjust the striker as required.

11   Refit the safety catch and check, that with the bonnet shut, there is a clearance between the catch and pin as shown in Fig. 12.3. Adjust the catch as necessary and check that the lock operates correctly.

2   Prise back the front tabs.

3   Unscrew the mounting bolts at the top, rear pillar, bottom and front inner wing panel.

4   Withdraw the wing, together with the inner splash guard.

5   Refitting is a reversal of removal, but seal all seams with an appropriate sealant, and apply sound-deadening compound to the inner surface.

9   Front wing – removal and refitting

1   Remove the front bumper/shield (Section 22) and the relevant direction indicator (Chapter 10).

10   Doors – removal, refitting and adjustment

1   On models with electrically-operated windows, first remove the trim panel and disconnect the wiring.

2   Using a pin punch, drive out the door check pin (photo).
3   Similarly drive out the hinge pins and withdraw the door from the car (photo).
4   Refitting is a reversal of removal, but check that the door is central within the body aperture when shut and that the outer surface is flush with the surrounding panels. Ideally the front edge should be slightly recessed and the rear edge slightly raised. If adjustment is necessary remove the trim from the front pillar – on the driver's side also remove the fusebox. Loosen the hinge nuts to position the door within the aperture and use shims under the hinge to adjust the door in or out.

11 Door trim panel – removal and refitting

1   Prise off the top of the armrest (photo).
2   Prise off the exterior mirror inner trim (photo).

3   Unscrew the map pocket top and bottom screws (photo).
4   Remove the screw from the remote door handle cover and withdraw the cover (photos).
5   Remove the screw from the remote mirror control cover and withdraw the control as far as possible (photo).
6   On manual window models prise off the regulator handle cover, unscrew the centre nut, and remove the handle and bezel.
7   Where applicable, prise the cover from the loudspeaker, remove the screws, withdraw the loudspeaker and disconnect the wiring (photos).
8   Lift the map pocket from the dowels and, where necessary, disconnect the wiring plugs for the electrically-operated windows (photo). Remove the switches if necessary.
9   Using a wide-bladed screwdriver, prise the trim panel from the door, feeding the wiring through the hole where necessary (photo). Lift the panel from the top bracket and guide it over the remote door lever and mirror control.

10.2 Door check pin (arrowed)

10.3 Door hinge pin (arrowed)

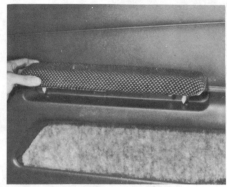

11.1 Removing the armrest

11.2 Removing the exterior mirror inner trim

11.3 Removing the map pocket screws

11.4A Remove the screw ...

11.4B ... and withdraw the remote door handle cover

11.5 Removing the remote mirror control cover

11.7A Prise off the loudspeaker cover ...

11.7B ... remove the mounting screws ...

11.7C ... and disconnect the wiring

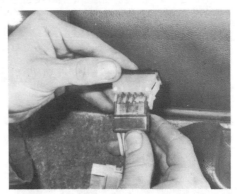

11.8 Disconnecting the electrically-operated window switch wiring

11.9 Feeding the wiring through the door trim panel

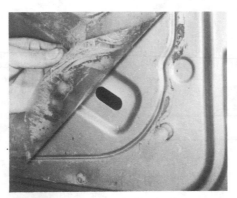

11.10A Removing the plastic sheet

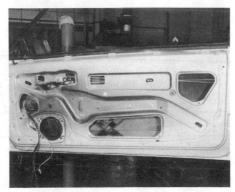

11.10B View of the door with trim panel removed

Fig. 12.4 Correct location of door trim plastic sheet (Sec 11)

Arrows indicate direction of water flow

10   Carefully pull off the plastic sheet (photos).
11   Refitting is a reversal of removal, but locate the plastic sheet as indicated in Fig. 12.4.

12 Door rubbing strip (inner) – removal and refitting

1   Remove the trim panel, as described in Section 11.

2   Pull the rubbing strip from the inner flange.
3   Prise the strip firmly onto the flange then refit the trim panel, with reference to Section 11.

13 Door striker – removal, refitting and adjustment

1   Remove the rear wing panel trim, as described in Section 24.
2   Remove the two screws and withdraw the striker (photo). Recover the plate from behind the pillar.

13.2 Door striker and tailgate lock lever

14.2 Door inner remote handle

14.3 Door lock retaining screws

14.4 Inner view of the door lock

3   Refitting is a reversal of removal, but before tightening the screws fully, close the door with the inner remote handle held open. Open the door and tighten the screws. With the door fully shut, check that the rear edge is flush or slightly raised in relation to the rear wing panel. If necessary move the striker in or out as required.

14 Door lock – removal and refitting

1   Close the window then remove the trim panel as described in Section 11.
2   Disconnect the lock control rods from the remote handle (photo).
3   Unscrew the Torx screws from the lock (photo).
4   Release the control rods from the clips, and withdraw the lock and rods from the door (photo).
5   Refitting is a reversal of removal.

15 Door lock barrel – removal, checking and refitting

1   Close the window then remove the trim panel, as described in Section 11.
2   Pull out the retaining clip and withdraw the lock barrel assembly.
3   To dismantle the unit use a pin punch to drive out the pin then remove the arm.
4   Extract the circlip and withdraw the barrel. Recover the spring.
5   Reassembly and refitting is a reversal of the dismantling and removal procedure, but make sure that the spring is fitted in line with the slot in the body.

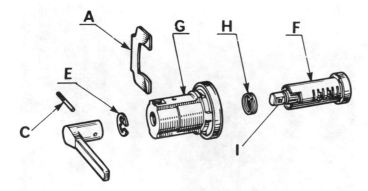

Fig. 12.5 Door lock barrel components (Sec 15)

A   Retaining clip   G   Body
C   Pin   H   Spring
E   Circlip   I   Slot
F   Barrel

16 Door window and regulator – removal and refitting

1   Close the window to 50.0 mm (2.0 in) from the top and use a wooden wedge to hold it in this position.
2   On electric window models disconnect the battery negative lead.
3   Remove the trim panel, as described in Section 11.
4   On electric window models disconnect the regulator motor wiring (photo).

16.4 Wiring for the electric window regulator motor

5   Unscrew the nuts and push the regulator in to release it from the studs.
6   Slide the regulator from the window rails and withdraw it through the aperture in the door.
7   Remove the wooden wedge, tilt the window forward so that its point is downwards, then lift the window from the inside of the surround.
8   Unscrew the nut and remove the fixed rail from the door.
9   Refitting is a reversal of removal, but make sure that the lug in the fixed rail engages the hole in the door.

17 Exterior mirror – removal and refitting

1   Remove the screw from the remote mirror control cover and withdraw the control as far as possible (photo).
2   Loosen the screw behind the cover and remove the cover.

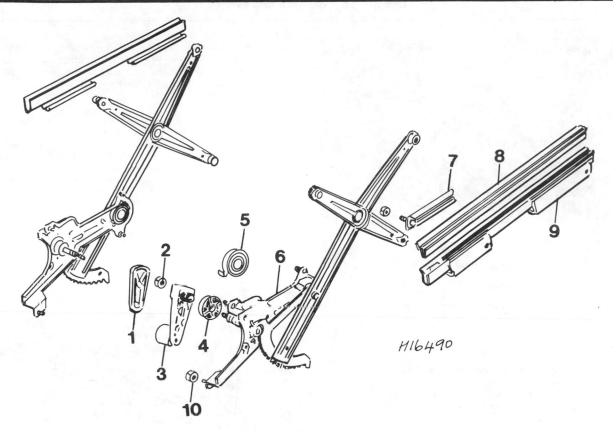

Fig. 12.6 Manual window regulator components (Sec 16)

1	Cover	4	Bezel
2	Nut	5	Spring
3	Handle	6	Regulator

7	Fixed rail	9	Window rail
8	Window channel	10	Nut

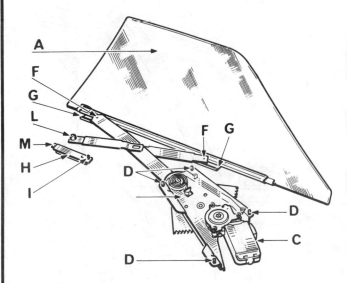

Fig. 12.7 Electric window regulator components (Sec 16)

A	Window	H	Fixed rail
C	Motor	I	Stud
D	Studs	L	Roller
F	Rollers	M	Lug
G	Window rail		

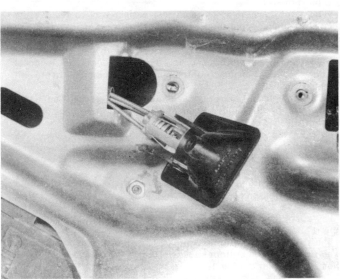

17.1 Exterior mirror control (it is not necessary to remove the door trim panel)

17.3 Exterior mirror control cables with trim removed

3   Prise off the exterior mirror inner trim, and use a Torx key to unscrew the mirror retaining screws (photo).
4   Fix a length of string to the control end of the cables, withdraw the mirror and cables from the door, then untie the string leaving it threaded through the door.
5   Refitting is a reversal of removal.

18 Windscreen – removal and refitting

Note: *The windscreen on certain models is bonded in place and several specialist tools and compounds are required to fit it, therefore this Section does not cover the procedure for those models.*
1   Removal of the windscreen will be required for one of two reasons; the glass shattering or cracking or deterioration of the rubber surround causing water leaks into the interior of the vehicle. Remove the wiper arms.
2   Where the glass has shattered, the easiest way to remove the screen is to stick a sheet of self-adhesive paper or plastic sheeting to each side and push it from the inside outwards, seal the air intake grille on the scuttle and air ducts and radio speaker slots in the facia panel to prevent glass crystals from falling into them during the removal operation. Protect the surface of the bonnet with a blanket to prevent scratching.
3   Where the glass is to be removed intact or just cracked (laminated type) or to renew the rubber weatherseal, make up two pads of cloth and, with the aid of an assistant, press the two top corners of the screen from the inside outwards and at the same time pulling the rubber surround from the upper corners. Remove the rubber surround as soon as the screen is withdrawn and clean the edges of both the glass and the body screen frame.
4   Commence refitting by positioning the rubber surround round the edge of the windscreen glass. Place the assembly flat down on a bench or table.
5   Lay a length of string or thin cord in the channel in the inner side of the rubber surround.
6   The string should be about 3 mm (0.125 in) diameter and the ends should overlap at the bottom edge by 100 mm (4 in) and leave a few inches to grip with the hands.
7   Place a bead of sealing mastic in the lower two corners of the screen frame.
8   Locate the lower edge of the screen surround in the body frame so that the two ends of the string hang inside the car, then pull both ends of the string while an assistant presses the glass and surround into position as the operation progresses.
9   The string will finally emerge from the top centre of the rubber surround and the screen and rubber surround lip should be in correct engagement with the screen frame.

10   Using either a sealing mastic gun or tube, insert the nozzle between the rubber surround lip and the outer surface of the screen frame and insert a thin even bead of sealant. Press the rubber surround hard to spread the sealant and to ensure correct location. Wipe away any excess sealant with a paraffin-moistened cloth.
11   Refit the wiper arms.

19 Rear quarter window – removal and refitting

1   Remove the cross-head screw from the latch on the window.
2   Fully open the window and release it from the pivot points.
3   If the rubber points are worn it will be necessary to drill out the rivets and remove the embellisher in order to fit new pivots. Secure the embellisher with new rivets.
4   The latch can be unbolted if necessary after removing the trim panel.
5   Refitting is a reversal of removal.

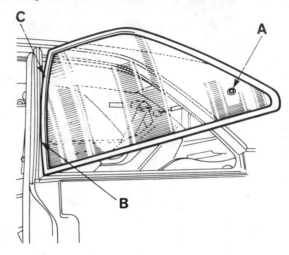

Fig. 12.8 Rear quarter window screw hole (A) and pivot points (B and C) (Sec 19)

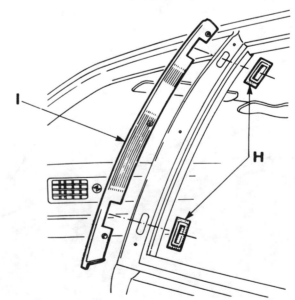

Fig. 12.9 Rear quarter window embellisher (I) and rubber pivots (H) (Sec 19)

20 Tailgate – removal, refitting and adjustment

1   Open the tailgate and pull back the rubber covers from the top of the pneumatic struts (photo).

20.1 Tailgate strut end

20.4 Tailgate right-hand hinge and earth wire

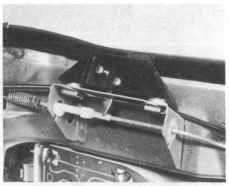

21.5 Tailgate lock housing showing operating rod and return spring

2   Disconnect the demister wiring.
3   Support the tailgate, then lift the tabs on the arms and release the arms from the balljoints.
4   Unbolt the earth wire near the right-hand side hinge (photo).
5   Unscrew the hinge nuts and, with the help of an assistant, withdraw the tailgate.
6   Refitting is a reversal of removal, but if necessary adjust the position of the tailgate so that it is central within the body aperture and level with surrounding panels. The hinges incorporate slots for up-and-down and centering adjustment, and the gap between the roof panel and tailgate is adjusted by shims under the hinges.

21 Tailgate lock and cable – removal and refitting

1   Remove the rear interior trim panels.
2   Pull the rear end of the outer cable, release the ring and withdraw the cable from the slotted bracket.
3   Unhook the inner cable end from the rear rod, and release the cable from the body.
4   Remove the screw from the release lever cover then withdraw the lever and cable.
5   Unbolt the lock housings and disconnect the rod return spring (photo).

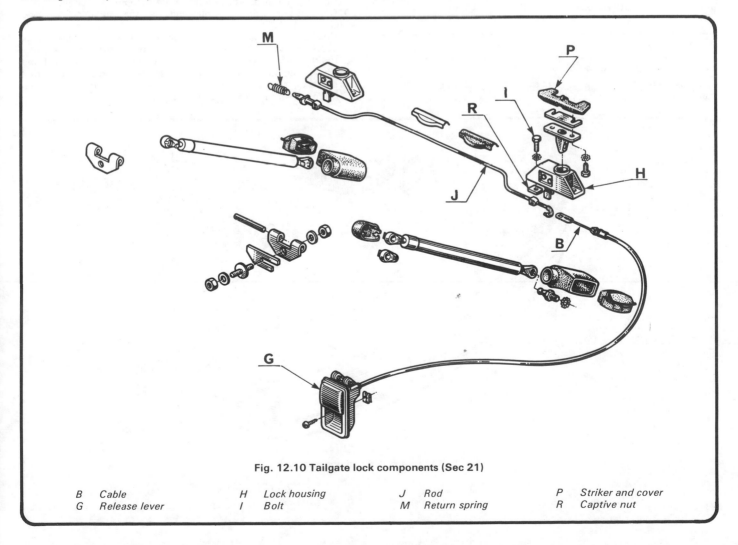

Fig. 12.10 Tailgate lock components (Sec 21)

| B | Cable | H | Lock housing | J | Rod | P | Striker and cover |
| G | Release lever | I | Bolt | M | Return spring | R | Captive nut |

21.7 Tailgate striker

6　Turn the bushes and end fitting to align with the bracket slots and withdraw the rod. Remove the lock housings.
7　If necessary remove the plastic cover and unbolt the strikers (photo).
8　Refitting is a reversal of removal, but fit the striker plastic cover using an appropriate adhesive.

22　Bumper/shield – removal and refitting

Front shield (except R1368)
1　Jack up the front of the car and support on axle stands. Apply the handbrake.

2　Remove the foglights, where applicable.
3　Remove the side mountings from the shield.
4　Unbolt the brackets from the underbody.
5　Unscrew the bolts from the end brackets, and withdraw the shield.
6　Refitting is a reversal of removal.

Rear shield (except R1368)
7　Jack up the rear of the car and support on axle stands. Chock the front wheels.
8　Unscrew the side mounting bolts, then pull out the shield slightly in order to disconnect the number plate wiring.
9　If necessary unbolt the plastic absorber and brackets from the body.
10　Refitting is a reversal of removal.

Front bumper (R1368)
11　Remove the battery, direction indicator lights, and headlight bezels.
12　Remove the clips from the bottom of the bumper.
13　Move the windscreen washer reservoir to one side, then unbolt the bumper facia.
14　Unscrew the shock absorber bolts and withdraw the shock absorbers, together with the metal bumper bar. Unbolt the metal bar.
15　Refitting is a reversal of removal, but align the bumper with the body before tightening the shock absorber bolts.

Rear bumper (R1368)
16　Remove the rear trim panels and the rear light units.
17　Loosen only the inner mounting nuts.
18　Jack up the rear of the car and support on axle stands. Chock the front wheels.
19　Drill out the rivets at the front of the bumper side extensions.
20　Unscrew the facia side bolts and the inner mounting nuts and withdraw the facia.
21　Unscrew the shock absorber bolts and withdraw the shock absorbers, together with the metal bumper bar. Unbolt the metal bar.
22　Refitting is a reversal of removal, but align the bumper with the body before tightening the shock absorber bolts, and make sure that the side extension supports are correctly engaged. Fit new 4.8 mm (0.189 in) rivets to the front of the extensions.

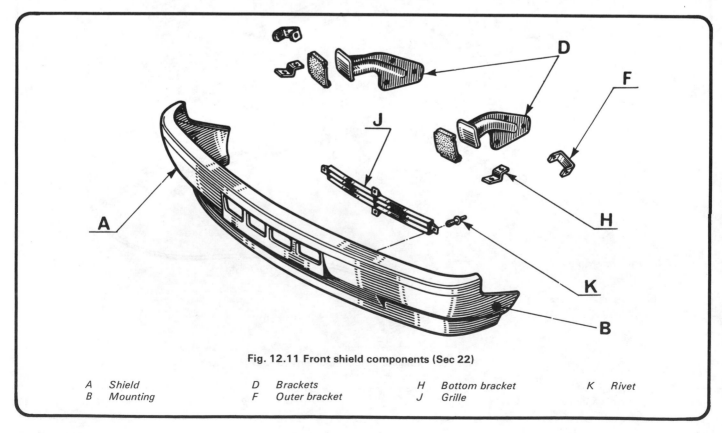

Fig. 12.11 Front shield components (Sec 22)

A	Shield	D	Brackets	H	Bottom bracket	K	Rivet
B	Mounting	F	Outer bracket	J	Grille		

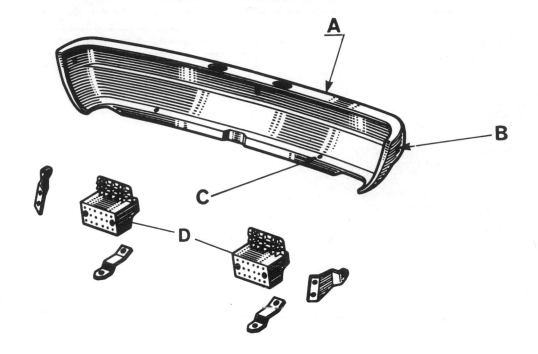

Fig. 12.12 Rear shield components (Sec 22)

A   Shield   *B   Mounting*   *C   Mounting*   *D   Absorbers*

Fig. 12.13 Front bumper shock absorber components – R1368 models (Sec 22)

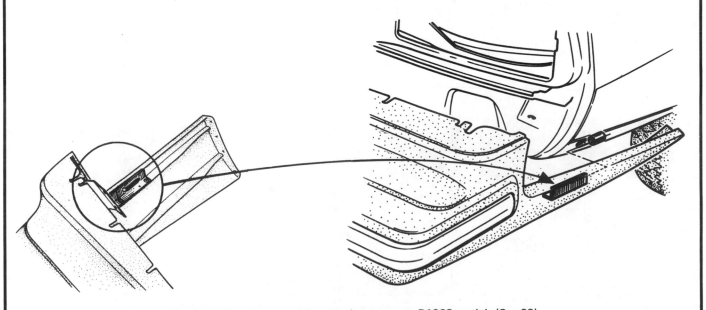

Fig. 12.14 Rear bumper side extension support – R1368 models (Sec 22)

23.1 Removing grille upper mounting screw

23 Front grille – removal and refitting

1   With the bonnet open, unscrew the grille upper mounting screws (photo).
2   Lift the grille from the lower rubber mountings.
3   Check the mountings for damage and renew them if necessary.
4   Refitting is a reversal of removal.

24 Rear trim panels – removal and refitting

1   Remove the screws and withdraw the rear corner trim panels (photo).
2   Pull the armrests upward to release the plastic clips.
3   Turn the screws to release the bottom of the trim panels beneath the quarter window, then lift the panels from the top retainers.
4   To remove the map pocket and support panel, remove the screws, then prise out the plug by the door striker and remove the recessed screw.
5   Remove the screws and withdraw the quarter panel.
6   Pull out the shock absorber cover and remove the seat latch.
7   Unbolt the seat belt runners and remove the tailgate struts, as described in Section 20 (photos).
8   Unclip the rear pillar panels and remove them.
9   Unbolt the seal belt rear mountings and remove the panels.
10 Refitting is a reversal of removal.

25 Seats – removal and refitting

Front seat

1   Unclip the rubber retaining strap under the seat and slide the seat fully to the rear.
2   Unscrew the Torx screws from the front of the runners and the nuts under the rear of the runners (photos).
3   Withdraw the seat, noting the location of the spacers.
4   Refitting is a reversal of removal.

Rear seat

5   To remove the cushion, pull out the plastic clip then lift the front from the brackets and withdraw it (photo).
6   To remove the backrest pull the cover from the pivot pin, then fold the backrest forward. Release the centre pivot pin and slide the backrest from the outer pivot pin.
7   Refitting is a reversal of removal.

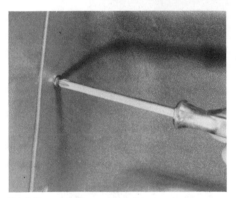

24.1 Removing a corner trim panel screw

24.7A Remove the tailgate strut end cover ...

24.7B ... and disconnect the wiring

25.2A Front seat front mounting screw

25.2B Front seat rear mounting

25.5 Demonstrating removal of the plastic retaining clip with the rear seat cushion removed

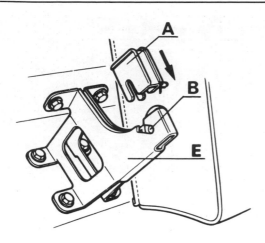

Fig. 12.15 Rear seat backrest fixing (Sec 25)

A   Cover   E   Bracket
B   Pivot pin

26 Seat belts – removal and refitting

Front belt

1   Remove the trim panel beneath the quarter window, as described in Section 24.
2   Unbolt the retractor, upper runner and lower runner bar, and withdraw the seat belt.
3   Refitting is a reversal of removal.

Rear belt

4   Remove the rear quarter trim panels, as described in Section 24.
5   Unbolt the seat belt from the front mounting.
6   Refitting is a reversal of removal.

27 Electric sunroof – removal and refitting

Note: *This work is best entrusted to a Renault dealer, however, the procedure is given for those who wish to carry out the work themselves.*
1   Open the sunroof approximately 300 mm (12 in) and remove the two front screws on the sunroof.
2   Lift the stiffener and push it back to release the retaining pegs.
3   Close the sunroof to the position shown in Fig. 12.16, and release the lever from the roller.

4   With the front of the sunroof folded back pull back the left-hand guide plate, loosen the bearing nuts and push the bearing to the motor.
5   Remove the headlining from the rear of the sunroof and disconnect the wiring.
6   Remove the rear crossmember screws, release the lining stretchers one by one and withdraw the sunroof.
7   Refitting is a reversal of removal, but adjust the rear crossmembers as necessary to tension the sunroof and inner lining.
Note: The motor will not cut out at the correct position unless the gear and worm are engaged as shown in Fig. 12.18 with the gear on the last tooth of the rack.

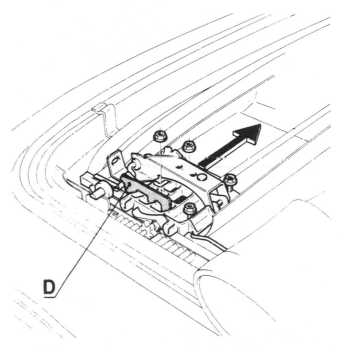

Fig. 12.17 Electric sunroof guideplate (D) (Sec 27)

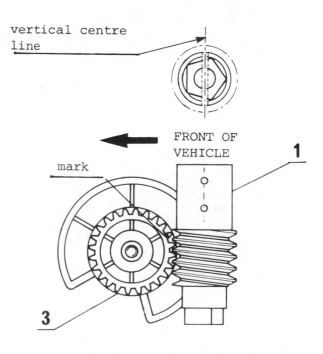

Fig. 12.18 Electric sunroof gear and worm setting (Sec 27)

1   Worm   3   Gear

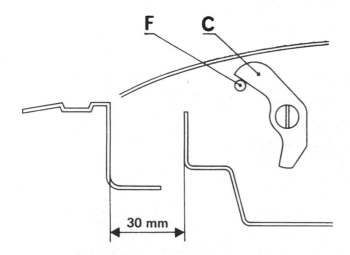

Fig. 12.16 Releasing the lever (C) from the roller (F) on the electric sunroof (Sec 27)

28 Facia panel – removal and refitting

1   Remove the instrument panel (Chapter 10), the steering wheel and column shrouds (Chapter 11), and the fusebox (Chapter 10) without disconnecting the wiring.
2   Pull out the top of the console and disconnect the clock wiring (photo).
3   Pull out the bottom of the console and disconnect the cigar lighter wiring.
4   Remove the glove compartment and facia bottom screw.
5   Remove the console side panels, heater control panel and, if applicable, the choke cable.
6   Disconnect the glove compartment light wiring.
7   Unscrew the remaining screws then unhook the facia and withdraw it; at the same time dismantling the air duct.
8   Refitting is a reversal of removal.

29 Heater control panel – removal and refitting

1   Disconnect the battery.
2   Remove the console, unscrew the heater control panel, and remove the console bracket. Leave the glove compartment in place.
3   Remove the lower steering column half cowl.

28.2 Removing the console

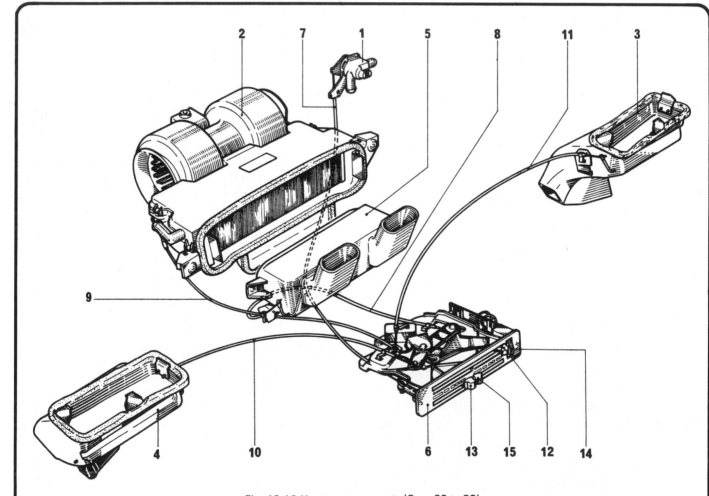

Fig. 12.19 Heater components (Secs 29 to 33)

1	Heater valve	4	Left heater duct	8	Ventilation flap cable	12	Distribution lever
2	Heater-ventilator assembly (with blower motor and heater core)	5	Ventilation box (fresh air only)	9	Airflow flap cable		(high-low)
		6	Control panel	10	Left heater duct cable	13	Heater valve lever
3	Right heater duct	7	Heater valve cable	11	Right heater duct cable	14	Fan motor dial
						15	Fresh air intake lever

4   Remove the accessories plate bracket, leaving the wires connected.
5   Pull off the rheostat and control panel illumination leads.
6   Remove the clips from the five control cables, and disconnect the cables from the panel.
7   Remove the panel.
8   Refitting is the reverse of the removal procedure.

30 Heater control cables – adjustment

1   The adjustment procedure for each cable is identical. First remove the control panel, with reference to Section 29.
2   With the cable connected at both ends, but with the outer cable clip removed, move both controls to the closed position.
3   Move the control knob back approximately 2.0 mm (0.08 in) then clamp the cable with the clip.
4   Check that the control operates correctly, then refit the panel.

31 Heater valve – removal and refitting

1   Clamp off the coolant hoses to the valve (photo).
2   Disconnect the hoses from the valve (photo).
3   Remove the clip on the valve cable, and free the cable from the valve.
4   Pull the valve forward and out, freeing it from the securing clips.
5   To refit, offer up the new valve until secured by the clips.
6   Refit the hoses, and remove the clamps.
7   Refit the cable to the valve, and adjust it as described in Section 30.
8   Bleed the cooling system (see Chapter 2) and top up if necessary.

32 Heater motor – removal and refitting

1   Disconnect the battery.
2   Clamp off the hoses to the heater matrix, and disconnect them. (Apply the clamp to the left-hand hose on the engine side of the bleed screw if necessary) (photos).
3   Take the clip from the airflow flap cable, and disconnect the cable.
4   Disconnect the electrical lead to the fan motor, and the screen wiper junction block (photo).
5   Remove the screws (3 positions) securing the casing on the engine side (photos).
6   Under the facia on the passenger side, remove the console side panels then unscrew the nut securing the motor casing. Similarly remove the nut on the driver's side, after removing the lower half steering column cowl (photos).
7   Lift out the heater assembly complete (photos).
8   Remove the main seal round the edge of the heater assembly, remove the clips and the centre screw, and separate the two halves of the case. (Note that the halves are stuck with a sealant) (photos).
9   Lift out the motor assembly, which cannot be repaired. If defective, obtain a replacement unit. Note the orientation of the fan blades in the case, and disconnect the hoses (photos).

31.1 Heater valve

31.2 Disconnecting the heater valve hoses

10 To refit, first clean the joint faces.
11 Reposition the motor assembly in the case, ensuring that the direction of rotation is correct. Check that the blades do not touch the case, particularly at the ends.
12 Lightly smear a sealant on the joint face, reposition the half casings, and refit the centre bolt and clips.

32.2A Removing the right-hand heater hose

32.2B Removing the left-hand heater hose

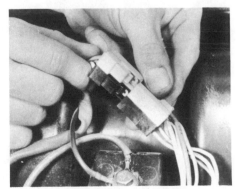

32.4 Disconnecting the heater motor wiring

32.5A Right-hand heater motor mounting

32.5B Centre heater motor mounting

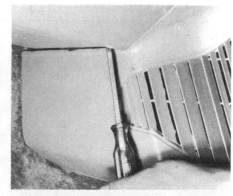
32.6A Removing the screws ...

32.6B ... retaining the console side panels

32.6C Heater assembly inner mounting beneath the facia

32.7A Removing the heater assembly

32.7B Heater assembly mounting grille

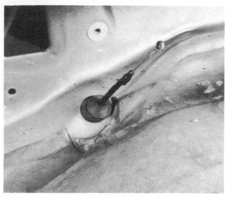
32.7C Heater airflow flap control cable

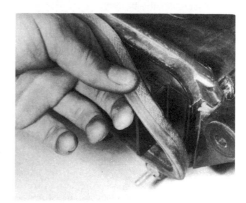
32.8A Removing the heater seal

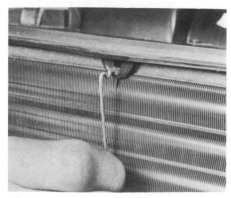
32.8B Removing the heater rear clip

32.8C Removing the heater side clips

32.8D Removing heater centre screw

32.8E Removing the heater upper half

32.9A View of heater motor with upper half removed

32.9B Removing the heater motor

32.9C Disconnecting the heater matrix hoses

32.9D The heater fan rheostat windings

13 Check that the fans are still free to revolve.
14 Refit the main seal, and relocate the heater assembly on the bulkhead. Check that when the studs are pushed through the bulkhead, they also locate the ventilation on the passenger side.
15 Refit the bolts on the engine side, but do not tighten. Remember to secure the earth leads for the heater and screen wiper motors.
16 Fit and tighten the two nuts on the passenger side of the bulkhead.
17 Tighten the two bolts on the engine side of the bulkhead, followed by the remaining front centre bolt.

32.18 Refitting the heater airflow flap

18 Refit the remaining items in reverse order, adjusting the airflow flap cable as necessary, as described in Section 30 (photo).
19 Bleed the cooling system (see Chapter 2).

33 Heater matrix – removal and refitting

1 Remove the heater motor, as described in Section 32.
2 Lift out the matrix and disconnect the return hose.
3 Refitting is a reversal of removal, with reference to Section 32.

34 Air conditioning system – precautions and maintenance

Never disconnect any part of the air conditioning system unless it has previously been discharged by a qualified refrigeration engineer. Where the compressor, condenser or evaporator obstruct other mechanical operations such as engine removal, it is permissible to move them to the limit of their flexible hoses, but not to disconnect the hoses.

Regularly check the condenser for clogging with flies or leaves, and if necessary hose clean with water. Also check the tension of the compressor drivebelt. The belt deflection should be approximately 3.5 to 4.5 mm (0.140 to 0.180 in) at the centre point under firm thumb pressure.

35 Air conditioning fan motor – removal and refitting

1 Disconnect the battery negative lead.
2 Remove the side panels from the console and unscrew the console lower mounting bolts.
3 Disconnect the fan motor wiring.

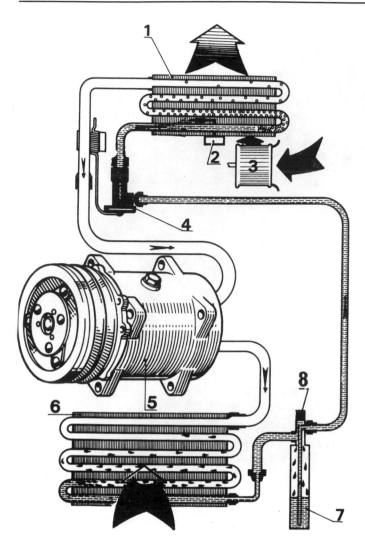

4   Unscrew the motor mounting bolts, then lift the centre console and withdraw the fan motor.
5   Refitting is a reversal of removal.

36 Air conditioning thermostat – removal and refitting

1   Disconnect the battery negative lead.
2   Remove the left-hand side panel from the console.
3   Disconnect the cable from the thermostat.
4   Disconnect the wiring and remove the thermostat.
5   Refitting is a reversal of removal, but adjust the cable as follows: Move the control lever to maximum cold and also set the thermostat at the maximum cold position; then lock the outer cable in this position. After refitting all the components check the thermostat operation as follows:
6   Move the blower rheostat to the lowest position then depress the air conditioning button. Set the control knob to maximum cold, and check that the fan motor switches to maximum speed. If it does not, either the cable is not adjusted correctly or the thermostat is faulty.

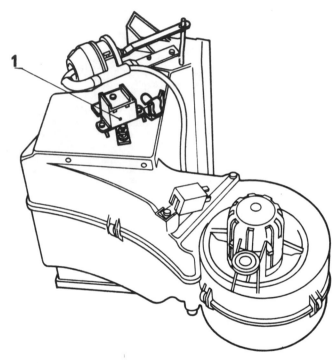

Fig. 12.21 Air conditioning thermostat (1) location (Sec 36)

Fig. 12.20 Air conditioning components (Sec 34)

1 Evaporator	5 Compressor
2 Thermostat	6 Condenser
3 Blower	7 Receiver/drier
4 Thermal expansion valve	8 Pressure relief valve

Chapter 13 Supplement:
Revisions and information on later models

Contents

1 Introduction

This Supplement contains information in respect of modifications made to later models built after 1984. It is suggested that this Supplement is referred to before the main Chapters 1 to 12 if working on later model vehicles.

2 Specifications

Engine
Torque wrench settings

OHV engines	lbf ft	Nm
Cylinder head bolts:		
Stage 1 (all engines)	28	38
Stage 2 (847 engine)	40 to 47	54 to 64
Stage 2 (all engines except 847):		
Hot	61 to 65	83 to 88
Cold	56 to 59	76 to 80
OHC engines		
Cylinder head bolts:		
Stage 1	36	49
Stage 2	58	79
Stage 3	Loosen 180°	Loosen 180°
Stage 4	70	95

Fuel system
Solex 32 SEIA – 795 carburettor

Choke tube	24
Main jet	127.5
Idling jet	45
Air compensating jet	160
Fuel inlet needle valve	1.5
Enrichment device – Econostat	80
Initial throttle opening (choke on)	0.80 mm
Float level	11.7 mm
Defuming valve gap	3.0 to 4.0 mm
Idling speed	750 to 800 rpm
CO%	1.5 to 2.5

Solex 32 MIMSA – 800 carburettor

Enrichment	50
Fuel inlet needle valve	1.5
Float level	33.0 mm
Accelerator pump jet	50
Initial throttle opening	0.90 mm
Mechanical part-open setting	2nd step high side
Defuming valve	1.0 mm
Accelerator pump rod clearance	1.7 mm
Idling speed	600 to 700 rpm
CO%	1.0 to 2.0

	Stage 1 (Primary)	Stage 2 (Secondary)
Choke tube	23	24
Main jet	105	112.5
Idling jet	41	45
Air compensating jet	155	125
Emulsifier	X3	X2

Weber 32 DARA 53 carburettor

Initial throttle opening (medium cold – second notch)	0.90 mm
Fuel inlet needle valve	2.25
Float level	7.0 mm
Float travel	8.0 mm
Accelerator pump jet	60
Pneumatic part opening	5.5 to 10.0 mm
Idling speed	750 to 850 rpm
CO%	1.0 to 2.0

	Stage 1 (Primary)	Stage 2 (Secondary)
Choke tube	25	26
Main jet	132	145
Air compensating jet	170	160
Idling jet	47	42
Mixture centralizer	3.5	4.0
Emulsifier	F58	F6

Weber 32 DARA 54 carburettor

Initial throttle opening (medium cold – second notch)	0.85 mm
Fuel inlet needle valve	2.25
Float level	7.0 mm
Float travel	8.0 mm
Accelerator pump jet	60
Pneumatic part opening	5.5 to 10.0 mm
Idle speed	875 to 925 rpm
CO%	1.0 to 2.0

	(Primary) Stage 1	Stage 2 (Secondary)
Choke tube	25	26
Main jet	130	145
Air compensating jet	155	140
Idling jet	47	42/55
Mixture centralizer	3.5	4.0
Emulsifier	F58	F6

Garrett turbocharger

Wastegate opening pressure on full load	610 to 640 mbar at less than 3000 rpm
Static opening pressure	725 to 795 mbar

Ignition system
Ignition timing (vehicles with electronic ignition)

The following table gives ignition timing figures at three engine speeds, to enable the integral electronic ignition (AEI) unit to be checked for correct operation.

Vehicle	Engine	Advance Curve	Idle speed	Advance (degrees) 1550 rpm	4050 rpm
R 1360	847	RE 030	9 to 12	8 to 13	24 to 28
R 1361	A2M	RE 015	6 to 10	9 to 14	19 to 25
R 1362	A6M	RE 010	9 to 13	12 to 16	24 to 29
R 1363	829 or J6R	RE 001	8 to 12	10 to 15	26 to 30
R 1363 (Switzerland)	J6R	RE 020	6 to 9	9 to 12	22 to 29
R 1365	A5L	RE 033	10 to 16	21 to 26	16 to 23
R 136A	A7L	RE 022	8 to 15	8 to 12	14 to 19

Tests should be carried out with the distributor vacuum hose disconnected. For advance curve identification, see the sticker on the AEI unit casing.

Suspension and steering

Tyres

Tyre pressures (cold):

	Front	Rear
TL, GTL	1.9 bar (28 lbf/in²)	2.1 bar (30 lbf/in²)
GTS, TX, GTX	2.1 bar (30 lbf/in²)	2.3 bar (33 lbf/in²)
Turbo	2.0 bar (29 lbf/in²)	2.1 bar (30 lbf/in²)

---

3 Engine

Oil filter – identification

1   It is most important that the correct oil filter is used as the threaded sleeve onto which it is screwed may be of 19.0 of 20.0 mm outside diameter depending upon the particular engine.

2   The oil filter which fits the larger sleeve is marked M20 x 1.50. This filter will screw onto the smaller threaded sleeve, but thread play will be evident just before tightening and the filter will loosen in service.

Rocker cover gasket – modification

3   Later 1647 cc engines are fitted with a thicker gasket and longer sealing sleeves under the rocker cover.

4   Do not use early type gaskets with later type sleeves, or *vice-versa*. Tho lator type gasket and sleeves may be used on earlier models.

---

4 Fuel system

Turbocharger boost pressure regulator – adjustment

Note: *Special tool MOT 1014 (pressure gauge) and a dial gauge will be required for this operation.*

1   The performance and reliability of turbocharged engines are dependent upon the correct adjustment of the boost pressure regulator.

2   Remove the air cleaner.

3   The test equipment consists of a reducing valve (1) Fig. 13.3 which can be adjusted, a test pressure gauge (3) graduated from 0 to 1.6 bar, and fitted with a zeroing screw and bleed screw (4).

4   Before commencing the test, zero the pressure gauge and release the screw (1) completely on the reducing valve. Also release the bleed screw (4).

5   Connect pipe (A) to a compressed air supply and pipe (B) to the take-off on the wastegate capsule, then tighten the bleed screw (4).

6   Slowly tighten the reducing valve screw (1) until the specified air pressure is obtained or the wastegate rod travel is within tolerance. Use a dial gauge for this.

Checking pressure 720 to 785 mbar
Setting pressure 755 to 785 mbar
Wastegate rod travel 0.36 to 0.40 mm

7   If the pressure regulator cannot be adjusted satisfactorily, the wastegate rod assembly will have to be renewed in the following way.

8   Disconnect the hose from the capsule (1) (Fig. 13.5).

9   Extract the circlip (2) and disconnect the end fitting (3). Unscrew the end fitting.

10 Unscrew the bolts (4) and remove the capsule.

11 Bolt on the new capsule, tightening the bolts to specified torque, see Specifications.

12 Screw the locknut and threaded end fitting onto the rod.

13 The calibrated pressure must now be set; except on capsules which have pin-punched end fittings, these are preset.

14 Connect the test equipment (MOT 1014) to the take-off (7) and then apply air pressure equal to the setting value (paragraph 6). It is essential that there are no air leaks between the test gauge and the wastegate valve.

15 Hold the wastegate valve closed by means of the arm (8).

16 With the setting valve maintained, adjust the length of the threaded

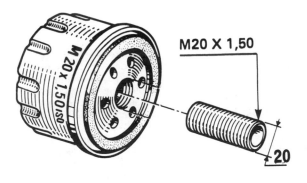

M20 X 1,50

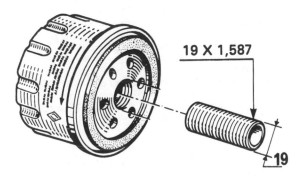

19 X 1,587

Fig. 13.1 Oil filter identification and threaded sleeves (Sec 3)

Dimensions shown in millimetres

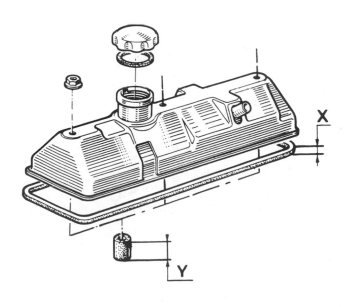

Fig. 13.2 Rocker cover gasket and sleeve dimensions (Sec 3)

Early type:	X = 5.0 mm (0.20 in)
	Y = 25.0 mm (0.99 in)
Later type:	X = 6.5 mm (0.26 in)
	Y = 26.5 mm (1.04 in)

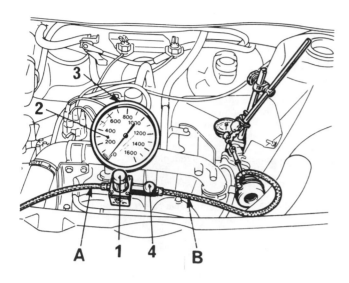

Fig. 13.3 Turbocharger boost pressure regulator test equipment (Sec 4)

A	Pipe to compressed air supply	1	Reducing valve screw
B	Pipe to wastegate capsule take-off	2	Pressure gauge
		3	Test pressure gauge screw
		4	Bleed screw

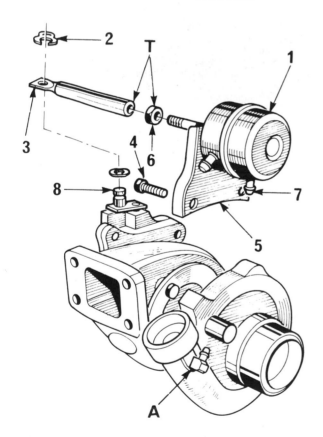

Fig. 13.5 Turbocharger wastegate components (Sec 4)

A	Angled union	4	Fixing bolts (one hidden)
T	See text	5	Mounting bracket
1	Capsule	6	Locknut
2	Clip	7	Take-off point
3	Threaded end fitting	8	Wastegate arm

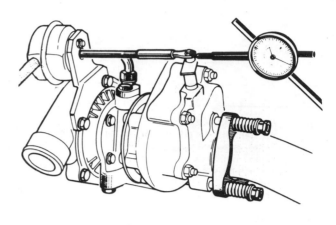

Fig. 13.4 Dial gauge connected to wastegate rod (Sec 4)

end fitting so that its hole just drops onto the control arm pivot pin (8) with the wastegate valve still held closed.

17 Zero the pressure at the take-off (7).

18 Using a dial gauge with its stylus against the end of the wastegate rod, and zeroed, gradually increase the air pressure until the rod travel is within the specified tolerance (see paragraph 6) and read off the pressure indicated on the test gauge. This should match that given in paragraph 6. Turn locknut (6) so that it touches the threaded end fitting (3), then tighten it up. Mark the locknut and fitting with a blob of paint at 'T' – do not get any on the capsule rod.

19 The boost pressure regulator is fed through a T-piece union (a) (Fig. 13.6). This has a calibrated bleed.

20 Should low boost pressure occur, check the T-piece for obstruction. When assembling the T-piece bleed union, screw it in two or three threads and then apply thread locking fluid to the remaining threads before tightening it.

Cruise control system ('Normalur' Type)

21 This system is fitted to certain models, and has two distinct functions – regulation of top speed, to avoid exceeding speed limits, and normal cruise control, which enables a predetermined roadspeed to be maintained without the need to keep the foot on the accelerator.

22 In order to set a particular top speed, activate the Normalur system by pressing switch (2) (Fig. 13.7). The set speed is indicated by LEDs around the speedometer dial (1), and it can be adjusted by pressing rocker switch (3). This sets the position of a stop under the accelerator pedal, which may be overridden if required.

23 To use the system as a cruise control, set the desired cruising speed as described in the previous paragraph, then with the accelerator held against its stop, press switch (4). The accelerator will then remain on the stop and the car will cruise at the desired speed.

24 The cruising speed can be varied by pressing switch (3).

25 If the throttle stop is overridden when in cruise control mode, simply lifting off the accelerator will reset the selected speed. If, however, the clutch or brake pedals are touched, the system cuts out and the driver resumes normal control.

26 When the system has cut out, hold the accelerator down against its stop, and press switch (4) to reset the cruising speed.

27 Apart from checking the system electrical connections and the vacuum hose to the throttle actuating diaphragm capsule, any fault occurring in the main components will have to be checked by your Renault dealer.

Solex 32 MIMSA carburettor – description

28 This carburettor is fitted to certain models with type A2M (1647 cc engines).

29 The carburettor is a dual-barrel downdraught unit with a manually-operated choke and coolant-heated throttle valve block at the base of the carburettor.

30 An interlock is used to prevent the secondary throttle valve opening if the choke is actuated.

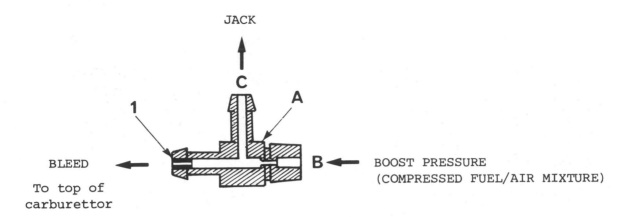

Fig. 13.6 Turbo boost pressure regulator calibrated union (Sec 4)

A Union	C Jack pressure (245 to 305
B Turbo pressure (610 to 670	mbar)
mbar)	1 Calibrated bleed

Fig. 13.7 Cruise control system switches (Sec 4)

1	Illuminated speed indicators	3	Speed regulator switch
2	'On' switch	4	Cruising speed control

31 A cam-operated accelerator pump is used, together with a vacuum-operated choke flap initial opening system.

Solex 32 MIMSA carburettor – idle speed and mixture adjustment
32 The idle speed is adjusted by means of the screw arrowed in Fig. 13.8.
33 The idle speed and mixture should only be adjusted when the engine is at normal operating temperature.
34 The mixture screw (Fig. 13.9) is set in production and should not be altered unless essential. If adjustment is necessary, remove the tamperproof cap from the screw and adjust using an exhaust gas analyser as described in Chapter 3.

Solex 32 MIMSA carburettor – overhaul
35 Complete overhaul of a carburettor is rarely required. A well-worn unit is better exchanged for a new or reconditioned one.
36 However, access to the jets and orifices can be obtained after extracting the screws and removing the top cover. It is not necessary to remove the carburettor from the engine, just the air cleaner. Before the top cover can be taken off, the choke flap vacuum unit and the flap control link must be removed.

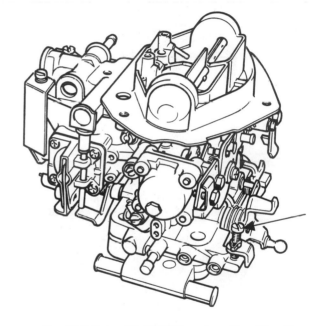

Fig. 13.8 Solex 32 MIMSA carburettor (Sec 4)

Idle speed screw (arrowed)

37 Clean out the fuel and sediment from the float chamber and remove the jets.
38 Clean the jets and passages using air from a tyre pump. Never probe them with wire or their calibration will be ruined.
39 This will normally be the limit of overhaul. Obtain a repair kit for your particular carburettor. This will contain all the necessary seals, gaskets and other renewable items.
40 Before fitting the top cover, check the jet sizes against those listed in Specifications, in case a previous owner has changed any of them.
41 The following checks and adjustments should be carried out if there is any doubt as to the performance of the carburettor. Some adjustments will require the removal of the carburettor as described in Chapter 3.

Float level
42 Invert the top cover and measure dimension (A) (Fig. 13.11) between the furthest point on the float and the surface of the top cover (gasket removed). This setting is not adjustable and can only be altered by fitting a new sealing washer under the fuel inlet needle

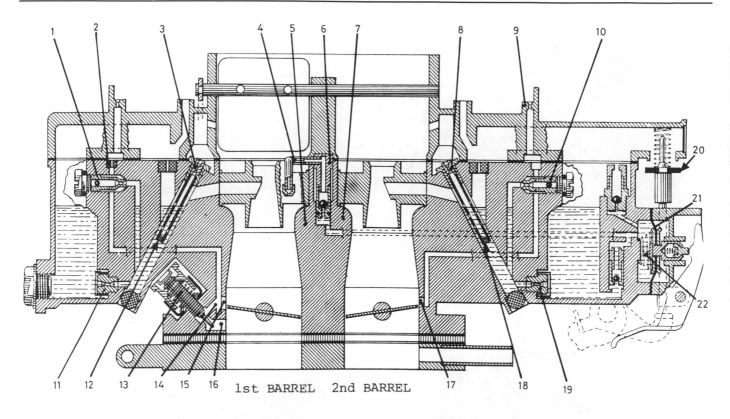

**Fig. 13.9 Sectional view of Solex 32 MIMSA carburettor
(Sec 4)**

1	Idling jet	7 Choke tube	13 Mixture screw (with
2	Emulsifier jet	8 Air compensator jet	tamperproof cap)
3	Air compensator jet	9 Air jet	14 Fuel duct
4	Fuel ball valve/jet	10 Fuel jet	15 Idle orifice
5	Choke tube	11 Main jet	16 Idle orifice
6	Fuel ball valve/jet	12 Emulsion tube	17 Progressive orifice

1 Idling jet
2 Emulsifier jet
3 Air compensator jet
4 Fuel ball valve/jet
5 Choke tube
6 Fuel ball valve/jet

7 Choke tube
8 Air compensator jet
9 Air jet
10 Fuel jet
11 Main jet
12 Emulsion tube

13 Mixture screw (with tamperproof cap)
14 Fuel duct
15 Idle orifice
16 Idle orifice
17 Progressive orifice

18 Emulsion tube
19 Main jet
20 Valve
21 Diaphragm
22 Spring

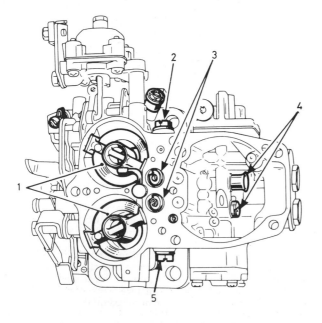

**Fig. 13.10 Location of jets in Solex 32 MIMSA carburettor
(Sec 4)**

1 Choke tube
2 Idling jet
3 Main jet

4 Air compensator jet
5 Idling jet

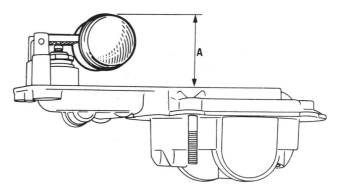

Fig. 13.11 Float setting diagram (Sec 4)

A = 33.0 mm (1.3 in)

valve. Check the tightness of the needle valve using a close-fitting spanner. The float can be removed for better access by driving out the pivot pin. Take care to support the pivot pedestals during removal and refitting of the pin.

Secondary venturi throttle angle

43 Adjust the screw (1) (Fig. 13.12) until the secondary throttle valve plate is fully closed, and then turn the screw until the valve plate is opened 0° 30'.

Initial throttle opening

44 Turn the screw (2) (Fig. 13.13) until the gap at the edge of the

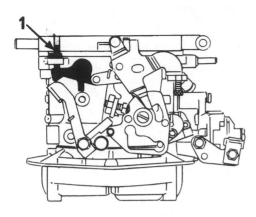

Fig. 13.12 Secondary venturi throttle angle adjustment screw (1) (Sec 4)

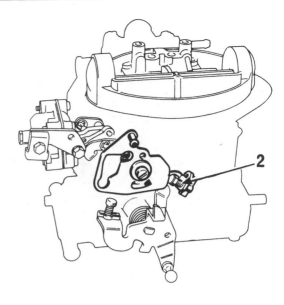

Fig. 13.13 Initial throttle opening screw (2) (Sec 4)

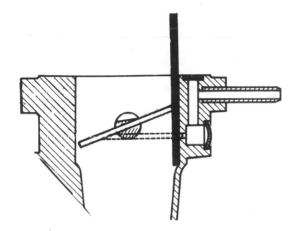

Fig. 13.14 Checking initial throttle opening (valve plate gap) (Sec 4)

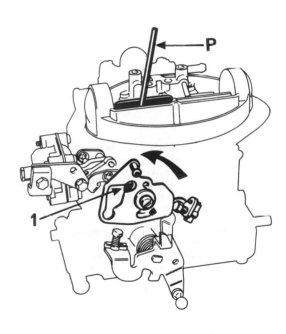

Fig. 13.15 Choke flap initial opening (Sec 4)

P   Gauge rod or twist drill   1   Pin

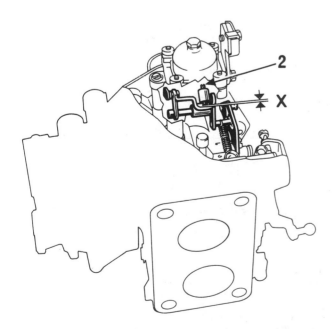

Fig. 13.16 Clearance (X) before diaphragm starts to move (Sec 4)

2   Adjustment screw   X   1.7 mm (0.07 in)

throttle valve plate will accept a twist drill or gauge rod of 0.90 mm in diameter.

Choke flap initial opening
45 Close the choke flap control and then close the choke flap against its stop with the fingers.
46 Measure the choke flap opening at its upper edge, using a gauge pin (P). It should be 2.0 mm. A slight adjustment may be made by bending pin (1) (Fig. 13.15).
47 With the choke flap closed adjust dimension (X), which is the clearance before the diaphragm starts to move, to 1.7 mm by turning screw (2) (Fig. 13.16).

Secondary venturi throttle locking system
48 When the choke flap is closed, the lever (1) (Fig. 13.17) prevents the throttle valve plate of the secondary venturi from opening.
49 When the choke flap is open, the lever (1) swings out of the way to

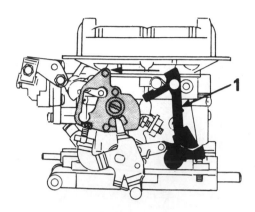

Fig. 13.17 Secondary venturi throttle locking system (Sec 4)

1   Lever

free the secondary throttle. When the choke control is pulled out by 5.0 mm, the secondary throttle valve plate should still be able to open. Any adjustment should be made by twisting the lever.

Accelerator pump

50 The pump on this carburettor is operated by a lever and cam. No provision is made for adjustment.

Carburettor overhaul – types Solex 32 SEIA/32 DIS – Weber 32 DARA/32DIR and Zenith 32 IF

51 The remarks made in paragraphs 35 to 39 for the Solex 32 MIMSA will generally apply to the other carburettors described in Chapter 3.

52 All the checks and adjustments which may be required to these carburettors are described in Chapter 3.

Carburettor preliminary setting after overhaul – all models

53 Should the adjustment screws be removed from the carburettor for renewal or for blowing out the passages in the carburettor body, preset them in the following way so that the engine will start. Adjust the screws once the engine has reached normal operating temperature, as described in Chapter 3, Section 12.

Idle speed screw (limited CO idle system)

54 Unscrew the throttle stop screw until it just loses contact with the throttle lever, and then turn the screw in two turns.

Idle speed screw (constant CO idle system)

55 Turn the volume (air) control screw gently until it just seats, then unscrew it through three turns.

Mixture screw

56 Turn the screw in gently until it just seats, then unscrew it four to five turns.

5   Ignition system

Integral electronic ignition

AEI unit and distributor – identification and advance curves

1 The unit used on the Fuego is the 'D' type shown in Fig. 4.16, Chapter 4.

2 The advance curve varies according to vehicle model and where suitable test equipment is available, the table given in Specifications can be used for checking operation of the distributor advance mechanism.

Distributor – overhaul

3 Remove the distributor from the engine – see Chapter 4.

Conventional type contact breaker distributor

4 Refer to Chapter 4 and remove the contact breaker points.

5 Remove the condenser by disconnecting its lead from the terminal post and extracting the condenser fixing screw.

6 Record the relationship of the serrated cam to the end of the

vacuum capsule rod. Failure to refit the cam so that the original notch engages with the rod will upset the advance curve when the engine is running.

7 Extract the spring clip and take off the serrated cam.

8 Extract the fixing screws and withdraw the vacuum capsule.

9 Remove the pivot post terminal, adjuster nut and adjuster nut bracket screws, and lift out the baseplate assembly.

10 If the driveshaft or centrifugal weight and spring assembly must be removed, mark the drive dog in relation to the slot in the cam at the top of the driveshaft, and then drive out the fixing pin. Take off the washers and dog, withdraw the shaft and counterweight assembly.

11 Defects in the bearing bushes, counterweight assembly or springs will probably mean that the most economical course is to obtain a factory exchange unit. Care should be taken that the correct distributor is obtained. Individual spare parts are unlikely to be available, but it may be possible to have items such as bushes locally made and fitted.

12 Clean all parts, lightly lubricate as necessary, and reassemble in the reverse order to the dismantling procedure.

Cassette type contact breaker distributor

13 Remove the condenser and cassette as described in Chapter 4.

14 The counterweight and cam assembly can be removed after extracting the screw from the recess at the top of the driveshaft. Mark the relationship of the cam slot to the offset drive dog at the bottom of the shaft.

15 Refer to paragraphs 10 and 11 of this Section.

Transistorized type distributor

16 Remove the distributor cap, rotor and dust shield.

17 Extract the circlip and, using two screwdrivers as levers, prise off the pulse rotor (reluctor).

18 Extract the fixing screws and remove the vacuum advance capsule.

19 Extract the remaining screws if the pick-up coils are to be removed.

20 Removal of the distributor driveshaft and counterweight assembly

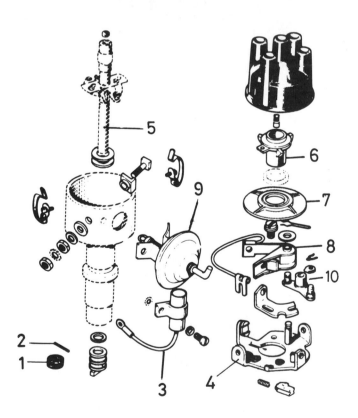

Fig. 13.18 Exploded view of conventional contact breaker type distributor (Sec 5)

1	*Coil spring*	*6*	*Rotor*
2	*Pin*	*7*	*Dust shield*
3	*Condenser*	*8*	*Contact breaker*
4	*Baseplate*	*9*	*Vacuum capsule*
5	*Driveshaft*	*10*	*Counterweight pivot*

is similar to the procedure described for the conventional contact breaker distributor in paragraph 10.

21 When reassembling this type of distributor, check the pulse rotor (reluctor) air gap and adjust it as described in Chapter 4, Section 5 if necessary.

6 Clutch

Clutch cable trunnion – lubrication

1 In order to ensure smooth operation of the clutch cable, the trunnion at the release arm end of the clutch cable must be kept well greased.

7 Manual transmission

Synchromesh baulk rings

1 The synchro baulk rings for 3rd, 4th and 5th gears are manufactured from molybdenum on later models, and this type of ring may also be used on earlier models.

2 When fitting this type of synchro baulk ring its inner surface should be smeared with 'Molykote M 55+', available from your Renault dealer, or an equivalent lubricant.

Type NG transmission – secondary shaft modification

3 As from March 1984, the circlip and splined washer grooves on the secondary shaft have been widened.

4 If the secondary shaft is renewed during overhaul of the transmission, only 1st gear can be used on the later type of shaft.

Starter motor locating dowel – modification

5 If a new transmission (types NG0, NG1 or NG3) is being fitted, check that the correct starter motor locating dowel is used, otherwise the starter motor or transmission casing could be damaged.

6 Measure the depth of the dowel recess (D) (Fig. 13.20) in the starter motor, then the recess (G) (Fig. 13.21) in the transmission casing. Add the dimensions together and use a dowel which is slightly smaller in length from the three sizes available.

    7.25 to 7.75 mm long – part no. 7705010006
    9.25 to 9.75 mm long – part no. 7705010080
    11.10 to 11.60 mm long – part no. 7705010087

8 Automatic transmission

Fluid filter (type MJ transmission) – renewal

1 Whenever the transmission fluid is being changed, it is recommended that the filter pick-up screen is renewed at the same time.

2 Having drained the fluid as described in Chapter 7, extract the screw and remove the transmission sump pan.

3 Extract the fixing screws, remove and discard the filter screen.

4 Fit the new filter screen using a new rubber sealing ring.

5 Wipe out the sump pan using a non-fluffy rag. On type MJ transmission, inspection may show only one magnet located in the sump pan. If this is so, obtain a set of four larger magnets and position them as shown in Fig. 13.22.

6 Using a new gasket, refit the sump pan. Refit the drain plug.

7 Fill the transmission with the specified type and quantity of fluid. Operate the car for a distance of at least 8.0 km (5.0 miles) and then check the fluid level and top up if necessary.

Automatic transmission computer – earthing

8 A poor earth at the computer can cause the transmission to stay in 3rd speed or change at random.

9 On later models, the earth wire of the six-way connector located at (E) is deleted and an earth wire (G) is fitted at the multi purpose switch – see Figs. 13.22, 13.24 and 13.25.

Starter motor locating dowel – modification

10 Refer to paragraphs 5 and 6 of the preceding Section. The information applies if a new or replacement automatic transmission (type 4139 or MJ1) is being fitted.

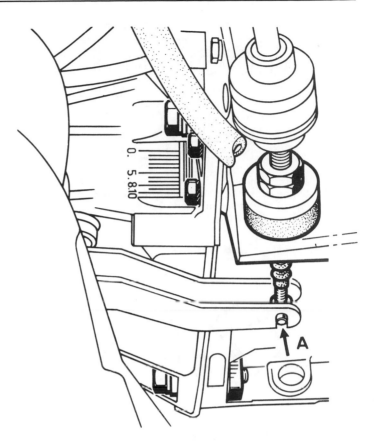

Fig. 13.19 Clutch cable grease application point (A) (Sec 5)

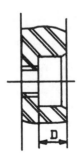

Fig. 13.20 Starter motor dowel recess (D) (Sec 7)

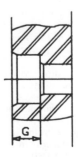

Fig. 13.21 Starter motor dowel recess (G) in transmission (Sec 7)

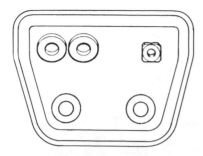

Fig. 13.22 Location of swarf-collecting magnets in Type MJ transmission (Sec 8)

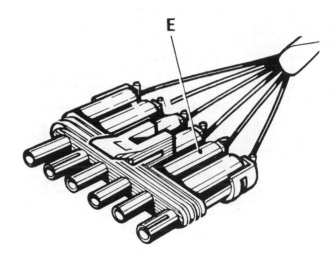

Fig. 13.23 Computer six-way connector (Sec 8)

E   Earth

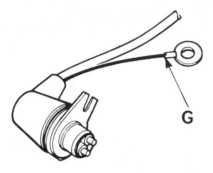

Fig. 13.24 Multi-purpose switch earth (G) (Sec 8)

9 Driveshafts

Coupling (GE 86) – bellows renewal

1   Later models are fitted with a modified GE 86 driveshaft joint at the roadwheel end. Beaded bellows are used and axial play is adjusted by means of a shim.

2   To renew the bellows on this type of joint, carry out the following operations.

3   With the driveshaft removed, cut off the bellows retaining clips, slide back the bellows and wipe away as much grease as possible. Cut the bellows and discard them.

4   Free the bell-shaped section of the joint from the driveshaft by gently prising up the starplate arms one by one. Take care not to twist the starplate arms.

5   Take out the thrust button, spring and axial play shim (2) (Fig. 13.28).

6   The special expander tool (T. Av 537-02) referred to in Chapter 8, Section 4, must now be used to slide the new bellows (smaller diameter end) over the joint yoke. A piece of sheet metal rolled to form a long cone will serve as a substitute fitting tool, but take great care that any sharp edges are taped to prevent cutting the bellows. Plenty of lubricant will be required to ensure that the bellows will slide up the expander. Stretch the first fold of the bellows onto the expander, then work the remaining folds slowly up the expander, lubricating as required.

7   Once the bellows is on the driveshaft, place the spring and thrust button in the joint spider without inserting the shim.

8   Move the roller cages towards the centre of the joint.

9   Locate the starplate so that each arm is centralised between each spider trunnion.

10 Engage the driveshaft yoke with the bell-shaped stub axle. Tilt the shaft, and locate each starplate arm in its slot using a screwdriver blade, ground as shown in Fig. 13.30.

11 Now tilt the shaft in the plane of one of the starplate arms – the thrust button will disengage under the pressure of the coil spring. Insert the original shim fully under the head of the thrust button.

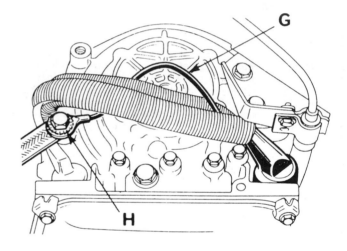

Fig. 13.25 Multi-purpose switch earthed to transmission casing (Sec 8)

G   Multi-purpose switch earth   H   Earthing point
    wire

12 Divide the sachet of special grease supplied equally between the joint and the inside of the bellows.

13 Slide the bellows into place, release any trapped air and fit the clips as described in Chapter 8, Section 4.

14 Refit the driveshaft, Chapter 8, Section 3.

10 Braking system

Bendix disc pads – modification

1   Later models are fitted with offset disc brake pads. This type of pad will be supplied as a service replacement for all models equipped with Series IV Bendix brakes.

2   Each pad incorporates only one corner indent and the anti-squeal groove is offset.

3   Particular care must be taken when fitting this type of pad. The outboard pad must be fitted with its indentation and groove offset

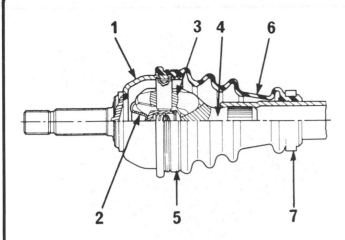

Fig. 13.26 Sectional view of Type GE 86 driveshaft joint (Sec 9)

1 Bell-shaped joint section
2 Starplate
3 Spider
4 Yoke
5 Bellows retaining clip
6 Bellows
7 Rubber bellows retaining ring

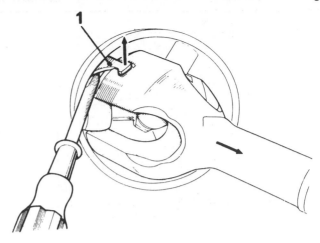

Fig. 13.27 Prising up a starplate arm (1) (Sec 9)

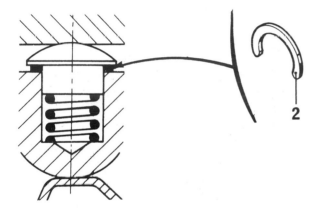

Fig. 13.28 Driveshaft joint thrust button and axial clearance shim (2) (Sec 9)

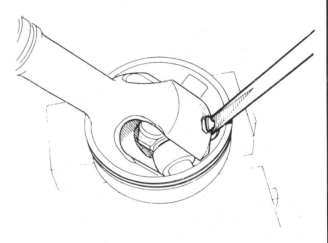

Fig. 13.29 Relocating a starplate arm (Sec 9)

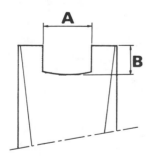

Fig 13.30 Screwdriver grinding diagram for relocating starplate arms (Sec 9)

A = 5.0 mm (0.2 in)   B = 3.0 mm (0.12 in)

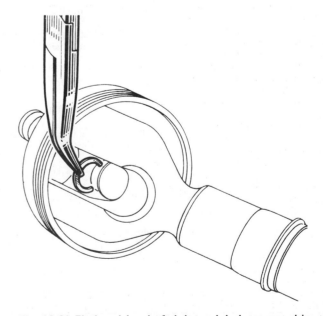

Fig. 13.31 Fitting driveshaft joint axial clearance shim (Sec 9)

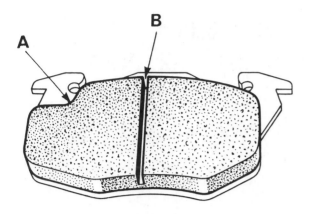

Fig. 13.32 Later type Series IV Bendix offset disc pad
(Sec 10)

A   Single corner indent   B   Offset groove

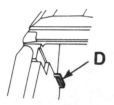

Fig. 13.34 Tab (D) outboard disc pad (Sec 10)

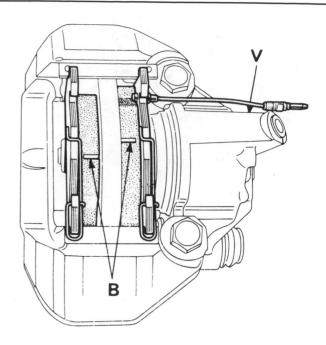

Fig. 13.33 Disc pad grooves offset (B) and wear sensor wire
near caliper bleed screw (V) (Sec 10)

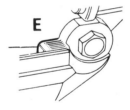

Fig. 13.35 Tab (E) inboard disc pad (Sec 10)

towards the front of the car. The inboard pad must be fitted with its indentation and groove offset towards the rear of the car.
4   Make sure that the pad wear warning lamp wire is routed close to the bleed screw (V) (Fig. 13.33).
5   For extra safety, each pad is marked with a white arrow which must point towards the front of the car when the pad is fitted.
6   The pads also incorporate a tab which would prevent a pad being fitted to the wrong side of the caliper in the case of all but very worn pads. The tab on the inboard pad, if fitted to the wrong side, prevents the pad retaining key being slid into position.

Handbrake (cars with rear disc brakes) – revised adjustment method
7   On cars equipped with rear disc brakes, the handbrake should be adjusted in the following way.
8   Working under the car, slacken the handbrake cable adjuster sleeve until there is a clearance (J) (Fig. 13.36) of 5.0 mm (0.20 in) between the cable nipple and the caliper lever.
9   Move the handbrake cable levers on both calipers several times, checking that they return freely.
10 Turn the cable adjuster sleeve until the clearance (J) is just eliminated.
11 Now pull the handbrake control lever inside the car. It should be fully applied after 10 to 11 notches (clicks).
12 It is important not to over-adjust the cable, thereby reducing the number of 'clicks', otherwise rapid wear of the rear disc pads will occur.

11 Electrical system

Electrical connections and relays
1   Due to roadspray entering the engine compartment and to condensation in cold weather, relays and other electrical connections

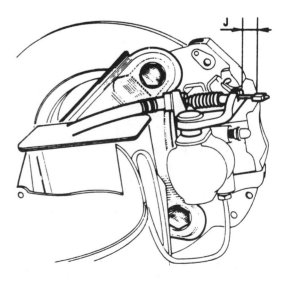

Fig. 13.36 Handbrake cable slackened (Sec 10)

J = 5.0 mm (0.20 in)

Fig. 13.37 Trip computer speed sensor (Sec 11)

can corrode relatively quickly and cause a malfunction of the particular accessory.

2 Later models have improved sealing but on all models it is advisable to apply petroleum jelly to the connector and relay terminal spades and sockets. If high temperatures are likely in close proximity to the component, use special electrical silicone-based grease.

3 Clean away any corrosion using a wire brush or by careful scraping.

4 If a new relay is fitted make sure that the wiring harness cable entry is sealed against moisture by application of a suitable sealant, also seal the joint of any connectors in the same way.

Trip computer

5 This device was fitted to some models from 1984 on. Its function is to supply the following details as required for a particular journey:

(a) The time
(b) The distance covered
(c) The average speed
(d) The average fuel consumption
(e) The range
(f) The amount of fuel left
(g) The outside air temperature

6 The information is obtained by four sensors, these being a fuel flow sensor, a speed sensor (located above the pedal unit and attached to the speedometer cable), a thermistor unit and a special fuel gauge sender unit which supplies fuel information to the instrument panel and the trip computer unit.

7 The system wiring diagram is shown in Fig. 13.38.

8 A digital display provides information to the driver in the following way (see Fig. 13.39).

Button 4

9 When depressed, starts and zeroes the device.

Button 1

10 When 'rocked' to the right (A) the time and outside temperature will be displayed.

11 When 'rocked' to the left (B) the display will indicate the quantity of fuel remaining in the tank. There will be no display if there is less than 5.0 litres (1.0 gal) in the fuel tank. After a minimum distance travelled of 400 m (440 yards) the range possible with the fuel carried, the average fuel consumption, the average speed, the distance covered and the quantity of fuel remaining will all be displayed.

12 When switching from B to A, the time is displayed first. When switching from A to B, the last item of information calculated is displayed first.

13 Reset buttons are provided for minutes and hours (buttons 2 and 3).

14 Automatic zeroing of the displays takes place whenever any of their capacities is exceeded.

15 Whenever the car battery has been disconnected, depress the 'start' button (4) on reconnection to stop the display flashing and to restart the computer functions.

16 In the event of a fault developing in the system, check all wiring connections for security and continuity.

17 Any faults which may develop in the computer or associated system components must be checked and if necessary, repaired by a Renault dealer.

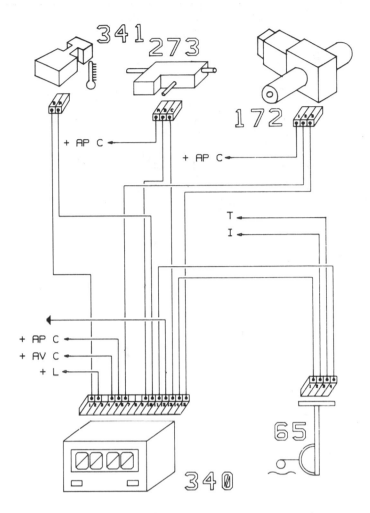

Fig. 13.38 Trip computer wiring diagram (Sec 11)

65	Fuel gauge	+AVC	+ before ignition switch
172	Speed sensor	+L	Lighting bulbs +
273	Flowmeter		accessories +
340	Trip computer	T	Min fuel level warning
341	Temperature sensor		light bulb
+APC	+ after ignition switch	I	Fuel level gauge

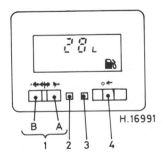

Fig. 13.39 Trip computer digital display unit (Sec 11)

A	Time/temperature	3	Minute reset
B	Fuel	4	Computer 'Start' – zeroing
1	Rocker switch		key
2	Hour reset		

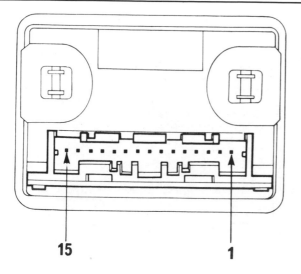

Fig. 13.40 Trip computer connections (Sec 11)

Note: only the 1st and last connections are shown on the diagram

1 Temperature sensor earth	9 Flowmeter information
2 Lamps (+)	10 Temperature information
3 Spare	11 Fuel gauge
4 (+) before ignition switch	12 Trip computer earth
5 (+) after ignition switch	13 Flowmeter earth
6 Speed information	14 Fuel gauge earth
7 Spare	15 Speed sensor earth
8 Spare	

Heated rear screen – care and repair

18 Care should be taken to avoid damage to the element for the heated rear window.

19 Avoid scratching with rings on the fingers when cleaning, and do not allow luggage to rub against the glass.

20 Do not stick labels over the element on the inside of the glass.

21 A voltmeter or ohmmeter can be used to assist with location of defects. Look for an open-circuit or a sudden change in voltage reading along the resistance wires.

22 If the element grids do become damaged, a special conductive paint is available from most motor factors to repair it.

23 To repair, degrease the affected area and wipe dry.

24 Apply tape at each side of the conductor, to mask the adjacent area.

25 Shake the repair paint thoroughly, and apply a thick coat with a fine paint brush. Allow to dry between coats, and do not apply more than three.

26 Allow to dry for at least one hour, before removing the tape.

27 Rough edges may be trimmed with a razor blade if necessary, after a drying time of some hours.

28 Do not leave the heated rear window switched on unnecessarily, as it draws a high current from the electrical system.

12 Suspension and steering

Wheels and tyres – general care and maintenance

Wheels and tyres should give no real problems in use provided that a close eye is kept on them with regard to excessive wear or damage. To this end, the following points should be noted.

Ensure that tyre pressures are checked regularly and maintained correctly. Checking should be carried out with the tyres cold and not immediately after the vehicle has been in use. If the pressures are checked with the tyres hot, an apparently high reading will be obtained owing to heat expansion. Under no circumstances should an attempt be made to reduce the pressures to the quoted cold reading in this instance, or effective underinflation will result.

Underinflation will cause overheating of the tyre owing to excessive flexing of the casing, and the tread will not sit correctly on the road surface. This will cause a consequent loss of adhesion and excessive wear, not to mention the danger of sudden tyre failure due to heat build-up.

Overinflation will cause rapid wear of the centre part of the tyre tread coupled with reduced adhesion, harsher ride, and the danger of shock damage occurring in the tyre casing.

Regularly check the tyres for damage in the form of cuts or bulges, especially in the sidewalls. Remove any nails or stones embedded in the tread before they penetrate the tyre to cause deflation. If removal of a nail *does* reveal that the tyre has been punctured, refit the nail so that its point of penetration is marked. Then immediately change the wheel and have the tyre repaired by a tyre dealer. Do *not* drive on a tyre in such a condition. In many cases a puncture can be simply repaired by the use of an inner tube of the correct size and type. If in any doubt as to the possible consequences of any damage found, consult your local tyre dealer for advice.

Periodically remove the wheels and clean any dirt or mud from the inside and outside surfaces. Examine the wheel rims for signs of rusting, corrosion or other damage. Light alloy wheels are easily damaged by 'kerbing' whilst parking, and similarly steel wheels may become dented or buckled. Renewal of the wheel is very often the only course of remedial action possible.

The balance of each wheel and tyre assembly should be maintained to avoid excessive wear, not only to the tyres but also to the steering and suspension components. Wheel imbalance is normally signified by vibration through the vehicle's bodyshell, although in many cases it is particularly noticeable through the steering wheel. Conversely, it should be noted that wear or damage in suspension or steering components may cause excessive tyre wear. Out-of-round or out-of-true tyres, damaged wheels and wheel bearing wear/maladjustment also fall into this category. Balancing will not usually cure vibration caused by such wear.

Wheel balancing may be carried out with the wheel either on or off the vehicle. If balanced on the vehicle, ensure that the wheel-to-hub relationship is marked in some way prior to subsequent wheel removal so that it may be refitted in its original position.

General tyre wear is influenced to a large degree by driving style – harsh braking and acceleration or fast cornering will all produce more rapid tyre wear. Interchanging of tyres may result in more even wear, but this should only be carried out where there is no mix of tyre types on the vehicle. However, it is worth bearing in mind that if this is completely effective, the added expense of replacing a complete set of tyres simultaneously is incurred, which may prove financially restrictive for many owners.

Front tyres may wear unevenly as a result of wheel misalignment. The front wheels should always be correctly aligned according to the settings specified by the vehicle manufacturer.

Legal restrictions apply to the mixing of tyre types on a vehicle. Basically this means that a vehicle must not have tyres of differing construction on the same axle. Although it is not recommended to mix tyre types between front axle and rear axle, the only legally permissible combination is crossply at the front and radial at the rear. When mixing radial ply tyres, textile braced radials must always go on the front axle, with steel braced radials at the rear. An obvious disadvantage of such mixing is the necessity to carry two spare tyres to avoid contravening the law in the event of a puncture.

In the UK, the Motor Vehicles Construction and Use Regulations apply to many aspects of tyre fitting and usage. It is suggested that a copy of these regulations is obtained from your local police if in doubt as to the current legal requirements with regard to tyre condition, minimum tread depth, etc.

13 Bodywork

Plastic components

With the use of more and more plastic body components by the vehicle manufacturers (eg bumpers, spoilers, and in some cases major body panels), rectification of damage to such items has become a matter of either entrusting repair work to a specialist in this field, or renewing complete components. Repair by the DIY owner is not really feasible owing to the cost of the equipment and materials required for effecting such repairs. The basic technique involves making a groove along the line of the crack in the plastic using a rotary burr in a power drill. The damaged part is then welded back together by using a hot air gun to heat up and fuse a plastic filler rod into the groove. Any excess plastic is then removed and the area rubbed down to a smooth finish. It is important that a filler rod of the correct plastic is used, as body components can be made of a variety of different types (eg polycarbonate, ABS, polypropylene).

If the owner is renewing a complete component himself, he will be left with the problem of finding a suitable paint for finishing which is compatible with the type of plastic used. At one time the use of a universal paint was not possible owing to the complex range of plastics encountered in body component applications. Standard paints, generally speaking, will not bond to plastic or rubber satisfactorily. However, it is now possible to obtain a plastic body parts finishing kit which consists of a pre-primer treatment, a primer and coloured top coat. Full instructions are normally supplied with a kit, but basically the method of use is to first apply the pre-primer to the component concerned and allow it to dry for up to 30 minutes. Then the primer is applied and left to dry for about an hour before finally applying the special coloured top coat. The result is a correctly coloured component where the paint will flex with the plastic or rubber, a property that standard paint does not normally possess.

Conversion factors

Length (distance)

Inches (in)	X	25.4	= Millimetres (mm)	X	0.0394	= Inches (in)
Feet (ft)	X	0.305	= Metres (m)	X	3.281	= Feet (ft)
Miles	X	1.609	= Kilometres (km)	X	0.621	= Miles

Volume (capacity)

Cubic inches (cu in; in³)	X	16.387	= Cubic centimetres (cc; cm³)	X	0.061	= Cubic inches (cu in; in³)
Imperial pints (Imp pt)	X	0.568	= Litres (l)	X	1.76	= Imperial pints (Imp pt)
Imperial quarts (Imp qt)	X	1.137	= Litres (l)	X	0.88	= Imperial quarts (Imp qt)
Imperial quarts (Imp qt)	X	1.201	= US quarts (US qt)	X	0.833	= Imperial quarts (Imp qt)
US quarts (US qt)	X	0.946	= Litres (l)	X	1.057	= US quarts (US qt)
Imperial gallons (Imp gal)	X	4.546	= Litres (l)	X	0.22	= Imperial gallons (Imp gal)
Imperial gallons (Imp gal)	X	1.201	= US gallons (US gal)	X	0.833	= Imperial gallons (Imp gal)
US gallons (US gal)	X	3.785	= Litres (l)	X	0.264	= US gallons (US gal)

Mass (weight)

Ounces (oz)	X	28.35	= Grams (g)	X	0.035	= Ounces (oz)
Pounds (lb)	X	0.454	= Kilograms (kg)	X	2.205	= Pounds (lb)

Force

Ounces-force (ozf; oz)	X	0.278	= Newtons (N)	X	3.6	= Ounces-force (ozf; oz)
Pounds-force (lbf; lb)	X	4.448	= Newtons (N)	X	0.225	= Pounds-force (lbf; lb)
Newtons (N)	X	0.1	= Kilograms-force (kgf; kg)	X	9.81	= Newtons (N)

Pressure

Pounds-force per square inch (psi; lbf/in²; lb/in²)	X	0.070	= Kilograms-force per square centimetre (kgf/cm²; kg/cm²)	X	14.223	= Pounds-force per square inch (psi; lbf/in²; lb/in²)
Pounds-force per square inch (psi; lbf/in²; lb/in²)	X	0.068	= Atmospheres (atm)	X	14.696	= Pounds-force per square inch (psi; lbf/in²; lb/in²)
Pounds-force per square inch (psi; lbf/in²; lb/in²)	X	0.069	= Bars	X	14.5	= Pounds-force per square inch (psi; lbf/in²; lb/in²)
Pounds-force per square inch (psi; lbf/in²; lb/in²)	X	6.895	= Kilopascals (kPa)	X	0.145	= Pounds-force per square inch (psi; lbf/in²; lb/in²)
Kilopascals (kPa)	X	0.01	= Kilograms-force per square centimetre (kgf/cm²; kg/cm²)	X	98.1	= Kilopascals (kPa)

Torque (moment of force)

Pounds-force inches (lbf in; lb in)	X	1.152	= Kilograms-force centimetre (kgf cm; kg cm)	X	0.868	= Pounds-force inches (lbf in; lb in)
Pounds-force inches (lbf in; lb in)	X	0.113	= Newton metres (Nm)	X	8.85	= Pounds-force inches (lbf in; lb in)
Pounds-force inches (lbf in; lb in)	X	0.083	= Pounds-force feet (lbf ft; lb ft)	X	12	= Pounds-force inches (lbf in; lb in)
Pounds-force feet (lbf ft; lb ft)	X	0.138	= Kilograms-force metres (kgf m; kg m)	X	7.233	= Pounds-force feet (lbf ft; lb ft)
Pounds-force feet (lbf ft; lb ft)	X	1.356	= Newton metres (Nm)	X	0.738	= Pounds-force feet (lbf ft; lb ft)
Newton metres (Nm)	X	0.102	= Kilograms-force metres (kgf m; kg m)	X	9.804	= Newton metres (Nm)

Power

Horsepower (hp)	X	745.7	= Watts (W)	X	0.0013	= Horsepower (hp)

Velocity (speed)

Miles per hour (miles/hr; mph)	X	1.609	= Kilometres per hour (km/hr; kph)	X	0.621	= Miles per hour (miles/hr; mph)

Fuel consumption*

Miles per gallon, Imperial (mpg)	X	0.354	= Kilometres per litre (km/l)	X	2.825	= Miles per gallon, Imperial (mpg)
Miles per gallon, US (mpg)	X	0.425	= Kilometres per litre (km/l)	X	2.352	= Miles per gallon, US (mpg)

Temperature

Degrees Fahrenheit = (°C x 1.8) + 32   Degrees Celsius (Degrees Centigrade; °C) = (°F - 32) x 0.56

It is common practice to convert from miles per gallon (mpg) to litres/100 kilometres (l/100km), where mpg (Imperial) x l/100 km = 282 and mpg (US) x l/100 km = 235

Index